PRISON PUZZLE PIECES

The realities, experiences and insights
of a corrections officer
doing his time in
Historic Stillwater Prison

By

Dave Basham

Volume 1

Published by eBookIt.com

Paperback ISBN-13: 978-1-4566-2727-0
Hardcover ISBN-13: 978-1-4566-2734-8

TABLE OF CONTENTS

THE SHORTEST CHAPTER EVER.................................1

DEDICATED TO 2

NOT DEDICATED TO – PREFERABLY DEAD 3

BOOMER 4
   OUR FIRST ENCOUNTER
   OUR SECOND ENCOUNTER
   BARBER BOOMER
   BUILDING A GOOD CREW
   GOOD TIMES
   LOCK YOURSELF IN
   TO THE FAMILY OF SERGEANT DODGE
   FRIENDS FIGHT FEROCIOUSLY
   CO 1 OBLIVIOUS
   IT NEVER HURTS TO HEAR THAT
   BOOMER'S DEMISE
   DA GANGSTA

INTRODUCTION – STOP READING NOW! YOUR
MIND IS AT RISK!...27
   THIS MONSTER
   TITLE EVOLUTION
   PLACEMENT OF PIECES
   CONFLICT
   RELATIONSHIPS
   UNDERSTANDING
   DOUBLE DUTY
   REASONS TO WRITE THESE BOOKS
   NAMES WERE CHANGED TO PROTECT THE IDIOTS
   SECURITY & SAFETY
   THE PITCH

SOME BACKGROUND ON ME 38
   WHY WRITE A SECTION ABOUT ME
   HOW DID I WIND UP IN HELL BEFORE I EVEN DIED?
   FRESH RAW MEAT
   MY PERSPECTIVES – WE ARE CREATED
   FEAR
   EMOTIONS
   NEVER LIE

WHAT HAPPENED AFTER THAT
WHY THERE ARE NOT A LOT OF BOOKS LIKE THIS
REGULAR MIND VS IRREGULAR MIND
CYA
SHIFT HISTORY
NUMBSKULL
BASHAM ERA ENDS IN B-WEST
MOVIN' ON OUT
BASHAM ERA BEGINS IN A-EAST
BACK TO B-WEST FOR ONE NIGHT

HISTORY OF STILLWATER PRISON IN BAYPORT ...68
WHY
FACT OR FICTION
SHOW ME
LOCATION, LOCATION, LOCATION
YOUNGER BROTHERS
NORTHFIELD BANK FIASCO
TWIN PRISONS BY THE TWIN CITIES

ACADEMY #81 97
MELDING MYSTICAL MINDS
ACADEMY X-PERIANCES
ACADEMY HODGE PODGE FOR 2000
ACADEMY GRADUATION SPEECH
THE GRADUATION SPEEECH
REACTIONS
PAST MODELING CAREER
IT BECAME OFFICIAL

ACADEMY INSTRUCTOR 127
IPC
ACADEMY LESSONS
I WONDERED WHAT HAPPENED TO THEM
TOP 10 LIST

DEFINITIONS, ACRONYMS AND OTHER STUFF..130
NECESSARY INFORMATION
ACRONYMS VERSES INITIALISMS
FLAG TIME
NO FLAG TIME FOR A LONG TIME
BUBBLE
THE A TEAM: A-LEVEL RESPONSE
B-LEVEL RESPONSE
SALLYPORT
WALKED OUT

TIER, GALLEY, GALLERY
UNIT, CELL HALL, CELLBLOCK
LOCKED OUT
BOSSES, HONCHOS
MEAT
CHIMO – CHOMO
REMEMBER ALL OF THESE, REALLY!

FIRST WATCH 137
BREAKING POLICY
DON'T TELL ME TO BE QUIET
WANNA BET
LAUREL & HARDY ROUTINE
NIGHTTIME UA
MSU – MINIMUM SECURITY UNIT
CAR PATROL
GHOST OF ATLANTIS
INDUSTRY
THE ROUTINE
DUCK FEET
HITTING THE WALL
THE BLOCKS
CURING AN ITCH
RACIST WANTED ME TO KISS HIS BLACK ASS
FAKER OR NOT
NIGHT TIME SHAKEDOWN
FORGETFULNESS, THEFT OR BOTH
ESCALATION & COPY CATS

COLOR BANDS 159
COLOR BANDS
AN EXAMPLE
LYING SCUMBAG AND VERBAL JIVE

DINING HALL DYNAMICS 164
NOT GOOD AT MAGIC
TIMING
REPUTATION
INMATES KNOW WHAT EACH OFFICER WILL DO
TO SHUT DOWN OR NOT TO SHUT DOWN
WANTING TO GET CAUGHT
TOO FRUGAL
NORGE REPAIRMAN
SOMETHING STUPID
MENTALITY THAT GOT HIM HERE
SAGGING

DOCUMENT TRIVIAL DETAILS
FART MAN
WRONG PLACE TO FINGER
ONE OF MY ASSAULTS
THEY ACCUMULATE VIOLATIONS
A SERVING OF BLOOD
WE ALL KNOW THAT GAME
ADDING UP THE VIOLATIONS
THAT DOESN'T WORK WITH ME BUCKO
SHOULDN'T BE ALLOWED A CANE
MYSTERY SOLVED
ANOTHER ASSAULT
MYSTERY NOT SOLVED
DON'T MESS WITH A PSYCHO
HARD(LY) WORKER
AT A BOY
IT'S JUST A JOB
SOME THINK THEY HAVE CONTROL
WARDEN WAS AWARE
APPLE MAN
SAME OLD THING
WHERE DO WE GO
SO THAT'S HOW IT IS
NOT AS SMART AS HE THOUGHT
TOO MANY GANG BANGERS
AMAZING
FROOT LOOP BANDIT
BEST FOODS BEST COOKS
SEG WAS FULL
MYSTERY LIQUID
MORE PROTIEN
PROBLEM COMB
FAKE DROP GAME
YES, WE'RE ANAL
KEEP THEM HEALTHY
LESS SUGAR FOR LUNCH
FIVE WEEK MENU

KITES 201

REPORT WRITING 208
BE HARSH WITH ME
INVESTIGATIVE CELL RESTRICTION
LOSS OF PRIVILEGES
SECURITY CENTER OR ESCORTED OUT
SEGREGATION

HEARINGS
TECHNIQUES FOR REDUCING VIOLATION REPORTS
PROGRESSIVE DISCIPLINE & LOP

OAK PARK HEIGHTS 218
SEND ME NOW

A TYPICAL DAY ON SECOND WATCH 219
START GETTING READY THE DAY BEFORE
TRAFFIC
DON'T FRONT THEM OFF
FIRST SALLYPORT & VENTING
SECOND SALLYPORT
GEAR & MACE
MORNING BRIEFING & SOILED BRIEFS
THIRD SALLYPORT
BLOCK OFFICER

IT'S A CRIME, INMATE MENTOR 227
HOOCH TIP
DECISION MAKING
WHO TO LISTEN TO
GENIUS
STAYING HEALTHY
GETTING TO KNOW HIM

PHONES...241
STILL ABLE TO VICTIMIZE
NO PHONE LIST
PHONE ALARMS
PROTECT YOUR PIN NUMBER
GANG CONTROL
GOTTA STEAL SOMETHING

CAREER CRIMINAL IN TRAINING 244

INFAMOUS – CRAIG BJORK & EDWIN CURRY 247
EDWIN CURRY
CRAIG BJORK
THE KITCHEN MURDER

PAT SEARCH ROUTINE 258

WHEN PRISON BUDDIES SQUABBLE...................260

MORE PUZZLE PIECES 262
  FIRST STOP
  TOUGH GUYS WILL COMPLY
  WISDOM FOR THE INCARCERATED
  IDIOTS CAN BE FUNNY
  THE TERMINATOR
  CHANGED
  OUT, BACK AND OUT AGAIN
  CAPTAIN RESPECT
  DON'T WISH ME A MERRY CHRISTMAS
  LEARN ENGLISH
  TALK ABOUT BAD LUCK
  INMATE OBSERVATIONS
  PEG LEG PETE
  WHERE'D THE MEMORIES GO
  GOING STRAIGHT
  ONE PISSED OFF INMATE
  WHEN GEESE ATTACK
  TRYING TO MAKE IT BETTER, DESPITE THE SYSTEM
  WHAT COUNTRY AM I IN
  HORNY INMATE
  SO THAT'S HOW YOU DOIN' ME
  KICKING A SIGNIFICANT VIOLATION
  CAN'T SAY WE DIDN'T TRY
  SOME SENTENCES ARE NOT LONG ENOUGH
  NOT YOUR CHOICE
  REBEL FILMWORKS
  DENIED
  I NEED HERB
  GATE MONEY
  INDIGNANT INDIGENTS
  35W BRIDGE COLLAPSE
  GOOD HIDING PLACE
  STUCK FOR YOU

INFAMOUS – LARRY DONNELL HILL 286

GOOD, BAD, UGLY ME 288
  FIRST INCIDENT REPORT
  AN UNSAVORY EDUCATION
  A COMPLIMENT? IN THIS PLACE?
  REVIEWED
  FIRST DISCIPLINARY INCIDENT REPORT I WROTE; THE
      DEVIL MADE ME DO IT
  THE HISTORIC FIRST
  HE HAD MY BACK

LABELED A SNITCH
STEVEN SEGAL
ASSAULT AVERTED
PUPPET FOR PROMOTION
JUST FOLLOWING POLICY
ENOUGH IS ENOUGH
FIRE EYES
BEING BLIND SIDED
ORGANIZED INMATES, A BAD THING
SKILLED OMISSION
THEY'RE AFRAID, THEY'RE VERY AFRAID
RESTRAIN THYSELF
TIME TO LEAVE
BURNED BRIDGES
REQUESTED
CAPTAIN SCREW OFF
OFFICER THOUGHTFUL
LETTER OF APPRECIATION

INTAKE PACKET 317

ARE WE REALLY DEALING WITH THIS SHIT.......327
IT'S THE JOB
VAPORS
DRAMA QUEEN
PLAYING DUMB WHEN YOU ARE DUMB
HE IS OUT AMONG US
DOUBLE VIOLATION
I WANT TO JOIN THE TALIBAN
CHRONIC WEENIE PAIN IN THE ASS
ADULT SIZED CHILDREN
FRIEND'S FUN
ELEMENTARY PROBLEMS
TAKE MY SHIT, PLEASE
NOT SMART TO CUSS OUT A COP
INEFFECTIVE LIAR
PUNKS RETURN
TEMPTATION
BRING IN MY MA
LITTLE CONSEQUENCE
MUST LIE BETTER
JUVENILE BEHAVIOR
WE ARE HERE TO HARASS
IT'S PART OF THE JOB
THE ANSWER'S THE SAME
POWER PLAYS DO NOT WORK

GO AHEAD AND FREEZE
WHAT DID WE LEARN
LAUGHABLE IDIOTS
I DON'T LIKE YOU EITHER
LIFE OF A CHILD MOLESTER
HOW TO FLOOD
DEFIANT INMATE'S PLAN
DISRESPECTFUL INMATE, WELL DUH!
HARASSMENT
SOME NEVER LEARN
"NICE ASS" FROM AN ASS
KEEP THEM IN SEG
DISRUPTIVE RELIGIOUSLY
NOT A MODEL CITIZEN
I JUST TELL MYSELF, I GET PAID BY THE HOUR
NOTE FROM A SARGE
STRANGE IS NORMAL
PEER PRESSURE WORKS GREAT

ASSAULTS – EXTORTION – INTIMIDATION 359

ASSAULT BY OTHERS
EFFICIENT ASSAILANT
ALWAYS KEEP AN EAR OUT
TIPS APPRECIATED
CLUMSY
ATTEMPTED MURDER
INMATE CONNECTIONS
THREAT TO ACHIEVE A GOAL
HISPANIC GANG WAR
NOT ALL PENS ARE USED FOR WRITING
SOME WATCH THEIR LANGUAGE
PINBALL WIZARD
PMB VS NAZI LOW RIDER
ENTREPRENEUR
VIOLENT HOCKEY GAME
REQUEST TO BE BEATEN
DON'T FLUSH THE EVIDENCE
CONSENSUAL BEATING
REQUEST DENIED
QUICK TRIP TO THE HOLE
TWO FOR THE PRICE OF ONE
SNITCH OR NOT
SORTING IT OUT
SLEEP TIGHT
ASSAILANT LOSES
PAINFUL WEAPONS

WIENER
THE SIGN WAS THERE
IT'S NOT SMART TO FOOL WITH THE SARGE
NOT SO SMART
SOUTHERN EXTORTIONIST
PART OF THE GAME
PREDATOR
INTIMIDATION DENIED
RUSH CITY ASSAULT
REASON FOR ZERO HORSEPLAY TOLERANCE

MAIL 382
A FOR EFFORT & CREATIVITY
REOFFENDING IS FOR SURE
MAIL REFUSAL

OMBUDSMAN 384

RACISM 387
9-11
RACIST INTIMIDATION TACTIC
LITTLE HITLER, TRAINING BY A RACIST
LITTLE HITLER'S COWARDICE COMES THROUGH
RACIST GETS HIS COME UP-UNS
RACIST MUSLIM
HOW MANY MORONS CAN I PISS OFF
CULTURE?
MISTER INNOCENT MUSLIM
FAILING WITH USING THE BLACK CARD
ADVERTISING RACIST
WHY WIGGERS WHY
COUNT HIM RACIST
ACCURATE QUOTES

TIPS 404
GOING THROUGH THE MOTIONS
ASSAULT PLANNED
OBSERVING & LISTENING
FLOOR WAX THIEF

VISITING 408
FEMALE MALE RATIO
VISITING ROOM
FRONT DESK
VISITING ROOM BUBBLE
WHAT I HEARD AND OBSERVED

WHAT I WAS TOLD
DON'T VIOLATE VISITING ROOM POLICIES
COMING SOON – A BROTHER
WHERE'S THAT TATTOO!
INTIMIDATE TO MANIPULATE
AUNTIE LOVE
I SUGGEST NO CONTACT VISITS FOR THIS ONE
DISRESPECT OR CON GAME
VISIT OR CHOW
SEND HER TO SHAKOPEE WOMEN'S PRISON
NOT AS COOL AS HE THOUGHT
SEG CAN BE A GOOD PLACE
OFFICERS BLAMED AGAIN

NUTS & BUTTS 423
NOT FOR ME
MENTALITY OF SOME
DINGLE BERRIES ON A BLACK MAN'S ASS
UNABLE TO SHAKE IT
EAGER BEAVER
TA DAH

CHOW HOUND – MY MOST BLATANT ENEMY 429

CONCLUSION 440

THE SHORTEST CHAPTER EVER

Hi!

DEDICATED TO

Dedicated to all of the good officers that did their time along with the inmates.

Dedicated to all of the people who were unjustly convicted.

Dedicated to those who were injured or lost their lives protecting others on the inside.

Dedicated to all of the people who were treated unjustly by corrupt prison guards.

Dedicated to those officers and inmates that could not keep sane in this environment.

Dedicated to all of the inmates who treated poorly trained officers decent.

Dedicate to those officers that refuse to kiss the asses of those in power above them.

Dedicated to those officers that stopped climbing that corrections ladder in order to maintain their integrity.

Dedicated to staff and inmates that assisted in educating me on how to perform my duties the best way possible and as humanely as possible.

NOT DEDICATED TO –
PREFERABLY DEAD

Not dedicated to the small percentage of offenders, officers and supervisors that cause most of the problems.

Not dedicated to the people in power that treat good officers like criminals and coddle the trouble makers in the institution.

Not dedicated to those not having the stones to do their job in spite of the old boy network.

Not dedicated to the offenders who use technicalities in the law to get off and not dedicated to those that created and allowed those technicalities to set those offenders free to victimize others.

Not dedicated to those so ignorant and power hungry that they choose to believe the words of the criminal and the corrupt over the words of those trying to do good time and those trying to do their jobs fairly and consistently.

Not dedicated to those who create situations that caused good people to leave this job for jobs where such unfairness and frustrations does not exist.

Not dedicated to the politicians who don't know their ass from a hole in the ground, yet force knowledgeable experienced personnel to do as they dictate.

Not dedicated to the racists of any race that crate a negative culture within the system.

BOOMER

OUR FIRST ENCOUNTER

The first time I ever saw Boomer was when I was working in the visiting room. He was not allowed to have contact visits, so I saw him through the thick glass enclosure where they had to use phones to speak to their visitor. The officer I was with saw him there and started to tell me about him. Boomer saw us looking his way, got an angry look on his face and pointed at us. This was a large black man. He was tall, sturdy and had bulk that was more muscle than fat. Even from the distance we were from him, I could tell he was a force to be reckoned with.

The officer was telling me that Boomer had non contact visits because the last time he had a contact visit with a woman, he made it more than the allowable contact, if you get my drift. All hell broke loose when officers tried to get them apart.

There is a lot that I have no way to verify 100%. I never looked up Boomers records to see what he was in for or what he had done while being incarcerated. I found it easier to treat everyone the same if I didn't know their background. After working in this place awhile, I could generally tell just by looking at these guys the reason they got locked up.

Most things that people have told me about things that have gone on in this place, I was able to verify to a high level of accuracy.

One thing was for certain, this officer feared Boomer.

OUR SECOND ENCOUNTER

The next time I ran into Boomer, I was working in D Hall, which was where Boomer lived. I was working the door post which in this block was right by the desk. Boomer came down to the desk to speak to the sergeant. He had a loud low booming voice. Barry White had nothing on this guy. Standing next to him, I felt like a little guy. I felt like I was standing next to a bear that could take me out with one swipe of his paw. If I had to use one word to describe him at this point, I would say powerful.

Later, I had an opportunity to talk to him. I introduced myself and told him the first time I had seen him was in visiting. He clearly remembered. I told him he seemed angry at that time. He said that he thought we were talking about him and that he didn't like that other officer. I verified to him that we were talking about him; that the officer was filling me in on him. He said that officer had it out for him and made up stuff about him. I told him that I listen to what people tell me, but that I make up my own mind about people and their character. He seemed very cordial and had a good sense of humor. He also had a good sense of himself, oozed confidence and was extremely savvy about people and the goings on in this place.

BARBER BOOMER

Our next meeting was when he was transferred into B-West. I was a regular in this block at this time. He was unemployed at the time. Nobody wanted to hire him because of his reputation and most were afraid of him. Nobody wanted the headaches that came with having him around.

He talked one of our sergeants into hiring him as a barber. The problem was that he couldn't cut hair. He would get friends to come to him for haircuts and intimidate others into coming to him in order to get some business. I was in charge of the swampers, (*inmates that get paid for performing jobs in the cellblocks*), so I wasn't happy with having a barber that had no skills. Inmates were complaining to me that they wanted a qualified barber. I asked the sergeant why he had hired Boomer. He said he deserved a break. I had a lot of respect for both of the sergeants that were in this block at this time. I needed a solution. We are only allowed two barbers in each unit, but I needed two good barbers. Our other barber did a good job, but quit, leaving me with one unqualified barber. I wanted to hire the best barber in the institution and use him to train in Boomer properly.

The job posting went up and two really good barbers applied. After asking inmates and officers what they thought about these guys, the consensus was that they were both very good and that one was the best barber in the entire institution.

I wanted to hire both of them, that way the best guy could train in Boomer and we would have two qualified barbers while Boomer was learning. Problem was that we were only allowed two barbers per cellblock, but I had a plan. I could divide the utility position, miscellaneous jobs, up between all three barbers and still have the correct allotment of swampers. When I bounced my plan off the top sergeant, he liked the idea and told me to go ahead with it. The best barber was known to not be the most agreeable person in this world of many abrasive attitudes. The top sergeant said he knew him well and was fine with him. When I found out where he was housed, I went to talk with him. I told him my plan and he liked the idea.

Another plus to having the three barbers was that greater diversity was able to be achieved. Now we would have a white, black and Native American barber.

The best barber was white and a witch, so that's what we'll call him. I found out that there were a few witches in the prison. Being a witch is considered to be their religion. They are called wiccans and get whatever special privileges that religion recognizes in being necessary to be able to worship in their own way. This allows these guys to be able to keep special herbs and teas in their cells. If you want to be able to get these herbs and teas, you just have to become a witch. These witches worship in the chapel during what they call Wiccan Ceremonies.

When I told Boomer what I was planning, he didn't believe me. He had been lied to by officers too many times before. He went to the sergeant that hired him and told him Basham was going to fire him. That sergeant came to me and asked me what was going on. I told him. He said, "Really?" I told him I liked what he had done with hiring Boomer, but that I needed him to be able to do the job. He liked the idea and told Boomer that I could be trusted. Boomer knew enough not to trust anyone in here, but he had no choice but to wait and see. He definitely was not pleased with me. He saw me as just another officer screwing with him.

When Boomer saw the posting announcing who got what jobs he was convinced that I was going to fire him.

When Witch came in, he worked on training in Boomer. Boomer was a quick study. Anything Boomer put his mind to, he could do well.

Witch quickly became lazy and uncooperative. He was supposed to be putting in five hours of work each day, but was only putting in about five hours per week. As long as my swampers did their job, they had no problems with me. If they didn't do their job, they would find out that their lives would be much more peaceful if they just went ahead and did it. Firing people wasn't my first choice with these guys, but if I had accumulated enough documentation on their violations and didn't feel they would eventually turn around and do the job, I had no problem with canning them. I was constantly on this guy to do his job. He filed a grievance on me. The night sergeant reported to me that he was refusing to do his job. Witch said he didn't have to do it because the associate warden said he didn't have to. I informed him that if she wanted to allow him to sit around doing nothing, she can tell me that and until then he would either do the job, quit or I'd have to fire him. He applied for and got a different job elsewhere. From that time on he was my enemy and made it known. He never did anything to cross the line with me though. He was just a major pain in the ass.

Once Witch was gone, Boomer came up to me and thanked me for how I had handled everything. Never again did he ever doubt anything I said.

BUILDING A GOOD CREW

Because the sergeant had given Boomer a break and it worked out well, Boomer came to me and told me he had a friend that was in the same situation that he had been in. Boomers friend had been in so much trouble that he could not get hired anywhere. Boomer asked me if I would hire him and guaranteed me that this guy would do an outstanding job. He said that if his friend didn't do well, he would make him or do it himself. I told him I would talk to the guy and that if it seemed like a good fit, I'd try to get him. But I told him, I didn't need him to monitor him. I told him that his tip on a potential good worker was enough for me.

Getting this guy was relatively easy because no one else wanted him. He did a great job the entire time he worked for me.

Getting tips on inmates that no one else wanted was the start of building the best swamper crew in the entire Department of Corrections. We know this because every cell block in every Minnesota state prison was inspected and evaluated. B-West came out with the best score. This was even with Stillwater being the oldest prison. Our block was the cleanest, best organized, the best maintained as far as painting, repairs and everything working properly. We achieved this because these men were given the opportunity to prove themselves. When they found out we were the best, they worked even harder. Most of them had never gained recognition from positive efforts before. They all took pride in what they had accomplished. We were the block that people were brought to see if the honchos wanted to impress them. I told the crew to not be shy about what they achieved. When people came in and commented on the block, I told the crew to step up and let themselves be identified as being part of it. In most blocks you would see swampers come out and disappear within the first half hour. In this block you could come in at anytime during the day and see at least a couple of them out working. Boomer taking a lead role setting an example was a big part of it.

GOOD TIMES

If I could have fun and not get in trouble I would do it.

Sometimes I had fun and got in trouble, because all of my decisions weren't perfect. Imagine that! So as time went on, there were little if any deviations from protocol by me, because I had acquired too many enemies of, inmates, officers and big shots.

Boomers friend had a stylish walk that he had perfected. It was a kind of a walk that was similar to what I'd see bands in a parade do; a little bit of a hitch in the git-a-long. Watching him, I tried to copy him. He started laughing and gave me a few pointers to perfect it.

Boomer with his booming Barry White type of a voice would occasionally belt out a tune. At times I would join in.

One day Boomer and his buddy were walking down the flag. I came up behind them using the special walk. Boomer started walking like that too. Then he started to sing. We joined in. The three of us were walking down the flag doing the walk and singing. This grabbed the attention of other inmates that were out. They were smiling and laughing and some of them joined in singing. Yes, there were times in this place that were worth remembering.

LOCK YOURSELF IN

One of my most memorable incidents involving Boomer was the time he saved my ass.

Most of the work in the block had been accomplished for the day. A few swampers were out on the flag, but other than that, everyone else was either out of the block at work or locked in their cells.

Boomer was out on the flag sitting at a table.

I was up on the fourth tier with an inmate plumber who was trying to unclog a toilet in a cell. We were never supposed to be on a tier alone with an inmate, but rules were established that were impossible to follow. The number of staff we had, more often than not, didn't allow us to have another officer up there with us. We were told that if we needed more help to call the watch commander and he would get someone. Someone tested this out once. He was chastised and hung up on. If someone had to go up alone, I would volunteer to do it, as would most others.

While I was up there, an inmate returned to the block. He had been at work, went to health services and then returned to the cellblock. Instead of going to his cell, he was hanging out on the flag. After watching him awhile and seeing that he wasn't switching in, I called down to him and directed him to switch in. He did not like this. He was yelling up at me and made it clear that he had no intention of returning to his cell. I directed him again to switch in. He continued yelling and started pacing. I could not make out what he was saying and could not leave this inmate plumber up on the top tier alone. I directed him a final time to switch in or I would call for the squad to come and get him. He continued to disobey, yell and pace. As this was nothing urgent, at the time, I called over the radio to have an unruly inmate escorted out of the unit. Upon seeing me grab my radio and hearing me make the call, this inmate went off. He hollered up to me that he was going to come up and get me.

At this time it seemed rather humorous to me. From the distance I was above him and his bizarre movements, he had the appearance of a little cartoon character. Something like you'd see in a Gulliver's Travel cartoon with the little guy yelling, pacing and shaking his fist up at me. As I found out, in this place, if it doesn't look real, that's when it is probably the most real.

He headed toward the back stairway. I thought he might be going back to his cell because the center stairway was the most direct route for him to get to me. He disappeared from my sight.

I started to evaluate my options just in case he appeared. At the time, I had just finished a class to be a trainer for de-escalation classes. It was necessary to evaluate what my options were and decide upon the best one in case he actually did show up.

I could stay there and take him on if he appeared, but most likely either he or I would wind up going over the railing. Either way, I would be screwed; either by me laying on the flag all busted up or him laying there.

I could see the headlines if he went over. "Officer throws inmate off fourth story of cellblock." Also, if I lost, he would have access to the plumber's tools and be able to use them as weapons on those responding to the incident.

I could leave the area and avoid the altercation. The problem here was that getting the plumber to respond quickly with me would be near impossible. If I left him there, the guy coming for me would have access to the tools to use as weapons again. Also, I had an aversion to running from any situation, but I would've done that if that had been the best thing to do.

This is all happening very fast. The speed things run through your mind when you're in a tight spot is amazing. I was getting ready to take this guy on when Boomer yelled up to me and said, "Hey Basham! Lock yourself in. This guy is crazy."

Wow! I hadn't thought of that one. As I saw the inmate coming down the tier for me, I was weighing out the options. I didn't want to lock myself in the cell with the plumber with the tools, but as the crazy guy approached, it seemed like the best option.

Just as he was getting to me, I stepped into the cell. As he was grabbing for the cell door, he saw and heard it click shut. This enraged him even more. He said, "Come out here you bitch!"

I just stood there and watched him. I was locked in like a caged animal, but he was the one that looked like a caged animal as he paced back and forth in front of the cell bars.

Staying aware of the inmate plumber with the tools was important too. As when anything goes down, you never know who is going to get a buzz on and join in.

Unbeknownst to me, Boomer had gone to the bubble. (*Bubbles are small office areas surrounded by thick security glass where one or more officers are stationed.*) He told the officer in the bubble what was going down. The officer in the bubble was a good experienced officer. He made the emergency call and directed the unit camera to my location very quickly.

The tier started shaking. The A-Team had arrived and was coming down the tier from the front of the cellblock. There were at least five of them and two of them were a couple of the biggest officers in the prison. The crazy guy had started going toward them. I don't know why; probably because he was crazy. Right then I hit my radio button and called for the bubble officer to pop my door open. I figured that with the squad coming from the front, I could pop out behind the inmate and we would have him from both sides. The least that I felt could happen was that he would run down the center stairway and wind up in a safer location for apprehending him. The door did not open. Later I found out that my call did not go through. Someone else must have been on the radio first.

The crazy guy then passed by the cell I was in and was headed toward the back of the block. With the tier continuously shaking from the weight of the officers running along it, they followed after him. One held his can of pepper spray out in front of him with his other hand covering his nose and mouth.

What I could not see was them catching the inmate at the back end of the tier, him fighting back, landing a fist on one officer's mouth, and the inmate getting sprayed before they could take him down and cuff him up.

There were a couple of reasons that this inmate acted the way that he did. Supposedly, as reported to me by staff, he had been getting frustrated with health services. He wasn't feeling well and felt health services should be able to wave a magic wand and make him feel great.

The other one, as reported to me by inmates, was that he had run up a gambling debt in the cellblock so large that he couldn't pay it. Time had come for him to pay up or get his come upins'. He wasn't man enough to take his beating, so he figured if he attacked an officer, he would be sent to the more secure Oak Park Heights Prison and be able to avoid it.

This guy had been by Boomer before he blew up. Boomer said the guy had been acting and talking crazy before I ever said anything to him. He said the guy had a problem and was looking to create a bigger one.

After reports were turned in and the bosses evaluated everything, I was commended on how I handled the situation.

I ran into the B-East sergeant in the bathroom. He said that locking myself in the cell was a great idea. He said he wished he would've thought of it. He asked me how I thought of it. I told him that I didn't think of it, that an inmate gave me the idea. He wanted to know who it was. I told him that I couldn't say at this time, for that inmate's safety would be at risk for breaking the inmate's code of not helping an officer. I told him I would check with that inmate and see if he was OK with anyone knowing. He understood.

When I saw Boomer, I told him people were asking me about what happened and wanted to know the name of the mystery inmate. I told him I wouldn't say who it was unless he said it was alright. He said that it was alright, but not to blast it all over the place. If anyone could break an inmate code and get away with it, it was Boomer.

A member of the A-Team came to me and said they had heard an inmate tipped me off on going into the cell. He wanted to know who it was. For them to know information like this would be good for them as they have to rush into violent altercations all of the time. It's good to know that everyone isn't an enemy and that there are inmates around that might have your back.

Quietly, I told him, but not to spread it around. He got together with a couple of other squad members and went into the cellblock. No inmates were out on the flag. *(The flag is the ground level of the cellblock. It is made out of flagstone, so it is just referred to as the flag.)* Most of the inmates were out of the unit working in industry buildings. They had Boomer paged. Boomer showed up. They told him to turn around and cuff up. He complied, but asked what he was being arrested for. They let him stir just a bit. Then they started laughing and uncuffed him. They all reached out to shake his hand. They said, "We just wanted to thank you for what you did for Basham."

This was one of the coolest things I ever saw happen in this place or any place for that matter. Few people ever knew the full story.

However, this wasn't the end of it. I took a lot of heat from officers that thought I should've taken the crazy guy on. I was called a coward, behind my back; nobody had the balls to say anything negative to my face. Guess that makes them the coward. Many officers ostracized me. An officer that I thought was my friend was adamant saying I should've taken the guy on and stated that he would've.

My job was to enforce the policies of the institution. My job was to get the job accomplished in as low key a fashion as possible; to de-escalate situations. My job was the safety of others, including myself. My job was to be able to walk through those gates at the end of my shift in as good of condition as I entered them at the beginning of my shift. I did my job the way I was supposed to whether it was popular with everyone or not.

As time passed, I found out that the tape of the incident was being used for training the new recruits in the academies. It was being used as an example of how to do things.

TO THE FAMILY OF SERGEANT DODGE

There was a sergeant that was well respected by a lot of inmates and officers. In January of 2003, he died in an automobile accident. Boomer wrote a letter to the sergeant's family and asked me to type it up for him.

To the Family of Sgt. Dodge;

We here at Stillwater Prison send our deepest sympathy.

We knew and loved Sgt. Dodge very much. He was a strict man, yet he was a fair man, though we loved him unconditionally.

He never showed favoritism and treated us as human beings.

Sgt. Dodge taught us about change and forgiveness, yet he never judged us.

For his openness, kindness and strictness, we are changed men.

I remember Dodge telling me one day, "If your heart is good, you are good. And if it ain't good, you need to assess what's inside and make a transition. You can change if you want to. There's good in everyone."

He was right. We are changed because of his patience and consideration. He left a huge impact upon us.

I personally will miss him tremendously. We were close. I lived in D-House with Dodge for nearly 7 ½ years of my 13 years here. I knew him well. We would sing and play the guitar often. I'm sorry for rambling, but I really cared for Sgt. Dodge and will miss him very very much.

You have my deepest sympathy. In truth and in spirit, he shall live forever through his teaching and our learning. We

15

thank you for the glorious opportunity of knowing Sgt. Dodge. Thank you very much.

Thank You

Boomer & Inmates

FRIENDS FIGHT FEROCIOUSLY

Chub was quite a bit more than chubby, but the name Chub will work. He was on the swamper crew and did a good job. Boomer and Chub were friends, at least to some degree. Chub was related to a top gang member in the prison, so he had some clout. Boomer had been associated with a gang and most likely still was, but he was strong enough and savvy enough to establish his own rules.

Another member of the swamper crew decided to try to create a rift between the two of them by telling Chub that Boomer was speaking badly of him. What the reason for this was, I have no idea. Generally jealousy is a reason. Revenge another. And still another would be to try to create a job opening for a friend. Who knows what all else is a possibility in this complicated underworld that exists in prisons.

When Chub went to Boomer to ask him about what was going on, Boomer brushed it off as nothing and told him to stop buying into the gossip. Chub wasn't convinced, as he kept hearing things. Boomer kept brushing him off telling him to ignore what he was hearing. Chub let the rumors get the best of him. One evening, when Boomer was on the phone, Chub came up behind him and cold cocked him. Boomer was laying on the floor out cold.

This was not seen by any officer. The officer in the bubble had no vision of the phone Boomer was using. Other officers were spread throughout the unit. Many inmates were out socializing, playing games, having snacks, ironing, and other such activities. All of these bodies would block the view of an officer unless the officer was very close.

16

Chub was smart enough to watch and wait for the right opportunity.

Chub was large and had power, especially if he put his weight behind a punch, but he was no match for Boomer in a one on one fight. Because of this, he ran and locked himself in his cell before Boomer could gain consciousness.

When Boomer came to, he was informed by other inmates of what had transpired. He went up to Chubs' cell to get revenge. There was no way Chub was coming out of that cell.

Boomer knew Chub had to come out the next morning to do his job, so he got ready for him. Chub knew Boomer would have to come for him, so he got ready.

Morning came. I was in the bubble assigned to do the paperwork for the day. A very competent officer was the OIC in the cellblock this day, (*Officer In Charge*). His one big fault, as I see it, was that he liked to screw with people, officers and inmates alike. I will refer to him as Screw Master. Screw Master was sitting in front of the control board, which had buttons to electronically lock or unlock the doors to the cells. Screw Master opened everyone's cell doors using the control board. Then he watched what was going on so I could keep hustling on the paperwork. Inmates were out taking care of their business and getting ready to go to breakfast.

Critical to this story is the layout of the unit. The bubble is in the middle up against the outside wall. From here we can look forward and see the wall of cells. If we look toward the back of the unit, first we see a line of telephones, next a large ice machine, then exercise equipment, washing machines and dryers are next with the shower post stand at the end. All of these things are lined up against the outside wall.

At the end of the block are the showers. They are lined up against the back wall. The fronts are open, so we can observe any unauthorized activity. The back staircase, allowing access to the tiers, is against the inside wall. It obscures vision from about half of the showers unless you are close to the showers. There is a large sink underneath these stairs. This area is not visible from the bubble.

When Chub came out of his cell, Boomer went after him. He caught up to him by the back side of the ice machine; out of our vision. Boomer had a slender round firm piece of metal with him that he had kept hidden in a cell that housed cleaning supplies. It was believed to be the firm wire handle from a paint can. It was straightened and sharpened. Boomer rammed it into the blubber of Chubs' belly numerous times before Chub was able to escape and run down by the washers.

As Chub was escaping Boomer's on slot, he reached into his pocket and grabbed hair clippers that he had put there to use as a weapon for this anticipated revenge assault. He turned around and planted himself firmly to the ground with all of that weight of his. As Boomer was flying toward him, Chub threw a punch at Boomers face with all of the power he had. The clippers were in his hand with the sharp edge driving toward Boomers face. Boomer had little time to react. He got his arm up to his face in enough time to keep his jaw from getting ripped off. The clipper still made contact with the left side of his face and sliced it open.

Screw Master saw some odd activity going on down there, but couldn't tell what was happening from how far away we were. He asked me who was down there. I told him Boomer was the guy that was moving and that Chub was standing next to the washers. He paged Boomer to the bubble. Boomer normally follows directives instantly. This time he did not. He could not be seen with a hole in his face and bleeding or he would be hauled out of the block. He disappeared under the back stairway to the sink where he tried to stop the bleeding and get the blood cleaned up. Screw Master mentioned to me that it was strange that Boomer hadn't responded. I concurred. We were wondering what was going on as a bit of time had passed. Then we saw him walking across the second tier to his cell. The hole in his face was away from us. Shortly after this, he came out of his cell holding a waste basket on his shoulder in order to cover up his wound. He made like he was out emptying his trash and then came to the bubble. Screw Master asked him what was going on down there. Boomer was evasive and apologetic. Screw Master spoke to him about horseplay. Boomer assured him that he would never be goofing around like that again.

When their conversation was done, Boomer told me that he needed me to come to his cell; that he had to talk to me. I told him I was real busy and that I would get to him later. He said it was real important. I told him I would be there as soon as I could. He went back to his cell. Shortly after, he sent someone to speak to me. He said that Boomer really had to see me right away. Screw Master said he would cover for me.

When I got up to his cell, I could vaguely see him sitting on a chair in the back of his cell with the lights off. He told me to step inside. I entered. He turned the left side of his face toward me. Even in the dark, I could see a large gash in his cheek. He then held up the arm that he had blocked the blow with. His forearm was bulged up over twice the size in the middle and gradually tapered down toward the elbow and wrist; and this was a big arm! I am not easily surprised, but these wounds were wicked. He also pointed out that his mouth was swollen on the right side from him being assaulted the night before.

We both knew the rules. I knew the rules he had to follow in order to exist in this environment. He knew the rules that my job dictated. He knew he needed help. He knew I would do my job according to institution policy no matter how cool we were with each other. To make sure he was clear with that I said, "What can you tell me?" I emphasized the word CAN.

He told me the story the way he could tell it to me. It was a short version. He told me about the night before. He left out names. He left out that this morning he had shanked the guy first. He told me what I had to know in order to get him help.

I reported back to Screw Master. We talked about the incident. I checked the control panel and observed that Chub had locked himself in his cell. We figured the other person involved was Chub, seeing as how that is who Boomer was with by the washers when their activity appeared strange and especially now that he had switched in.

Screw Master escorted Boomer to health services to get fixed up. After repairs were made to his face, Screw Master locked up Boomer in his cell.

The squad came and escorted Chub to segregation; soon after Boomer was escorted back to seg. During the unclothed body search, while Chub was being processed, is when we first found out that Chub had been shanked. Due to the amount of blubber around his gut, no organs or anything vital were hurt; only fat was pierced.

Both of these guys were professional convicts. They never gave up any information on each other. I pieced together what I knew with information from informants. Also, over time, people that knew things but wouldn't be informants gradually spoke about details when it didn't matter anymore.

CO 1 OBLIVIOUS

There was an older female that made it through the hiring process. I'm guessing her to be around 50 years old. She really stuck out especially since she dyed her hair the red color of Lucille Ball. She was very friendly, too friendly. She didn't have many problems with the inmates because they saw her as a mother figure and not as anyone that would stop them from doing anything they wanted to do. Some of these people in here hate their mothers, but she didn't keep her job long enough for them to hassle her. She was oblivious to security procedures.

Officers know right away when someone has been hired that never should have been. She was one of them. One instance that sealed her fate with most officers was a time when she was working in the dining hall. She had a set of keys that an officer had given to her in order for her to complete a task. There was major emphasis in the academy training about never leaving keys lying around. When she was through with the keys, instead of returning them to the officer's hand, she just tossed them on the desk. This is an area that inmates had access to. By the way, she did this in front of an associate warden. Normally a new person would be sternly informed of their mistakes and they would eventually become a good officer. This however was a capper to her numerous other security violations that everyone had been putting up with. The female officer that should've received the keys saw CO 1 Oblivious toss the keys on the desk. She saw the associate warden observe what had happened. She knew that in order to cover her ass, she had to write a report on the incident, even though you can get in a lot of trouble with other officers by doing so. She also knew that this would probably be the nail in Oblivious's coffin. Other officers were fine with her writing the report due to the circumstances and due to the fact that they were fed up with dealing with all the mistakes that Oblivious made.

During Oblivious's final days, she worked in my block quite a bit. With Boomer being in my block and being able to be out of his cell all of the time due to his job, Boomer and Oblivious had opportunities to chat.

The following is a report that I found necessary to write to the warden. It should also be noted that this was winter in Minnesota – slipping off an icy road into a snow filled ditch on the side off a road is a common occurrence.

This is a confidential report about former CO 1 Oblivious. When she was working here, I helped her with learning the job, as I have with others. The difference was that by the time she worked in my

21

block, B-West; she had made mistakes, which caused her to be written off by most other officers.

The day before she was terminated, she had gone into a ditch on her way to work making her car inoperable. She asked me for a ride home and possibly to work the next day. I told her that if she couldn't find a ride that I would do it, but that she should try other options first. This is when I gave her my phone number. I never had to give her a ride, but she called me the next day, after she was terminated to thank me for helping her with the job.

Offender Boomer was a swamper in my block at this time. Within a week or so after CO 1Oblivious's departure, he told me that he had talked to her and her husband on the phone. I thought this was odd, but she no longer worked here, so I perceived no potential problem.

The day after Boomer was knocked out by Offender Chub, while Boomer was talking on the phone; Oblivious called me here at work. (It should be noted that I have never given my work number to anyone. I don't want phone calls at work. If people need to contact me, nothing is so urgent that they can't wait until I get home to get my messages.) She had nothing urgent or important to say, so I told her I had work to do. She called again later while I was working on count. I was not pleasant with her and hung up. When I got home she had a message on my answering machine asking me to call her. I did not call. Several days later, she caught me at home. It turns out that she was the person that Boomer was talking to on the phone when he got knocked out. She was wondering what had happened, as she hadn't heard from him. I informed her that she probably wouldn't be hearing from him for a while.

I informed my fellow block officers about this. They just teased me about her. But when I heard the rumor of her sending a picture of herself in lingerie to Boomer, the progression of these things seemed quite strange. I informed my sergeant about this and he suggested that I call OSI. I informed OSI about this and was told to write this report.

She has not called me again. If she should call again, I will not just give her the polite brush-offs that I gave her previously, as she seems unable to take a hint. I will be informing her that she is not to call me again in my "painfully blunt" manner my friends tell me I am so good at. Helping her learn the job was my job; not an attempt to dig up a psychotic friend.

After this, I heard through the officer grapevine that she had sent Boomer $15,000 over 3 payments. The payments were in the increments of $7,000, $2,000 and $6,000. What was the reason for these payments? I don't know. However, I do know that Boomer knew that she was not competent to be working in the prison as a corrections officer. He had coached her on how she had to handle herself in this place. She may have felt very appreciative. Boomer was a very smooth con man. He may have worked his magic on her. There are so many possibilities, it would be near impossible to draw the correct conclusion. Another question that came to mind was that if she had that kind of money to spare, what was she doing working here? It was shortly after hearing of these payments that I found out that Boomer was transferred out of Stillwater's segregation unit to Oak Park Heights.

IT NEVER HURTS TO HEAR THAT

After teaching an Interpersonal Communications class to an academy, one of the officers from that class that worked at the Oak Park Heights Prison contacted me.

This officer had two purposes. One was that he was thanking me for the "tell it like it is" training that I provided.

The other was to inform me about Boomer who was in the Oak Park Heights Prison's Medical Unit. This officer was letting me know that Boomer was doing well. He also filled me in on what Boomer said about me.

"He said you were the finest CO he has ever known. He also said you were a great man. I just thought you would like know."

It is always nice to know that some people appreciate your efforts. Working in this place, you rarely hear anything good.

BOOMER'S DEMISE

While Boomer was at Oak Park Heights, I heard that he got hit with stomach cancer. I had never heard of this before, but many inmates told me they knew others that came down with stomach cancer while being in the prison. The water in this place was suspect, especially with the hundred year old plumbing. The administration said the water had been tested and that it checked out as being OK, however they put filters on the water lines going into the ice machines and water fountains. Water coolers with bottled water were also placed in strategic areas around the prison for staff to use. After I became aware of this, I either used water from the water coolers or brought water in from home. I figured it was better to be safe than sorry.

While Boomer was at Oak Park, I found out what was going on with him from an officer that I knew over there. At times, I had to go to Oak Park to teach a class. I asked if I could go see Boomer, but the lieutenant there would not allow me to do so.

Eventually, the word around Stillwater was that Boomer's life was nearing an end. I also received a couple of emails from Oak Park officers that knew about Boomer and me that verified his condition. It just so happened that I had to go to Oak Park around that time for a class. I asked a friend of mine to check and see if I could see Boomer before he died. He got the OK from the sergeant of that unit, but he said it had to be very quick. He escorted me to a medical cell. When I looked through the little window in the door, I saw a tall man that was just skin and bones sitting on the side of his bed. I kept looking for Boomer. I thought that I was at the wrong cell. He recognized me and cracked a big smile. That's when I recognized him. We were only allowed to see each other a minute or so. He wasn't giving in to the cancer, even though he knew he was losing the battle. The officer that brought me to see Boomer said we had to go. Boomer used all of his energy to stand up. Being close to an inmate is not acceptable. He reached out to give me a hug. Now, I've never been much of a hugger; generally a handshake at most. Over the years we had developed this bond that would not be considered acceptable with him being an inmate and me being an officer. We both knew the boundaries though and never crossed them. Now, I figured to heck with what's acceptable, this is right. We did the inmate hug where you put your arms around someone and bump your fists on each other's backs. We both knew this was the last time we would see each other.

Less than two weeks later, on June 21, 2005, an officer friend of mine at Oak Park Heights, emailed me that Boomer passed away that morning at 9:30am. I've always found it difficult to admit, even to myself, that an inmate was a friend of mine. But I have to admit, this man was my friend.

DA GANGSTA

"I'm down wit 'cha bein' da gangsta cause you was right wit da G." Decipher that one, why don't you.

On 11-22-05, I observed an inmate in an unauthorized area. He had not been in the block long, but I had spoken to him several times about policy violations already. He had never done anything really bad, but he was pushing the limits and becoming a problem child. I hadn't written him up for anything, I just had to speak to him too often about his minor violations. He wasn't even being sneaky about it.

When I spoke to him this day about being in an unauthorized area that is when he said, "I'm down wit cha bein' da gangsta, cause you was right wit da G."

Huh? What's that you say? I didn't want to let on that I didn't understand him. His manner was that he was accepting my directive. I wrote down what he said, so I could figure it out later.

When I had time, I broke his statement down. G was a nickname of Boomers. Fixing up the broken English helped.

The statement now was, "I am down with you being the gangster, because you were right with Boomer."

"Down with" meant that he was alright with, could accept or handle me being the gangster.

"The gangster" was how he perceived me. I enforced policies consistently when others were too intimidated or lazy to enforce them.

"Right with G" was that I had helped Boomer out. I treated him decent. I helped him as I would've anyone, but never crossed the line. While other officers were trying to find a way to write him up and put a notch on their belt, I was trying to assist him in functioning without being harassed; encouraging him to play it straight.

So, what I came up with from this guy's statement was that I wasn't going to have any problems with him because he respected what I had done for Boomer.

He was a player and a nuisance, but he knew when not to push the limits. If he was going to do anything major, it would be when I wasn't around. This was one guy that I never had to write up; due to my friendship with Boomer.

INTRODUCTION –
STOP READING NOW!
YOUR MIND IS AT RISK!

THIS MONSTER

These books are about what I experienced during my 7 years 8 months and 26 days (2825 days) as a corrections officer. When you are employed or incarcerated in a place like this, you are always aware of the time.

Corrections officers' job responsibilities are:
1. The safety of the public
2. The safety of ourselves, the officers
3. The safety of the offenders
4. The preservation of public property

The things we deal with most are trying to correct problems or problem people. It is best if you can take action to prevent problems in the first place. Most jobs I have had involved trying to fix or prevent problems both with inanimate objects and people. My life outside of work has been that way, but that's a whole other story. It just seems like most things in life have to do with preventing and correcting.

TITLE EVOLUTION

So, my first problem was what to name these books.

My first idea was to call it "Dingle Berries on a Black Man's Ass." This title would've made perfect sense by the time you finished reading the book, but friends told me it sounded racist. Racism is a subject that will be addressed, but it is not who I am, nor is it my perspective.

Another title was "Stillwater Prison." This could be confusing as there is a prison in Stillwater, Oklahoma too. Also, people from other parts of the country would probably care less about that title. Most people have probably never heard of Stillwater, Minnesota. Those who have heard of it would probably know of it from its' early days of housing members of the James-Younger Gang; Cole, Bob and Jim Younger. I will address some of the history of this institution and some of the stories that get passed around from one generation of officer to another.

Nicknames people called me were possibilities.

An early nickname was "Totally Basham" or just "Totally." It was derived from "totally awesome." This came from my style of being alert to what was going on and not being afraid to do my job.

During my time in the B-West cell block, after it was double bunked, a huge percentage of the offenders that were in segregation were there because of reports that I wrote. An inmate said that I always sent at least one inmate a day to the hole. He said it never failed. That's how "One a Day Basham" came about.

Many knew me as "The Terminator." Some inmates didn't even know me as Basham; they only knew me as the Terminator. This was a top contender, but I believe that title had already been used.

It was later, after I was no longer in double bunking hell that the less sinister nickname of "DaBash" began to evolve. That is how the inmates and officers who knew me well referred to me the last few years. That one almost got the nod.

I was called many other things that would've been totally inappropriate for little kids to see on a book shelf; however now-a-days it's common to hear those words come out of some of our youngster's mouths.

"I Stand Alone" was a strong contender. Considering my propensity for accuracy and telling it exactly like it is, this seemed to be a good fit. No matter what battle I was fighting, whether it was versus an inmate, officer or superior, I could only count on myself. Due to the politics of the place, it would be rare for anyone to go to the mat for anyone other than themselves. By the time you have finished this book, you will understand why. Also, I knew I could never count on certain people backing me up. This is why it was important to always know who was around. What inmate or officer was near and whether they were friend or foe.

In the process of writing these books, when I got to 1000 pages and still had a lot to write, I realized that there were so many little pieces to this puzzling prison environment that "Prison Puzzle Pieces" evolved.

PLACEMENT OF PIECES

In order to try to eliminate some redundancy, some pieces to this puzzle may not be categorized where you would think. An example is a lockdown that occurred during B-West double bunking. It is in the double bunked section rather than the lockdown section, as it seemed more pertinent to be there. B-West incidents are scattered throughout the book, as they seemed more pertinent to those sections. However, at times, I do mention some items off and on as reinforcements to certain sections. When you have read it all, all of the pieces will come together.

CONFLICT

While I was doing standup comedy, I took improve classes. I performed, taught and created several improv groups. One thing improv taught me was that you need some sort of conflict to drive a scene in order to make it interesting. You also need characters. This place was overflowing with conflict and characters. When asked if I liked my job, I would flat out tell them, "No, but it's always interesting." A lot of the conflicts I'll be relaying to you involve bad, lazy, egomaniac officers and bosses making unintelligent, uniformed, downright stupid or self serving decisions. If someone did something to save the taxpayers a million dollars, that would be good, interesting and worth telling you about, but those things rarely happen in a place like this. Even though there are many good officers here, most of our time is spent dealing with all of the crap that rolls downhill from those above us.

RELATIONSHIPS

These books are about a convicted mass murderer being the man I learned the most from, whether it was by him correctly informing me of institution policies, unwritten codes and inmate perspectives or if it was by lying to me, lying to officers about me, lying to inmates about me or lying to superiors about me to try to get what he wanted. These are all things he had to do in order to make his life as a lifer as good as possible.

The relationships in a place like this can get complicated. When they start to get complicated, there are questions I would ask myself in order to do the right thing. What is my job responsibility? What is right or wrong? What is just? Unfortunately and strangely, the answer to the first question frequently conflicted with the answers to the other questions. Just as odd, the correct thing to do at times is not the answer to any of these questions.

UNDERSTANDING

There are stories I will tell you about that would be more believable if told by someone other than who it happened to. But seeing as how they happened to me, I am the only one with the accurate information involving situations that were one on one between me and someone else. And believe me when I say some of these things seemed unbelievable to me at the time too.

You will realize that I am not a clone of anyone. You will see run on sentences and sentence fragments, but that's who I am. Not a run on sentence or a sentence fragment, but different and really not liking a lot of the rules that force us to do what we don't want to do; someone with a different kind of a mind; someone with the correct dysfunctions to be able to survive a job like being a corrections officer;

someone who is stepping into a different world every day that is extremely dysfunctional.

Making you aware of why and how I am different will require me to gradually inform you of things from my past that have made me who I am today. I had hoped to not give up so much of myself, but it is the only way that you will be able to understand my approach to this job and why I did things the way I did them. Normally, I would be extremely guarded about letting anyone so far into my mind, but these books, will probably never get published anyway. If they do get published, by that time, I'll probably be dead or close to it, so it won't matter much.

A friend of mine thought it was cool when I was doing standup comedy. We'd meet people and he'd say, "This is Dave Basham. He's a standup comedian." Once I started working in the prison, comedy wasn't the coolest thing about me anymore. His introduction of me changed to, "This is Dave Basham. He's a prison guard in Stillwater Prison."

People think they want to hear stories of what happens inside those prison walls. The problem is how you tell them about what happened. Even some of my hard core buddies would cringe and say, "Why did you tell me that?" "Hey, you asked!" I found out that most people don't really want to know the details of what happens. Most can handle a sanitized version, but not the graphic details. When I tell you of these incidents, I will make them as palatable as possible, but some things could turn your gut no matter how much creative phrasing I inject.

DOUBLE DUTY

There will be some minor repetition in this book. Some is intentional as I felt some things needed reinforcing. Some things crossed over into other situations. Some is because I wrote this over a period of several years; felt it was interesting or important and wasn't sure if I had written about it before. Some is just because I am an old man trying to get this finished before I croak.

Writing these books really sucked. I had to relive all of the frustrations and dysfunctional crap that I was elated to leave behind when I retired. There is a reason books like these don't get written. We just want to leave all of the bullshit behind.

REASONS TO WRITE THESE BOOKS

In order to be qualified to be a corrections officer, the Department of Corrections started us off with a six week training course. When I finished that course, I had filled three loose leaf binders with notes and handouts. This seemed hilarious to the other cadets, especially those that finished the course with nothing.

During my time working in the prison, I took extensive notes on my experiences. I documented the conflicts I encountered, the bizarre goings on and the way this place functioned.

I felt our training could've been a heck of a lot better, so I combined these notebooks with the other notes that I had accumulated. I figured that this would be invaluable to anyone deciding on how to approach this job. With the huge amount that there is to know about handling this job, if the DOC would be interested in using my books to fill some of the gaps in our training, I would just give it to them. Any new officer reading these books and then going to work behind those walls would be far more prepared than any of the rest of us ever was.

However, I knew that the reality was that this was most likely something that would be tossed in the trash when I croaked.

When I told friends of some of my experiences, they wanted to read about them. This resulted in formulating these notes into books that the general public would find interesting. By doing this, these books became even better training devices for corrections officers.

This was an immense task; especially considering that I had never written a book before. I had to condense thousands of pages of notes. It was necessary to add my commentary and to phrase things to make them more understandable and palatable to those that have never been behind those walls. Trying to eliminate redundancy from a project so huge was time consuming and frustrating. It was necessary to rewrite and reorganize this sucker several times; nothing enjoyable about that.

Over the years many people had asked me what went on in Stillwater Prison. It was a loaded question. It can't be answered quickly. There are so many pieces to this puzzling little world that no matter how much I wrote, there would still be pieces missing. I wanted to write about as many pieces as possible without getting sued and tossed into this place as an inmate. I wrote it for those people that wanted to know what went on behind those walls and how it all worked.

I searched the internet to find out about things I was told that didn't seem to make sense and to try to find out more about things I was interested in. I hate inaccurate information. It is difficult to sort out fact from fiction a lot of the time. I wanted this to be as accurate as possible; knowing that total accuracy was impossible. From research and my experiences, I feel that I was able to determine the most likely probability of how certain events transpired and phrased it as such. Some instances will be left up to you to draw a conclusion. If I experienced it, I took good notes and you can be assured of its accuracy. I wrote it for those people that are as anal as me.

This facility is historic. Most people do not know much about this place other than it is a prison. The fact that Stillwater Prison is in Bayport raised questions in my mind. I am interested in history and appreciated working in a place that actually had an interesting history. I wanted to know of the history and thought others might find it interesting too, such as the Younger Brothers connection to the prison.

There is corruption in the Department of Corrections in Minnesota, as there probably is most everywhere. I wanted people to know it existed, however I don't have a legal background to be able to protect myself if I printed the word of mouth things that I found out. By letting people know that this existed, and tossing out a few starting points, maybe someone would dig in and uncover enough facts to be able to end or at least decrease the amount of corruption. I wrote this for them. They must be careful because there is a powerful system out there that can squash most anything or anyone. Just writing this, I may become a target, but hey, I'm getting old anyway. If they don't get me, cancer or a heart attack will probably get me.

I needed this to be interesting from start to finish. I realize that 100% of this probably won't be interesting to 100% of the population. Some of this, I found a bit dry, but others told me to include it because it was interesting to them. I hoped that by interjecting my perspectives and different sense of humor that this would be interesting to most that thought about reading it.

In my opinion, showing how dysfunctional this system is, was important. It was also important to show how and why it actually works, but there could easily be massive improvements. Hopefully someone would read this that could and would do something about it.

Most people think that the inmates are the biggest problem in prisons; not this one! The officers and other staff were the worst problems that I had to deal with. If there was any consistency among staff and officers, the problems that did exist from inmates would've decreased drastically.

It was necessary to inform people how the relatives, friends and society that created the criminals put pressure on politicians to interfere with those that know how to handle situations in the prisons. The prison higher ups have paid some awful dues to get to where they are. Their lively hood is often threatened by a phone call from a politician. It all rolls downhill. Keeping politics out of the prison system would greatly reduce the problems that we have with inmates.

To show how the union protects bad employees was important to me. The jerks need the union to protect them from being fired, so they are strong supporters of the union. The rest of us better watch our backs.

I wanted to show that this could be a great job. If some of the problems were fixed, they could hire people that better fit the job and had better work ethics. Getting the good ones in charge is difficult. Getting the good ones to stay is difficult. Some of the best personnel they have wind up having to ride their time out so they don't get chewed up and spit out by those without ethics.

Training could be a lot better. Sergeants are not trained; they are promoted according to seniority.

During my time working in the prison, lieutenants were chosen more by diversity than anything else. Even though some of these people were qualified, many were not.

The historical society could use this as a rather detailed eight year history of life in Stillwater Prison.

These things and so many more, I felt were important for the public to know.

I realize that endeavors like this are generally not something that produces a cash flow; but if it does, I'd be darn happy about it. After working just under eight years, my pension is not significant. It was necessary for me to leave as soon as I could. Even though I had some supporters in the prison, the ones that weren't, were in much better positions to do me in.

NAMES WERE CHANGED TO PROTECT THE IDIOTS

Due to the nature of things inside the prison walls, I will not be using real names, even if they would be OK with that happening.

The only times I will use real names is if they were in some sort of a highly publicized event and a matter of public records.

I believe that I made only one exception to this. This man was highly respected by officers and inmates. He had a huge influence on everyone and the prison.

I have tried to come up with names for some that are at least somewhat descriptive of who they are, what they look like, personality traits, anything that would help you to keep track of the numerous people that I had some sort of acquaintance with in this weird dysfunctional world within these walls.

There are many varied instances and events where knowing the name of someone doesn't matter in the least. What happened is just another piece to this puzzling prison environment.

SECURITY & SAFETY

Anything important for the security and safety of the prison, inmates and officers is not divulged.

Some people may be able to identify themselves, which they may like or dislike.

Some may be extremely upset with what is divulged. I have been warned that some may choose to retaliate with violence. It would be best for them, and for me, for them to not front themselves off with such actions. I believe that most of them are intelligent enough to not want to wind up behind bars. If any of them want to be behind bars, I suggest becoming a bartender.

The only ones able to identify themselves or others would need first hand information to do so.

THE PITCH

Maybe I should pitch this like an old time movie trailer...

Experience the existence of a unique society within high walls, barbed wire and armed guards!

Discover how murderers, rapists, thieves and other violators of society's guidelines survive when locked up together.

Do you really want to know what goes on in this dysfunctional world?

Will you maintain your sanity once you have been exposed to the things these people do to each other?

How do the people employed to control this environment stay sane?

Could you stay sane behind these walls?

Must you be insane to survive here?

Perversions, drugs and violence, to twist your mind!

Do you dare enter this world where every move you make must be calculated in order to survive!

Who can survive and who won't!

So I've given you fair warning, if you continue to read, it is at your own risk.

SOME BACKGROUND ON ME

WHY WRITE A SECTION ABOUT ME

I was asked, why write a section about me? I was a unique corrections officer in my mindset and how I approached the job. By informing you a bit about me, you might be better able to understand the decisions that I made. When a decision seems ludicrous, knowing a bit about my life up until the point that I started working at the prison, might make my decisions more understandable. People have asked me how I could place myself in an environment like that every day and continue to exist as a normal person. The fact is that a normal person cannot exist in a prison and stay normal. The normal ones leave. Those that realize they are not normal are able to exist in this dysfunctional environment if their dysfunctions line up well with the strange situations that need to be dealt with.

HOW DID I WIND UP IN HELL BEFORE I EVEN DIED?

Many things determine the paths we take. We think we are in control of our lives, but things happen to us that push and pull us in different directions. How we process and act on these things determines the overall situations that we put ourselves in. Guess I really screwed up to wind up in Stillwater prison, even if it was me committing myself to doing time there.

There are many interesting stories I could tell you about my twenty years at McDonalds, my time doing comedy and my time in Toastmasters, but I'll just have to lay enough ground work for you to be able to understand the decisions I made that eventually landed me in the prison, so here it goes.

While in high school, I started working at McDonalds. Due to unsavory family situations, I moved out on my own as soon as I graduated high school. McDonalds, at this point, was to be my lifetime occupation. I was making a buck thirty an hour and dreamed of the day that I would be making five bucks an hour and be on easy street. This proves I was not properly educated on how the economy works or on politics in the work place.

Oh stupid me! I thought that if you worked your tail off, that if you stepped into a job and were a human dynamo, that effort would be rewarded. Wrong! Our society does not reward top performers, unless you are a jerk and toss fear into anyone that gets in your way. If you are a decent person, you will get screwed.

Why, you ask? Jealousy! There are many more people out there that are not willing to work hard, than there are out there busting their hump. Early on at McDonalds, a fellow employee got in my face and told me to slow down, that I was making everyone else look bad. I should have taken that advice, but I'm not programmed that way. I've been told I have obsessive compulsive personality traits. Supposedly that's a bad thing, but being aware of it, I look at it as a strength. I channel it toward doing the best I can possibly do; toward being as productive as possible; toward accomplishing everything I can in this life before I croak. I realized a long time ago how short life is and how fast time flies, especially when you stay busy.

I had a doctor that identified my traits. He gave me the name and telephone number of a psychiatrist he suggested I see. Then he said, "If you never see this guy and you ever start your own business, I want in on it."

While I was writing this chapter, nature called. While I was sitting there doing a puzzle and taking care of business, my lady walked by the closed door and teasingly said, "Aren't you done yet. I started after you and I'm done." I said, "I'm relaxing. This is my "me" time. This is as relaxed as I get." She said, "That's for sure."

If I could be like King Solomon and do ten things at a time or however many it was, I would. But I'm just your average everyday obsessive compulsive psycho doing his best to act as normal as possible to try to fit into what is acceptable behavior and actions in today's society. Try saying that ten times real fast.

A swing manager at McDonalds was a crew person doing the job of a manager. While I was working in this capacity and running every night shift, McDonalds established a ratings system for their stores. You could receive an A through F rating in the areas of quality, service and cleanliness. We were the first store to ever receive a triple A rating. Every store I went to after that was not doing very well when I was sent there, but received triple A ratings and increased sales while I was there.

I ran my stores as if the vice president of McDonalds would walk in at any time; and there were times when he actually did. My decisions were based on this perspective. Because of my reputation of my stores always running top notch, our advertising company would come to my store occasionally to film commercials.

The man from the advertising agency that came to produce these commercials was Peter Simmons. He was the agencies front man for McDonalds, a writer, an actor, Ronald McDonald for this area and a standup comedian. When I found out about the comedian part of his background, I had a lot of questions for him.

I was nearing forty years old at this time. I have always been shy to the point of being rude. It was time I found a way to change my programming. My mother died around this time. With her death came a release, a freedom, a mindset that I could do anything I set my mind to. I thought, "What's the best way to beat this shyness dysfunction; the toughest thing I can do, the most pressure I can put on myself, the best way to throw myself into the pit?" The answer came back, "Standup comedy!" Oh, crap!

Peter Simmons entered my life at the right time. I had been writing jokes, but didn't really know how to go about making things happen. It turns out that Peter had taught comedy writing in the past. He had me meet him in a remote McDonald's warehouse in St. Paul. There he looked over what I had written. He knew a lot and gave me the crammed course of a lifetime. He showed me how, by moving words around, the joke would have a bigger impact. He said, "Open with silver, close with gold." Or in other words, start with a great joke and close with your best.

One day he said, "You're ready. Go do it." This was good and bad. With him as my instructor, I knew I had good material and had been coached well on how to present it. Now I had to actually go to an open stage and perform in front of an audience. I had painted myself into a corner in order to make sure I couldn't back out. I had told everyone I was going to do it, so if I didn't do it, I'd look like a bigger fool than if I went up and bombed.

Stevie Ray had an open stage, so I went there. It went well; I received a lot of encouragement and continued doing it. I wound up taking comedy classes and improv classes with Stevie Ray. The improv classes brought me further out of my comfort zone. I entered "The Funniest Person in the Twin Cities" contest at the Acme Comedy Company.

In one of the rounds, I beat out a guy that had been to the finals the previous year. He came up to me and introduced himself. He was in a group called Toastmasters. I knew nothing about it at the time. Turns out it is an organization that has small clubs all over the world where you can go to improve your speaking skills. I felt I had to do things like this as much as possible to keep from regressing. The more I forced myself into uncomfortable situations, the better I became. He invited me to attend a meeting. I did and eventually I joined his club. Whenever he introduced me, he told this story and said, "If you can't beat them, have them join you."

A couple of years later, I was car pooling up to Thunder Bay, Ontario to compete in a Toastmasters humorous speech contest. The guy I was with, Keith Hardy, told me of a club they were trying to get started in Lino Lakes Prison. A man named Ken Kube was heading up the effort and

41

needed help. For some strange reason, people were afraid to go in there. No problem for me. The prison was less than 15 miles from my home. It was an interesting, uniquely rewarding experience. Both the inmates and staff told me they thought I would make a good corrections officer. I was pursuing comedy at the time, so brushed it off.

A few years later, upon returning from touring, primarily the Southwestern United States, pitching myself and my comedy, I returned home. The money I had set aside to use until I made it in the business was all used up. The trany on the van I lived in while I was out on the road was shot. I had promised myself that if I hadn't made it in the comedy biz by the time that money ran out, I would get a normal job. Guess I actually broke that promise, because the job I got would be the furthest thing from normal that I would ever run into.

Upon returning to Lino Lakes Prison to attend the Toastmasters meeting, I was informed that the state was hiring corrections officers. The fact was that they were always hiring corrections officers. It is a high turnover business. When I found out that doing cavity searches wasn't part of the job, I was still reluctant, but considered it. I was 47 years old and had discovered most places did not want to hire anyone that age. There were times I walked into a place, asked for an application and they literally laughed in my face. Lucky for me or unlucky, whatever way you want to look at it, the state could not discriminate against someone because of their age. Before applying, I checked with a few other people on that cavity search thing. Turns out there would be times I would have to be doing what was called at the time, a "strip search," but was changed to being called an "unclothed body search" while I was employed at the prison. We were told this was the politically correct way to state it, the way that was least offensive to the inmates. Heck, the inmates always called it a strip search, before and after the brains from above changed it. I'll explain the strip search procedures when I get to filling you in on the visiting room and shakedown areas. Boy, that's something to look forward to isn't it?

After filling out a job application, there were many more forms to fill out, tests to take and interviews to go through. From the time I applied until I got the job it took about three months.

When the inmates in the Toastmasters Club in Lino Lakes found out that I got hired, they gave me some advice. I always followed that advice because it was the right thing to do, but made my time working in the prison more difficult and more dangerous. They all said, "Enforce the policies. Your job is to enforce every one of the policies all of the time no matter who it is or what the situation. There will be a lot of pressure to try to get you to not enforce the policies, but don't ever let that get to you. Always enforce the policies." I promised them that I would and I did.

FRESH RAW MEAT

I was in Stillwater Prison before I put myself there.

It was sometime in the early 80's when I found myself in Stillwater Prison. I was assigned to go there and execute a job.

I was an engineer at Pan-O-Gold bakery in Minneapolis when the place closed down. It closing down wasn't my fault. The plant was run down and had been poorly maintained for years before I did my short stint there. If a machine broke down, we were not allowed to spend money to fix it correctly; we were just supposed to use bubble gum, glue, duct tape or whatever possible to keep the machine running.

A business named Pack-O-Mach, standing for "Pack of Machines", found out about me. Yes, it seems as though I was beginning to establish a trend of working for places that had hyphenated names. Pack-O-Mach primarily bought and reconditioned used bakery equipment and resold it. They bought all of the equipment in the entire bakery where I had been working. They needed someone to tear the machines out of the bakery and prepare them for shipping. They asked me if I would do it. I accepted. I may as well; I had just been laid off and had nothing better to do. I figured that I may as well keep trying to pay my bills. They figured the job would take about two weeks. I had it done in less than two days.

They liked my work and kept assigning me more. Months later they realized I had never been hired and then took care of the necessary paperwork.

One of my many jobs at this place was to install and tear out equipment in bakeries. This included the disassembly and assembly of large ovens and walk in coolers, that where sometimes as large as a small house, and flour systems among many other things.

I acquired a class "A" driver's license because of it being necessary for me to drive a truck in order to transport this equipment locally and across the country.

Because of my knack for being able to improvise and come up with strange efficient workable solutions for difficult job situations and the fact that I had the proper license for driving a truck into a government facility where that license would get checked, I was chosen to go to Stillwater Prison and tear out a flour system. Also nobody else would go.

This was an experience of a lifetime, I thought. I never could have guessed that I would wind up working here later in my life and experiencing continual experiences of a lifetime with people doing time and life.

There were two truck entrances to this place. I definitely wanted to get the right one, so I circled the prison before choosing where to go. I pulled up to a gate that happened to be the correct gate. The gate opened and an officer came out to check my paperwork, ID and ask me a few questions about my business there.

Satisfied, at this point in time, with my intent being business, he had me pull into the sallyport for trucks and other vehicles. The gate closed behind me. Before letting me through the next gate, two officers started searching my vehicle. They looked under the truck, under the hood, inside the cab, and between the cab and the box of the truck. There was an officer on the wall above with a shotgun that could view the top of the truck. They had poles with mirrors on the end to see into difficult to get at places. They had me open the door to the back of the box, so they could check out the inside.

This is where their suspicions grew and my interrogation began. I had equipment in there that was necessary for tearing equipment out of bakeries. The problem was that this wasn't any ordinary bakery. They inventoried what I had so that they knew what I went in with was what I would come out with.

My tool boxes were a problem. There were two items that I remember distinctively that they took. Hack saw blades were one. They can easily break and when you are out on a job, you can't be stopping to run out and buy more of them, so I carried a lot of them. They took all of them except for the one in my hack saw. They told me that if it broke, I had to bring them the pieces and they would let me have another one. They made it clear that anything I was taking in, I better be taking out when I go.

When doing tear outs, I always carried what I called my beater box. With the tools I had in there, I could hack out walls, chisel out concrete, smash out blocks, most anything necessary to take out supposedly permanent structures that were hindering my progress and do it quickly. An officer opened up that tool box and then turned to me with a scowl on his face. I explained about these items that he could identify with being perfect tools for anyone desiring to breakout. After my explanation, he didn't seem convinced. He pulled a hatchet out of the box and said, "What's this for?" I explained that it worked well for going through walls. He said, "You're definitely not taking this in there." So that was the second item that they were upset about me having.

As I could access my tools from them if I needed something, I volunteered to leave all but my very basic tools with them.

Eventually, I was cleared to enter. An officer hopped in the truck with me and showed me where to go. There was a cement dock at the back of a building that happened to be the kitchen and bakery area. He told me that whenever I left my truck to make sure it was locked up. He left me there with a different officer that escorted me to where I would be working.

The flour system was primarily on the second floor. Part of it was positioned over a hole in the floor that led to a hopper on the ceiling below. This hopper was positioned over a large mixer. With this system, flour could be metered from the system above, into the hopper and then the exact amount desired could be dropped into the mixer.

They no longer needed this system as they were now using bags of flour that were shipped into the prison on pallets. This was simpler for them and more security friendly.

Once he had me briefed, he left me with two inmates to help me. They were good workers with a good sense of humor.

On the second floor, hidden behind part of the flour system, was an old dirty jar. There was corrosion on the inside as if it had been full of some sort of a liquid that had fully evaporated over time. One of the inmates told me that it must have been full of hooch that someone was hiding. Once they stopped using this flour system, inmates no longer had access up there and thus couldn't get at this hooch jar.

We made good progress on dismantling this system. We got to the more difficult part of disconnecting the hopper from the bin. The hopper was by the ceiling on the first floor hanging above a large mixer. It was attached to the bin on the second floor.

I needed to rig up a system to keep control of the heavy hopper by the ceiling. I needed to be able to lower it slowly so it wouldn't crash and damage something or hurt anyone.

The officers in the sallyport had a rope that I brought with me. I needed it, so I went to get it from them. They measured it before they gave it to me, so they could make sure I came back with the same length.

Tying the rope many different ways onto many different points on the hopper in order to control its descent took some time. Just as I finished and the two inmates and I were going to take out the last couple of bolts and start lowering it, a loud alarm rang.

One of the guys in the bakery told me that alarm was letting us know we had to shut down because two things were going to happen. Inmates had to go to their cells to get counted and that they had to go start serving lunch to the inmates.

I bent over at the waist, because I still had a waist then, and started to pick up my tools. One of the inmates told me never to bend over in here. He said it was dangerous. He said to always stoop down so that nobody gets any ideas.

There was a small bathroom near with a toilet and a hand sink in it. I was going in to wash my hands when one of the inmates told me to look around before I went in there, make sure no one follows me and to lock the door behind me. He said you never know when someone will be sneaking around trying to take advantage of someone that isn't savvy to this place. Need I say that I have greatly cleaned up the actual language that was used?

At this point a baker came yelling at me. He said, "You're taking that rope down aren't you? You can't leave it hanging there. You never know when one of these idiots will decide to hang themselves or someone else."

There is no way to be totally prepared for going into a place like this. There are things that normal people just don't think of and aren't aware of. At this point in time, I was still somewhat normal; or at least I could act normal enough so that I could blend in with normal people.

Working in this place, I realized that in this situation, as the saying goes, I didn't know my ass from a hole in the ground; however, it was pointed out to me that some of the people inside these walls did and would have an interest in it.

Luckily the rope came down quicker that it went up. I wasn't allowed to stay in this area. I had to wait in an area where supposedly no inmates would be. I would be doing nothing for a couple of hours while the prison went though their routine of serving some inmates lunch, conducting count and then serving the rest of the inmates their lunch.

When the prison was through with their business, my two inmate helpers came back. I rigged up my rope again. We got the hopper loaded on the truck and all of the smaller pieces down off the second floor and loaded on the truck.

There was one large piece to get down from the second floor. This is where I got in big trouble. This piece was so large; I couldn't figure out how it got up there, much less how I was going to get it out.

Have you ever heard that a little knowledge is a dangerous thing? Well, I had knowledge of elevators from working at the Pan-O-Gold Bakery. The freight elevator there was old, decrepit and the inspectors were always threatening to shut it down. Whenever the inspectors came in, they were bestowed with a massive amount of bakery goods. This caused the bakery to avoid citations, avoid properly fixing the elevators and it caused the inspectors to come in a lot for their free food. I learned a lot about jury rigging elevators in order to get a job accomplished.

I decided that I would try to get this large flour system part down the elevator by finagling the different switches and things to keep the doors open while I slowly dropped the elevator down and manipulated the large part while moving between floor levels. What I wasn't aware of was all of the security systems within this facility. A loud alarm went off. I mean it really went off. What I was doing was the kind of thing inmates would do if they were trying to escape. Hey, I was just trying to finish a job that would've been impossible to do any other way.

Instantly there were several officers on the spot. They weren't happy. I explained what I was doing. They radioed what was going on while other officers kept showing up. My inmate helpers looked very concerned with being involved in this. As the elevator was between floors at this time, I was allowed to finish what I was doing so they could get things back to normal. Maintenance engineers showed up to fix, reset or whatever they had to do to get things back to normal from what I had done. By the time I got the piece off the elevator and they got the alarm shut off, there was a huge congregation of officers and big shot looking people around. I was sternly chastised as this congregation started to dissolve. I was glad this happened at the end of the job rather than earlier or the atmosphere here would've been even more uncomfortable than it was already.

As we finished loading the truck and securing the load, I noticed inmates out in the yard. There was a guy that was well over 300 pounds with a shaved head and lots of tattoos walking around the track. There were two guys walking with him. They were on each side of him, a half a step back. There was a large group walking orderly behind them. The guys I was working with told me the big guy was the leader of the gang.

I drove the truck to the sallyport. The officers were all over and inside my truck. They were looking inside every piece that I had picked up. I thought they checked everything out thoroughly when I came in. This search made the first one look like nothing. I suppose my elevator escapade didn't help matters any. They gave me the tools and equipment that I had left with them. They made sure I was leaving with the same amount of rope that I came in with and they made sure I was leaving with the hack saw blade that I had brought in.

When they opened the outside gate, I drove off hoping that I would never have to go back there again.

MY PERSPECTIVES – WE ARE CREATED

Some people believe that criminals are born criminals. I don't believe that. I believe they are created. I believe we are all a product of what has happened to us in our lives. Speaking with many an inmate, things they told me about themselves, their environment, what happened to them in their lives, how they spoke, these and so many other things gave me clues as to how they became who they were and justified the things they did.

As I stated previously, I have always been extremely shy. Dysfunctionally shy. This was instilled in me by my mother. The attitudes of "don't speak until your spoken to", "you can't do that", "who in the hell do you think you are", "nobody else in our family has ever done that," "what makes you think you're better than the rest of us" rang loud and clear from her. This mentality was beaten into me really well.

My mother definitely did not believe in the phrase "Spare the rod and spoil the child." Every day she made sure I wouldn't become spoiled. We won't get into her psyche; only as to how it created who I am and how it relates to how I did my job in the prison. Sometimes I just got slapped or pulled around by my hair. I could really use some of that hair back now. Sometimes, getting beaten with things like belts, yardsticks, fly swatters and branches from weeping willow trees was my cure. Oh how I still hate weeping willow trees.

I remember really well the fly swatters that she had. They had wire handles with a plastic swatter part on it. She would swat me with them until the plastic broke off. Then she would get really angry that I broke her fly swatter. Her level of rage would go off the charts and she would continue whipping me with that wire. She was very good at making sure that no marks were left where anyone would be able to see what was going on.

I remember reading the book "Mommy Dearest." I thought, "Boy, I sure wish she had been my mom. What's this kid complaining about. She had it easy."

Other people have been abused like this and worse. Some whine and want sympathy; I feel I gained strength from this. There is little anyone can do to me or say to me that would deter me from doing what I am supposed to do. My mind stays on task and pain cannot stop me.

It was good for her to do this to me though, because as she explained it, I was a rotten little kid and she was doing it for my own good.

For my own good? Well, yes and no. I've wondered at times what I could have done in life if I had been brought up not as something to use and control, but as something to guide; something to train to be able to do anything I desired to do in this short life. I've wondered what it would be like to have the power that goes along with being a fully functional human being with a normal thought process.

But, you must use to your advantage what you get and not do the "poor me" routine that many of the incarcerated do.

In order to function in this world, I had to look at what others considered to be normal. Taking an A – B – C approach has been quite beneficial to help me blend in with normal society, as much as I can any way. But my mind also looks around corners and jumps from A to X to D to Z. Basically my mind gets me there, but provides me with many options; some better than the normal, some worse and some that make me see how the criminals mind got to where it went.

FEAR

The fear of public speaking is the number one fear of most people. I have now conquered that.

People are afraid of getting beaten, injured or of pain. I was beaten so much as a kid that I got used to it and didn't fear that. Actually when I got big enough so that my mother feared me and the beatings stopped, it was like something was missing.

People fear embarrassing themselves. I've done that so many times, I'm used to it now and intentionally do things that others would never consider doing.

People fear dying. People in my family generally don't live a long time. I figure that because of some of the crazy stunts I've pulled over my lifetime, I should've been dead or killed long ago.

I have a logical mind; at least that's the way my mind sees it. I see things as "shit happens". I can't control what someone else does, natural disasters or accidents. Dealing with things to the best of my abilities is all I can control. Whatever the consequences, "que sera sera". (For those of you who have never heard that phrase, it means "Whatever will be will be." It is in an old Doris Day song.)

I have self preservation instincts to some degree, but I also like challenges, both physical and mental.

My beatings and the way I was handled gave me a different kind of power that I have used frequently during my lifetime. The power to be beaten and not have it affect me. The power to not have fear. Now, the power of no fear is a dangerous one to have, but it has made my life much more interesting than if I were normal.

EMOTIONS

Showing emotions were a sign of weakness in the environment I grew up in. Like vultures seeing a wounded animal and ripping it to pieces, some people will take advantage of that weakness.

Sometimes emotions are difficult to control, but not doing so leads to greater problems. When you let emotions take over, you can't think clearly.

Everyone is going to feel emotions at times. Most people's lives are controlled by their emotions. It's a human thing; an animal thing.

Everyone is different as to what emotions they feel, why they feel them, when they feel them and how they deal with them.

More often than not, I am able to rule emotions out of my decision making process. This makes me better able to do what has to be done, but it also makes me appear as a non caring person.

I have been alone the greater part of my life. The only one I could rely on was myself. Due to people saying things and not following through, I don't count on anyone but myself. If someone is dependable and does what they say, I appreciate that and respect that, but I also realize that there are other things that happen that could change that. I never get my hopes up or count on anything going right.

Working at this institution was like being out on the highway. You keep on trying to do exactly the right thing by going the speed limit, but there's always someone flying past you riding your ass trying to force you to do what you are not supposed to do.

NEVER LIE

As an officer in this place, I heard a lot of lies. When I instructed academies, I stressed to them that no matter what happens, what boner you pull, NEVER LIE. This is a place where it is impossible to train officers on every situation that may develop. What is correct to you, may not be correct to your superior. Most can accept that, but they cannot accept not being able to trust you.

Officers do expect inmates to lie to them, but it is a certain type of lie that would get them in trouble with me. If their lie was to try to lead me to a wrong conclusion or get someone in trouble that did nothing, that kind of lie would make me aggressive in writing them up. If they were trying to play me for a fool, that was another type of lie that would make me write up their violations.

Lies I could accept were lies that they had to tell me. For instance, if they were in a fight and needed medical help. The inmate code would not let them tell me who hurt them. They would have to tell me that they fell down or some such thing. That is an expected and necessary lie for them to tell me so they wouldn't get attacked again later. Generally if they had been assaulted, their business with the assailant had been concluded.

I would find it difficult to write up an inmate for a minor violation that they were straight up about and sincerely told me it wouldn't happen again. I found so many violations of so many types, that any that I could justify not writing was a blessing.

WHAT HAPPENED AFTER THAT

There is an important thing to realize when reading this account of my experiences in this place. Part of my job was to observe and report. When I observed violations or potential problems, my responsibility was to report it. That was the end of my responsibility.

More often than not, after I turned in my report, I did not know what happened after that. If my report caused someone to go to segregation, I would see them get hauled out, but rarely would I know what happened after that. If a deal was struck, I would not know. If they were shipped to Oak Park, I would not know. Some of these things, I could've found out if I had the time to dig or had better connections with officers that worked the areas where this information was easily accessible.

The amount of work I did, time spent manning my posts, helping offenders with their problems, supervising the swamper crew, trying to get the block in order and things repaired, and so on; filled my day and then some.

It was a challenge just to get out of there at the end of the day. Many days, I was the last one to leave from my shift. I wouldn't submit overtime unless it was someone else or the institution causing me to stay late. If I stayed late because of being aggressive at doing my job well, that wasn't normal here, so I didn't submit an overtime slip. It was easier to get out if I didn't take time to write up a slip. After over 8 hours at this job, I just wanted to get out.

What happened after writing a report was none of my business. Some people checking over this book and giving me their input stated they wanted more than just what I wrote about each incident. More often than not, I did not know or care. My job was done; as far as that incident was concerned.

There were general conclusions to most violations where the inmate was taken to segregation. Most were handled by investigation officers that would offer the violator a certain number of days in segregation. The number of days was standard per type of violation. The worse the violation and the greater the number of violations, the more segregation time they were charged with. The inmate would have to sign a paper accepting the segregation time, which was an admission of guilt, or contest it and ask for a hearing. Rarely did any of them ever contest what I had written. They would generally wind up back in my block when their time was served. They would either behave, make sure I didn't catch them again or if they did it again and I caught them, go back to segregation for another series of days there.

If their violation was extreme, they may be sent to Oak Park Heights. Violations like this would be things like them assaulting someone viciously, assaulting an officer, trying to escape, and the such.

WHY THERE ARE NOT A LOT OF BOOKS LIKE THIS

In writing these books, I realized some things.

I did not find many books on how prison life really is. There are reasons for that. When you get home, you definitely do not feel like inflicting more of this place on yourself. You need to get your head out of this place in order to try to maintain who you are and your sanity, even though that is not possible.

Working in this place 8 hours a day changes a person, and not for the better. You find out a lot of things you never knew. You have a darker perspective of life.

Sitting down and writing about this after I was out of this place, was not a pleasant experience. There were many times that those angry feelings came back; those feelings that I always worked so hard at trying to get rid of; those feelings of people that are supposed to be bad that appear to be good and those feelings of people that are supposed to be good that are bad; the feelings of friends that are enemies and enemies that become friends. The inner conflict is frustrating and confusing. It wears you down. It is difficult to maintain being the person you are or perceive yourself to be.

REGULAR MIND VS IRREGULAR MIND

Once you walk through those series of doors to start your shift, you have to force your mind into an entirely different place. I always related to it as pulling my mind out of my head and placing it on a shelf. My normal mind, at least as normal as my mind could possibly be, was not functional in this environment. Ok, instead of calling it my normal mind, let's call it my regular mind; the one I use regularly even when I'm not regular.

My abnormal mind made it so I could function in this place. Inmates told me that the way they survived and kept from going nuts was to close their eyes and imagine they were with their family, playing with their dog and many other things that made them feel good.

They told me many things that would not be appropriate for me to describe to you even in a book like this, if you know what I mean. If you don't know what I mean, you are obviously quite young. Read this book again in a few years and vivid pictures will pop into your head and you will be in a place just like those guys.

The reason it was difficult going into prison with my regular mind was because that mind feels compassion, anger and all of those other emotions that control what we do. Entering a prison is a place where my actions couldn't be governed by emotions. They had to be governed by the rules of the institution.

Quite often, my regular mind would creep in and get in the way. I would have to fight to get it back out of my way.

You can't be around some of these guys without being friends with them. There are others you can't be around without wishing Minnesota had a quick death penalty system with no appeals.

It was a great feeling when I retired knowing that I would never have to step back in that place again. At the same time it was quite sad. There were a lot of those guys that I knew I would miss.

There are people I had conflicts with that I miss, because there were people in that place that were intelligent enough to realize that my decisions were based on doing my job. I could respect people who came to me that disagreed with me. Those people helped me and the institution a lot. An inmate having the guts to tell me exactly how they viewed things was what I needed in order to make the most intelligent decision possible. I have always looked at things with the perspective of the more informed one is the better decision one can make and the better one can feel about having made the best decision possible. I was always open to hear what anyone had to say. I truly miss the diversity of perspectives and ideas these guys had. It felt good when I could incorporate that additional information into my decisions.

It was a constant battle in my head when I realized I was friends with an inmate. I felt like it was wrong. I felt like it was forbidden and against the rules. I can say that I was able to maintain objectivity and treat everyone the same, but that was becoming more and more difficult as time went on. Obviously, there were people I communicated with more and had a good time with. I frequently miss those conversations with so many of those guys. I saw things the way they saw things more than I saw things the way institution policy was laid out.

I can see how so many institution policies came about, even the ridiculous ones. One person does something stupid, so a policy is made that states that it is a violation, just in case anyone ever tries it again. Because of common sense not being allowed in courts, someday there may be a policy specifically stating how much snot an inmate is allowed to blow into a piece of toilet paper and the only allowable process acceptable to dispose of it.

There I go with my regular mind creeping in and letting out a bit of anger, but I caught it in time, I think.

It is difficult to write about feelings, especially when my persona was not to be feeling. According to a lot of the guys, I failed quite often at this.

CYA

In case you didn't already know, CYA is the acronym for "Cover Your Ass." Those three words cover everyone's responsibilities in the joint; inmates included. Those three words should be going through everyone's mind before they do anything here.

The best way to CYA is to "Know the Rules." If you know the rules and follow them you won't get in trouble as often as someone who doesn't. A problem here is that when I started working here there were supposedly three huge volumes of rule books in every lieutenant's office. Officers could've taken them and read them at a shower post or during a slow time at a door post. In their ultimate wisdom, someone higher up got the bright idea that once we got computers in the blocks, they would get rid of these manuals. They had all the information put into the computer and felt there was no longer a need for the books. Wrong! Someone always had to do work on the computer and guess what? There are no computers at the shower post or door post. These are areas that during certain parts of the day, it would be safe to read these books.

Even if you knew all of the rules forward and back and knew every angle to them or around them, you can still get in trouble. Every big shot saw things differently and enforced things differently. Every lieutenant, sergeant and officer saw things differently and enforced things differently. Everyplace in the institution was run by someone different, so the rules were different. If a different person was in charge of a cellblock from the day before, the rules were different. If a lieutenant walked through your assigned area, no matter what, you better know their pet peeves or you could get in trouble.

There was one lieutenant, who was not in charge of any cellblock that would pop into any cellblock at anytime, quickly walk down the cellblock and try to catch anyone he could at anything he could, whether or not the lieutenant in charge of that block was fine with it or not. He would even write someone up if they had their foot on the railing at the shower post.

If a situation arose where there was no cut and dried way of handling it, you could get in trouble if someone above you would've done things differently; even if the results of your actions were positive.

I schooled the inmates on CYA. I told them to just figure there was a rule against everything. This was a slight over statement, but only a slight one. I told them, when in doubt, ask an officer and that it wouldn't hurt to have a buddy or two close to hear what was said. I also told them to remember the date, time and name of the officer they asked and specifically what was said. This was because anyone ranking higher than that officer, that didn't like what that officer said, or didn't like the officer or the inmate, might put pressure on that officer to lie. You have to be able to say "so and so told me this was OK." That way your ass is covered, so long as they don't lie about it.

Here is a mild example of CYA that I ran into toward the end of my time in Stillwater. I received a call at work from an inmate that had been released. He had been a cell hall worker for me. He called wanting me to be a job reference for him. They are not allowed to contact us. If something like this happens, we have to notify our superiors. I notified my sergeant, lieutenant, case worker (past sergeant), investigations and the Watch Commander. It was necessary to notify all of these people in order to CYA.

SHIFT HISTORY

After about 3 months of jumping through hoops, interviews, tests, medical examinations, I started academy on August 30, 2000. My rate of pay was $10.71 per hour.

After completing academy, I started out on the 2nd Watch Utility position with Tuesday's & Wednesday's off.

"Utility" means that you can be assigned anywhere in the prison. You could be in segregation one day, tower the next, visiting the next... You go where ever you are needed.

Wednesday was the first day of the pay period. I had my last day of the academy on Tuesday, so they gave me Thursday off. This made my first day of actual work Friday, October 13, 2000. How's that for starting off on the right foot in a place like this. I started on Friday the 13th.

Eventually I was told that I was being forced to 1st Watch. I had expected this and it was OK as far as I was concerned. Being forced into a position still leaves you being able to bid elsewhere if something pops up that you are interested in. If you bid on a position, you are not allowed to bid on anything for another 3 months. If your dream position becomes available during that 3 month period, you are out of luck. If you perceive that there is a dream position in this place, you have been out of luck for a long time.

One week after being informed that I was being forced to 1st watch, I was informed that things had changed and that I was being forced to the visiting room instead. I told them that they told me they were forcing me to 1st watch and I was holding them to it. They found no humor in that. Hey, it was worth a shot.

I started in the visiting room on February 28, 2001. Checking out nuts & butts all day was not my idea of a great career move. I let it be known that if I got stuck there for long, I would be quitting. Little did I know at the time what a good career move that would've been.

The place I had worked most up until this time was segregation. Most people did not like to work seg because it was loud and smelly. You had to work hard and put up with more pissed off assholes than if you worked other areas. Pissed off assholes can be quite entertaining at times. I liked being busy, it made the time go faster. A job like this isn't a dream job; it's a job to pay the bills. Many officers here have a second job, especially if they have a family to support.

The lieutenant in segregation liked my work ethic. He wanted me in seg and seg was my preference. I liked the officers there, the sergeant and the lieutenant. That is the biggest plus in this place if you can find it. The lieutenant spoke to the sergeant in the visiting room and requested that she keep me out of shakedown as much as possible, so I wouldn't quit before he had a chance to get me in his unit. She did what she could, but any time in shakedown was repulsive to me.

I had to do the visiting room for two weeks with Monday's and Tuesday's off.

An opening came up on 1st watch, so I bid on it in order to try to get out of visiting. I got it, so I went to 1st watch with my days off being Wednesday's and Thursday's which is Tuesday's starting at 10pm & Wednesday's starting at 10pm. My first day on First Watch was March 14, 2001.

Second watch was my preference. It ran from 6am to 2:30pm. I knew that was a long shot at this time because I had very low seniority.

Third Watch ran from 2:10pm until 10:10pm.

Convincing myself that being on first watch was my best move was necessary, so I made up a list of what I perceived to be the pros and cons.

It gave me the best shot at getting overtime, which I needed badly.

It was easier to get people to switch shifts with me than if I was working in the visiting room, but I rarely did switches anyway.

First watch made it so I could get workout times in the gym when the gym wasn't very busy, which I really didn't take advantage of very well.

It made it so my day hours were available for appointments, running errands, making phone calls, doing yard work and doing comedy gigs around town. This one actually did pan out a bit.

It was a shift where there was lower stress, because the inmates were locked in and most were asleep.

It made it possible to do things with friends, but rarely.

What I found out was that it cuts your evenings short. Just when things are getting rolling around town, you have to leave and get ready to go to work.

Getting to sleep was impossible. Trying to sleep during the day is tough. My toughest job in life has always been trying to get some sleep. Now I'm trying to get to sleep with it being light out and with many more noises that are much louder than at night. I found it difficult to shut my mind off. I had the urge to get up and make my daylight time productive. The cycle that evolved was that I spent all night trying to stay awake, all day trying to go to sleep and the only time I could actually doze off easily was when I was driving home from work. Luckily, I never crashed into anyone. Hitting the gravel on the side of the road would wake me up enough to go a little further, then conk out, then hit the ditch, and on and on. By the time I got home, I was so rattled that I couldn't get to sleep. Working this shift, I was always way too tired to accomplish anything needing energy or brain power.

On this watch I had to work with some wienie snitches, not my favorite type of person. I'm fine with anything they tell a boss about me that is accurate, but don't make things up.

By bidding, I was frozen for 3 months.

After being on 1st watch for 4 months, two opportunities came up in the same week. Both of them were on 2nd watch. One was a position in segregation and the other was in B-West. The seg position was my preference, but getting to 2nd watch at this point was critical. My health was going down and my weight was going up. The position in seg had better days off, so I lost out on that one, but I was lucky enough to get the B-West position with the low seniority that I had.

Starting on July 18, 2001, B-West became my home with Tuesdays and Wednesdays off. I was in this block until February 21, 2006. This block had a reputation from the past. It was called "The Wild Wild West." Little did I know at this time that while I was there, changes would be made that would make it wilder than it ever was before.

One year after graduating from the academy the rate of pay was increased from $13.86 to $14.26. This was the step 2 classification.

NUMBSKULL

My time in B-West was near an end. One reason for leaving was that for some time, my head would gradually go numb. This day, by the time I left, my head was totally numb again.

I had been to doctors to try to find out what was wrong. The doctors ran me through a lot of tests.

One day they gave me a brain scan. The doctor said, "We couldn't find anything."

I said, "I'm paying you to tell me that? My mother told me that for years."

Once I got out of B-West, the numbness went away.

BASHAM ERA ENDS IN B-WEST

The morning started off with Officer Cutter creating problems again. She caught two guys taking sugar packets. They weren't hooch makers. They wanted some flavor for their coffee.

If we caught it, the best way of handling it was to give them a verbal warning and document it in their file.

She started yelling at them and told them she was locking them up. She was spazzing out again. Her physical antics and yelling created a huge scene and was escalating the situation. I had to step in. First I had to get her to chill out. Then I had to calm one guy down that was tired of putting up with her superiority trip.

Before the morning had ended, we had to send four inmates to segregation for making hooch.

MOVIN' ON OUT

Later in the day, I emptied my locker and moved the items to a locker in A-East. Officers were like vultures waiting for me to evacuate. Two officers took shelves that I had in my locker and another moved his things into what was no longer my locker.

When I stepped into A-East, one of the swampers already wanted a favor. He wanted me to appoint him to the laundry job. I told him I'd decide once I found out what was actually going on in the block. I didn't want to step on anyone's toes.

Three block officers and two sergeants were working in B-West on my last day in that block. They gave me a going away party at the Crab House in Stillwater after work. They picked up a card and signed it. I didn't expect anything like that. It was a very nice gesture. I appreciated it.

And so the "Basham Era" ended in B-West.

BASHAM ERA BEGINS IN A-EAST

My first day in A-East was February 22, 2006. I was there until I retired with my last day being May 24, 2008.

I was on a round with another officer. An inmate, who didn't know who I was because he was new to the institution, asked what was going on.

I said, "He's training in the rookie".

An inmate on the flag said, "You ain't no rookie. Far from it."

An inmate in his cell on gallery three heard what was going on. He stepped out of his cell to see what was up. When he saw me he froze. He just stood there with a shocked look on his face. I could hear him say, "Oh shit!"

He turned around and went back in his cell. Obviously, my reputation came with me.

There was a barber in A-East that I had worked with in B-West. We had knocked heads many times before. When he saw me, he gave me a lot of attitude. I could guarantee that he would not comply with the job standards that I required. That means that I could guarantee that he would not be a barber in A-East much longer. Before I went to A-East, I was informed that the lieutenant wanted me to take over the swamper crew and get this block squared away. Those inmates that would cooperate and assist me in that endeavor would be around. Those that resisted and created problems would either leave on their own, be fired or leave by way of segregation.

I could tell that the other officers were feeling a little bit of pressure from me being there as they were well aware of my reputation for taking care of business.

The sergeant, that rarely wrote a report, wrote up three inmates that day.

Trying to get up to speed as fast as possible, I asked the other officers what was enforced in this block and what they didn't enforce. They told me what they were supposed to enforce, but I never saw them enforcing those policies.

The lieutenant told me that he definitely wanted the policy stating that, everyone is supposed to have their ID in the slot by the phone they were using, enforced and unauthorized area violations enforced. By the time I left that day, everyone on the phones had their ID's up and everyone was staying on their assigned side of all black lines that were painted on the floor.

When I cruised the flag enforcing policy, the inmates thought it was kind of strange because the other officers just sat in chairs passing the time of day. The inmates definitely liked the other officers' style better than mine.

One inmate that wanted to go out on a visiting pass gave me attitude. I told him I wasn't taking that attitude and that if he wanted to settle down, maybe we'd have a chat. He eventually squared himself away and apologized.

Being in A-East was like being on vacation compared to working in B-West. I didn't have to answer a thousand questions every day, there were only a few. These inmates were much more cooperative than those in B-West, even though they weren't exactly happy with me enforcing policies.

My second day in A-East the lieutenant called me into his office. He thanked me for bidding into his block. This was unexpected, appreciated and rather cool. It was a total flip flop from the way I had been treated by my last lieutenant.

And so began my stretch in A-East.

As I had just entered this block, a lot of policies were not being followed. During a security check, I observed 14 inmates using footlocker lids as headboards. I issued verbal warnings to the 11 that had this as their first violation. This was the second violation for three of the inmates, so it was necessary for me to lock them in their cells.

BACK TO B-WEST FOR ONE NIGHT

On a Friday night, I worked for another officer In B-West. They asked me if I would work the bubble. I told them that I would. Entering the bubble, I detected odors. It stunk. Trash was piled up and rotting. Everyone was too lazy to empty the trash. The place was a disaster. Junk was lying around everywhere. It took a while to get the clutter cleared out so I could actually do my job. Before the end of the shift, I had everything squared away, clean and in order.

I went through all of the bunking requests. When the inmates saw me in there, many of them came asking me to do things for them. More bunking request slips started pouring in. I told them that I would set up paperwork, but it would be up to the block officers tomorrow whether or not they would make the moves. The next morning, I received an email from one of the block officers thanking me for all the work I did. They made all of the moves that I had lined up.

A 3rd watch officer in B-West told me that the books had not been the same since I left. He said they needed me back. I told him I appreciated it, but I would never be back.

Another 3rd watch officer in B-West had been enforcing policies. The inmates give him static and called him Basham Junior.

One of my block sergeants, when I was in B-West, became a caseworker. He said, "Most of my memories of B-West are bad, but you're a good one."

HISTORY OF STILLWATER
PRISON IN BAYPORT

WHY

Why write a section about the history of Stillwater Prison? It's because that is the main character in these books and it's very interesting. People come and go. Programs come and go. The prison changes, but it is always there. Without it none of these stories would exist. My time in this prison is the largest portion of these books because that is what I have firsthand knowledge of. Working in the prison, I heard other stories and developed more questions about the place. Researching these questions and trying to verify accuracy of some stories I heard took a long time and raised more questions, but I had to stop somewhere. This is the tip of the iceberg. Anything in these books will relate in some way or another to this prison. Items from the past will give you more of a perspective of the place and add a bit more flavor to this institution. People are always curious about what happens in prisons and how they work. These books will give you an excellent perspective of this specific prison by giving you pieces of its puzzle. However, most things will relate to any prison.

FACT OR FICTION

The information in this chapter was acquired from the Minnesota's Department of Corrections web site, the Washington County Historical Society, information I received while attending the academy, information I received about the James-Younger Gang from visiting museums in Missouri and Kansas, information I received by visiting the Northfield Historical Society, some information from the prisoner's newspaper "The Prison Mirror", information I received from people inside Stillwater Prison (staff and inmates, of course the old timers were very interesting) and numerous internet sites. Information from one source to another varied.

The information from the DOC web site was a good chronological guide line; however I would call the information close but not 100%. The DOC was always good at covering up what actually happened in the prison. Stories that got out were generally watered down. Information from that site is what is in the public record and not necessarily all of the facts.

The internet was the best resource for information on the Younger brothers; however information varied from one source to another.

My opinion has always been that criminals are created; that people are not born to be criminals. Environment, how they have been treated or mistreated and the examples that are set for them are a few of the areas that dictate how they view the world and process information. Visiting the museums in Missouri and Kansas solidified my opinion. By learning events that shaped the lives of the Younger brothers and the James brothers, from the area and time they grew up in and getting varying perspectives, I could see how they made the choices they made. Had they not grown up in the time and area that they did, I don't believe we would've ever heard of them.

SHOW ME

There are some excellent old pictures available on the internet that can give you some visuals of what I'll be writing about in this section. The cost to obtain these was far beyond my means. The cost to put them in this book would've increased the price of the book beyond what most would want to pay.

I admit to being frugal, because I have to be. These pictures are interesting, but in my opinion, not worth the cost. However, should you like to take a peak; here is a list of web sites and some of the paths necessary to find some of those pictures, at least of 2016.

Minnesota Historical Society
http://sites.mnhs.org/library
How Do I
Ordering a Photograph
Searching for Photographs
Search MNHS Research Material
Type "Stillwater Prison" in the search box

Minnesota Department of Corrections
www.doc.state.mn.us
Photo & Video Gallery
About
DOC Background/History

www.google.com/maps
Minnesota Correctional Facility Stillwater
970 Pickett Street North, Bayport, MN 55003, 651 779 2766

www.google.com/maps
Old Prison, 604 Main Street North, Stillwater, MN 55082

Google or Bing "Younger Brothers"

LOCATION, LOCATION, LOCATION

Stillwater prison is a registered historical site. Stillwater prison is in Bayport. How did that happen, you ask? Well, I'll tell you, eventually.

On July 2, 1839, a member of a Sioux tribe was killed and scalped by two Chippewa near Lake Calhoun. This caused the Sioux to send out war parties to find them and get revenge.

The next day, the Sioux found the Chippewa camped in a marshy ravine on the shore of the St. Croix River and attacked. This area is on the north end of Stillwater.

The Sioux caught them by surprise. 21 Chippewa were killed, 29 were wounded and the Sioux had no injuries or deaths.

This bloody battle in this ravine became known as "Battle Hollow". This site was chosen for the Minnesota Territorial Prison.

Minnesota became a territory in 1849. Alexander Ramsey was its governor. At this time prisoners were held at Fort Snelling and Fort Ripley as counties had no jails. On September 3, 1849, Ramsey addressed the territorial legislature. He stated that "there should be proper and safe places of confinement." He requested that they ask the federal government for money to build a prison.

In June of 1850 the government appropriated $20,000 to the territory to be used to build the prison.

Both Stillwater and St. Paul were being considered to become the capitol. Stillwater was important because its logging industry was booming.

Battle Hollow had an area of 4 acres, which was enough space for a prison at that time. This area was surrounded on three sides by bluffs. This worked well for the Sioux to be able to contain and conquer the Chippewa without receiving any casualties themselves. The legislature felt that this would be a great location for containing inmates in their territorial prison. That is why in February of 1851, St. Paul was designated to be the capitol and Stillwater was chosen to be the site for the prison.

Construction began in May of 1851. The prison was ready by April 4, 1853. Francis Delano, one of the contractors building the prison was appointed to a five year term as its first warden. There were a total of 13 wardens running this prison until it was abandoned in 1914.

Buildings completed by the time the prison was open for business were a three story housing unit with six cells and two dungeons for solitary confinement, a workshop and an office. They were constructed of limestone taken from nearby quarries. The wall surrounding the prison was 12 feet high. A warden's house was built outside of the walls on the south bluff overlooking the prison.

(As the prison population began to grow, the original building that held only six cells was torn down and replaced by a building that held 158 prisoners.)

The cells measured five by seven feet and had steel floors. The ventilation was poor and the small cell hall windows allowed very little light to enter. It was always damp and dingy. There was no running water or toilet.

Flat out the location sucked. Whenever it rained or there was snow melt, the prison had water flowing into it that was running off from the higher elevations around it.

Water constantly flowed into the prison. Cellblock workers had to try to get the water out of the prison in order to keep it livable for the inmates. They had to sweep out the water, squeegee it or do whatever they could to try to get all of that water out of the prison. Because of this, they acquired the name of "Swampers." That name is still what the inmates that clean the cell halls are called to this day.

(Even as recently as 2000, in the infinite wisdom of the Minnesota politicians, the prison in Rush City was built on swamp land because the state could acquire that land cheap. This created greater expense problems after it was built due to parts of the prison sinking.)

Warden Delano built up a profitable business for himself using the prison, its prisoners and hiring about 15 people from Stillwater to come into the prison to work. He used eight thousand dollars of his own money to buy steam powered machinery for the manufacturing of shingles, sashes, doors, flooring, wagons, and plows.

Factory owners worked at getting the wardens job so they could rent prison shops and use cheap inmate labor.

There were very strict rules governing the old prison. Inmates were required to be kept busy from sunrise to sunset, so they worked less in the winter due to fewer hours of daylight. They were allowed thirty minutes off to eat each meal. Inmates were not allowed to talk except on rare occasions. Dungeon cells were used for the unruly or disobedient. When in the dungeon cells, they were allowed only bread and water. If that didn't take care of the problem, they would receive 20 lashes a day for 5 days.

Escapes were frequent by such methods as prying, digging, dismantling and sawing. There were no night guards. In 1856, seven men and one woman escaped. On June 27, 1857, every prisoner escaped. Francis Delano was still the warden. As his background was as a contractor, he was more concerned with using the prison and prisoners to make money rather than having a secure facility.

Minnesota became a state on May 11, 1858. The territorial prison became the first state prison. The new warden tightened security, ordering muskets and bayonets to be used by guards; reduced prison accessibility by outsiders; and refused to accept county prisoners.

In 1860, the prison started making the prisoners wear black and white striped uniforms. They were used until 1921.

In 1861, an addition included three cells for women.

In 1862, the legislature passed a law allowing prisoners to have their sentence reduced three days for every month of good behavior that they racked up.

In 1864, a 24 x 24 foot stable was built on the lot adjoining the Warden's House. The construction of the stable was completed in July for the cost of $75. The stables eventually evolved into a two-story framed carriage house. By 1910 the carriage house was used as an automobile garage.

Female convicts were generally locked up in local jails or county jails. In 1870, the prison started locking up females there on a regular basis. Nellie Sullivan became the prisons first female inmate since Minnesota had become a state. She was 19 years old. The best that I could find about her crime was an inference that she was a sexually promiscuous person. It became necessary to build a different area in which to house her and other women.

Matrons were assigned to care for, control and discipline the women prisoners. The wives of prison staff were generally assigned to be the matron. The work for the female offenders was washing, ironing and mending clothes. This set up went on for 50 years, which is when the Shakopee Correctional Facility for Women was opened.

In 1874 the Minnesota legislature passed a law that allowed prisoners to be paid for the work that they did.

November 22, 1876, the Younger Brothers, (Cole, Jim, and Bob) arrived to serve life sentences for the Northfield Bank Raid.

What did the prisoners eat in 1879? The Minnesota Department of Corrections web site states that "typical prison food consisted of boiled meat, potatoes, vegetable and two slices of bread on a tin dish with a cup of water. Coffee, tea and porridge were also served. Milk was a delicacy reserved for the sick. Fruit, butter, salt and pepper were not provided."

The prison had two fires in 1884, both in January. The first fire was on the 8th. The second and worst was on the 25th. This fire started in the wood working shop. The state militia was called and helped get about 350 prisoners out of their cells. The temperature was below zero. The inmates were held in different parts of the prison yard before being moved to a foundry where they were guarded by the militiamen. An inmate who did not obey the order to leave was the only casualty. About the only objects saved were the prison records.

The Younger Brothers had been in Stillwater prison seven years at this point in time. Cole Younger later wrote, "There was danger of a panic and a terrible disaster." The prison shopkeeper, who trusted the Younger's, released them and handed a revolver to Cole, an axe handle to Jim and a small iron bar to Bob.

According to a quote attributed to Cole, "We stood guard over the women prisoners, marched them from the danger of fire, and the prison authorities were kind enough to say that if it had not been for us there might have been tremendous loss of life."

The next day the prison was flooded with telegrams, and newspaper headlines that read such things as, "Did the Younger's escape?" and "Plot to free the Younger's." The warden suggested to his chief deputy that the Younger's be put in irons, not because he feared them, but to soothe the public. The deputy refused. Instead he took the Younger's to the county jail downtown, where they stayed three to four weeks. It was the only time they were outside the prison from 1876 to 1901.

Cole Younger recorded, "I can say without fear of contradiction that had it been in our minds to do so, we could have escaped from prison that night, but we had determined to pay the penalty, and if we were ever to return to liberty, it would be with the consent and approval of the authorities and the public."

Governor Hubbard worked on finding cell space for the prisoners by telegraphing county jails and the Wisconsin State Prison in Waupun. Most inmates were transferred by train. A few were housed temporarily on the prison grounds.

A matron and six female inmates were guests of the warden and his wife at their home adjacent to the prison before being taken to Winona. Three of them were doing time for murder.

As soon as they could put a roof on the burnt prison, the prisoners were brought back.

Most reconstruction was completed by the middle of 1886. There were now 582 cells and work space with machinery to employ over five hundred people. At the time there were only 387 prisoners.

On July 11, 1887, fifteen inmates put up $200 to start a prison paper. Three of the fifteen were the Younger brothers. Cole and James each gave $20 and Bob gave $10.

On August 10, 1887, the first edition of "The Prison Mirror" was published at the old Minnesota State Prison in

Stillwater. It is the oldest continuously published prison newspaper in the country.

Cole Younger was a printer's assistant, called a "printer devil" back in those days.

In 1885, the legislature began the process of creating the Minnesota State Reformatory for Men. St. Cloud was chosen due to the granite quarry there that could be used to build the facility. The purpose was to be for correcting "criminal tendencies before they became chronic". It was felt that a younger prisoner could not be reformed by locking him up with the hardened criminals at Stillwater. In 1889, inmates began being transferred from Stillwater to St. Cloud.

In 1916, construction began at the St. Cloud site on the largest enclosed granite wall in the world. It is over one mile long, 22 feet high, and four and one-half feet thick. It was constructed from granite quarried within the prison grounds. This wall transformed the reformatory into the prison where all convicted felons first enter. Here they are evaluated. Some stay here while most get transferred to other Minnesota Correctional facilities.

Between 1858 and 1889 the cell capacity at Stillwater grew from 22 cells to 582.

In 1892, the forerunner of the parole system began. This allowed prisoners considered to be good risks to be released from prison before their sentence expired.

The twine factory banged out one million pounds of twine this year.

In 1893, a new parole law was passed by the legislature authorizing release of prisoners on parole prior to the expiration of their sentence.

There were three different classes of prisoners, each with its own uniform and its own set of rules and privileges.

Prisoners could be leased out to do work for others up until 1895. After that, only the sale of finished goods from the prison shops was permitted.

Inmates convicted to life sentences had not been allowed to be paroled. In 1901, the law was amended to allow lifers to be eligible for parole. This is when Jim and Cole Younger were paroled.

If you want Minnesota to have the death penalty, it's not going to happen. That is the fault of the Ramsey County Sheriff's Department. In 1906, they failed to properly hang murderer William Williams. There must not have been a budget crunch that year, because they used some extra rope on this guy. When the trap door was dropped and he fell through expecting to be hung, it did not happen, being hung that is. His feet touched the ground. No, it was not a divine intervention. The idiot that determined the length of the rope must have been bad at math. The three wizard deputies that were standing on the scaffolding were quick to find a solution. They pulled up on the rope and held him there thrashing around. It took fourteen and a half minutes before he stopped moving. Strangulation was not considered a proper way to be executed. Having one's body weight plop down at the end of the rope is a main ingredient in helping to help snap the neck and spinal cord. This was considered the humane way to kill. This hanging was like watching the end of a basketball game where one team keeps intentionally fouling the team that is leading and getting further behind. It seems to go on forever when you want it to end. You keep watching because you want to see how long it will take before the stupidity ends. The spectators expected a quick show and instead wound up with a marathon. I don't know if they were upset with all of the wiggling around or if they had other plans, but they were upset. Newspapers that printed this fiasco generated the public to put pressure on the legislature to end death sentences. This change took five years to execute no more executions. Before this change passed, however, they took a shot at consistency. They thought about performing all hangings at Stillwater prison. The thought was probably that one group of officers could dispose of prisoners more efficiently than various hacks across the state. I worked with plenty of officers that would have liked to have been on a death squad like that.

(While going through the academy and working in the prison I heard this story many times. Only the version being told was that the sheriff grabbed the rope and started dragging the guy around the grounds until he died. This is an example of how the truth gets distorted over time.)

As time passed, the state needed a larger prison to accommodate their increasing number of felons. They chose a location two miles south of the Battle Hollow location in South Stillwater. They secured 160 acres on a bluff overlooking the St. Croix River. This location also solved the problem of water flowing from the surrounding area into the prison.

The prison didn't open officially until 1914; however some prisoners were transferred there in 1909 to work in the twine factory.

The powerhouse, water tower and industry buildings were the first to be built. The prisoners lived on the third floor of the south industry building in a dormitory. They went to work on the first floor in the twine factory. Making twine was a staple of the prison industries program from early on at the first prison until a few decades ago when the demand for twine diminished.

In 1914, the new larger prison in South Stillwater officially opened to replace the prison in Stillwater. With the construction costs, the state was able to direct funds toward education and recreation activities for the inmates. This Minnesota prison was a model for countries around the world to come to see. The same thing happened when Minnesota built the Oak Park Heights Super Max Prison 68 years later.

In 1920, the Minnesota State Reformatory for Women was opened for business. The female prisoners housed in Stillwater entered their new homes in Shakopee.

With the new prison on line, the state expanded its prison industries program. In 1921, all of the prison industries became known as the Industrial Department. They produced twine, rope, barrels, shoes, farm machinery and other farm equipment. The prison industries program is now called MINNCOR. They have recently phased out of producing most of the farm machinery, however they will produce whatever they can get a contract for. While I was working there around 2006, they received a contract to assemble tractors.

On September 26, 1922, South Stillwater became a separate city from Stillwater. They changed the name of their new city to Bayport. That is how Stillwater Prison wound up in a town called Bayport.

During the 1930's, most of the old prison's buildings were torn down to provide stone for public works projects.

In1941, the state sold the warden's house to the Washington County Historical Society and the two remaining prison buildings were sold to a dairy. The old warden's house is still there and is being used as a museum.

In 1953, there was a riot in Stillwater Prison. The inmates tore the place up. They were protesting conditions and rules. The riot was so loud that people living near the prison could hear the noise.

I found information that stated that during an incident in 1960, it took 150 guards with bayonets to get inmates back into their cells. Where they got all of those guards and all of those bayonets, I have no idea. Another time tear gas was needed to regain control of the prison.

Two televisions were put in each of the A and B cellblocks in May of 1965. The inmates were allowed to buy televisions for their cells by the time the early 1970's rolled around.

A work release program was instituted in 1967. Inmates that met specific guidelines were allowed to work at paid jobs outside of the prison. Others were allowed to participate in community vocational programs.

In 1970, the "twine factory was closed by the warden, primarily because it did not provide marketable vocational training for inmates."

Warden Jack Young prevented an escape by firing a shotgun at a cellblock where inmates were cutting bars with a stolen piece of machinery known as a "Cincinnati Grinder."

During this incident, three officers were taken hostage. Inmates tried to walk out wearing the officers' uniforms. These inmates were not successful. Not that this could not happen at some point, but during an uprising, this would be expected. Inmates gave up after listing grievances for a reporter.

Later, another disturbance was ended with the use of shotguns and tear gas.

In 1971, an inmate stabbed the warden several times. This got the stabber committed as mentally ill and dangerous. Why wasn't this inmate committed before he tried to kill the warden? It's because massive buildings would have to be built to house all of those guys that could be listed as mentally ill and dangerous. A lot more staff would need to be employed. Those people would require higher rates of pay than correction officers. Housing those committed would cost much more than housing them in prisons. The warden lived, but obviously the physical and mental scars remained.

In 1972, a program called Legal Aid to Minnesota Prisoners (LAMP) was created to help inmates with problems other than criminal in nature. The program was run by the state Public Defenders Office.

"The Ombudsman for Corrections was authorized by the state legislature as an independent state agency." This was the first program of its kind in the United States. There is a section later that explains this program.

In 1975, a murdered inmate was found in his cell. We find plenty of inmates that have been beaten, but rarely is anyone murdered. Suicide is the larger problem. I should say that we assume that they have been beaten, because most often they assure us that they just fell. From the inmate's statements of so many falling down, vertigo must be something a lot of inmates must catch upon entering prison. Our country's surgeon general should check into this problem, maybe not.

May 30, 1975, after a one hour riot, an inmate with his throat cut was found on the flag after being tossed off the third tier. Yes, he did die shortly thereafter.

In 1977, in order to establish more control of the prison, housing assignments, unannounced cell block searches, extended inmate work days and other restrictions were implemented at Stillwater. Truckloads of contraband were removed from cells.

Even with the higher security measures, four inmates escaped by sawing through the bars and getting over a fence. They were all caught. Two of them never got very far. One was able to turn his escape into a two day vacation. The other was able to party for five days before being found.

In 1980, sentencing guidelines were created. This established consistency within the system for like crimes. This way, those choosing to commit a crime could see what their sentence would be if they got caught. If you felt like taking a three year vacation from freedom, you could look up crimes that would get you three years and commit one of them. However, this system established a new type of parole system. If sentenced to three years, you would only have to do two thirds of your sentence and be paroled for the final year if you behaved in the slammer. If you wanted to do the full three years, you would have to be a bad boy, bad boy, what ya gonna do; go for three or two.

In 1982, the Oak Park Heights Correctional Facility opened. This was called a super max prison at the time. It was designed differently than any other prison. Being the first of its kind, people came from other countries to examine it and still do. This is now a common design for states and other countries to build.

Escapes are preventable if officers are alert and question anything that does not seem normal. It took more than one security breech from officers for two inmates to be able to escape in 1982. The inmates did like little kids would do. They hid in cardboard boxes, were loaded on a truck and driven out of the prison. No further escape attempts have been successful from Stillwater since then. Inmates have walked away from minimum security outside of the walls, but no one has escaped from within the prison walls.

In 1983, the nice young gentlemen residing in cells in the prison got a little rowdy. When that many people of that type are placed in one place, bad things can happen. In this case, the public had to bear the cost of replacing 900 windows.

In 1985, sex offenders became the largest group locked up in Minnesota prisons. There were 430 of them which was eighteen and a half percent of the total population. This caused the Department of Corrections to mount a huge effort to increase the number of programs for these smarmy characters.

In 1989, the legislature increased the amount of time criminals would be doing. Many sentencing guidelines were doubled. I don't know if this was to be a deterrent to committing crimes or if they wanted to keep these guys off the streets longer. It did create a need for more prisons.

In 1993, Stillwater's warden got the bright idea to create a controlled movement system. Guess what? I'm not being sarcastic. This was actually a bright idea. Instead of inmates being able to wander anywhere in the prison, groups were restricted to who could go where and when. Fewer numbers of inmates were allowed to be out of their cells and cellblocks at one time. This made it more difficult to be able to victimize other inmates. It also made it more difficult for groups to organize and create problems.

In 1995, Minnesota was the first in the nation to establish a restorative justice program with a full-time staff person. This has been a very successful program that allows victims and/or victims' families to interact with the criminal. This can create closure or healing for all involved. Criminals can put a face and feelings to the negativity that they caused.

In 1996, the city of Stillwater bought the site of the old prison for $845,000 to preserve it as a historical site.

In 1997, Minnesota's prison population reached over 5,000 inmates. The constant rise came from criminalizing more offences and increased length of sentences.

As of August 1, 1997, the state banned tobacco from being in their prisons, inmates and staff included. This was not popular. Tobacco became a highly sought after form of contraband and thus worth a lot of money. An old timer told me that before this policy went into effect, it was not possible to see from one end of a cellblock to the other because the smoke was so thick. Imagine the affects of that second hand smoke on those living or working in that foul air.

In 2002, Stillwater opened a new health services unit inside the main building. The old health services' building was separate from the main prison building. It had been built on a hill within the perimeter of the wall in the early 1900s. The old building was torn down and the hill was removed in order to make room for the new segregation unit.

On Tuesday September 3, 2002, fire destroyed the old prison's historic three story brick twine factory that had been built in 1890. Witnesses reported seeing three people running from the building shortly before the fire was reported around 8pm. It took more than 150 fire fighters from 15 neighboring fire departments to put out the fire. Due to its secluded location, vandalism on this site had been an ongoing problem. Two of the three men, that did not set the fire, turned themselves in two days later. They identified the man that started the fire. An 18-year-old St. Paul man was apprehended and charged with arson the next day. This crime carried a penalty of 10 years in prison and/

or a $20,000 fine. When police asked him why he set the fire, he replied, "I was bored." The two accomplices told the police investigators that they entered the building to investigate rumors that it was haunted by the ghost of Cole Younger. The three men explored the old twine factory building for 40 minutes. The arsonist stated that when he became bored, he placed a piece of cardboard under a shelf and lit it with a cigarette lighter. However, the next day he said that he might have thrown the cardboard into an open can, also igniting spilled liquid. The State Fire Marshall's office confirmed the use of a flammable liquid to start the fire. Due to this historic site being destroyed, the city sold the land to a developer for the same amount ($845,000) that they paid for it back in 1996.

In 2004, the prison population was continuing to rise. The DOC had been trying to maximize the number of beds in their prisons. They made future plans for more beds. In the mean time, they contracted with county jails to house their overflow of criminals.

Wisconsin even took some of our prisoners. I don't know when this started, but I believe it is no longer necessary.

Methamphetamine became very popular causing the prison population to spike. By January 1, 2005, the number of inmates locked up in Minnesota prisons due to being involved with meth was at 1,087 verses only 139 just 4 years earlier.

A prisoner attempting to escape was found in the basement of a prison industry building by a trained dog. He was captured 90 minutes after it was discovered that he was not where he was supposed to be. He had made a dummy and positioned it at the sink in his cell as if it were washing up. A seasoned corrections officer identified that something was wrong when checking that cell during the mid day count. That same prisoner was caught trying to escape from a jail in 1985. Escape materials were discovered in his cell in 1992.

In 2007, the warden's house across the street from the prison was refurbished and dedicated as the Jack & Adele Young Conference Center. They were the last ones to live there when Jack was warden from 1968-1971. This would have been a good house for one of those remodeling shows to cover.

(While I was working at the prison, a training instructor was hired for both the Stillwater and Oak Park Heights Prisons. This house was being used for training and had not yet been refurbished. Bats lived in this house and were frequently seen flying around. One day this instructor was bitten by one of these bats, thus his nickname became "Batman.")

The new segregation unit opened shortly after I retired in 2008. "The 150-bed unit provides a safer, more functional and energy efficient means of supervising offenders who must be segregated from the general population. The $19.6 million building features solid doors, electronic locking, and wider hallways."

YOUNGER BROTHERS

Thomas Coleman Younger
(January 15, 1844 - March 21, 1916)
Cole was paroled in 1901, pardoned in 1903 and died in 1916 at the age of 72.

James Hardin Younger
(January 15, 1848 - October 19, 1902)
Jim was paroled in 1901 and committed suicide in 1902 at the age of 54.

John Harrison Younger
(1851 – March 17, 1874)
John died from a gunshot in 1874 at the age of 23.

Robert Ewing Younger
(October 29, 1853 - September 16, 1889)
Bob was frequently sick in his cell and died in 1889 of tuberculosis. He was 36 years old.

These four brothers had 10 other siblings.

The main historical aspect of Stillwater prison is entwined with the Younger Brothers being incarcerated there after getting caught at the Northfield bank robbery that they attempted with the James brothers.

I use the word entwined because one of the occupations used to keep the inmates busy at the first prison was the making of twine. The twine factory is where the fire started in 1884. It is also where a vandal started a fire in 2002 wiping out this historical building.

The Younger brothers were ideal inmates. This helped to get them released from their life sentences. They helped maintain order during the fire in 1884 and kept other inmates from escaping.

How did the Younger's become criminals and wind up in Stillwater Prison?

Missouri was an organized union state, however many residents owned slaves or sympathized with the South. In 1861, those siding with the union and those siding with the confederates began fighting a guerrilla war.

The James and Younger brothers belonged to slave owning families. The mother of Frank and Jesse James was pro south.

In July, 1862, the Younger brother's father, who was reported to be pro union, was killed by Union Soldiers while on a business trip. Because of this, several of the Younger brothers, including Cole, joined Quantrill's Raiders. John and his younger brother Bob were too young to join so they stayed home to look after their mother and sisters.

William Clarke Quantrill was the most famous "bushwhacker" of them all. Frank James was with him at one point in time.

Later, in 1864, when Frank was fighting under Archie Clement and Bloody Bill Anderson, Jesse joined them at the age of 16.

Cole eventually joined the regular Confederate army.

When the war ended, Frank surrendered in Kentucky; Jesse surrendered in Missouri after being shot through a lung; Cole Younger returned from a mission to California; Quantrill and Anderson had both been killed.

The James brothers continued to associate with their old guerrilla buddies, who remained together under the leadership of Archie Clement. This began their criminal career.

On February 13, 1866, the first daylight, peacetime, armed bank robbery in U.S. history was executed, when the Clay County Savings Association was held up. Archie Clement was suspected of leading the raid. Frank James and Cole Younger were implicated. Some say Jesse was there, some say Jesse was at least involved in the planning of it, however, nobody knew anything for sure. The only thing I can say for sure is that this little building is an interesting tourist attraction.

When Archie Clement was killed in 1868, his followers stayed together. They became known as the James-Younger Gang.

With the exception of Cole, the Younger's tried to live a peaceful life after the war, but they were harassed.

At one point, Bob was knocked unconscious and John was hung four times by people that didn't like what Cole was up to and those still having opposing viewpoints from the civil war. They finally cut him down and hacked at his body with knives. He survived. John was quicker to anger and retaliate than was Bob. That is probably why there was such a vast difference in the violence levied upon him at this instance. If this story is true, it shows a high level of incompetence and indecision if they actually raised and lowered John on a rope four times, knifed him and still did not kill him. This would be pure lack of dedication to a cause. They must have been like the people of today that have nothing better to do than to accumulate and picket for a cause they know nothing about, just to get on television news shows.

After their mother's death, John, Bob and Jim Younger moved often because it wasn't safe for them to stay in one place very long.

On Jan 20, 1871 John shot and killed two Texas Deputy Sheriffs that were trying to arrest him. Why? Don't know! I guess I would relate the two deputies to rogue correction officers and John to an inmate of the smart mouthed variety. Without anyone else around, a situation like this could escalate.

In 1873 Jim, John and Bob Younger joined Cole in the James-Younger Gang.

The James-Younger Gang now included Frank and Jesse James and Cole, Jim, John and Bob Younger. Over time, many others joined up with them but left. You might say that their employee retention rate was quite low. Working conditions and their benefit package was undesirable

On March 17, 1874, Jim and John Younger were headed to see some friends in Roscoe, Missouri. Pinkertons were hired to capture outlaws that had robbed a safe. A Deputy Sheriff and two Pinkerton agents suspected the Younger's. The three men were tracking Jim and John when the Younger Brothers ambushed them. One of the Pinkertons ran off successfully. While the Younger's were interrogating the others, Detective Louis Lull, drew a hidden pistol and shot John through the neck. Jim killed Deputy Daniels while John pursued Lull on horseback into the woods. John shot Lull in the chest and left him. John rode out of the woods and fell to the ground, dead. Jim buried him by the roadside. Later he dug him up and buried him in an unmarked grave in a cemetery. Louis Lull died three days after being shot.

On the night of January 25, 1875, the Pinkertons surrounded the James farm. Frank and Jesse James had probably been there earlier, but had already left. The Pinkertons threw what they said was not a bomb into the house. This non-bomb exploded when it rolled into the fireplace. The blast nearly severed the right arm of Zerelda

Samuel, the James boys' mother. Her arm had to be amputated at the elbow that night. The blast killed their 9-year-old half brother, Archie Samuel.

Continued injustices perpetrated upon the James and Younger families by post war authorities and people of dissenting viewpoints continually pushed the James and Younger brothers into justifying their criminal activities. This is an example of why I believe criminals are created and not born to be criminals. Learning about the backgrounds of inmates that I have been associated with and read about constantly reaffirms this point. Those scientists that say otherwise should quit trying to write papers to the contrary to get themselves notoriety and stoke their egos.

NORTHFIELD BANK FIASCO

This link is to a video on YouTube called "Faithful Unto Death."
https://www.bing.com/videos/search?q=Faithful+Unto+Death%2c+Northfield+raid+video&view=detail&mid=09594C1A8AABB7E255FC09594C1A8AABB7E255FC&FORM=VIRE

This 12 minute video played at the Northfield Historical Society when I visited there. (This video is good; however it varies slightly from the information delivered on the historical society's tour.) The bank is part of the building. I like to support these places by buying their products. They did have Cole Younger's autobiography that he wrote while in Stillwater Prison, so I bought that, but they did not have this video available.

On September 7, 1876, at 2 p.m., Cole, Jim and Bob Younger, Frank and Jesse James, Charlie Pitts, Clell Miller and Bill Chadwell (aka Bill Stiles) attempted to rob the Northfield Bank in Minnesota. The Cannon River flows through the northwest side of the town. This is a very short distance behind the bank, so they had to cross a bridge to get into the main part of the town. They entered town in three groups so as to not draw attention. Frank, Bob and Charlie rode into town first and were the ones designated to enter the bank. Cole and Clell crossed the bridge next and swung around the block so they could come in from the south. Jim, Jesse and Bill crossed the river and hung out in the town square, which is right by the bank.

They were supposed to call off the robbery if there were a lot of people in town. There were a lot of people in town, but they felt these Minnesotans would be oblivious to actually having a bank robbed in their town, so they went ahead with the robbery. (A television show I saw on the history of this event stated that there were more people than normal in town on this day because it was the first day of hunting season. This was the only source that I found that stated this; however the other information was quite credible.)

When they entered the bank, Charlie closed the door. This was a warning sign to a man that had just left the bank, because the door was kept open for cross ventilation. While word of a holdup was spreading through the town, inside the bank the trio was getting on with the robbery.

Three people were working in the bank. Joseph Heywood was in charge of the vault. He was ordered to open it. The large door to a more secure area was open. The other area had a time lock on it, but it was new and was not yet operable. The robbers were told that they could not open it because of the time lock. The nature of this gang's success in the past had to do with getting in and out quick. This was taking too long and the total time reached 7 minutes. Charlie decided to try to bust into the vault himself. As he was passing through the large door leading to the vault, Heywood was able to slam the door on Charlie's arm. Charlie pushed back on the door, knocking Heywood to the floor. Frank put a bullet in Heywood's head. This robbery was not going well. One of the other three employees tried escaping through the back door. As he was running away, one of the robbers was shooting at him. The first shot missed, the second shot hit him, but he did get away. It was time to admit it was a bad day at work and to call it quits. What they never knew was that the vault had never been locked. If they would've tried opening it, they could've been in and out with $15,000 before the shooting began. One other point was that while Charlie was dealing with Heywood, the others were shaking the place down. They missed checking the cashier's drawer that had $3,000 in it. All they got away with was $27.

While all of this was going on inside of the bank, there was action going on outside. When the towns' folk became aware of the hold up, they got their weapons and started blasting away. One source stated that some were throwing rocks at the gang members. Clell Miller and Bill Chadwell were killed. All of them were wounded; Bob got it in the elbow, Cole in the hip, Jim in the jaw, Jesse in the thigh, Frank and Pitts both got hit in the leg. Bob's horse was shot.

By this account we can tell that there were definitely some people shooting that had extremely bad aim. These would be the people that get hired to have long shootouts in television and movie westerns. Maybe the town had a contest going where they got more points for hitting smaller more difficult areas to hit. Those who killed Miller and Chadwell were most likely the ones who lost the contest. Whoever shot the horse was probably eliminated from any future contests.

The death of a Swedish immigrant named Nicolaus Gustafson was attributed to a 75 foot shot by Cole Younger. It was suspected that because Gustafson did not know English that he couldn't understand what people were yelling when they hollered to clear the street. His tombstone reads, "A SWEDISH IMMIGRANT SHOT BY ROBBERS."

So that you can get a perspective of where this happened, Northfield is about 35 miles south of the Twin Cities.

The Youngers, James and Pitts got away into the woods. Many posses were formed. Over 1000 people were after them. Several days later, they were near Mankato which is about 60 miles southwest of Northfield. According to an interview with Cole, the gang decided to split up. This is common in old television and movie westerns in order to water down the size of the group pursuing you. If they were the first outlaws to do this, maybe their heirs could get residuals from all of those shows, probably not.

There are many varying accounts of the Younger Brothers and James Brothers. My guess is that the perspectives of many people confuse the facts. After this amount of time, it is doubtful that we will ever know many of the true details of these guys' escapades. Researching them and trying to find out the accurate details raised many more questions. I just had to pick a few interesting pieces to show how the Youngers wound up in Stillwater Prison history.

It's said that the Younger's and Pitts were on foot when a posse caught up with them near Madelia, Minnesota. This is primarily west, but a little south of Mankato by about 24 miles. There was a gunfight. The Younger's got wounded again. Pitts was murdered by a posse member. I say murdered, because he was shot while waving some type of a white flag trying to surrender. The Younger's were allowed to surrender. They could either plead guilty to murder and live or lose in court and be hung. Once again, they made a wise choice by pleading guilty to murder and staying alive. They were sentenced to life in Stillwater Prison on November 20, 1876.

The James brothers rode west across southern Minnesota to the Dakota Territory. They made it to Missouri and then continued on to Nashville, Tennessee where they lived without incident for three years. Frank was doing well as a farmer.

Jesse was restless, eventually recruited a new gang and started up again with his shenanigans. On October 8, 1879, they held up a railroad near Glendale, Missouri. One of the gang was captured by a posse. His name was Tucker Basham.

Tucker Basham? Was this a relative of mine? My family is from that part of the country. I was always told that my family lineage contained pirates, horse thieves and President Truman. I couldn't find anything on Tucker Basham to verify if I was or wasn't related to him. That's OK though, especially since one piece of information stated he was dim witted. Hey, watch what you think. I didn't have to tell you about that, but it does seem to make sense that he would be the only one captured.

Frank eventually got sucked back in with Jesse's criminal activities. On July 15, 1881, they robbed a train with a conductor and a passenger being killed. On September 7, 1881, Jesse robbed his last train, probably because he would be killed before he decided to hold up another one.

On April 3, 1882 Jesse was living with his wife, Zee-who was his cousin, and his kids in St. Joseph, Missouri under the name of Thomas Howard. A somewhat friend of his, Bob Ford, had conspired with the governor of Missouri. Ford was to receive $5,000 for killing Jesse. He shot Jesse in the back of the head in Jesse's own home that he was renting for $14 a month.

Thus, the chorus from the "Ballad of Jesse James":
Poor Jesse had a wife, a lady all her life
And three children, they were so brave
But that dirty little coward that shot Mr. Howard
Has laid ol' Jesse James in his grave

The house Jesse was shot in is a tourist attraction, but it has been moved to a different location two blocks away. You can enter the house if you get there at the right time on the right day as long as the person running the place decides to show up then. I know. I was there. It was impossible to enter.

Eventually, Frank turned himself in on robbery and murder charges on the condition that he would not be extradited to Minnesota. He was found not guilty.

Jim and Cole's parole in 1901 was on condition that they stay in Minnesota. Cole was pardoned in 1903 on the condition that he left the state and never return. Both Cole and Frank eventually joined a Wild West show in Missouri.

TWIN PRISONS BY THE TWIN CITIES

We were notified that there was an attempted helicopter escape foiled by a snitch on 11-18-00 at the Oak Park Heights super max prison.

Their plan was to have some people on the inside create a diversion by starting a fight in the chapel. While this was happening, people in a helicopter would take out the officers stationed on the roof and then swoop down and make their pick up. The inmate or inmates they intended to pick up would've been out in the yard at this time for recreation.

This was significant as the Oak Park Prison is just across the swamp from Stillwater Prison.

These are pictures that I took of the prisons from a hot air balloon. They show how close the prisons are to each other.

Oak Park Heights Prison

Pond between the two prisons

Stillwater Prison

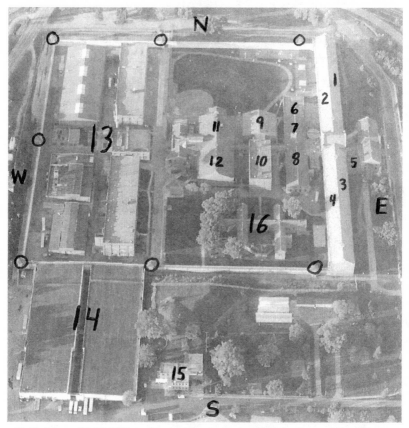

1) B-East 2) B-West 3) A-East 4) A-West, South half was
seg until the middle of 2008 5) Visiting & Shakedown
6) C-Hall (also called Atlantis) 7) Security Center
8) Health Services 9) Recreation, gymnasium upstairs,
weight room and other activities downstairs 10) D-Hall
11) Education 12) Dining Hall 13) Industry
14) Warehouses 15) MSU, Minimum Security Unit
16) Replaced with new segregation unit
The 7 small circles are towers along the wall.

ACADEMY #81

MELDING MYSTICAL MINDS

For the institution, academies are about getting their numbers up. These numbers are actually people, but that doesn't matter to them. They just need enough numbers to cover every shift. We are all assigned eight digit numbers.

This is a security institution run militaristically, so we must all be indoctrinated into this type of mentality no matter what our mentalities may be. And believe me when I tell you that with the mentality of some of the people they hired, it was evident that all of the hoops they had us jump through in order to get this job were just a formality to satisfy government procedure. By the time I filled out all of their forms, so they could evaluate my criteria, passed all of their tests, was interviewed by several people, waited a long time between every process to hear anything, notified that I was accepted to be hired with a 100% rating, I was feeling pretty good about myself for being so damn good.

As time passed, I found out that everyone hired that I spoke to had received that 100% rating. As time passed, and I worked with some of the people that had been hired before me and after me, I no longer felt proud to be classified in the same group as some of these morons, idiots, jerks and criminals. Yes, I said criminals. Some of these guys actually wound up living behind these bars. Some who aren't living behind these bars should be locked up here.

What about those people in my academy? Who were they and what happened to them? I numbered them in the order of which they left and the final three as to how I expect that they will leave.

0 was a female that left during lunch break the first day of our academy and never returned. She was probably the smartest one.

1 wanted to be a cop. Coming to Stillwater was his way of getting some training and experience to try to get into a county jail. His short time at Stillwater got him a job at the Hennepin County Jail. He figured he could make contacts there to help him in getting a career as a cop. Also, the state prison and county jail experience were great for his resume.

2 came to the big house in the big city to try to get better pay and benefits to support his wife and kids. He had worked in a private prison for awhile where the pay was very low and there weren't many benefits. He left Stillwater to become a meat packer in the town his wife and kids were in as he had never moved them here. He had been on first watch all of the time.

3 had one of the most interesting stories. He was the first one from our academy to catch a couple of inmates having sex. It was right after we finished our academy. He was flustered, didn't know what to do, so he just kept walking by the cell and didn't say anything about it. The next morning when we were in the briefing room, before our shift started, he filled me in about those guys filling each other in. No, that's not the interesting part of his story but it seemed worth noting.

He had been acting strangely for awhile. One morning, in the briefing room, I asked him what was up. He told me that he was walking the tiers doing a security check. He looked into a cell and saw a guy. He said it was like looking into a mirror when he was younger. It was like this guy could've been his son. It turns out that it was his son. He did some research and found out that he used to date that kid's mother. The timing worked out just right for this kid to be his. He gave money to the inmate's mother, the gal he didn't know that he had knocked up. This was so she could put it in the kids prison account. When the institution found out what was going on, they locked him out.

How did the institution find out? There are some really good people that work here. Some of them are paid to watch us, watch tapes of us, monitor phone calls and investigate us. Sometimes people are harassed or terminated unjustly, but more often than not, they get it right.

4 was walked out for not cooperating, refusing to do her job and being a bitch. At least that's what the officers on first watch told me. I'm sure the formal record doesn't read that way. She had been on first watch all of the time. Seems she knew more about the job than people who had been there for years, according to her anyway. I was surprised about this, because in academy she never showed me this side of her. She may have just pissed off the wrong people. One possibility was that it was reported that she was speaking negatively about blacks. She said these things to an officer she didn't know was black. She thought he was Hispanic. He was an officer with a chip on his shoulder and a snitch. They had a rather intense discussion about the black comedy duo "Amos and Andy" that he was unhappy about.

For those of you too young to know about Amos and Andy, it started out as a radio show, in the early days of radio, with two white guys speaking in a stereo-type black language of that time. It was so successful that black people were hired to play all of the parts on a television show in the early days of television. Today, some people find it offensive. As a kid growing up in that era and watching that television show, I loved that show, the characters and the actors playing those rolls. I would watch it whenever I could. I also watched "Mac & Meyer", "Laurel & Hardy", "Toody & Muldoon"... These were white people that did ridiculous things. They acted and spoke humorously. It's entertainment. Some people will try to make an issue about anything rather than having an intelligent discussion about ones differences. I learned a lot in prison by having conversations with people that viewed things differently than I did.

Anyway, we have a six month probation period after we get out of the academy. This period of time allows the institution time to check us out to see if we are competent or if they don't want us around for any reason what so ever. She was walked out on the last day of the sixth month. She fought it, but to no avail.

Her daughter, who was a 27 year old virgin, started working here a couple of academies after us. 4 was canned around the time that her daughter finished academy. Her daughter was worried that she would be canned because of her mother. I assured her that anything her mother had done would not negatively affect her. Maybe if she had been dealing drugs, she may have been investigated with a fine tooth comb, but she wouldn't lose her job because of some things they didn't like about her mother.

5 had been a Minneapolis cop. She was an honest cop that did not go along with the rules of the department's old boy network. She left the cop job because she was worried about other cops taking her out; and not on a date. She was pretty tight lipped about the whole deal, but over the time we knew her, we were able to piece together this scenario little by little.

She was very good. She was smart and had the necessary skills to do the job, but she wasn't very big. Being aware of her lack of size, when a fight broke out in the cellblock she was in one night, she went to the officer's desk and had the larger male officer respond to the fight rather than responding herself. She received a lot of criticism for doing this.

She took a job in Austin, Texas as a police officer. There was a rather strange officer working in Stillwater that she hooked up with. He went down to Texas with her to be her kept man as he was a loser and there was no way this guy would ever pull his own weight. She left a little over a year after she started.

6 would have instantaneous mood swings and was generally in the negative mood mode. He never got along well with anyone. I was the only one that could even half way get along with him, but that was when he wasn't swinging off the deep end. He transferred to Rush City the end of 2001.

7 was a personable enough guy. We got along quite well. He was a bright guy and very strong for his slightly above average size. Another strong area he had was his smell. One day when we were doing drills outside, my van was parked nearby. I called him over to my van, pointed to a can of deodorant that I had sitting on a counter in there and told him people were talking. He thanked me, went in the van and sprayed down. It helped, but not a lot. I thought he would come in the next day without this problem, but that wasn't the case. A few days later, we had to practice putting holds on each other. This required touching each other and wrestling around. No one wanted him as their practice buddy because no one wanted to get that close to him. On a break, I grabbed the can of deodorant, walked into the room, slammed it down on a table and yelled, "It's not a secret anymore. Use it."

By the time we got out of the academy and were working in the cellblocks, word had spread throughout the institution about this guy that stunk. Officers complained to bosses about having to work with this guy. He was eventually assigned to a tower almost every day, because towers were a one person operation.

One day when he wasn't in a tower, he was in segregation. Seg had an odor of its' own. He got urine in his face back there, rode out stress leave, got 65% of regular pay and sued for 100%.

By the end of 2001, he showed up on first watch for a short time. First watch is a place where he could sit alone in a cellblock all night. Eventually, he was gone with no one knowing what went on other than the assumption of him getting canned for abuse of the system, being late, not showing up for work, etc.

8 worked 3rd watch in the first turnkey when he got out of the academy. This was a good place to be if you didn't want to deal with the inmates. He was very personable, hung in there for a few years, but eventually left for a different job.

9 hey, that's me! I retired. You will find out more about me than you would ever want to know as you read this book.

10 transferred here from a state janitorial job for better pay and benefits. He had 14 years in with the state when he walked into the prison job. That fourteen years counted as seniority for getting time off, so there were a lot of officers that were real upset about him just stepping in the door and having seniority on them He worked 3rd watch. This watch was filled with people that didn't have a lot of seniority, liked the hours, found it easier to get the days off that they wanted or they had kids so they could avoid paying a babysitter if their spouse worked a different shift. I see him retiring when he hits 55.

11 is a former professional wrestler.

He has toured with well known wrestlers from the Twin Cities. He spent a lot of time in Japan and other oriental countries. He told me that wrestlers are looked at and treated like gods over there.

He was also a bouncer at the Minneapolis strip club called Déjà vu. He ran into famous people at this club. A super famous NBA hall of famer pulled up in a limo one night. This black man had a white gal in the back with him, but it wasn't his wife. She waited in the limo when he went inside.

11 is a big friendly guy that chose to work 3rd watch.

A guy like this is good to have on your watch. He would be very easy to hide behind.

I see him working as long as he is physically able. He has a lot of pain from his wrestling career and nothing to show for it. He has an easy time with the inmates because of his size, the interest they have in his past career, his demeanor and the wise way he has learned to play this game.

12 is very intelligent. 5, 12 and I got the best grades in our class. 5 got them because of her previous experience. 12 rarely studied, but it all came easy to him without having to study. I took a lot of notes and studied my tail off.

12 acquired the name "snack boy" in our academy. He was assigned this name because he came to class everyday with a back pack filled with snacks. He guarded this satchel like it was full of cash from some heist. He was always eating or drinking something and this guy was slender. His weight changed quite a bit to the plus side when he started working security in the kitchen. He grew larger, but I never considered him to be fat. A lot of weight landed on his rear. An inmate awarded him the name "Bitch Hips." The inmate camouflaged that title as Mr. Bishop, so he wouldn't get in trouble.

12 could be very abrasive and started out working 3rd watch. He later bid onto 2nd watch in segregation. He was not getting along well with the other officers back there, so he bid into B-West with me.

With all of us starting at the same time, our seniority was established by drawing numbers. He had seniority on me because the number he drew was slightly lower than the one I drew. He abused that seniority every chance he got.

When he started, he was very immature. He abused sick days. He took pride in keeping his sick time under 8 hours.

When he got eight hours built up, you knew he would be calling in sick soon. He had a daughter. Anyone with a kid had a better chance at calling in sick and not getting disciplined for it than those without. He had called in sick so much though, that it eventually caught up with him. His boss drew a line in the sand and told him to shape up or he would be gone.

He took pride in being lazy and didn't hold back on proclaiming that to any boss. If he saw violations, he would ignore them unless they were really bad ones.

Before I retired, he started getting his act together. He started treating his girlfriend with respect, married her and had another kid. This pretty well locked him into the job. Up until this time, he was always talking about going back to school and getting out of this prison job. Now he was talking about going for promotions. I see him as being the last one to leave. With his brains, if he even half way applies himself, he could go a long way in the DOC, depending on the politics of the time, of course.

ACADEMY X-PERIANCES

The following are things that happened or that I was told during the 6 week academy.

Our first day in academy was 8-30-2000. There was seating for 12 of us in our room. 16 people were scheduled to be there. Only 13 of us ever showed. After lunch, one did not return, so we were down to 12.

Our training room had no doors on the hinges. Supposedly they were taken for repair and never brought back. Well, so much for security in this place.

Most of our class had graduated college, had previous experience in corrections or been in the military. Of course I didn't fit this profile. However, the combination of all my life experiences made me a good fit for this job.

The main excitement on this first day was when a person from psychology freaked out when she had a wasp in her hair. I wonder what she would have to say about how her fear of bees manifested in her psyche and how it has negatively impacted her life. Maybe I should have a talk with her and help her sort out her fears and other psychosis.

They took our picture, gave us our photo ID's and finger printed us.

I had my first painful experience today, when I took my pants off. Turns out there were four of those fabric inspection stickers on the inside of them that attached themselves to my legs during the day. I lost a few hairs with their removal from this sensitive area.

Our class could take on the Vikings. We had size and speed. There was not a wimp in the bunch.

Only 10 of us showed the second day. One was out getting divorced and one was at a funeral.

They took us into a cellblock the third day. At one point, a swamper came running along the platform toward us yelling, "216 is slashing his wrists." One officer stood securing the door to the cellblock and one cleared the flag area. One went to cell 216 to verify the situation and then called for the A-Team. Within seconds reinforcements were on the scene. Before a minute was up, all kinds of people arrived from around the prison; the A-Team, nurses, even someone to clean up the blood. In an instant everyone was back in their cells. The slasher was whisked off to segregation. The mess was cleaned up and the incident was entered in the logbook. The only thing left to be done was for everyone to fill out an incident report and have the slasher transported to the Oak Park Heights prison where they have a medical unit; kind of a mini hospital and psyche ward.

The inmate was using a razor blade to cut himself. They are allowed to have Bic razors for shaving. They smash the plastic to get the blade out. We are instructed never to run our hands under anything during a search. We are to look under things or use a mirror. The inmates will hide razor blades on the underside of things like their bed frame by sticking them there in toothpaste. If this guy had really wanted to kill himself, he wouldn't have done it during flag time. Doing it during any other time, nobody would've known until they found his body during a security check, which happens every hour; the security checks that is. People who do things like this can be seeking attention or help due to some mental conflict. They may want to go to segregation or Oak Park for security reasons. They may view that their only way to survive or avoid being beaten is to be in isolation.

The instructor informed us about an email the institution had just received from a prison in California. The purpose of this was to give us as broad a base as possible to the kind of situations that can develop. A prisoner and a female officer had been left alone in the kitchen area. Another officer eventually came in and upon seeing no one started looking around. He noticed a barrette from her hair on the floor. He found them in a stock area. The inmate started pulling up his pants. The officer yelled, "He raped me!" The male officer obtained control over the inmate. He had beaten and raped the female officer. His next step was to kill her in order to keep her quiet. What did he care? He had his fun. What more can be done to him? A few less privileges... Time in segregation... They just don't have much more to take away from them.

Later, I found out that a female officer at the Lino Lakes Correctional Facility was raped. That California incident may actually have been the Lino Lakes incident. No one was supposed to know about it. The Minnesota State Prison system is very good at keeping things like this secret. If we speak up about it, we could be terminated. The story and some details gradually seep out, but this generally happens later after it is no longer news. Several years after this, I was in a class at Lino. A person from Lino, that had firsthand knowledge of the incident, filled me in on details at that time. The female officer had left the prison system and received a nice settlement which she was bound not to disclose.

Having females in a male prison is dangerous for them. However, it does decrease the chance of inmates finding my butt cheeks a worthwhile endeavor. Sorry, I just had to pop in some sick prison humor.

Another day in the academy, 29 liter bottles of hooch were confiscated from an inmate. This is considered a good sign. A sign that the flow of drugs into the prison had slowed down or they wouldn't be hassling with making hooch. Some of the ingredients are obtained through the commissary, but they smuggle bread and sugar packets out of the dining hall. It can take a long time to get enough stuff together, but they have plenty of time. After a cell has been checked, they may move the stuff to that cell figuring the odds are low for that cell to be checked again very soon. The stuff moves to different cells according to alliances, threats, a piece of the action, etc. If a strong or powerful inmate is making hooch, it probably won't be in his cell. The weaker or less connected inmates are forced to hold the hooch, so that if caught, they take the fall.

Drunks are dangerous and very undesirable. They lack all inhibitions. Hooch is not a high quality beverage and the inmate's system is no longer accustomed to it, so you can expect it to be spurting out of them. They will be put in segregation where they can throw up, urinate and crap all over themselves. Either they or a swamper will do the cleaning up when the effects have worn off.

We are told that we will get used to seeing strange things. One officer told us of the first time he saw an inmate with a Hilex bottle stuck up his ass. Another told us that the first time he found a guy hanging in his cell with his eyes popped out it was rather freaky. Now, it's just one of those things you deal with on your job.

We received our first of 3 Hepatitis B shots. The next one would be one to two months later. The third one must be 4 to 6 months after the first shot.

The warden spoke to us. The main point that he said was, "In Minnesota we lock up who we are afraid of, not who we are mad at."

I was talking to an inmate who came to Stillwater prison from the Oak Park Heights prison. He spoke of some poor conditions he got himself into there. He had been raising holy hell consistently, so they took everything out of his cell. They even pulled out his mattress because he was destroying everything. He was letting his water run and flooding the cell, so they turned the water off to his cell. Getting a drink of water was accomplished by drinking out of the toilet. He tried to clean the toilet with a bar of soap, but he got sick anyway. Eventually he decided he better chill out for a while.

Inmates see so many things. They analyze every move we make, everything we say, the way we breathe, and the look in our eye. They have nothing better to do than to become psychologists. They have to do this in order to survive. They look for weaknesses in every one in order to be able to exploit those weaknesses.

No matter what kind of a rapport we develop with someone, we must never trust them. Their job is to get out. Our job is to keep them in.

They must never trust us either. Officers are pawns following orders. Especially when an officer or big shot has been around for some time; staff will do most anything and turn on most anyone in order to not get canned before they can retire. We may have told an inmate one thing and right after that we get ordered to do just the opposite of what we told the inmate, making us look like a liar.

There have been instances where an officer has been attacked and an inmate has helped out, but it is rare, so don't count on it. We were told that if they respect you, the best you can hope for is if some of them have shanks and are going for someone, they may tell you to step aside.

People in our class were starting to get sick with the flu. Two guys dropped a load in their pants and had to go home.

We were on a tour of the Oak Park Heights facility when an "Injun" incident occurred. They had just been released from their pipe and drum ceremony when some moron in our group saw the Native Americans coming toward us and stated, "Here come the Indians." They heard this and as they were passing us in the hallway they started saying things like, "Here come the Injuns. Look out! The Injuns are coming." They started making whooping noises and pushing each other. Just as they passed us, they turned a corner and started fighting. Officers immediately came running from around the institution to break it up. It doesn't take much to set things off in a place like this.

Some inmates will have a lot of items from the canteen. Food, toiletries, etc. are used as money in here. If they have an excessive amount, they are probably running a store. Stores are generally run by a powerful connected inmate. It used to be that they would have someone else hold their supplies, so they couldn't get caught with it. I found out that this is not the case anymore as it isn't anything most officers hassle with tying to enforce.

They are allowed to spend $120 per week at the canteen, plus $50 per week for the telephone, and whatever else they choose to buy like TV, clothes, etc.

Where do they get the money? Some have jobs in the prison where they can make from 25 cents an hour up to $2 an hour. In the past, some of them made more than the officers, so they made strict guidelines reducing the pay scale. Their pay will vary depending upon the job they do.

Some Indians get huge amounts of casino money every month. Some guys are pimps with their women running tricks on the outside to supply them with money. Some have family members that send them money, others con people into sending them money.

As actual money is contraband, the money is placed in an account that they can use to buy their canteen items.

To try to make us realize the positive effects of CPR, they told us that a guy that was dead was a grey color. When CPR was applied he became pink. He was still dead, but they figured telling us this would cause us to at least attempt CPR if we found someone not breathing.

They told us that all officers once carried mace. It stopped when a couple of officers were spraying mace at each other and hit some inmates. Eventually we were all assigned and required to carry it again.

Most of the officers here are not good trainers. They are extremely bad at explaining anything. When asked how something was supposed to be done they say, "Technically......" This way they tell you how it should be, and then how they do it. They infer that their way is best.

Radios for A-West & A-East are in the seg bubble. Don't expect them to be in the proper spots because most everyone is lazy and when it comes to getting out of this place and going home, nothing is more important to most officers.

A-East was the stated to be the "homo" block. Have you come to the conclusion that this is not a politically correct environment? They had pimps there. There was a little black dude that would take it from anybody. So long as you're "pitchin'" and not "catchin'", these guys don't consider themselves to be homosexual's.

Another rookie and I were in the bubble in B-East when these two real negative guards came in pissing and moaning about everything. This one guy had just got through writing someone up for sucking his teeth. The inmate was doing it to intentionally annoy the officer. The inmate was sent to segregation for it, because the officer had given him a direct order to stop doing it. These officers went into the computer to erase the cookies so nobody could find out that they were visiting sites that they weren't suppose to be visiting, like the Vikings and porno. This one guy had a large file of personal e-mails with all kinds of jokes and graphic pictures that had been sent to him. Eventually, because of officers abusing the internet at work and viruses shutting down the computers, only a few top brass were able to access the internet. The rest of us could send emails only to those employed by the DOC.

Out in D block there was a gal that was a major pain in the ass to everyone including herself. She inflicted her attitude on the inmates. You could see them steaming. I definitely didn't want to be in the same area as this gal when the inmates blew. The first thing she asked us was, "What the hell are you doing here?" Actually, this negative attitude seemed to be a humorous persona that she created, probably to deal with the dysfunctional environment.

Wasps were constantly flying around the class room. This was particularly annoying. The windows did not have screens on them, so we just figured that they were flying in from outside. We kept the windows open as it was a hot day and the room did not have air conditioning. Later, when on a break, we noticed a large number of wasps in the hallway. There was even a nest of them there. A couple of us started smashing the wasps as most of the other cadets left the area. We were smashing them on the walls; jumping up and knocking them off the ceiling. Some we knocked out of the air to the floor and crushed them. Others, we clapped our hands together to kill them. Our break ended with dozens of wasps littering the hallway floor. We kicked them into piles against the wall, so people walking by would not have to squash them on the bottom of their shoes in order to get back in the classroom. Some cadets were afraid to pass by these dead wasps. We had eradicated most of them. Throughout or time in the academy, we only had to do minimal kills in order to keep people from hopping around the room.

One day we went out to the minimum security area to work on riot control drills in a field out there. We had to learn some marching techniques, so we could be easily controlled as a unit if that became necessary. We had to learn commands and how they wanted us to move. It was nice to be outside moving rather than having to sit in a classroom. That is until they had all of us enter a shed and set off gas canisters. We started with gas masks on. Once the room was consumed with gas, we were instructed to take the masks off. We were told to see how long we could handle the gas before running out of the building. A couple of us idiots stayed in trying to be the last one out. Finally we decided to run out at the same time and call it a tie. We should've thought of that sooner. We had been instructed to run to the top of a hill close by, so the wind could blow in our faces to help with the eye irritation and breathing. We were also told not to touch or rub our eyes as that would make the irritation worse. I definitely did not touch my eyes as this was miserable the way it was. Most of the effects had dissipated by the next day. Why did they feel it necessary to put us through this? It was so that we would know how to handle it when a situation occurred in the prison when we would have to perform our duties in this gas. I did not have to deal with it very often, but when I did, I was glad I knew how to deal with it.

Officers are supposed to be very alert to every little detail. We must stay focused at all times. This was not the case during one of our breaks. Several of us went straight to the lavatory. There were two urinals in this lavatory. They became occupied immediately. I grabbed a stall with a toilet, as I have no problem having my release resonate. Also, we were issued long pants to wear, so I was unable to feel any splatter. When I was finished, I went to wash my hands. Not that I had soiled them, or that what I had grabbed onto was dirty, it's just a habit I got into years ago. I heard one of the guys at the urinal yelling. It turned out that one of the guys was not paying attention to his aim. He was watering one of the other guy's legs. I felt it interesting to note this as it was the worst aim I ever became aware of. Sure I've seen dudes get watered this way before, but never unintentionally. Also, I made a point of never relieving myself when Mr. Super Bad Aim had to take care of his business. I have always wondered if this guy's aim was that bad when he was at home.

ACADEMY HODGE PODGE FOR 2000

My academy was in the year 2000. The information we received pertains to that point in time. The academy was a good start and a good guideline, but that is all. It was full of opinions, which were beneficial if presented that way. A problem was that some opinions were presented as fact. The following are bits and pieces of information presented in the academy and some things I observed or researched.

The #1 medical call in the prison is a seizure.

Tobacco addiction is stronger than that of weed, so some will buy tobacco before buying weed.

A gang member with El at the end of their name means he is a soldier. A gang member with Bey at the end of their name is a more passive member of this gang.

If a person is in a mindset to kill themselves, they won't hesitate to kill you.

If you like sausage or have an interest in the law, don't watch either of them being made.

If you hear of somebody escaping from Stillwater, it means somebody walked away from the minimum security unit outside of the walls.

Prison is the state's most expensive resource; it is saved for the worst offenders.

1 in every 46 people in the state is on some kind of community supervision. This costs us $16 per day verses the $86 per day in prison.

Ground up marijuana, one teaspoon is 7 grams (1/4 ounce) and goes for $50 in prison and $30 on the outside.
I don't know how this officer that told us this knew this, but he was darn positive about it.

Officers that have to go defecate found a less offensive term. They say they have to go give birth to a new warden.

Inmates whose crimes were against people are never allowed to go to minimum.

When inmates feel like hanging themselves, they hang themselves with things like shoelaces, elastic underwear bands and cut bedding or towels. Where there's a will there's a way.

We were told not to go into the liquor store with our uniform on as it looks bad to the public. We can be fired for doing it.

Money is contraband in the prison. We must keep the amount of money we have on us to a minimum. Inmates can't have money. The money they earn is put on account for them to use at the canteen. They use canteen items to barter with. Their currency used to be cigarettes, but they are contraband now too.

There has been no parole board for 20 years. We are on a Target Release Date Method. Past sentences were Indeterminate, 0 to 10, 25 to life. Now we are Determinate, 2/3 definite, 1/3 supervised or parole. If they create a lot of problems in the prison, they may end up doing 100% of their time in prison. SRD = supervised release date. All sentences are now in months.

Oak Park is level 6, which is maximum, but was once called super max. Stillwater & St. Cloud are level 5. They are maximum-security facilities, but are now referred to as Close Custody. Rush City is a level 4. Lino is level 3. Level 2 is minimum with a fence. Level 1 is minimum without a fence. Stillwater has a level 1 section outside the walls. It is called the farm, because it once was a farm being worked by Level 1 offenders. Later, due to double bunking, Oak Park was changed to a level 5 and Stillwater and St. Cloud were changed to a level 4.

Tennessee and Minnesota have comparable populations. Tennessee has 28,000 inmates as compared to Minnesota with 6,000. We also have 100,000 on supervision in Minnesota.

A 10th grade reading level was required for an inmate to get one of the prison jobs. In 2001 they needed at least a GED. Without a GED, inmates are only allowed to be in school or locked up. Educated inmates are less likely to reoffend. If not in school or at work, they are locked up 23 hours per day. Over 90% are going to be released someday.

Minnesota's inmates serve more time than anywhere else.

Our recidivism rate is not as good as the national average. That means more of these guys come back to our prisons.

From what I've experienced in Minnesota prisons, coming back to them is not a great deterrent.

At Oak Park, the only human contact some of them have is from an officer. They are out of their cell about 4 hours per week in order to shower and get exercise. They have nothing in their cell except their toilet, sink and bed. Food is delivered to them through a slot in the cell called a book slide or book pass. In time, if they aren't crazy all ready, they can go crazy. However, they chose this through the many decisions they made that got them to this point.

In segregation, there is a restraint board or surfboard. This is a sheet of plywood with numerous Velcro restraints on it. It is used when someone is going totally nuts or won't stop resisting violently; any situation where they would be dangerous to others and themselves. They can be secured on this for up to an hour, which is generally enough time for them to wear themselves down enough so they aren't as dangerous. After an hour, their situation must be reviewed by a health services professional.

Gas is used in segregation more frequently than anywhere else. It is only used for safety. They have the choice to comply with directions. If not, apply 2 to 3 seconds of gas into their cell, let set for a few minutes and you have an instantly cooperative inmate; more often than not anyway.

There are security cameras covering a lot of the facility. They primarily are a deterrent. If somebody decides to do something, it will probably happen. The cameras are used to look back on the tapes to see what happened and who did it. They are also used to follow up on the officers.

The institution got a new machine today called a scanner. This thing will detect if anyone has come in contact with any drug within the last month. It cost $20,000; a cheap price to pay for something that will seal the fate of many, so we were told. They tested it out in the visiting area and found traces of cocaine and marijuana all over the place.

We had a class that was based on a theory of Hypocrites that basically made it easier for us to stereo type people.

It costs $1.82 per day to feed an inmate 3 meals per day.

#1 problem area is the kitchen, due to the volume of people; also, due to the access to food and hooch making supplies.

#2 problem area is industry, due to access to items to make weapons.

We were told to keep the lines moving in the dining hall; that this would make it less likely for problems to develop.

We were told that there were over 6 million in prison across the US and that was expected to reach 10 million by the year 2005. This was incorrect information. There were 2 million locked up and possibly a total of 6 million cumulative in prison, on probation and on parole. By 2011 there were 2 1/4 million in prison and 7 million cumulative in prison, on probation and on parole. So that projected 10 million by 2005 never came about, but projecting numbers like that do help for trying to get more money out of the legislature.

Canteen is marked up 25%. This money goes to social welfare (their victims) and provides the inmates with cable TV access and other amenities.

Approximately one inmate per day is released from Stillwater Prison.

Inmate TV's burn out in 4 to 5 years because they are almost always on.

No officer can prevent getting sued. A nuisance law has helped. Many inmates have nothing else to do except to create law suits.

The prison system hopes to get 2 years of service out of us. They will be happy with that.

Be yourself. Don't lie to inmates. Don't try to be their friend and then try to enforce policy.

Staff is suggested to bid out of segregation after one year in order to help maintain their sanity.

Stillwater has a $32 million budget with 82% going for salaries and benefits.

We get free steam from the NSP power plant across the road. This ended during my time working in the prison.

There are a lot of former military people employed here.

Remote control weapons are being worked on in addition to guns that fire nets.

We have a gangster war room. There is a board with everyone on it that is confirmed or suspected as a gang member. Stillwater has the most people identified. People identified as the leaders are not the leaders. They are assigned to be the fall guy in order to protect the real leaders.

Minnesota has 8 prisons, while Wisconsin has 26.

Legal mail – We open it in front of the inmate and then we keep the envelope.

Paperwork is our friend.

No Minnesota Corrections Officer has been killed, yet. Plenty have been beaten, but no one has died.

We were told the "Hole" used to be a hole in the floor. The violator was locked in it with nothing. I saw the place they referred to. What I was told seemed possible early on, but also seemed very unlikely. More than likely, it seemed like a large drainage pool in a mechanical area.

A guy from Alaska was in here for having sex with a walrus.

A guy nick named Shep was in here for having sex with a St. Bernard.

There was a karate dude that was crazy and assaulted staff. Once, when they cuffed him, he broke the cuffs.

At one time inmates were constantly changing their names. They can now change their name once, but if a check is run of them, it goes back to their original name when they were committed to the prison system. People were changing their names to things like Peppy Dog, Frito Bandito and the Lord God Almighty.

They used to have huge metal safety pins for the ends of their laundry bags. They bent them out to a 90-degree angle and fastened them to the end of a stick. They would then smash people in the head with them, so they were eliminated.

A guy riding a motorcycle had an accident. He was holding on so tight his hands ripped off and were still holding onto the grips.

Another guy, riding a crotch rocket, rear ended a car and wound up in the trunk with his leg lying on the ground. He was awake and screaming.

From incidents like this it was learned that bones have a purple satin appearance.

I have no way of verifying this to be fact or fiction, but the guy that told us this held our interest.

A chimo raped a boy so badly that the pressure caused the kids meat sack to explode. The rapist was killed in prison with a piece of conduit.

One dude tried to burn his house down with his wife in it. He accidentally blew himself up at the same time and is in Stillwater severely disfigured.

A Jewish guy was put in prison for insurance fraud. He was a millionaire by the age of 13. He monitored fire calls and arrived on the scene with lumber to sell to board the building up. At 19 he purchased an air force base for $120,000, turned it into a retirement home and made $2.8 million. His mother had been in Auschwitz. At his trial she told the judge not to fuck with her son. The son was sent to prison. The mother hired a private investigator to tail the judge. She got pictures of him molesting a 13-year-old. She met up with the judge at his trial and said, "I told you not to fuck with my son."

The atmosphere in this building is kind of like the old reptile building at Como Zoo. There is no air conditioning in the cell blocks. When it gets hot in the summer, the building heats up like firebrick. If you place your hand on the inside of the thick brick walls, they are uncomfortably hot.

"If you haven't driven for a while, it's murder out there.
It can make you feel like killing people. Again. Which is exactly what got some in here in the first place."
This is a quote from an inmate.

"The government is supposed to be the ones to protect us, but they are often the ones that make us feel like killing. Then they throw us in the slammer for doing it."
This is another quote from an inmate.

I never saw a guy in curlers before I came here, then I saw it frequently.

Inmates are not allowed to read material on guns, ammo or the martial arts.

The inmates once had a work stoppage. This was part of an attempted escape plan.

Some officers walk around eating and drinking all of the time. Some officers have a bad habit of spitting sunflower seeds all over.

What does the prison provide: Handball, football, softball, basketball (inside & outside), track, weight room, leagues, video game area, cable TV, jobs, education, canteen, 24 hour medical, washer, dryer, ice machine, 3 hot meals and a cot.

ACADEMY GRADUATION SPEECH

Upon completing our six week course, a graduation ceremony is held in the prison chapel. I guess it's held there so we can pray we survive this dysfunctional paradise.

Staff from around the institution come to these. Some come to speak. Some come to see the new faces they will be working with. Some come just because they can. Some come because it creates a break in their day. Some come because there are higher ups at events like these to hob knob with if they are trying to climb the promotion ladder. At times a commissioner or some other higher up from outside of the institution might even show up. Being new to this place, I wasn't able to identify a heck of a lot of them at this time.

A member of every class is chosen to give a graduation speech. At the end of our last day, the instructor notified our class that they had to choose someone. Everyone in my class either pointed to me or called out my name and started laughing. I had one evening to prepare.

Being together, in this kind of a class for six weeks, bonds you together in a strange sort of way. People that you would never associate with in real life wind up being your homey's. We all realized the collection of strange minds that the Department of Corrections brought together in this class. Knowing that and knowing my background in comedy, they knew whatever I said would be representative of our how our minds worked. They knew I could get some points across without getting into trouble, at least not getting them in trouble.

THE GRADUATION SPEEECH

Howdy! This sure is a nice looking group. Obviously I have no problem with telling lies.

When we first came here we were told that we would have to go through a cavity search. I thought, WOW! Free dental!

On our first day there were 13 of us. One lady left for lunch and never came back. Guess she must've been normal and that just won't fit in around here.

We were told that there are a lot of real mental cases here. Well, now, there are 12 more.

A lady from psychology got a wasp in her hair and never returned. The wasps provided us plenty of recreation. We spent a lot of our time as wasp exterminators. We would leave little piles of them around. Bet we killed over 250 of them.

My first day was quite a painful experience. I was never informed of the inspection stickers that are put in the crotch of the pants that they issued us. It felt like I had wasps down there.

After a few days together, we found out that among our group we could say anything we felt and it would be taken the way we meant it to be taken. Yes, we discovered that we all had the same sick sense of humor.

Before we started our training, we were all for the death penalty. Now, we're all against it. We call our change in viewpoint, job security.

A large percentage of our population find love where they work. We found out that if we find love here, we should write them up.

They took our picture and gave us a photo ID. Then they finger printed us. I never had to do this for a job before, just after pulling a job.

In here money is considered contraband. With my financial condition, I won't have to worry about this one.

We have learned a lot here at Stillwater. We now know how to make hooch. But they never told us not to tighten the bottle caps. It was only 65 degrees out when the bottles of hooch I had in my trunk exploded. The force of them blew my trunk lid over the Anderson Window stack into the river.

Instructors! There's a huge flaw in this training program that I suggest be changed immediately for your own good! We were run through riot control drills and gassed one day. After that, they armed us with shotguns and M-14 rifles. For your safety, I suggest you gas the next class, "after" firearms training.

We were trained on how to conduct unclothed body searches. I feel there were a couple in our class that spent a little too much time in this area. However we will just write them off as slow learners until proven otherwise.

During our tour of Oak Park, there was a great sounding rapper displaying his craft. However I don't believe we would ever be allowed to repeat his lyrics without being arrested ourselves.

There was a major down side to our training. They forced us to take weekends off. Thank God we won't have to worry about crap days off like those for a couple of decades.

The reality training was much appreciated, but I think they have to learn where to draw the line. In my opinion it's not necessary for the CPR dummy to be able to vomit.

Part of our bonding experience was getting enough time to go to lunch together. We cleaned them out at the Pizza Hut buffet. We created a line at Wendy's. But going to an oriental buffet and eating Chinese was my favorite, except that their fingernails would get caught in my teeth.

We were asked numerous times, why with the economy being so good did we come here to work? We asked, good economy or not, why did you hire a dozen people like us?

They told us we were crazy. We say, play to your strengths.

We discovered that we had three die hard Packer fans among us. To our amazement, we found out that they were a lot like real people.

We discovered that there is no one in this class that could be described as being normal. We're all a little strange; some a little more than others. That is one thing that helped us bond the way we did. We realize that we're not perfect, but together, we're the best. And we intend to spend our time here proving that.

It was necessary for us to learn how to survive on the inside. It was necessary to get trained in the realities of life here. Numerous excellent instructors gave us that knowledge and skill over the past 6 weeks. I think there were about 357 of them, but it worked. I was taking care of a job last night when I decided to write them all down. (At this time I pulled out a roll of toilet paper and let it unroll down the aisle) I guess I don't have time to read them all, but our primary instructor was "Master Instructor." He got stuck with us most of the time. We are prepared primarily because of him. We would like him to come up here now.

(At this time we presented him with gift certificates to his favorite restaurant and my part of this ceremony was over.)

REACTIONS

This speech seemed to anger some of the higher ups; as I noticed some of them conveying disgust and disapproval by scowling and with other types of facial expressions and body gestures. A couple of them never treated me decent the entire time I worked here. However, I noticed most sergeants, a few lieutenants and some case workers trying not to get noticed by some of the big shots as they laughed and shook their heads in agreement.

The warden came to me after and said they would have to work on me to see if they could get me to come out of my shell.

News of my speech spread like wildfire throughout the prison. Lots of people came up to me to talk to me about it. When people met me and heard my name, the comments were, "Oh, you're the one that gave that academy speech." Word travels fast in this place. Every little thing becomes a big thing. I realized that if I hadn't given that speech, and I would've passed some gas, I would've been that guy that broke wind at the graduation. However, they were talking about how it really pissed off some of the honchos, but my piers loved it.

Saying things with humor, allows us to get by with stating viewpoints that can torque off some people, but because of the humor, they are less likely to respond or take action against us. Through humor, I said a lot with my speech. Master Instructor said, "Dave, you're really deep." This was appreciated, because it meant that he got everything I was saying. My graduation speech wound up being used as an example in other academies, but they never told me if that was in a good way or a bad way.

PAST MODELING CAREER

The warden was always pleasant towards me. He told me I looked familiar. We couldn't figure out why. I told him I had never been an inmate, so he didn't have to worry about that one.

We were in a sallyport with others one day when the subject came up again. An assistant warden had seen my picture on a government website. Then I figured it out. A friend of mine, which was in my improv troupe, had a state job where one of his responsibilities was to produce a quarterly magazine for the Minnesota Department of Human Rights. One issue he did was on discrimination and disabilities. He wanted to put people on the front cover that had disabilities; some that were obvious and others that weren't. For the photo shoot, I sat in a wheelchair and posed as a Viet Nam War Veteran. The beard, moustache and long hair tied back was exactly the look he wanted. The extra weight I carried around fit someone who couldn't get out of a wheelchair to get much exercise. The warden had seen the magazine.

My speech and this magazine gave people a way to identify with me; some good and some bad.

IT BECAME OFFICIAL

The graduation ceremony was on a Tuesday. They gave me Wednesday and Thursday off. That meant that my first day of work would be on a Friday. It just so happened that it was Friday the 13th. I guess I should've taken that as an omen to get out while the getting was good. I was oblivious to the warning or you wouldn't be reading this now.

ACADEMY INSTRUCTOR

IPC

The most boring class in the academy was IPC, Interpersonal Communications. I guess I had cut down this class so badly, that they asked me if I would be the instructor for it. I accepted. It got me out of the blocks for a couple of days every 6 weeks, or whenever they ran an academy. I worked hard at injecting my style into it. This class was the final 2 days of the academy. I wanted to make sure that they were better prepared to do this job than I had been. Telling it exactly like it was without sugar coating anything was important, whether they wanted to believe it or not. Obviously, I would use humor a lot. Informing them that they could have problems with other officers and staff members was important for them to know before it happened. Getting them to know how to handle the bizarre happenings was important. Learning how to handle any situation was imperative. Upon the end of my two days with them, many of the new officers would come up to me, thank me and tell me it was the best class they had attended. Afterward, I would frequently get emails from them informing me of situations they encountered that they were able to easily handle due to what they learned in my class. Some of them would seek advice on how to handle different situations. Mission accomplished.

ACADEMY LESSONS

Every once in awhile, when instructing academies, we get someone who believes they know more than us that have been chosen to instruct these classes. I love these guys, but I hate them too. They irritate the hell out of me, but I love to have the opportunity to humiliate them until they shut their mouths; just like Judge Judy does with big mouthed arrogant idiots in her court room.

This guy tried telling me how to do the job. I raked him over the coals and humiliated him until he shut up.

Later, after academy was over and he had been on the job for awhile, he came to see me in A-East. He apologized for being disruptive in my class. He said that once I had shut him down, he started listening to what I was saying. He said he found out that I was right. He said that what he learned from me had been the most beneficial of any class he had and that my advice had kept him out of some trouble. He thanked me and shook my hand.

I WONDERED WHAT HAPPENED TO THEM

While taking the academy on a tour of the Oak Park Heights Prison, we heard inmates yelling my name. One yelled out, "Hey Basham!" He asked, "What you been up to? What you doing here? How you been?"

I recognized him as an inmate that I got along well with back at Stillwater. I wondered what had happened to him.

A trainee asked him how he wound up here. He said, "Basham. But it was my fault. Basham's cool."

We didn't have much time to talk, as we couldn't stay in one place very long. Also, when an officer seems to be getting along well with an inmate, there is always someone to make either you or them get moving.

I asked him how I put him here, as I had no idea. He said that he wound up here on a report that I had written.

There were a couple of other guys with him that said the same thing. I just write what I find and what happens after that is no business of mine. My job is done.

I actually liked all of these guys. I don't know what they did to get locked up and I didn't care. We got along well, could joke with each other and knew where the policies drew the lines. We were able to live with that.

TOP 10 LIST

The education coordinator sent us instructors a list of ten expectations they had for instructors and cadets.

1) Be honest, but not negative.
2) Share knowledge.
3) Be prepared for your class.
4) Share personal stories and how you coped.
5) Build confidence ...thru encouragement and reassurance.
6) Pay attention to instructors.
7) Be professional.
8) Good sense of humor.
9) Encourage participation.
10) Be on time.

DEFINITIONS, ACRONYMS AND OTHER STUFF

NECESSARY INFORMATION

There will be some sections in these books where the informational and educational value is higher than the interesting value. This is one of those sections.

However, I believe many will find this information very interesting. This section and others definitely contain major pieces of the prison's puzzle. They are vital to understanding the prison system and how it works.

There is no way to remember all of the details in these sections, so they will be a great resource to look back on as you read through these books.

Some of it you will probably use your fastest reading style to consume.

If you are considering corrections as a career, these sections will do a lot to prepare you for that occupation, as will everything in these books.

Talk about speaking in code! This place is acronym hell! There are numerous terms specific to prisons, the Minnesota Department of Corrections or even just this prison, that create road blocks to effective communications. Need I say how important clear communications are in a high security facility like this? OK, I will. If you make one mistake by using ineffective communications there could be dire consequences. The wrong person could be released. Someone could be beaten or killed.

The Natives once put a hit out on a sergeant in my cellblock. There was a miscommunication. They beat down a sergeant in a different cellblock. When they got him down, they kicked and stomped on him until they were stopped. Once this sergeant recovered, he tried to come back to work, but his mind wouldn't let him enter an area where inmates were housed ever again. He had to leave this job.

Had the assault been attempted on the correct sergeant, there may not have been any assault. The other sergeant had been around longer. He was well aware of how the inmates felt about him. He knew he was on the top of their hit list. He knew how to implement CYA (Cover Your Ass).

With how critical communications is in this job, it is amazing that some of the people they hire can't communicate effectively. People were hired that could hardly speak the English language. People were hired that had such a strong accent that we had to guess at what they were saying. Most of these people never improved their speaking ability. They had no incentive to improve. They had the job. Why would you hire someone like this? Have them learn the language and learn how to speak clearly before you hire them.

Why would you promote someone like this? Just before I retired, an African man was promoted to lieutenant. His accent was so strong most of us could understand only a few words that he spoke. His accent was so thick, I don't even know if he was speaking English. Was this man qualified to do the job? Not from what I or anyone I knew saw from the decisions he made.

ACRONYMS VERSES INITIALISMS

To be accurate, most of what is below are "initialisms." I had never heard of these and as I wrote this, it seems as though spell check never had either.

Both are generally created by taking the first letter of a phrase.

If the letters create a pronounceable word, it is called an acronym. SORT, Special Operations Response Team would be an example of this.

If the letters do not create a pronounceable word, it is called initialism. BCA, Bureau of Criminal Apprehension is an example of this.

I know, I really don't care either, but I'm trying to be as accurate as possible.

FLAG TIME

The floors in the prison are made of flagstone. The inmates can come down off of their tiers when they are allowed out of their cells. They mingle on the flagstone, play cards, work on exercise equipment, use the phones, do laundry, take showers, iron clothes, use the micro waves, assault each other, etc.

This is how the time that inmates are allowed out of their cells to roam the cell block became known as "FLAG TIME." If someone asked where an inmate was that was on the ground level, we would say that he was on the flag.

NO FLAG TIME FOR A LONG TIME

Upon completion of non worker flag time, an inmate did not switch in. He came into the block that morning on IHS status (**I**n **H**ouse **S**egregation). I made a second page. He did not switch in. When I paged him to the bubble, he secured his door. This was his 5th unauthorized area violation within 90 days. Any 5 violations of the same type within 90 days will send that inmate to segregation. Also, any violation of anyone on IHS status sends them straight back to the hole.

Being aware of these guys and their violations and not ignoring them was a bit of a curse for me. A large percentage of the inmates that were back in seg, were there because of what I saw them doing and wrote reports on them. The number of them that were there because of me writing them up far exceeded those of any other officer.

BUBBLE

There are secured areas throughout the prison where officers are stationed. There is thick security glass on one or more sides. Most are small office areas. All have items that offenders should not have access to; like rifles, ammunition, keys, computers, electronics to open cell doors, items like barber equipment that could be used as weapons ... These areas are called bubbles. The officer inside has good vision as to who is close and what is going on. This officer controls the door or doors to that area, so no unwanted or unauthorized individuals can enter. Actually, there are often people that you don't want to enter, but you have to let them in because they are your boss.

THE A TEAM: A-LEVEL RESPONSE

The A Team are officers posted around the institution that are assigned to respond to emergency situations like fights, fire, medical emergencies, escape attempts, ... They are also referred to as the squad. They are the ones that run to any area of the prison to provide an emergency response or handle any lesser security business. Emergency responses are called A-Level responses.

B-LEVEL RESPONSE

If more personnel are needed than what the A-Team has available, a B-Level response is called. All areas of the prison are locked down at this time to allow for more officers to be able to respond.

SALLYPORT

A sallyport is the area between 2 security gates. No one can move out of this small area until someone else opens one of the gates. Only one of these gates is allowed to be open at any time. Both gates being opened would be a security violation during normal operating procedures.

WALKED OUT

This refers to a staff member that has been fired, quit or retired being escorted out of the institution. Generally a lieutenant or higher ranking staff member does the escort. They make sure anything necessary is recovered from the terminated employee.

TIER, GALLEY, GALLERY

They are all the same thing. They refer to the level of cells in the cellblock. In a normal building it would be the first floor, second floor, ... or third story, fourth story, ...

UNIT, CELL HALL, CELLBLOCK

Again they are the same thing. The entire grouping of cells that are separate from other groupings of cells. These isolated areas can be locked down without affecting any goings on anywhere else in the prison.

LOCKED OUT

Locked out is someone that is no longer allowed to enter the institution. This would generally be due to some unacceptable behavior or action they did.

BOSSES, HONCHOS

These are everyone ranking higher than me, which was a lot of people. This could be people not even working in the prison. It could be anyone from a sergeant up to the governor.

MEAT

That is the inmate's term for new officers.

CHIMO – CHOMO

These are terms used for child molesters. I preferred to use CHIMO as that seemed to sound more like **CHI**ld **MO**lester.

REMEMBER ALL OF THESE, REALLY!

The following is a trimmed down list of acronyms and initialisms that was given to me that I was expected to know. Did I know the entire list? Not even close. Most of them I never even heard of, so I cut them out.

A-E	Cell Hall A-East
A-W	Cell Hall A-West
A/W	Associate Warden
ACA	American Correctional Association
ACLU	American Civil Liberties Union
ADM	Administration
AFSCME	American Federation of State, County & Municipal Employees
ATO	Alert Tone Oscillator
B-E	Cell Hall B-East
B-W	Cell Hall B-West
CCTV	Corrections Cable Television
CEO	Chief Executive Officer (Warden)
CHC	Cell Hall C
CHD	Cell Hall D
CHPLN	Chaplain
CM	Case Manager
CO	Corrections Officer, CO1 (First 6 Months)
CO1	Corrections Officer, first 6 months
CO2	CO from the 7th month until promoted
CO3	Sergeant
CO4	Lieutenant
CO	Central Office
DOB	Date of Birth
DOC	Department of Corrections
DOER	Department of Employee Relations
FTO	Field Training Officer
HS	Health Services
ICR	Investigative Cell Restriction
IR	Investigative Restriction, same as ICR
IMS	Incident Management System
IPC	Inter-Personal Communications
KITE	Inmate Request Form, prison letter

K-9	Canine
LOP	Loss of Privileges
MCF	Minnesota Correctional Facility
ML	Medical Lay-in
MSU	Minimum Security Unit
NC	Non-Contact
OD	Officer of the Day
OIC	Officer In Charge
OID	Offender Identification
OJT	On-the-job-training
OSI	Office of Special Investigation
PC	Protective Custody
PROBV	Probation Violator
REC	Recreation
SEG	Segregation
SRD	Supervised Release Date
TRIAD	Treatment & Recovery From Independence of Drugs & Alcohol
TRV	Technical Release Violator
TU	Temporarily Unemployed
UA	Urinalysis
UI	Unassigned Idle
WC	Watch Commander
WR	Work Release

FIRST WATCH

I was informed that I was being forced to first watch. This was the 10pm to 6 am shift, the graveyard shift. Before I could be forced there, things changed and they forced me to the visiting room instead. I didn't want to be checking nuts and butts all day, so I bid onto first watch and got it.

By being forced to bid to first watch, I was frozen for 3 months. This means that I would not be able to bid on any other position for this period of time. If a day shift came up that I would be able to get, I wouldn't be able to bid on it. If I had been forced to first watch like I was supposed to, I wouldn't have been stuck in this situation.

Some of the officers on first watch are quite different. If you ever wondered where the dweebs from school ended up, some of them are here. People that are extremely afraid of the inmates are on this shift. People that are attending college and need time to study are here. Some of the older people work at this time. Life situations make people bid onto this shift. Those requiring a second job during the day in order to provide for their families work this generally calmer shift, more boring shift. My rocket scientist degree went to waste on this shift.

Some inmates feel this is a good time to sleep. There is a lot of TV watching going on, some reading, and a whole lot of looking at nudie magazines, of women and men, while yanking their whackers. Maybe that's why they tell us not to shake inmate's hands.

BREAKING POLICY

Some officers feel this is a good time to sleep. One of the toughest jobs on this shift is to stay awake. Some of us fight it and others find an inconspicuous place to crash.

When working D-Hall, two officers are assigned to this block. One would go in the lieutenant's office and sleep, while the other kept an eye on things. You are locked in the block without a key to get out, so if the watch commander did his rounds and came into your block, you would have a little notice from the rattling of the keys. Also, these doors are so solid and heavy that it is near impossible to open and close them without some significant noise. I wasn't in this block very often, but most often, when I was, the other officer would go in the lieutenant's office and sleep. When he had his fill, he would come out and tell me it was my turn. I would always decline.

When you don't go along and do the same wrong thing that they do, you are suspected of being a snitch. They become very leery of you and wonder if you can be trusted. In order to get by in this place, I went by the no harm no foul rule. If nothing went wrong, there would be no reason to say anything. If something went wrong and it was necessary to write a report and an officer sleeping was a factor; it had to go in the report.

I'd let them know that if something went wrong and it was necessary for me say something, they better be the first one to step up and speak before I had to.

I'd let officers know that I wouldn't be broadcasting things they did that they weren't supposed to do, but that I would never lie for anyone.

I was here to do a job and if what they did didn't cause any problems, it was none of my business.

If they went someplace to sleep, I would make sure I didn't go to that place during that time, so I wouldn't see if they were sleeping. That way, if asked, I could honestly say I never saw them sleeping.

This is a place of laws, rules and regulations. We deal only with facts and not what we think or believe to be true. This way the facts were that I actually could not say they were sleeping. It may have been their intent to catch a few winks, but it's like an inmate that might intend to steal something. We can't do anything until he actually does. We can suspect something and keep an eye out, but there can be no conviction on something that there is no proof of.

DON'T TELL ME TO BE QUIET

When working the flag back in segregation, the main job is to try to keep the guys quiet. The unsuccessful officers tell them to be quiet. Especially back in segregation, inmates do not take to being told what they can and can't do. Considerate phrasing goes a long way in a place like this. We all know the rules and we don't need someone hounding us or micro managing us, inmates and officers. I just talk to them a bit, crack a few jokes and inform them of how little time they have left until the others wake up and start making noise. Mutual respect goes a long way in a place like this.

When I went on my first security check of the night, it would take me a while. If someone wanted to ask me a question or have a brief chat, this was the time for it, in my opinion. Mostly, they wanted to be sure that if they had a problem that someone would be there to help them. After this, the block would generally be relatively quiet the rest of the night.

One night I was doing this first round with another officer that saw things the same way. It took us a while.

This night, an officer that was an inmate hater and didn't like our approach, informed a sergeant, that was an inmate hater, of our approach. The sergeant gave us orders to never do it that way again. He told us to just get the round done fast: that if they were loud to tell them to shut up and if they didn't to write them up. Inmates in segregation are the most disruptive people in the institution and we were given orders to tell them to shut up by a sergeant. This is why promotion to sergeant should be on merit and not on seniority. You wind up with idiots like this in charge.

We protested to no avail. An order is an order so we had to comply. We had to tell them to be quiet. We tried phrasing it as nicely as possible, but it all meant the same thing. They viewed it as "the cops thought they could tell us what to do." These guys raised hell all night. The sergeant

139

came over and asked us what was going on. We told him that we just followed his orders. He told us to get them quiet; that they were disturbing the two blocks next to us.

Getting these guys quiet now was impossible. The fuse had been lit and the bomb was bursting. The watch commander came to see what was going on. When he asked what got them going, the officer I was with told him.

Before the night was over, some of the inmates were flooding the place by clogging their sinks and turning the water on; they clogged their toilets and kept flushing them. Once this starts and these guys have it in their heads, they generally do it a few more days.

The sergeant that jumped on us for doing the first round our way never came over to tell us to shut those guys up again. I believe he got some heat from the watch commander, possibly from higher up too.

Oh, and the guy that called the sergeant; he was a dweeby weenie type of a person that eventually quit. He was the type that fits an old phrase my mother used to say. "Thinks he's hot snot on a silver platter but is only a cold booger on a paper plate." We had other words for him.

WANNA BET

One night, when I was working back in segregation on first watch, I had to go up on the tiers to do a security check. Keys were needed in order to get through an end gate, a center gate and an end door on each tier. I grabbed a set of keys. The other officers told me that the keys I took wouldn't get me through the center gates. I asked one of them how much he wanted to bet that I couldn't get from one end of the tier to the other with the set of keys I had taken. He was amazed when I got through. After that, whenever another first watch officer stopped by the block, he would pull out the key and show them. Whoever trained these guys had never shown them every key and what they were for. It is every corrections officer's responsibility to know what every key is for. Hopefully, everyone would start finding out the purpose of every key they were responsible for using. OK, that is not reality, but now more would know now than before.

It is important to be able to identify every key on every key ring. If the shit hits the fan, you and everyone else are much better off when everyone can respond as effectively as possible.

I knew a lot about segregation, because when I graduated out of the academy, I was placed on what was called a second watch utility position. This is where every day you come in, you may be assigned a different place to work in the institution.

I worked segregation a lot. When you are a rookie, you get assigned to segregation more than any other place. This is because more officers are needed in seg than any other block. Also, senior officers prefer to be elsewhere; and this is a seniority system.

I liked seg. It was busy back there. Being busy made the time go faster than if you were just sitting at a post for hours.

Watch Commanders liked placing me there because I wouldn't complain about being assigned there, unlike many other officers. The lieutenant and sergeants told the Watch Commander that they liked having me back there too.

I was back there so much; the inmates thought I was a regular.

I liked the officers that I worked with back there. They had a good sense of humor. They liked having me back there, because I would volunteer for anything and everything. That made it so they didn't have to interrupt their card game.

LAUREL & HARDY ROUTINE

One night, the A-Team, which consisted of two officers on first watch, brought a guy back to segregation. He had been attacked on third watch and had just returned from the hospital where they had sewn his face back together. He said that nobody hit him, that it was an accident. You don't snitch out people in here or you will be worse off. He was put in segregation for his protection. We checked up on him and found out he was a white supremacist, which was a darn good possibility for being the cause of his injury.

The problem on this shift is that the A-Team is more like an F-Team. It is rare on this shift to have to move any inmates. Between the F-Team and the first watch officers assigned to seg this night, everyone was telling everyone else what to do. None of them actually knew. These people wouldn't admit that they didn't know what to do. I stood back and watched the Laurel & Hardy routine. One guy was throwing clothes around.

Finally, I had seen enough and stepped in. I told them how it was supposed to be and told them that was what I was going to do. Some of the people here have never been on any other shift, so they haven't learned much. I never received good training, but I watched what was going on and also had inmates that filled me in on lots of things.

When one guy started showing me what to do in the bubble, I showed him the checklist on the wall and informed him that I was the one who wrote it up. That checklist was still being used when I retired.

NIGHTTIME UA

A lieutenant came into A-West with two members of the A-Team. They were here to do UA's. UA in this place does not stand for United Artists. It stands for Urine Analysis Test. Two inmates were scheduled to leave in the morning. Running a UA is routine for anyone leaving. If they come up clean when they leave and they come up dirty once released, they know they have made a connection on the outside and have started using again.

MSU – MINIMUM SECURITY UNIT

The Minimum Security Unit is just that; minimum security; just making sure the number of inmates remains the same.

This is where if you hear of an escape, someone decided to walk away. This area is outside the prison walls, so if they get an itch to take a hike, they can. It's a stupid thing to do, because they will get caught. They will then do the rest of their time inside the walls and razor ribbon. They will do more time because of the escape and have more restrictions than the others because of it. Some have at times snuck into the town of Bayport, only a few blocks away, to pick up a few items at a gas station or convenience store. The local bar, Woody's, is real close too. If they get caught outside the assigned perimeter, they are placed inside the prison.

These guys are in jeans and t-shirts, not striped pajamas, so if you saw them you probably couldn't tell them apart from anyone else. Shortly before I retired, ankle bracelets were being tried out on these guys.

This area is also called the farm, because there is land out there that was used to raise crops for feeding the inmates years ago.

Once you got the inmates upstairs in their bunks for the night, they had to be counted. 128 of them were housed here. There was a desk in about the middle of the place where you would sit with those 128 felons. All lights were turned off except for a very small light on the desk and lights in the lavatory. The light on the desk was so we could read something to try to pass the time. The lights in the lavatory were for safety, so they could see where they were going and to help prevent assaults and extracurricular activities. A few of the inmates would be watching their televisions which provided a little light until they turned them off. Headphones were required so they wouldn't disturb anyone. Sometimes pictures would come on the tube that any normal adult male, semi adult male or lesbian could appreciate, but you really didn't want to get excited sitting in the middle of 128 guys. There would just be something wrong about it. Anyone living in MSU could not have committed a crime against a person or they wouldn't have been allowed there.

Two officers are supposed to be out at MSU, but when we were short people, the car patrol officer would do a security check of the perimeter and then report to MSU. One officer would be posted upstairs and one would be posted downstairs.

Turns out that watching the movie "Breaking Point" out at MSU on a big screen TV was on the agenda one night for whoever was posted downstairs. Someone had rented it for the inmates. The movie was about a serial killer that killed women by slicing their spinal cord at the base of their neck. This caused them to appear lifeless. They were still able to get the benefits of a horrific death, however. This is because this caused the victim to be unable to breathe or move but still feel the pain and terror associated with suffocating. This was a great movie to be renting to show felons. It was a good training flick for those that wanted to continue their careers when they got released. Hopefully, you detect my sarcasm here.

CAR PATROL

When on car patrol, it is required to carry a shotgun in the vehicle. The car is actually a small pickup truck, but I guess car patrol sounds more common than truck patrol. One night, the person scheduled for car patrol was not certified on firearms, so I was assigned that position. Having never been on car patrol before, I was quickly briefed on it and then did it.

My first night, I found the gate by tower 5 to not be closed properly, a lock missing off of a gas pump, a door lock ripped off of a door on a warehouse in the MSU area and the fence and gate for the firing range in bad shape, but the Watch Commander said all of these things were OK.

There is a cemetery within the block where the prison and MSU are located. I had heard about inmates hiding there when they were trying to escape, so I would drive through there every so often. Later, after I was not on first watch anymore, I heard that we were not supposed to drive through the cemetery. There was nothing pro or con about it in the post orders book, so I considered it a CYA thing to do.

You will see a lot of critters out and about when you are working car patrol. Rabbits are all over. It is necessary to be on the lookout for skunks. You don't see them as often as the rabbits, but you sure do smell them. There are quite a few raccoons. I came across an opossum when I was in the cemetery. When I was checking the lock on a building, a flock of bats popped out of an evergreen tree next to me. One night during the start of the St. Croix River flooding, a huge wounded beaver was lumbering up by the institution. Another night, I had to brake fast in order to keep from hitting a deer.

Once again, the hardest part of this job was fighting the boredom and staying awake. There was a female officer that I stopped seeing around. I heard that she would pull over in a grassy area, lie down in the grass and take a nap. She was eventually caught when they were calling her on the radio. They got no response. An officer was sent out to look for her. She was sound asleep outside of the truck lying on the grass.

There is a small creek that runs through part of the MSU grounds. A small bridge goes over it. An officer told me about the time he avoided using the bridge and got stuck in the creek. It took him some time, but he eventually got the truck out. The truck was covered in mud from spinning his tires trying to get out. Once he got out, he splashed water from the creek up on it to try to wash the mud off. He got away with it. I had driven through that creek before and never got stuck, but I always chose a low area where the bottom had a lot of gravel.

I was told of a time when a guy was out on car patrol and found a fun but inappropriate way to pass the time. He started pulling shit hooks (I have heard people that are more politically correct than I am call them donuts). He was having a blast until he rolled the truck.

GHOST OF ATLANTIS

Atlantis was the more common name used for C-Hall. This is a small block with 36 inmates going through Chemical Dependency Treatment. This is the last requirement they have to fulfill before they are allowed to be released. This block housed Cubans after the Cuban flotilla years ago. One officer is in this cell block alone on first watch. It is the most desired place to be for inmates and officers; except on First Watch for those that believe in ghosts. I was only in this block a few times. Officers told me there was a ghost there. Inmates told me there was a ghost there. I believe anything is possible, but I never saw one there. I did hear noises coming from areas where there were no inmates, officers or other semi-humans that I could see. When I explored the source of the noises, they would stop. One benefit to trying to solve this ghost mystery was that it helped to pass the time. Some officers were afraid to work there alone. If there was a ghost there, at least it could've come forward, so we could chat awhile. Imagine the stories a prison ghost could tell.

INDUSTRY

One of the duties on this watch was to search industry for weapons. Instead of being trained on what to do, how to do it and where to go; the officer that was supposed to train me escorted me out to an industry building and just told me to look for shanks. He told me he'd come back out to get me after he had a nap. He told me that I could lie down on a table and take a nap too. Sorry, but my father always taught me an honest day's pay for an honest day's work, even though it was night time.

Here I am in a dark prison industry building in the middle of the night with only my mini flashlight for light. I had never been there before and I'm supposed to shake the place down.

There were three levels to this building above ground along with a basement and underground tunnels. I knew nothing about this area. I had no idea what was supposed to be accessible to the inmates and what wasn't. To me, most everything looked like a weapon or a shank. I started to grab things to turn in to evidence. As my hands instantly filled up with potential weapons and I had to hold my flashlight in my mouth, I knew there was no way I could carry all of this stuff. I concluded that there was no way this many weapons could be lying around out here. I put everything back and continued going through the place with my little flash light.

After I started, I had no idea where I was. I just kept going through the building. I was not sure if I had passed through an underground tunnel to another building or not. It was difficult enough to find my way around this place in later years, much less as my first time out in industry buildings in the dark. Eventually, I passed by the place I entered. From that point on, I took shorter journeys from that spot and back again. I kept searching the building that way until the officer that dropped me off came and retrieved me. When he asked me if I found any shanks, he had a big smile on his face. I told him that everything looked like a shank to me. I can't say for sure if this was incompetency on his part or just a prank they pull on officers new to this watch. I did learn an awful lot about the nature of this place no matter what.

THE ROUTINE

First Watch began at 2210 hours. We counted and verified that all equipment was accounted for. Then the third watch officers were allowed to leave. Keys, barber equipment and small tools like scissors had to be accounted for. Radios had to be accounted for and they had to have the numbers on them that were assigned to that block.

Most lights had to be turned off.

Our first security check had to be conducted at 2230.

We had to check all doors, nooks and crannies and the showers. We had to make sure things were turned off like the shower fan. We had to unplug the washers and dryers. Unplugging them was routine, so that anyone putting laundry in them late had no reason to complain. We had to get the block quieted down so these guys could get their beauty rest. Also, with a good night's sleep, there might be fewer of them that were cranky and looking to create problems the next day.

By the time these things were accomplished we were about an hour into our shift. Radio checks were then conducted to make sure who had what radio; that the radios were on the right channel, that the radios were working properly and to document the officer's location.

Then we rode out the night doing rounds every hour and checking in with the officer in the control center every half hour so they knew we were alright and awake.

We did counts at 2330 and 0330. This was to help ensure that no one had creatively slipped out in the middle of the night. It was rare for someone to get out, but it has happened. We had to do a lot of routine tasks to make sure that anything that had ever happened before wasn't going to happen again. Or at least we would be aware of it sooner than if we didn't conduct these routine mundane tasks. The main thing we would find on security checks was inmates having difficulty with their health. The two counts were conducted at the same time as scheduled security checks.

The rule for checking on the inmates in the middle of the night was that you had to see skin or movement. Movement at this time was generally to identify if they were breathing and to know that there was a live body in that cell.

Doing rounds, we were walking in the dark. We had to use a flashlight and shine it in the cell so we could see skin or movement. The walls of the cells were white. I found that if I directed my mini flash light on the white wall, it would generate enough light so I could quickly see what I had to in order to determine if a live body was in there. No matter how hard you try, there was always someone that would complain that the light was directed in their eyes. Granted, once in a while, if they were in some odd position or if you had to check further for signs of life, you might hit their eyes. The complainers just wanted to create problems. I used a dinky little flash light and if they were sleeping, they would never even know I had been there, even if my flashlight hit their eyes.

Some of these guys were so skinny that when they were under the covers, you couldn't tell that anyone was in there. This was especially the case when they had a foam rubber mattress that was worn down in the middle and they had sunk into it. It was necessary to try to see the covers move from them breathing before you could continue your rounds. Then again some of the bumps on those beds were like mountains. If I could see no skin and see no movement, I'd call out to them and try not to wake any others up. When they moved a little bit or gave me a disgruntled groan, I could move on.

I was as quiet as possible doing rounds. The keys in my pocket would make noise as I walked, so I would keep the hand that wasn't holding the flashlight in my pocket when doing rounds at night so they wouldn't make any noise.

DUCK FEET

An officer, that I was on rounds with one night, told me to walk more quietly. He was a little guy and made hardly any noise at all. I was walking as quietly as I could. I felt that I was pretty quiet and never received any complaint from any inmate. I wore black tennis shoes that blended with my uniform. Tennis shoes made much less noise than those clod hopper boots that were issued to every officer when we started.

I didn't think I was too darn noisy. I would think that anyone up to any activity that they didn't want to get caught doing would appreciate my feet warning them that I was coming. I did develop kind of a shuffle walk where I would just push my foot forward rather than lifting it up and having it slap the floor when it came down.

My feet are wider than most at the toes, narrower than most at the heel and they are flat; "quadruple E" toes and "single A" heels. Yes, they are shaped like a ducks foot. They slap the floor a bit with each step. They are great for swimming, but it is difficult to walk without getting a bit of an echo off of them in a quiet cell block in the middle of the night.

When I flapped them suckers hard and fast, I would rise a ways out of the water when I went swimming. Feet like that slap a little bit when you walk no matter what you do. Mikhail Baryshnikov would've never made it in the ballet if he had feet like mine, but Jacque Cousteau would've loved to have them. He would've saved a lot of money on flippers.

HITTING THE WALL

I dreaded the time around 0300 to 0400. I called it "Hitting the Wall." My body wanted to shut down. Speaking to other officers, many of them felt the same thing. It was extremely difficult to stay awake with the place so quiet and sitting in the dark. When I got through that time period, it was downhill from then on. I'd try walking quietly around on the flag. I'd do stretching exercises. I'd drink or eat something.

That created another problem. I have never been known to be a petite man. When I was a kid, my brother, who was slender, and I would have a contest hitch hiking to the lake in the summer to see who would get picked up first. He always got a ride and I NEVER did. Our mother said that I was too big and ornery looking; and this was when I wasn't even fat. During my four months on this watch, I porked up considerably. Eating in the middle of the night was a contributing factor. Fighting to stay awake all night and not being able to sleep during the day kept me exhausted and inactive except for accomplishing the bare necessities. The only time that I actually conked out was while driving home from work in the morning. I'd wake up when I hit the ditch. This definitely was not the shift for me. I'd walk about 4.5 miles doing rounds every night, but in the course of a day, that isn't a heck of a lot.

As it got closer to morning, newspapers were delivered to the blocks for those inmates that had subscribed to them. We had to count them and put the number in the log book. If someone got shorted their paper, there would be hell to pay. When you don't have much, little things become big things.

On the last round of the night, we put passes on the cell doors of any inmate needing to leave their assigned area during the next day.

THE BLOCKS

When this prison was built, the main prison had two wings. The south wing is the A Block. The north wing is the B Block. There is a large stairwell in the middle of each cell block with the tiers stacked 4 high. These blocks could house 504 inmates each. Over time these blocks were divided in half to cut down on the number of inmates in one area. Each half could hold 252 inmates. 252 inmates raising hell would be preferable to 504 inmates raising hell. The fewer inmates in one area, the easier it would be to try to maintain control if things went awry. The halves on the front or east side of the building are called A-East and B-East. The back halves or west sides are called A-West and B-West. In addition to this, A-West was divided in half with the south half being adapted for segregation.

In the middle of the A cell block, in the stairway area, a sally port was built. This made it so that once the A blocks were all locked down at night; officers posted in these blocks could access each other's blocks.

The institution has a rule that there must be at least two officers in each block. There is generally a sergeant in A-East, another officer in A-West and generally three officers in segregation with one of them assigned to the bubble controlling the sallyport. This allowed for a five officer potential in this area if there was trouble. If there was trouble, segregation was most likely where it would be.

B-East and B-West each have large heavy steel doors in the wall separating the blocks in the stairwell area. The B-West door is always kept locked when inmates are out of their cells. The B-East door is open in the morning for the swampers as there is a sink and storage area between those two steel doors that they need access to. When the swampers are finished, this door is locked. When the institution is locked down at night, these doors are unlocked so that the one officer in B-East and the one officer in B-West have access to each other's cell blocks. When rounds are done at night, the B-East officer observes while the B-West officer does rounds and the B-West officer observes while the B-East officer does rounds. These doors are locked back up before first watch leaves.

C-Hall has one officer posted in there during the night, but the officer posted in the control center with the Watch Commander has quick access to that area through a door in the control center.

D-Hall has two officers locked in there with 200 inmates. In this cell block the tiers are stacked 5 high.

There used to be a hill behind the main prison with a building on it. I was told that there were some cells in there that were used some time ago as segregation. It was used as the Health Services building when I started working there. Eventually, a Health Services area was developed inside the main prison while I worked there. This allowed the old building to be torn down, the hill removed and a new segregation unit was built there. This segregation unit opened shortly after I left. The plans were to turn the old seg back to being part of A-West.

CURING AN ITCH

One night, as I was up on a round, I passed by a cell where the offender had his light on and was vigorously scratching his leg. After I passed, I thought that this guy might need medical attention because of the intensity with which he was scratching. If he continued scratching like that, he would scratch the skin right off of his leg. I returned to his cell to ask him if he needed medical attention. I didn't have to ask him. Upon a longer glance, I realized that he wasn't scratching; he was rubbing, and it wasn't his leg. The reason his light was on was so that he could view pictures while he rubbed. I went on my way immediately without saying a word and with this guy probably thinking that I was some kind of a voyeur.

I never wrote anyone up for this kind of activity. I realized that it was going to happen. No one was ever overt about it when I was around. I was glad about that, because I saw more than I ever wanted to see any way. If someone were standing there ogling me with their tongue hanging out, that would be a different story. I'd rather have them in their cell taking care of their needs and then needing a nap than out and about releasing that energy in a disruptive manner. I figured that if they could pull off this activity discreetly, good for them. One time I had a medical problem and my doctor needed a sample. He gave me a jar and sent me off. I had never partaken of this activity and was not successful. It was disheartening to discover that I wasn't my type, but I guess that's a good thing.

RACIST WANTED ME TO KISS HIS BLACK ASS

While on rounds in A-West at 0500, I past by an inmate's cell. I could hear his headphones. I informed him that they were too loud. He proceeded to argue about it. I again told him to turn them down. He eventually did but continued to argue about it and kept raising his voice. I gave him a direct order to quiet down. He kept getting louder and stated that I should throw him in the hole. As I walked away, I could hear him yelling even after I was inside the segregation bubble sally port.

After talking with the sergeant, he told me to write the inmate up and place him on ICR. When I passed by his cell to do this, he started yelling again calling me "a white piece of shit."

As his poor behavior escalated, the A-Team came to escort him to segregation. When back in segregation he started to come towards me, at which point the A-Team forced him into a cell. I told them to let him come to get me, so we could conclude our business together that he was so intent on getting to, but it seems as though that was frowned upon.

During his entire time being escorted, he was yelling comments like, "I hate all you fuckin' white bastards. You can kiss my black ass."

He was charged with disrupting the unit, disobeying a direct order, verbal abuse, harassment, disorderly conduct and violation of special unit regulations.

Six weeks before this, I was doing count in segregation on 2nd watch. Yes, he was back in segregation at that time too. He was back and forth to seg frequently. At that time, I had to write him up for refusing to stand for count. This was probably part of his anger toward me. However, he was always angry about something. I believe he had TAS, Terminal Asshole Syndrome.

FAKER OR NOT

While conducting security checks, an inmate in B-West called for the CO as I was passing his cell. He asked me to get the nurse. He was complaining of neck pain and pain and heaviness in his chest on his left side. I radioed for an emergency medical response. A sergeant and a CO1 (Trainee) entered the unit within one minute. Another officer entered the unit with medical equipment within another minute. The watch commander entered the unit within another minute. The nurse entered the unit within two more minutes. She talked with the inmate and then cleared the medical response within 8 minutes of when I called it. The nurse brought the inmate an ice pack a few minutes later. He told her to leave it on the bars. I checked back with him about half an hour later and he was still not using the ice pack. Checking back with him an hour after that, he was asleep.

From this account, you get the idea of how quickly officers and Health Services personnel can respond, even in the middle of the night.

The most bizarre situation that I was involved in happened after this response was over.

Before the watch commander left the block, he called me into the bubble to speak with me. He jumped on my case for calling the emergency response. He told me that I shouldn't have called it. He told me that I knew this guy was a faker. He said if this guy ever complained again, I was not to call an emergency response!

I didn't argue with him. I just let him rant. The fact was that if it ever did happen again, I would call it the same way. It's my ass on the line if this guy croaks and I didn't make the call. I am not a Health Services professional, even though we do learn quite a bit doing this job. It is not my place to determine whether or not an inmate is faking a health problem. My responsibility is to get a Health Services professional to that inmate as quickly as possible and let them make a determination.

Picture this scenario. An inmate complains of chest pains. I don't call for an emergency response because the lieutenant gave me orders not to. The inmate dies. There is an investigation. I tell the captain that the lieutenant gave me orders not to make the call. First, do you think the captain is going to believe something that sounds that ridiculous? Second, do you think that when the lieutenant is asked if he gave me that order that he would actually admit to it? There is nothing on paper. It is not documented. It's contrary to our training. Just because the lieutenant is watching a television show in his office and doesn't want to be interrupted, I should put my ass on the line? You know the lieutenant is going to throw me under the bus and I will be smeared all over the corrections highway.

Then, the inmate's family could sue me and press charges against me. The institution is not going to back me up because I didn't follow documented policy. I could wind up penniless and in prison with these guys. Because I'm an officer that does my job as I was trained to do, the inmates would be real pleased to be able to take their shots at me.

No, there is definitely no way I was ever going to follow that order. Some lieutenants are excellent. Some lieutenants are not qualified. They just had more time in than any other sergeant when a spot opened up and no one else was qualified either. Some of these lieutenants just hob knobbed with the right people in order to get promoted.

NIGHT TIME SHAKEDOWN

One night, when nobody called in sick, they had a few of us available to conduct a shakedown of the kitchen area.

This covered the dining room, all food preparation areas, bakery, clerk's office, meat locker, fruit and vegetable cooler and upstairs storage area. This included inspection of the scattered plastic pails and containers which kitchen workers used for storing personal items, clothing, tools, spices and food they wanted to eat.

We found a variety of food items being diverted for personal use such as peppers and other items commonly smuggled into the units.

I found one of the food cart straps folded behind several boxes. This strap was about four feet shorter than the others and appeared to have been cut. I also found broken pieces of glass near a window.

Other officers found three bottles of pills containing at least ten different types of pills.

One reason for this shakedown was that hooch had been being found frequently in the kitchen. This night we found none.

FORGETFULNESS, THEFT OR BOTH

While on car patrol, I found the two locks for the Unleaded and Diesel pumps on top of the pumps. The pumps were on, working and had fuel in them. 25 gallons were registered as having been drawn from the unleaded pump. 10 gallons was registered as being gone from the diesel pump. I did not have a key for the locks, so I brought them to the first turnkey where the sergeant found a key to open them. I then returned to the pumps and locked them up.

While conducting my initial security check, I found the side door half open on the maintenance garage north of the gas pumps. I radioed to the first turnkey and was instructed to pick up the A-Team. They checked the building. Finding nothing out of the ordinary, they secured it.

Were these simple mistakes or did someone find a way to save a few extra bucks by having the State of Minnesota pick up the tab? Theft is always a problem, especially in a prison. Professional thieves are here; and they aren't all inmates.

ESCALATION & COPY CATS

Inmates flooding their cells in seg were a common event. Once one person does it, many times a lot of others join in. There were times that this went on a grand scale for weeks. It could go on day and night.

I was posted on the flag one night when I heard a dripping noise and saw water flowing off the second tier. On my was to shut of the water to that cell that was located in the tunnel behind the cell, I radioed to the Officer In Charge (OIC) what was happening. He checked out the situation. He couldn't get the inmate to stop flushing the toilet he intentionally clogged up, so he radioed for the A-Team. The inmate was cuffed up and moved to an observation cell on the flag and given an unclothed body search.

The OIC's shirt was soiled from this interaction, so he was issued a replacement. This is necessary due to the water being contaminated with urine and feces. (For the first couple of years that I was at Stillwater, there was a room in the basement where clothing could be issued to us. Fouled clothing could be replaced from this area. Eventually this method was eliminated. Instead clothing issue was contracted out to different uniform companies where we could order our uniforms and have them shipped to us or we could go to their location and pick them up.)

While I was finishing cleaning up the mess, water started raining down upon me again. We had to go through the same process all over again.

COLOR BANDS

COLOR BANDS

Color bands are colored zip ties. They are typically clear or black plastic in hardware stores. You will see them used to group electric wires together. They are now so versatile in their use that they are second only to duct tape in how many ways they can be used. You will see large ones used by police officers and in corrections in place of handcuffs.

In Stillwater prison, they are used to attach to inmate's identification tags. Every group of cells is assigned a different color. Whenever an inmate enters a cell block, a colored band relating to the assigned color of the cell they were placed in was zip tied onto the clip of their ID (Identification Tag). This was beneficial to know if they were in an unauthorized area such as on a tier they were not allowed to be on, on a phone they were not allowed to be on, out of their cell when they were not supposed to be, etc.

The color bands were a major tool in trying to keep inmates safe from each other. When an inmate entered the institution, their background was checked to see if they had any major incompatibilities with anyone in the institution. Some of these guys were incompatible with everyone and there wasn't much that could be done about that. However, if someone had been in a fight with someone or threatened to kill someone, it was best to place them in different cellblocks.

Sometimes the best that could be done was to house them on different tiers in the same cell block. The color bands helped insure that enemies would not wind up sitting at the same table in the dining hall and having a possible altercation that could escalate. The colors were painted on the edges of the tables in the dining hall. Inmates were to sit at a table with their specific color. They had to wear their ID on their chest, so we could see the color on their ID and see if it matched the color on the table they were sitting at.

If it did not, they could be written up for being in an unauthorized area.

With a policy like this, the inmates try to find ways around it. Not wearing their ID was a common one. This way when we approached them on not seeing their ID, they could say they forgot. They are to have their ID clipped to their chest area at all times or they can be locked up. There was not uniform enforcement of this policy throughout the institution, because it was much easier to not say anything instead of having the constant confrontation with the inmates.

Inmates would switch their ID with a different inmate. Their pictures are on their ID, but the color code system made us focus more on the color rather than the picture. If they were caught with a different inmate's ID, it was a worse violation.

Some of these guys would take a pin, poke it in the back of the color band to release it and put a different color band on their ID. How could they get different color bands? It was easy to lie to inexperienced officers or busy officers that wouldn't take the time to check out the inmate's stories.

There were quite a variety of lies that were used on us officers when confronting these guys. "When I came in from my last cell hall, the officer checking me in never gave me a new color." "It fell off and this is what the officer on last night put on my ID." "When I switched cells, nobody changed it."

When searching a cell, I once found a stash of different color bands that the inmate would rotate to his ID depending on where he wanted to be allowed to be.

The color band system wasn't a fool proof system, especially with so many fools around, but it was the best we had.

AN EXAMPLE

The sarge noticed an inmate pass him without his ID on.

"Where's your ID?"

He pulled it out of his pocket.

"You need to wear your ID when you are out on the flag." The sarge noticed there was no color band on the ID. "Give me your ID so I can put a color band on it."

"Don't bother. I'm going to take it off like the other one that was just put on."

"Switch in. I'm placing you on ICR."

"Whatever."

Removing the color band that identifies which group of cells an inmate lives in is considered tampering with a security device. That charge can get you from 30 to 90 days in the hole. Maybe he won't be such a wise guy after doing that time. You're right; I doubt it too.

LYING SCUMBAG AND VERBAL JIVE

The following is a report that I wrote.

Offender Lying Scumbag came to the bubble yesterday to get the color band changed on his ID. He stated that his name was Lying Scumbag and that he needed a purple band on his ID. There is a Lying Scumbag in 525 and this area requires a purple band. The ID he gave me had a different inmate's name on it and a white band. I asked him about the contradiction of what he had told me. He was not answering my questions and not making any sense with what he was saying.

I checked our gallery book and found him to reside in 108 which requires a pink band. I put the pink band on his ID and gave it to him.

He was ICR'ed last night for a tier violation. He was caught in 523. The color assigned to this area is purple.

Today, after receiving 3 days LOP for that tier violation, he was instructed by the lieutenant to go directly to the bubble and get the color changed on his ID. Somehow, the pink was gone and he had a purple band on it. He did not do as the lieutenant ordered him to do. He chose to switch in instead. I paged him to the bubble. When I asked him questions about him not following the lieutenants orders, he started with the same misdirection type of dialog that he used yesterday. He was uncooperative. Officer Smiley witnessed this exchange and changed the color band on his ID.

I discussed these series of events with the sergeant. The sarge talked with Lying Scumbag. Lying Scumbag was giving him half truths. The decision was made to send him to seg.

Whenever one of these guys started doing what I refer to as the "Verbal Jive," I knew that I would be having some fun throwing the same techniques back at him before I sent him to segregation.

Lying Scumbag was a master at using verbal jive to confuse officers. If you know the game, it can't be played on you. I knew the game, as did the sarge that sent him to the hole.

Lying Scumbag wrote the following to our unit's top sergeant.

While over there in B-West Officer Basham verbally abused me and almost assaulted me with a blunt instrument. He told me to shut my mouth instead of asking me, then he pulled the drawer shut with force barely after I raised my face and hand out of it. I was told by the Grievance counsel to write a informal grievance to you before writing to them again. I need your response to this kite.

Lying Scumbag – Please Comply – Thanks!

This is the note that I wrote and attached to the inmate's kite for the sergeant:

I would like to file charges against this inmate for misrepresentation, slander, whatever fits these lies. Screwmaster said you could tell me how to go about it. The exchange he is talking about was witnessed by Officer Smiley.

After talking to the sergeant, he directed me to a lieutenant to notify.

The lieutenant told me to get a copy of the kite to him, which I did.

I saw the lieutenant a few weeks later and asked what was happening with this deal. He said that Central Office allows them to lie all they want. They have to threaten us before we can do anything.

That is what we have to put up with in this place. The inmates have more rights than the officers. They dish it out and we have to take it.

Nothing ever came of this because Lying Scumbag was and always will be a LYING SCUMBAG.

Yes, I do feel better for having written this.

DINING HALL DYNAMICS

Dining Hall = Hot, Noisy, Volatile

Due to the high number of inmates packed into this one small area, it was a dangerous place to be. A fight between two inmates could quickly evolve into a riot. Any violation down there would be met with a more severe penalty than if it were committed in a different part of the institution.

The dining hall had an extremely high ceiling; at least 30 to 40 feet high with a couple of skylight areas in it.

There were large windows around three of the walls. The windows start about 2 ½ feet above the floor and go up close to the ceiling. They were functional for the purpose of seeing what was going on with inmates passing by outside. They were greatly needed to try to cool the place down, however in the summer, nothing, not even fans mounted around the dining hall could make it comfortable.

The seating contained small square tables that would seat four. The seats were round metal discs welded onto the frame of the tables, making it so that chairs and tables were too heavy to be lifted up and thrown around or used to smack over someone's head.

When this prison was built, the seating area was wide open. Eventually, a brick wall roughly 8 feet high was built down the center separating the seating area into two halves. This was in hopes that if inmates got out of control, there would only be half as many out of control. 250 inmates could sit on each side of the wall. 250 inmates going crazy at one time were preferable to 500. Not that the wall would stop them, but it could allow some time for things to settle down before the other side could get involved.

The wall also helped control serving these guys in a more orderly fashion. The largest cellblocks housed 252 inmates, so each side would hold one of the largest cellblocks. Blocks were released one at a time. Once the first group was served and seated, the next cellblock would come down. Once they were served and seated on the opposite side of the wall, the first group would be sent back to their cellblock. Once they were all back in their cellblock with the door secured, another cellblock would come down. We rotated like this until all blocks were served. This would take over 2 hours to get all of the inmates fed in the entire institution.

When B-West became double bunked, they initially were fed in the cell block. When it was decided to try to feed them in the dining hall, the front half of the block would come down at one time and the back half would come down at another time.

The front of the dining hall is where the serving lines are. The wall in front of the serving lines is the north end of the room. Entry to this room is through the east end of this wall. The kitchen is through the west end of this wall. On the north wall, in the center, is a platform that I'm guessing is about 15 feet or more above the floor. I was told that years ago an officer with a rifle would be posted on this platform. I don't know why an officer is not posted there anymore. There is no better place to observe these guys than this platform. Other officers could easily be sent to a problem location by directing them over the radio. At least this was one place in the dining hall that was a clear cut great place to be posted.

Up front, separating the seating area from the serving area, there is a fence with a gate in it about 3 feet high. This is where the officers in charge of the dining room would be. There was always supposed to be a lieutenant in this area while meals were being served. They did not always arrive. If there happened to be more than enough officers to cover the 3 walls, the extra officers were to be at the fence.

Where did all of the officers come from? Every cell block except the very small C-Hall had to send an officer from the block to help provide security in the dining hall; this was 5 officers. A couple A-Team officers would be assigned to cover the serving area. These 7 plus the two assigned to the kitchen and dining hall area plus the lieutenant came to 10 officers that should be in the dining hall while meals are being served. Then why was I alone on a side by myself at times. It's because some officers did not do their job. Others had situations arise that pulled them away. Others congregated up front by the fence in a BS session.

I didn't care if I had to cover the entire side by myself, but first of all, let me know that will be happening. Next realize that if there is only one officer there, more inmates will be trying to get away with things. With that, realize that I do my job. That means I will need time to write reports, so don't bitch to me when you know that will be the end result.

Working the dining hall was one of my least favorite duties; however I would gladly volunteer for it if the other option were shakedown. The rules in the dining hall were clear.

The basics are as follows:

1 – Maintain order as the inmates passed through the chow line. Watch for things like people cutting in line ahead of others, inmates putting pressure on the inmates serving to give out more than they are supposed to, watch for servers smuggling food to those passing through the line, watch for those yelling or gang signing to other inmates, those being disruptive with inappropriate actions or with violence.

2 – Check to make sure they all have their ID card clearly displayed on their chest area.

3 – Check for those not sitting in their assigned area.

4 – Watch for those roaming around the dining hall

5 – Watch for those trying to smuggle any food out of the dining hall, especially sugar packets that could be used for making hooch.

These would not be a problem if every officer did the job as we were told. The big problem was that most officers are intimidated to be standing in the middle of 250 inmates, most inmates of whom are pissed off that you are there watching them eat. Also, there was no clear area to post up (A designated or unobtrusive spot for officers to stand and observe). You stand with your back to a wall and you are literally closer to inmates that are eating than they are to the people that are sitting next to them. This causes officers to go up to the front gate and socialize with other officers instead of staying among the inmates and maintaining order.

In order to leave the place where we were posted, to take care of a problem, many times it was impossible to not brush up against someone. For the institution to create negative situations like this, be aware of it and not solve this easily solvable problem is utterly ridiculous. How would you like it if someone was standing over your shoulder while you were sitting down eating? It didn't create a good environment. With the big shots not caring to solve the problem, inmates and officers knew we just had to live with the stupidity.

At one time a couple of unit directors were frustrated with officers not doing their job in the dining hall. They decided to create a training class on what they expected officers to be doing when they worked this area. I thought, great, now everyone will be on the same page, doing the same thing and I won't be the target for the inmates. Wrong! Without consistent follow up it is never going to happen. In this place, anybody trying to improve things never gets cooperation for very long.

When I took the class, I was surprised by the things they said to do and how they wanted them done. If I followed their directions, I couldn't be as effective as I had been. After the class, I went up to them to address these issues. I started to tell them how I did things different and the reasons why. They cut me off. They said, "This class was for everyone else. We don't want you to change a thing. You do a great job. Keep doing it the way you have been." I was relieved, thanked them and headed back to my cellblock.

At this point you're probably thinking that I'm full of myself and making something like this up; I know that's what I'd be thinking.

Within the rest of this chapter, I'll give you instances that will help justify this to be accurate and not just a load of crap.

NOT GOOD AT MAGIC

As officers, we were assigned to be food monitors at times. We had to watch inmates going through the food line and make sure they didn't take more than they were supposed to take.

On this day, an officer was to make sure that inmates took only one piece of cake. An inmate took two pieces, so the officer told him to throw the extra piece in the trash. The inmate hit the lid to the trash can to try to make it seem like he tossed it away, but he had not.

This guy thought we were as dumb as he was. He was locked up.

TIMING

There was a time where a lieutenant called me from my post to the front of the dining hall. While he was talking to me, a fight broke out in the exact place I had been posted. I was frustrated that I hadn't been there, but I was just following orders.

REPUTATION

Another instance was rather funny, to me anyway. When it was time for inmates to return to their cellblock, a green light would be switched on and a gate would be flung open so that it made a loud bang.

Some of the guys would make a mad dash out of the place. Most would get up and file out in an orderly manner. Still others would loiter, sit around talking or continue eating.

If they weren't done eating it was generally because they spent their time flapping their jaw while they were down there rather than using it to chew.

Nobody likes to be told what to do. You don't and I don't. Not being told what to do is a great motivation for me to do my job properly.

If these inmates got up and left when they were supposed to, I didn't have to say anything to them. I started at the back of the dining hall and if some people weren't getting up to leave, I slowly walked over that way. If they got up and left when they saw me coming their way, I didn't have to say anything to them, thus no confrontation. If by the time I got to them and they didn't get up to leave, I still wouldn't say anything, I'd just stand there briefly. Most of them would generally leave at this point.

If I had to say something, it would generally be something like, "How's it going guys?" At this point things either got humorous or confrontational. A humorous comment from someone might be, "You really don't care how things are going. You just want us to leave don't you?" I always liked these guys, if they were having fun with it. We could get some witty banter going back and forth while they got up and walked out.

However, one time when I asked how it was going, an inmate, new to the joint, turned around angrily and yelled, "What do you want?" The guy sitting next to him was a guy that I had numerous confrontations with over the years. He had obviously learned his lesson because he quickly grabbed this guys arm, held him down and said, "Shut up! Don't say anything! Don't do anything! Don't even look at him! That's Basham! Just get up and leave or he'll toss you in the hole!"

INMATES KNOW WHAT EACH OFFICER WILL DO

Another time I walked up to an inmate to enforce a policy. He looked surprised. He said, "I'm sorry, I didn't know you were here today."

If everyone did their job the way they were supposed to, I wouldn't have to deal with situations like this. It wouldn't be, this officer enforces this and that officer enforces that. If we all did our jobs the way we were supposed to, the inmates would know there was consistency among us. They would know that if we saw an infraction, we would address it. They would know there would be consequences for their violations. Consequently there would be fewer violations and fewer people being carted off to segregation for the accumulation of menial violations. Stiffer penalties and longer terms in segregation could be handed out creating a greater deterrent for those thinking about violating rules. Thus, we wouldn't have to keep putting up with so much stupid behavior all of the time. The trouble makers would be doing most of their time in segregation.

Believe it or not, most of these guys just want to do their time as peacefully as possible, get out and never come back.

TO SHUT DOWN OR NOT TO SHUT DOWN

When I first started working in B-West, there were two excellent sergeants there to learn from. One was a "rule guy" and one was an "old school find a way to get it done without getting into too much trouble guy." The combination of styles became who I was and how I got things accomplished.

I always approached a problem first with the rule method. If this couldn't accomplish a "just" end result, I would try the other method. It didn't involve breaking rules; it was more like finding a loophole.

While working the dining hall one day, an inmate approached me and stated that he had been having chest pains on his left side. He stated that he would like to be checked out by Health Services. I escorted him to Health Services. They took him right in and checked him out.

That is the way I had to write the report. Reports are as brief as possible. They contain only facts, not opinions. This report is accurate, but there is always more that could be written.

This inmate had first reported to the officer in charge of the dining hall. This officer was quite savvy. I had learned a lot from him over the years. He was one of the few officers that weren't afraid to do his job the way it was supposed to be done.

The inmate complained of having chest pains. This is generally an instance where we are to call for an emergency response from health services. The inmate should be made to sit down to wait for them. The alarm would sound. All movement in the institution would stop. The squad would run for testing equipment. Health Services personnel would come to check the inmate out. Everyone in the dining hall would be gawking to see what was going on.

The inmate told the officer that he didn't want this to happen. He was concerned about the pain, but he had been lifting weights the night before. Most every officer working in a prison has lifted weights at one time or another. We know that you may have more pain the day after lifting than the day you lifted.

This is lunch time. This had been a trying day throughout the institution. Several emergency responses had already been called and the schedule was running way behind. An emergency response to the dining hall would really foul things up. Things were rather hectic down there already. It would be difficult to get everyone fed and back to where they belonged before our shift was over.

This officer knew pretty much what was up. If he wanted this situation handled properly, he would've called for an emergency response. He obviously didn't want it handled that way, so he called for me to find a solution as he knew that I found ways of getting things done that weren't necessarily wrong but that others might not do that way.

I asked the inmate questions in order to find out what was going on. He was adamant about not having me call an emergency response. He was concerned though. He just needed to be seen in order to have peace of mind.

In this place, you need peace of mind or your mind travels all over the place and will create bigger problems. Prevention is the name of the game here. If you can keep these guys minds at ease, larger problems won't develop.

I told the guy that I saw three options. The best was to call for help which he definitely didn't want. The next was that he felt that there was no problem, that it was a false alarm, return to his seat and if he later felt it necessary, schedule a doctor appointment. And the worst option was for me to escort him to health services, which I knew I could possibly get in trouble for doing. Obviously, he chose the latter.

I escorted him to Health Services to see the doctor who verified the inmate's hope of just muscle strain. The inmate had peace of mind. Mission accomplished, except for me getting in trouble.

Once I had written my report, I took it to the watch commander. I stood there while he read it, as I knew I would be getting a talking to.

This lieutenant was very smart. Nobody could get anything over on him. That made it so officers that thought they could lie to him and get away with it didn't like him very well.

He knew how I thought. He could probably predict what I would do in any situation. That's why instead of reaming my ass, he just informed me that the proper way to handle a situation like this was with an emergency response call.

I was expecting this. He was doing what he had to do. He was trying to keep my tail out of trouble, but was also somewhat appreciative that I handled it the way I did.

However, I knew I could never pass a situation like this off as me being naïve ever again. There was no grey area for an instance like this for me again. The kitchen officer had already used his naïve card up in a situation like this years ago, that's why he passed the situation off to me.

The problem was that if this inmate had actually had a heart attack, I could've been held accountable. However, he was definite about not calling for an emergency response. Because of this, I figured that he must not be in dire straits. That's why I handled this the way that I did.

He was a man of color. I knew heart problems were a high risk factor for his group. I believed his pain had to do with muscle pain from working out, but I am not a doctor.

He was extremely appreciative that I got him to the doctor and that I had handled it the way I did. I basically had left all of the decisions up to him.

The officer that he had first reported to that was running the kitchen was thankful for the way I handled it. He was able to get the serving of inmates concluded without any further problems or delays.

The day concluded smoothly with things getting back to normal; at least as normal as this place gets.

WANTING TO GET CAUGHT

There was a time where I saw an inmate in the dining hall blatantly front himself off on an unauthorized area violation. He made sure I was watching him when he went to an area of the dining hall he wasn't supposed to be in. I had never had any trouble with this guy before, so I went over and told him to go back to his seat. He was acting rather strange, but went back and sat in his assigned seating area. Shortly after, I saw him make it clear to me that he was in an unauthorized area again. I knew something was up. I thought he may be getting harassed where he was supposed to be, so I told him to sit down right where he was and to stay there when everyone else left.

I would have inmates stay back frequently when I thought they might have a problem that they couldn't speak about if others were around. Also, I'd have them stay back if they were the type of guy that would try to stand up to me and play big shot in front of their peers. Another reason was to talk to them and see if I could get compliance on a policy without having to write them up. Just that they had to sit there through the rest of chow and wait while everyone else exited, gave them time to think about what they had done and whether or not they really wanted to face the consequences of their actions knowing that I would be dealing with them.

When the inmates started returning to their block and enough of them were out of the area for our conversation to not be overheard, I went to speak to him. He wanted to talk. He was being harassed. A group was not allowing him to sit where he was assigned. There was going to be a fight between a couple of groups when everyone got back to the cellblock. He was a member of one of the groups and didn't want to be involved. I quickly called the watch commander who rushed all available officers to that block and had them spread out throughout the block. This was done without calling an emergency response. Officer presence is the biggest deterrent that we have and in this case it worked quite well. I got the informative inmate out quickly so he could blend in with the rest of the group. This was so that I wouldn't front him off. (Not let other inmates know he gave me information) After everyone was secured in their cells, an investigation was conducted. Instigators were removed from the cellblock and the fight never happened. Many violent confrontations were never given the chance to happen due to an inmate giving us information and investigations being conducted. I have to say that with all of the failings in this system, this area was not one of them.

TOO FRUGAL

When the state acquires surplus food, finding a way to serve it to the inmates is a good budget saving maneuver. But carrot cake! Why? Do we need vegetables in our junk food? Did they grow too much and didn't have enough friends, relatives and rabbits to ditch the stuff on? Do we really need to grind this stuff up and put it in something sweet so we will eat it? It's not really like a vitamin is it? This proves that if you camouflage something with enough frosting, we'll eat anything. This is an example of the kinds of things that went through my mind on a slow day in the dining hall.

NORGE REPAIRMAN

If you were around in the early days of the Saturday Night Live television show, saw reruns of it or heard of the Norge repairman, you will know what I'm telling you about this next guy.

In this comedy bit, that was one of the most hilarious ever, a repairman came to a house to fix a Norge refrigerator, if I remember the appliance correctly. He is stooped over working on it and the crack of his butt is rising over the top of his pants. The kids in the house are laughing at him behind his behind and cracking jokes. Yes, just like those puns I laid out there.

Well, there was a time when an inmate had the same problem. He was in the dining hall eating and the "Moon Was Rising." Some inmates saw this and started laughing and cracking jokes. Gradually more and more people noticed. Anyone that could see this rear end cleavage was having good natured fun at this guy's expense. Part of the problem was with the amount of moon that was out. You could harvest crops at night from the brightness of this thing. It may not have been a full moon, but with how big it was, it didn't matter.

I definitely saw the humor in it. My problem was that there were a lot of guys that did not appreciate coming to eat and having this bright white blubbery cleavage on the lower back side of a man drawing their attention. They had just come down for a meal and not for this type of a show. Had it been on the upper front side of a woman, I believe it would have been a different story. Heck, I know it would've been a different story. Unfortunately, once the novelty wore off, it was my responsibility to say something.

I walked over by him and as quietly and as discretely as possible, as if that were possible, said, "The moon is coming out early today." He didn't catch on. I had to bend over and explain it to him. He did not seem concerned about it, but tugged his pants up a bit.

The next time I saw him in the dining hall; it was the same thing all over again. I went over to him right away and explained that it was inappropriate to have his rear uncovered. I told him that he needed to solve the problem, which he did.

The next time I saw him down there with his pants down there; I went to him. I told him that I did not know what his problem was, but that it was necessary for him to solve it. I informed him that I would not be warning him again. Solve it now and forever or I'd have him escorted out of here. He wasn't happy with me, but never did I ever get that disgusting view again.

SOMETHING STUPID

One day, I saw an inmate wrapping a piece of cake in paper towels, so he could take it back to the cell block. You are probably wondering why I viewed that as being something stupid when there are probably many of them doing it. It was the way he went about it. Intelligent inmates will smuggle items out discreetly. Most stupid inmates will at least try to smuggle things out discreetly. This guy was standing up at an empty table only three tables away from me, carefully and slowly wrapping this cake in several paper towels. I was watching him. Most of the inmates in the dining hall were watching him. They were all watching me watching him. I was laughing at this spectacle as were most of the inmates that were viewing this display of idiocy. Seeing me still just standing and watching this guy, an inmate next to me asked me if I was going to go get him. I said, "No. It's useless. He obviously does not comprehend where he is." Any inmate within ear shot of me laughed and shook their heads in agreement. I knew other inmates would be speaking to this guy about the break I gave him.

MENTALITY THAT GOT HIM HERE

An inmate was wandering around the dining hall stopping and talking with different inmates. He was also watching for someone going through the serving line. I spoke to him and explained that wandering around, loitering and making contact with those in the serving line was against policy.

The next day, after eating, he moved up 8 tables to the front of the dining hall and again was watching to hook up with someone from another cell block. I had him escorted back to his cell hall and locked in his cell for being in an unauthorized area.

Some of these guys are just plain stupid. I guess this is the kind of mentality that allows some of these guys to get caught and convicted of crimes.

SAGGING

An inmate came in the dining hall with his ID in his pocket. I had discussed this with him several times before. Another officer told me that she had spoken to him before. Another officer told me that he had spoken to him about sagging twice before.

Sagging is when someone walks around with their "Pants on the Ground" as the man from American Idol sang about in 2010. This guy was sagging again. It's hard to say if this is a style thing or if some of these guys are advertising for sexual activity.

I had him locked in his cell on both violations.

DOCUMENT TRIVIAL DETAILS

An inmate that I had informed numerous times to have his ID displayed came into the dining hall again without it on. I sent him back to the cell block to be locked in his cell. He couldn't be deprived of a meal, so when he got back to the block, he was offered a bag lunch, but he refused it.

It was necessary to state in the report that a meal was offered. It was also necessary to document that he refused to accept it, as he may state later that he wanted one and we wouldn't give him one. Documenting what may seem to be a trivial detail is one way for officers to keep out of trouble.

FART MAN

An inmate was having a lengthy conversation in the dining hall at a table he was not assigned to. When he saw me coming, he headed back to his table. When I was making sure he was aware of the policies in the dining hall, he would not respond. Once he started talking, he became loud and uncooperative. He made statements like, "I left when I was through passing gas." Toward the end, he said, "You can go now."

I locked him up for being in an unauthorized area, disobeying and attempting to incite others in a volatile area.

His attitude encouraged me to go into more detail in the report and issue more charges than I would have otherwise. That along with him being a wise guy in the dining hall made it so I would not have to deal with him again for a long time.

WRONG PLACE TO FINGER

While checking inmates coming through the gate in the front of the dining hall, an Asian inmate came running up to me yelling and pointing to the back of the dining hall. His statement was rather unintelligible to begin with, but after he said it a few times, it sounded like, "He assault me! He assault me!" Or maybe he was asking for a salt shaker.

He seemed quite frantic however, so I went with my first assumption.

If you are going to get tossed in a Minnesota prison, it would be helpful if you learned the English language first. Many years ago, the United States chose English to be the language of our nation in order to try to not have these types of communications problems, but things seem to be changing. I wish I had been notified of this before I got so old. At this age, I think I'll be dead before I could learn another language.

This inmate was escorted back to the cell block for his safety.

It would be investigated later. To have him finger the perpetrator in front of all of these other inmates would not be healthy for him. He was probably in a lot of trouble now any way because of the way he notified us in front of about 250 other inmates.

ONE OF MY ASSAULTS

The day before this report, I told an inmate to move his ID from the bottom of his shirt to his chest area. Later, when I saw him at his table, I noticed that he had ignored me. I then went over to him and had him move it to his chest area.

The next day, he came in again with the ID on the bottom of his shirt. I went up to him to speak to him. After getting only a few words out, he yelled at me, "It's high enough."

I told him to go back to the block. He threw his utensils at me. As they bounced off my arm, he turned and went back to the block.

This is technically viewed as an officer assault, so his refusal to comply with policy combined with his temper and trying to make like a big shot in front of so many other inmates was going to get him a lot of time in the hole and maybe even a trip to a box in Oak Park Heights.

THEY ACCUMULATE VIOLATIONS

I was working in the dining hall when an inmate came through the gate without his ID displayed. When I asked him about it, he pulled it from his pocket. Because he was carrying his tray and a full glass of pop, I directed him to put the ID on as soon as he got to his table. I observed him sit down, prepare his food and start eating. He still did not put on his ID. Later, I took his ID and had him come to the front gate where there was a sergeant. He started yelling and making a scene, so the sarge had him escorted out of the dining hall. He would do some time in segregation for disobeying a direct order, being disruptive and trying to incite others when all he had to do was have his ID displayed in his chest area.

A SERVING OF BLOOD

When A-East was leaving the dining hall, two inmates started fighting toward the back of the dining hall. Two officers and I made our way through the crowd of inmates to get to them. The two officers got there just before me, drew their mace, aimed it at the inmates and directed them to stop. They stopped fighting. I cuffed up one of them and another officer cuffed up the other. They were escorted to segregation by the A-Team. The other officer cleaned up the blood.

WE ALL KNOW THAT GAME

I observed an inmate sit at three different tables, all of them with different colors painted on the sides. They are only allowed to sit at tables with the same color as is on their ID.

Later, I observed him standing up front loitering. He filled his tray at the salad bar a few minutes before having to go back to the block and then threw most of it away. Filling their tray at the salad bar was one of the ways these guys tried to justify being where they were not supposed to be.

When I went to shag them from an unauthorized area, they would say they had the right to be there. In this case, he said he had the right to be there because he was getting more to eat. We all know the game.

I had him locked in his cell for being in an unauthorized area, loitering and wasting resources. Like I said, there is a policy against most anything in this place. If they want to test me, I can lay a pile of violations on them.

Many times, when I saw someone violating a policy that there wouldn't be much of a consequence for, I'd try to give them a break and seek cooperation later by letting them know I was aware of their actions and let them off the hook. Other times, like this time, these guys would violate more policies thus forcing me to have to write them up.

FYI: When I first started working in the prison, there was a salad bar at the front of each side of the dining hall. This was eliminated later due to abuses of the system like this.

ADDING UP THE VIOLATIONS

An inmate drew attention to himself by standing up in the back of the dining hall and raising his arm straight up over his head with his fist clenched. This was unacceptable behavior and ridiculous for anyone to be drawing attention to themselves in this way.

He also fronted himself off on not having his ID on. I notice these things easily from most any distance. It's kind of like a cop that notices if you haven't put the tabs on your license plate. I knew he had the ID on when he entered the dining hall because I check them all and don't let them enter unless it is on. These guys take them off after getting in the dining hall so we can't see their color code when they go to an unauthorized area.

When he returned his tray and proceeded back to his table, he stopped and talked to some people for awhile. This was his third violation. When he got back to the table, I approached him and asked him for his ID. He refused to hand it over. Disobeying me was his fourth violation.

He asked me why I was coming all the way over to his table. This was a misdirection tactic to try to take the focus off of his violations. I don't respond to these tactics. I am the one that asks the questions, not the perpetrator.

I directed him again to give me his ID. This time he complied. He was sitting at a burgundy table. His ID was pink. This was his fifth violation.

When he was leaving, he stopped and asked, "What you pickin' on me for?" The poor boy was feeling sorry for himself and thinking that I was picking on him. Actually, it was no such thing. It was just another tactic these guys use to try to divert attention away from their own improper behavior. They don't deserve acknowledgement. The only thing this guy deserved was to be locked up and spoken to by the lieutenant like the delinquent that he was.

THAT DOESN'T WORK WITH ME BUCKO

An inmate was not in his assigned area. He was talking with people at a different table. I directed him to go back to where he belonged. I was going the same way as he was as I had to speak to another inmate.

He stood by his table and was looking to the front of the dining hall. I directed him to sit down. He refused this directive. Again I directed him to sit down. Again he did not follow this directive. I took his ID and told him to switch in when he got back to the unit. At this point he told me he couldn't because his leg was sore. He sure was walking around a lot for having a sore leg. You would think he would want to sit down. As you can see, most of these guys are really bad liars.

He came up to me later and wanted to talk. I had to tell him several times to go back to the block. When I got to the block, he was still not switched in and was talking to the door officer. At this point he wanted to get a kite. (Form to write an institution letter on) The door officer told him to get one and take it to his cell with him. He did not go back to his cell. He wanted to write it before going to his cell. He wanted my name and the name of a couple of other officers. I had to tell him several times to switch in before he finally did so.

This was typical behavior from someone that is a chronic trouble maker. Making a point of letting us know they are going to write us up is an intimidation tactic. I actually should've pushed the button on my radio and had this guy hauled to segregation, but I'd be sending guys all day if I tossed them for things like this guy was doing.

My hope was that one day, these guys would get tired of having to speak to the lieutenant and curb their inappropriate behavior, at least to some degree. Well, I could hope, couldn't I? Actually, some did eventually turn around.

SHOULDN'T BE ALLOWED A CANE

An inmate that was supposed to be seated in the front of the dining hall came to the middle of the dining hall and started grabbing at the food of two other inmates. One of them called me over. The disruptive inmate then started grabbing at the salt and pepper shakers that one of them was holding. I told the man to go back to where he belonged. He refused. He stated that if they didn't give him the salt and pepper shakers now, he was going to hit them with his cane. I made a call on the radio to get this guy picked up. He was escorted to the Security Center. This was a crotchety old black man that got away with more than he should have in this place because he was a crotchety old man. His antagonistic animated behavior would be quite humorous at times. It would be like when little kids are being bad, yet funny, so you try not to let them see you laughing, because you don't want them to think it's alright to act like that.

A big problem with this guy is that he wasn't goofing around. With his attitude, he should not have been allowed in this prison with a cane.

MYSTERY SOLVED

An inmate entered the serving area with his ID in his hand. I saw the black color band when he went through the gate. He took a seat at the back of the dining hall. Black tables were in the front. I went back and asked for his ID a couple of times. When he took it out of his pocket, he held his thumb over the color band. I directed him to give it to me. He didn't. I took it. He was not cooperative. He wanted to argue about it. I went back to my post. After returning his tray, he still didn't take a seat at a black table. He sat in a green area next to black.

In order for him to be so blatant with this violation, I figured that this guy was a moron, wanted to go back to segregation or was getting punked out.

I went over to him and asked him if he was getting punked out at the black tables; if others were not allowing him to sit there. He stated he wasn't and gave me a lot of attitude.

When I got back to my block and started writing the report, I found out that this guy was on In House Seg status. This meant that segregation was full. He didn't have a lot of time left on his sentence in seg, so he was released to a cell block to make room for other new violators. This status comes with very few privileges. Any violation that one gets caught at when they are on In House Segregation gets them sent right back to segregation. The mystery was solved. He was being mouthy, violating more policies and playing big shot in front of his buddies because he knew he would be going right back to segregation as soon as I discovered his status.

ANOTHER ASSAULT

An inmate stopped at a table next to me where 3 people were sitting. He seemed agitated as he walked away, so I went over to him to make sure nothing was going on. He was sitting at his proper table. He said something to me that I couldn't hear, so I bent over to try to hear him. He then raised his voice and told me not to bend over his food.

I was not over his food. This is one of their little techniques that they use to try to misdirect attention away from them and at others. He wanted to argue. I directed him to give me his ID. He did not and stood up speaking even louder. I reached for his ID. He grabbed my hand and pushed it away as he pulled back.

I reached for my radio. He instantly got a scared look on his face. Inmates are not allowed to lay a hand on us. If they do, it is an officer assault. I radioed for this guy to be taken out. He was taken directly to segregation where he would be doing a chunk of time and might even get sent to Oak Park Heights.

MYSTERY NOT SOLVED

While at my post in the dining hall, I noticed an inmate staring at me. I looked to see if there was a reason for this. He continued staring, bugging his eyes out and making weird gestures with his head and hands. I went to his table and asked him what was up. He told me not to lean over his food. Again this tactic! He kept going on about this and got louder and more disruptive. I asked him for his ID. He complied. I went to my post. He went to the front of the dining hall to talk to the officer in charge of the kitchen. I followed. The officer called a sergeant over. He was informed of the situation and had the inmate hauled out to the Security Center. He was placed in segregation after all the inmates in the institution had been fed. This was a way of keeping this as low profile as possible, not having the mater escalate and being able to handle it later when we weren't as busy.

Did this guy want to go to the hole, want to make a name for himself by standing up to me or just another arrogant idiot? I have no idea.

DON'T MESS WITH A PSYCHO

A kitchen worker was filling the salad bar while I was checking the ID's on the last few inmates coming through the gate from B-West. I heard yelling, so I looked over and observed an inmate with ketchup and pickles on his shirt. An inmate from my unit that had just entered with his tray of food did not have a tray in his hands, so I called him over and asked him what happened. He stated that the other inmate had put pickles on his tray, so he gave his tray to him. He had given his tray to the other inmate by tossing it at him. I had the tray thrower step to the other side of the gate, escorted back to B-West and placed on Investigative Cell Restriction. This guy was always a problem child.

HARD(LY) WORKER

A kitchen worker was talking to an inmate at the front of the dining hall. When he saw me coming to speak to him, he went back in the kitchen. Later, he was talking to a different group. This time he did not leave when I approached him. I informed him that he was not to be there having a conversation with other inmates. He told me that they were just giving him a compliment on what a good job he does and that I didn't know what he was supposed to be doing. I told him that I had seen his work, so I knew that no one would be complimenting him on doing good work. I informed him that I knew exactly what he was supposed to be doing. He continued to be uncooperative. I had him come to the railing and meet with an A-Team officer. He was still uncooperative, so he was sent back to his cell block to be locked in his cell. I never saw him working there again. Or not working, as the case may be.

AT A BOY

An inmate was sitting at a pink table. He had a red band on his ID. I instructed him to go to a red table. He came back to the pink table and said they were all taken. I directed him to an empty seat at a red table. Later I observed him back at a pink table. I escorted him back to A-West where he was placed on ICR for being in an unauthorized area and for disobeying a direct order.

This common occurrence is pertinent because a few days later, I had the report that I had written returned to me with the following writing on it.

David,

You consistently do an excellent job of enforcing dining hall rules. Just wanted to thank you.

This was from the director in charge of this area of the prison and a few other areas.

This is not an environment where you get an at-a-boy very often.

IT'S JUST A JOB

An inmate passed through the gate on the west side of the dining hall. I asked him if he had his ID. He stated in an irritated manner that he did, but he did not put it on. I followed him to the front table where he placed his food. I told him he had to have the ID on his chest.

He put it on as he was yelling at me, "Hey! It's just a job man!"

I said, "You're right, and I'm pretty good at it ain't I?"

He was sitting at a pink table. His ID had a black color band on it, so I took his ID and had him locked up for being in an unauthorized area, failure to display his ID and being disruptive in a volatile area.

SOME THINK THEY HAVE CONTROL

I noticed an inmate with a gold color band on his ID at a blue table. A-West was in the dining hall and does not have anyone assigned to this color of blue table. Nobody should be sitting at these tables when A-West is in the dining hall. He stated that he did not know where he was to sit. I showed him an empty seat at the gold table next to him. An inmate sitting at that table stated that seat was saved for someone else. I instructed the man at the blue table to sit there. The protesting inmate started to raise his voice and argue about this. I instructed him that the man was going to sit there and that he better not be hassled. He wouldn't let it drop. Another officer came over. By this time, another inmate came and sat in the seat. He proceeded to give me an attitude about being in his space. The two of them were getting quite loud. They went up to complain to the lieutenant. They were escorted out of the dining hall and locked in their cells.

WARDEN WAS AWARE

An inmate entered the serving area without his ID displayed. It was in his top shirt pocket. As he passed an officer and the warden, he was told to put on his ID. He put it in his mouth, entered the dining area and sat at a light blue table. He put the ID back in his pocket and settled in at this spot. I went over to him and asked him about his ID. He eventually put it on. His ID had a gray band on it. I sent him back to the block and placed him on ICR.

Did I ever get tired of doing this? Yes, but that was the job I was hired to do. I never had kids, so I guess this job made up for that.

APPLE MAN

I observed an inmate collecting apples from others in the dining hall. When the side of the dining hall that he was in was released, I directed him to get rid of all of the food that he had collected. After returning his tray, I called him over and had him empty his pockets. He took one apple out of his pocket and threw it on the table. It went flying across the table onto the floor. He stated that was all that he had. I directed him to continue emptying his pockets. He pulled out another apple. I took his ID and sent him back to the block to be locked in.

SAME OLD THING

While working the dining hall, an inmate passed through the gate without his ID displayed. I asked him if he had his ID. He was very confrontational when he stated that it was in his pocket. I directed him to put it on his chest. He grumbled something incoherently and kept going. After checking the last inmate to pass through the gate, I checked to see if he had followed my directive. He had not. I directed him to give me his ID 3 times. He did not comply. The third time instead of giving it to me, he pulled it out and put it on. The color code was brown. He was sitting at a pink table. I took the ID. He went to complain to the lieutenant who had him escorted to the security center.

It always amazed me as to why these guys thought they could get away with this when they saw me working. Actually, a lot of them probably did get away with it, but why not just comply when I catch them?

WHERE DO WE GO

B-East was in the dining hall for breakfast. When the B-East door opened up for the inmates to return to the block, two guys ran out. One had a foot long plastic shank and was chasing the other guy.

The man trying to get away was affiliated with people that had killed the other man's nephew on the outside. The man with the shank wanted vengeance. He caught up with the guy in the dining area. As the man being chased could go no further, he turned around to try to defend himself. He put up his hands as the shank was thrust forward. He got one of his hands sliced.

Officers were converging on them, so the attacker turned around and started running back to B-East. He had to get through B-East inmates that were returning from the dining hall. They were scattered throughout the hallway and the dining hall. The first radio call had mentioned B-East, so officers ran to B-East.

As the attacker approached B-East, he saw a mass of officers standing there. He did a 180 and headed back to the dining area. I guess he knew he was getting caught one way or the other, so he'd try to get to his victim and finish the job.

There were plenty of officers in that area too. A radio call, after the first call, identified the dining area. Many officers were confused as to what was going on and where, so there were plenty of officers all over the entire area, waiting to take care of whatever business came their way.

As the offender entered the dining area, officers got him cornered, tackled him, cuffed him and took him to segregation.

SO THAT'S HOW IT IS

One day, another officer and I were working the chow hall. He saw a guy smuggling bread. As the guy was leaving, the officer told him to get rid of it. The guy wasn't cooperating. He had always been a problem inmate. I went over by him to enhance officer presence and to assist if the inmate wanted to escalate the situation. He then threw corn in the trash that he had stashed in a bag. The officer hadn't known about that. He told him to get rid of the bread. The guy started protesting. I stepped right up next to the inmate as the officer got firm with him. The guy complied but walked away grumbling about the officer. He said, "So that's how it is." This is a common veiled threat.

NOT AS SMART AS HE THOUGHT

An inmate's status was Medical Idle. He had an authorization from Health Services to have his meals delivered to him in the unit.

I received a tip that he was going to the dining hall and laughing about having meals delivered to him in addition to sneaking out to the dining hall and getting another meal.

I had assisted in delivering his meal to him that morning. I observed him sitting at an orange table with a tray of food. If he had been authorized to be in the dining hall, he should have been sitting at a white table.

I directed him to come with me that he was going to the unit to be locked in.

He was uncooperative and refused my directive.

I directed him again to comply.

He refused again.

It took three directives to get him to stand up. I directed him to leave his tray of food on the table.

He ignored this directive by grabbing a sweet roll.

I directed him to put the food down.

He again ignored my directive. It took another directive before he put it down and went with me to the front of the dining hall.

He was escorted back to the unit and locked in his cell to have the Watch Commander decide his fate. By being disruptive in the dining hall with so many inmates around, he sealed his fate on going to the hole.

TOO MANY GANG BANGERS

B-West was going to the dining hall for the evening meal. An officer noticed about 18 black inmates grouped in feeding line #1 and only a few in lines 2, 3 and 4. An officer told them to move into other lines. They asked him why. He told them the other lines were almost empty. It was this officer's responsibility to keep inmates moving through the lines as efficiently as possible. This was important in order to get them all fed in a timely manner.

8 of them moved to line 2. The two groups appeared as though they wanted to stay together and did not want to split up.

As they were going through the gate, the groups were arguing. Officers instructed them to take their seats.

The sergeant notified the watch commander and the B-West OIC of the impending problem. A-Team members positioned themselves along the railing on the east side of the seating area, the side these inmates were to enter.

Several inmates got together at a table in a back corner of the dining hall. They then dispersed and went to speak with inmates at other tables. An officer told them to quit roaming around and go to their assigned seats. At this point, they got up and went toward the front of the dining hall, appearing to be taking their trays back. They began hitting inmates that were sitting at the front tables. This turned into a large fight by the racks where inmates return their trays. A B-Level response was called for. Orders were issued to break it up, to no avail. Chemical irritant was sprayed into the crowd by multiple officers. Only a few dispersed. As officers tried to take control of inmates to cuff them up, the officers became the objects of their violence.

As inmates were being cuffed up, they were placed on the floor by the serving lines. One inmate ran up and punched one of those cuffed up inmates lying on the floor, so he was added to the collection of cuffed up inmates.

Cuffed up inmates were being taken to several areas to secure them. Segregation was able to take 4, the security center took 4 and the front turnkey took 2 for a total of 10.

An inmate, identified to be a Vice Lord, was bragging to the inmates in A-West, "We got into it with some Crips." He had to be taken through A-West to get to seg.

An inmate in B-West was heard to yell out, "We gotta watch out for the Crips."

The inmates that were left in the dining hall were released three at a time to go back to the block to be locked in. They were checked for cuts and bruises as they left.

After the kitchen was cleared, it was some time before feeding could be resumed. Blood was in the area of the fight and dripped along the routes the inmates were taken to be secured. Pictures needed to be taken before the blood cleaning crew could clean up the blood. The blood needed to be cleaned up before people could be allowed to travel over those areas. All food that was contaminated by chemical irritant was disposed of. All secured inmates had to be showered due to the chemical irritants. They needed to be checked over by Health Services.

Because of B-West getting locked down, those that did not have an opportunity to eat had meals delivered to them in their cells, 350 of them.

An officer noticed blood on one of his fellow officers. He had a bump on his head and marks on his face. The officer stated that he had been sprayed in the face with a lot of chemical irritant. He notified the watch commander of his friend's situation. She directed him to escort him to Health Services where he was treated for head wounds. His bloody shirt was placed into evidence. He showered and was issued a clean shirt.

This was the beginning of a lot of friction, fighting and lock downs in B-West; not that it wasn't going on before, but now it increased a lot. With double bunking increasing the number of inmates in that block, it also increased the number of rival gang members.

AMAZING

One day the warden showed up in the dining hall. Because of this, six officers showed up on my side of the dining hall when I was frequently alone there.

FROOT LOOP BANDIT

An inmate got caught smuggling a partial bag of Froot Loops out of the kitchen when returning from breakfast. He was placed on ICR. The next morning, I made sure that his breakfast bag had Froot Loops in it. He did see the humor in it.

BEST FOODS BEST COOKS

Best Foods ran the kitchen here, at least at this point in time. They would send in cooks to supervise the inmates that made the food.

A Best Foods employee was not allowed into the prison when he arrived one morning. It was called a lock out. He was suspected of supplying the prisoners with drugs and tobacco. Six kitchen workers were sent to segregation for possession of contraband. One had 29 hits of acid and some marijuana. Another tried flushing what he had down the toilet. He was sent to the hospital and given something to clean out his system, REALLY REALLY clean out his system. One had nothing, but tested positive on his UA, (urine analysis test). The others had a combination of marijuana & tobacco. This happened on the first shift. It is rare for anything to be going on then, especially as much as this.

On the second shift, we got two more testing positive on their UA's. The investigation continued.

Two other Best Food workers were locked out this same week. They were women who decided to supplement their income by charging inmates $50 for each blowjob. The inmates have no money on the inside, so their friends or relatives outside of the prison pay for them.

SEG WAS FULL

In the dining hall, during supper, two inmates chose to sit at the wrong tables. They were told to move to their correct tables. One complied with no problem. The other got loud and mouthy, but went to his correct table.

Later, the mouthy inmate came up to the officer. He was yelling and waving his hands all around. He said, "I never sat down at that fuckin' table. I was leaning over it because the dude called me over. It's dumb ass officers like you that pick on petty ass shit that makes our life hard."

(No, it's dumb ass convicts like you that still don't follow rules and refuse to behave that cause yourself more grief and longer time locked up in this prison.)

The officer said, "Leave and don't argue with me."

The inmate continued making a scene and trying to escalate the situation, so the officer called and had him removed. He was placed on In House Detention. Normally, this would be an automatic trip to seg, so I can assume that segregation was full.

MYSTERY LIQUID

An inmate from B-West was seen passing off a small plastic bottle in the serving line after taking a tray. Officers tried to recover the bottle, but all five servers played dumb. All of them were searched and removed from the dining hall. The inmate passing the bottle was taken to the security center. The bottle was found on a cart that was used to move food to and from the serving area. The bottle contained an unidentified thick, yellowish white liquid. A lot of time would have to be used investigating this one, unless someone would snitch and that was a long shot. These kitchen workers would lose their jobs and have the privilege of residing in my cellblock.

MORE PROTIEN

An inmate went through the food line a second time. This should not have been possible. Some officer was not doing their job. Once they get a meal, they are to go through a gate that separates the food lines from the seating area. At least one officer is to be standing there. Nobody is allowed back in the serving area from the dining area without an officer allowing it to happen. This is one area that if a big shot is not around, officers get into little BS sessions and don't pay attention to their responsibilities.

Anyway, an officer noticed this inmate go through the line a second time.

"Why did you go through the line again?"

"There was a hair in my food."

"I saw you hand the other tray off and go back to eating off your first tray. I am placing you on ICR."

We are relatively sure that this guy was lying about finding a hair in his food. With the hygiene of some of these guys working with their food, I would think finding a hair would be the least of their concerns.

PROBLEM COMB

An officer that was always very observant, knew the rules and wasn't afraid to enforce them noticed an inmate going into the dining area with a comb in his hair. He directed the inmate to remove it; he shouldn't have even had it with him. There weren't any women here for him to try to look pretty for, oh, that's right, that doesn't make any difference now a days. As the inmate was leaving the dining hall, the officer saw that the inmate once again had the comb in his hair. When the inmate noticed the officer looking at him, he quick reached up and made like he was combing his hair. After he passed the officer, he stuck it back in his hair. The officer called him back and directed him to turn over his ID. The inmate wanted to argue. He was again directed to turn over the ID. The inmate said, "Fuck that!" He protested to the lieutenant to no avail. He was locked in his cell to have a chat with the lieutenant the next day.

As officers, we could care less about a lot of these rules. Obviously, over time, things have happened to make them necessary. For us, it's about doing our job.

FAKE DROP GAME

An inmate entering the dining hall did not have his ID displayed. He had been warned about this the day before.

The officer asked him for his ID.

The inmate said it was in his pocket.

The officer told him he wanted it.

He pulled it out of his chest pocket and extended his arm out toward the officer in a veiled attempt to give it to him.

As the officer reached for it, the inmate dropped it on the floor.

The officer stepped back to allow the inmate space to pick up the ID.

The inmate started to walk away and said, "Why are you being such a punk?"

The officer called him back and informed him that he would be placed on ICR when he got back to his block.

"It don't matter. I got a life sentence." In an attempt to stir up other inmates in the dining hall he raised his voice and said, "Why did you throw my ID on the floor and then tell me to pick it up."

"I did not drop your ID on the floor and tell you to pick it up."

"Why you talkin' shit to me?"

"I am not."

The disruptive lifer was removed.

YES, WE'RE ANAL

An inmate did not have his ID displayed.

An officer asked for it.

"You guys are kinda anal about this."

The officer agreed.

The officer was trying to issue just a warning to this guy, but the inmate kept interrupting.

Finally, the inmate said, "Whatever."

With the violation, along with not cooperating and the attitude, the officer decided to place him on ICR.

KEEP THEM HEALTHY

On November 14, 2005, Stillwater became the final Minnesota Correctional Facility to offer the inmates "alternate meals" for lunch and dinner.

These were healthier meals that the inmates could choose to have or not. The other institutions found that five to ten percent of the inmates chose these meals with less fat, less sodium, less calories and more fiber.

There were inmates that required special diets, so these meals would replace many of those.

LESS SUGAR FOR LUNCH

The DOC likes to have everything as consistent as possible between the different Minnesota prisons.

There are always changes being made to the menu as the knowledge of how different food affects our bodies' increases.

On January 7, 2007, the adult prisons started using 8 ounce cups for milk, soda pop and fruit flavored drinks. 4 ounce cups would be used for breakfast juices. This would aid in decreasing the liquid calories that the inmates took in and get all of the prisons using the same size cups.

To further try to decrease obesity in the institution, there was encouragement to choose water or sugar free beverages.

FIVE WEEK MENU

The meals are on a five week rotation. These guys may not have freedom to choose exactly what they want, but they eat a heck of a lot better with a lot more variety than I do.

Some Breakfast Meals:

All breakfast meals had coffee, milk and juice available.

On the rare occasion that juice was not made available, it was replaced with a fruit.

Either hot cereal (oatmeal, Ralston, Farina) was available or else varieties of cold cereal were available.

If toast was available, jelly was too.

Syrup was provided for waffles, pancakes and French toast.

Hard boiled eggs, toast
Cheesy eggs, tri-taters, toast
Eggs, grits, toast
Denver eggs, sweet roll
Scrambled eggs, hash browns, bran muffin
Scrambled eggs, turkey ham cheese, English muffin
Sausage-Gravy-Biscuit
Eggs, turkey ham, toast
Creamed beef, biscuits, apple
Waffles, apple
Pancakes, beef sausage
French toast
Corn bread, beef sausage

Some Lunch Meals:

Some type of salad, bread and beverage is almost always available with these meals.

Meatballs, gravy, egg noodles, stewed tomatoes, pudding
Salisbury steak, mashed potatoes, gravy, carrots, cookie
Spaghetti, sauce, dressing, peas, fruit
Taco meat, hard shells, Mexican rice, cheese, lettuce, fruit
Fish, tartar sauce, au-gratin potato, spinach, coleslaw, cake
Turkey ham, sweet potatoes, black eyed peas, corn bread
BBQ chicken, baked potato, rolls, veggies, jell-o cake
Smoked sausage, pinto beans, steamed cabbage, fruit
Meatloaf, potatoes, green beans, chocolate cake
Tomato soup, tuna salad, potato wedges, saltines, orange
Beef Stroganoff, egg noodles, carrots, fruit
Beef patty, mashed potatoes, gravy, corn, cookie

Other main courses: Baked chicken, BBQ meat balls, Hamburgers, Chicken patty, Beef stew, Roast Turkey, Roast Beef, Lasagna, Egg rolls, Roast beef sandwich

Some Dinner Meals:
Some type of salad, bread and beverage is almost always available with these meals.

Hot dogs, baked beans, potato salad, fruit
Navy bean soup, egg salad, tom/let, macaroni salad, cookie
Enchilada casserole, Mexican rice, corn, yogurt
Hamburger gravy, mashed potato, glazed carrots, corn salad
Minestrone soup, Italian sausage, potato chips, yogurt
Mac & cheese, turkey ham, green beans, carrot raisin salad, chocolate cake
Vegetable beef soup, submarine sandwich, corn chips, fruit

Other main courses: Tater tot hot dish, Turkey ala king, Turkey stew, Chicken fried steak, Cheeseburger, Corn dog, Beef chow mien, Spanish rice casserole, Chili, Creamy chicken with brown rice casserole

KITES

Definition of Kite: A prison letter from an inmate to someone within the prison system.

Over the course of doing my time in Stillwater Prison, I acquired many kites that inmates wrote. I saved some of them that portrayed how some of their minds work and the things that go on in this place. I used these while being an instructor for the Interpersonal Communications Course. These kites helped get the new officers to start to realize what they had gotten themselves into.

It was extremely difficult to type some of these up the way they were written. I did my best within the restrictions of a computer that is set up for proper methods of typed communications. You will notice that many of these men never received a proper education. As for the problems with my writing, a proper education was provided, but some of it was just too darn boring to listen too. Besides, lots of people like my STYLE!

KITE 1

AttentioN:
If you ARe A Child Molester StAy AwAy from My Cell!
I refuse to AsscoshiAte With your KinD
If you WAnnA Hang out with Me, Be PrePared to Show PAPeRWork.
I found out 3 PeoPle I haD tAlKeD to were Child Molesters
I'm SicK with it
ThAnK You
Dark Pagan
P.S. yes I AM A Witch AnD ProuD of It!
BlesseD Be

A picture of a skull with flames coming out of the top and fangs was drawn on this kite. This was a three pager that was taped to an inmate's cell bars.

KITE 2

I just made it out of segregation. I think it's very important that you move me and (X) in the room together. I have a history of confrontation with people I am really not comfortable with. If me and (X) could get in the room with each other I think it will resolve any risk of any kind and it will assure safty to the institution and inmate

Thank you for your concern and consideration.

P.S. (X) and I talk and he feels the same way he wouldn't have any problem if we were together.

We would get this kind of a kite all of the time. They try to make like they are doing us a favor by doing exactly what they want. Sorry, but we aren't as dumb as they are by thinking we would buy into that crap. Follow the rules. Put in a proper kite, one that has two of you requesting to be in the same cell. If there is no problem with doing it, we will. You have just fronted yourself off as a player. We will be watching you closely.

KITE 3

I wrote a Kite asking if (X) could move in my cell Hes in 60s I don't Think it would be a good Idea for him to move in with me I thinks its Best if I Live alone tell him if he ask IM Single cell reStricKion

We are not here to lie for you. Honesty is the best policy. If you are afraid of this old guy, find someone else to sign off on bunking with you. This was also a lame excuse for trying to be single bunked in a double bunked unit.

KITE 4

I have A strong SHArp pAiN by my private ARRA
Its bEEN gEtting woRstER And woRstER.
CAN I PlEASE SEE A doctor? I Put A Kite IN ONCE.

I called Health Services; this man was seen by a nurse that day.

KITE 5

Basheem, I thought it wAs falg time. I didn't even sighn up for chaple. We usually pop out for first flag. I don't know what to do.
I'm not trying to mess around.
My family is Driving up here from St. peter today.
That's A 2 ½ Hour Drive.
They should Be Here at 9:AM.
Every Body Knows Not to mess around when you're here, I wouldn't try it trust me.
Please let me get my visit when it comes. I'm sorry I really Didn't Know. Please I Need this visit.

This guy made me feel sorry for writing him up, NOT! I did feel sorry for his supposedly expected visitors. I say supposedly because you never know what to believe in this place. He was a chronic minor rule breaker. I had caught him the week before for the same violation and gave him a warning. This time his visitors would be inconvenienced due to his propensity to violate policies. I did let him out of his cell to call them and let them know he was still a screw up. If he wasn't telling me the truth, I preferred to error on the side of the visitors.

KITE 6

Bash
Them Two Tables That Are uP. Need To stay uP, oR Be Taken out of Here, Inmates throw Milk on Them Two Tables Everyday, An Nite An laugh, An They stop At Them Tables An put There Food ON Them, An use the Micro Wave DelAy going To There Cells All The Time Sir Things Will Move Faster If Know TAbles.

These were tables located on the flag in the cell block. They were large steel tables with a steel plate welded to the bottom and six seats welded to the steel plate. It took six of us to tip them up on their side safely to be able clean under them. Milk would get under them and stink. Inmates congregated at these tables much to the annoyance of the inmates living on the flag. Unfortunately for those on the flag, the best I could do was to have the swamper crew keep cleaning and for me to keep strictly enforcing policies.

KITE 7

As you know I'm in Seg. Right now due to the "incident" that happened last Saturday

When I read the narrative I was shocked and upset about what was contained in it. I thought about it for awhile. I am an honorable man and I am big enough to admit when I'm wrong. If you remember the religious pass incident that is proof enough.

I guess I should word this next part carefully because I don't want to be accused of "threatening or harassing" you again. I do feel the need to tell you this though.

I'm not going to have ill feelings or wish bad upon you because you lied on me. God teaches us to forgive, so I forgive you. (over) (back of the page)

If this was a play to seek revenge of some sort or retaliation for the grievances (informal) I wrote, so be it. I forgive you. It was totally unnecessary on your part, but I forgive you. That is the right thing to do.

I will pray that whatever it is in your heart that makes you do these things, leaves you. I don't hate or wish bad upon you, I simply pray that God will touch you in the same way to help you be a better person. That's how real I am. And in turn I'll feel better.

So I will end this kite now. If you choose to try and Squeeze additional "charges" out of it, fine. No matter what, I'll still be praying for you and hoping God changes that in you. Take Care. God bless.

I found this one hilarious. This guy was a chronic violator with an extremely bad attitude. This was even before I wrote the report that sent him to segregation for his bad choices. Nothing changed afterward. As far as praying to God, I believe a person like this just uses that as a manipulation tactic. I believe this con is out on the streets now conning unsuspecting victims.

He also inferred that I was seeking revenge for grievances that he wrote on me. I was unaware of any of them. I once asked one of my lieutenants about grievances written on me. I didn't think there were any because I was never informed of them. He told me that he gets them on me all of the time. He gets way more on me than anyone else. He had a place in his office where he stacked them up in a pile. I asked why he didn't tell me about them. He said there were too many; that he didn't have the time. I'm thinking I'm in big trouble. Then he said that he was glad to get these types of grievances. He could tell by what they were about and what they said that I was doing my job very well. He told me to keep up the good work and to keep those kinds of grievances coming.

KITE 8

CO Basham
Pre- Grievance attempt at informal resolution.
I do not know if you are aware of the fact that some of the things you are doing with the intercom paging system is very, very disturbing to myself & others who are trying to rest/sleep in early AM, which we have every right to, especially in my case when I was Terminated from my work assignment for no legitimate reason whatsoever. You are punching phone buttons(s) prior to speaking. I am asking you to discontinue doing this. The flag is fairly quiet from 6-10 AM & a normal tone of voice w/o repeating 2-3X who or what you are trying to make your point would be greatly appreciated. I hope that you are willing to make adjustments which would reflect you showing some respect for people like myself who are light sleepers & do not want to be continually upset & disturbed by intensely loud phone button prior to every announcement, which seem to be about every 5-10 minutes in the early A.M.

Some staff over the years have told me flat out that their attitude is that as long as <u>they</u> have to be up & wake and at work in the early AM, then they feel <u>we</u> are not entitled to any quiet or respectful level of noise by staff. I'm trusting that not only are you not like this, you were unaware of the devastating impact to much needed rest/sleep your up-to now (at least on me) techniques w/intercom have been having! Thank You

We had a major problem in the cell blocks that I complained about frequently. Only a few speakers were mounted high on the wall across from the cells. This made it so that when an announcement was made, those closest to the speakers got blasted out and those between the speakers had difficulty hearing anything.

The response I got from the administration was that they had worked this way for a hundred years and it will continue to be sufficient.

The cost of adding a few more speakers to every cell block would be very little and solve a lot of problems, but every big shot I pitched this to, brushed me off. Consequently, we had to deal with it.

As far as this guy complaining, the main point is that he was torqued off that he got fired from his job.

Another fact of the institution and B-West in particular at this time was that breakfast was served first thing in the morning, making it necessary for us to wake everyone up to go to chow. In addition to this, we had to announce all moves before they went to chow. B-west had more inmates than any other block and thus more moves and more passes. All inmates came to B-West before going to any other block, thus more moves. This all adds up to a lot more announcements that had to be heard. Because of all of the inmates, the block was louder than other blocks, so these guys put stuff in their ears and wrapped things around their heads so they could get some sleep. This made it so many didn't hear announcements.

Because of being a standup comedian, I know how to properly use a microphone; that caused me to be louder without speaking louder than anyone else.

You need to get people's attention for them to be able to listen to what you are saying. Many times people do not hear the first things you start to say, especially in a noisy place like this. The announcements, which are many, are for one of over 400 inmates. Pushing a button on the phone system made a loud tone to try to get people's attention. Most didn't pay much attention until they thought they heard their name. Repeating the announcement gives the best odds of them hearing it and not having to go through the process again later after someone calls us asking where that inmate was.

In a block like B-West, it was a no win situation.

I spoke to the inmate who wrote the kite. I told him that I would review my procedures and if I could cut anything out I would. He was an intelligent person, so I filled him in on what I just laid out. Him knowing that I wasn't trying to be a jerk, made all the difference.

KITE 9

UNLESS I INVITE You IN, GET THE FUCK OuT! You'RE TRESPASSING!!!!!!
NOW DON'T GO AWAY MAD, JuST GO AWAY!!!!
P.S. HAVE A NICE DAY!
FonZIE

This was one sheet that was taped to an inmate's cell bars.

REPORT WRITING

BE HARSH WITH ME

While writing this book, I would have my lady read chapters off and on. She would give me her opinion on things. You need someone that will be downright honest with you when taking on a project like this. Believe me when I tell you she had no problem with that, but she never made me cry; not very often anyway.

When she started reading the chapters where I had written reports, she had a comment that was necessary to address to anyone reading this book. She said that she wished there was more of a conclusion, so this chapter is an attempt to explain and offer an overall conclusion as best possible.

INVESTIGATIVE CELL RESTRICTION

Other than an "Informational Report," when I wrote a report, the inmate would be locked up in one way or another. The majority of all reports end in the inmate being placed on ICR (Investigative Cell Restriction). The last couple of years I spent there, it was changed to just IR (Investigative Restriction).

The "Minimum Security Unit" (MSU) is more like an army barracks at Stillwater. It is outside of the prison walls. It is also referred to as the "Farm" because it once was a farm that the prisoners worked. Some prisons have MSU sections where they have rooms or barracks instead of cells. The DOC likes to have uniformity, so they dropped the "cell" out of ICR.

As far as uniformity in the DOC is concerned, it will never happen. China and the United States are closer than the DOC and uniformity. The Sun and Uranus are closer than the DOC and uniformity. Common sense and Nancy Pelosi are closer than the DOC and uniformity. OK, I guess the DOC and uniformity aren't quite that far apart, but I think you get where I'm coming from.

When placed on ICR, not much happened. It was a waste of time overall, but it was my job. The discipline policy is so lax; it is a ridiculous waste of time. The system is much harsher on its officers.

Once placed on ICR, the inmate is locked in his cell and meals are brought to him. Within 24 hours, the lieutenant will call the inmate to explain himself. This is generally done mid morning the next day.

The inmate has to violate the same policy five times within 90 days in order to be sent to segregation. Do you catch how lame this is? These are adults that are allowed to be disruptive 5 times within 90 days before there is much of a consequence. If they go 90 days without violating that policy, their slate is clean and they can start all over again. There are hundreds of policies, maybe thousands. It is not just five of any policy violations within 90 days. It is five violations for each and every one of them! It would be funny if it weren't so ridiculous.

The first violation, they receive a verbal warning.

The second violation, they get 3 days of LOP.

The third violation, they get 5 days of LOP.

The fourth violation, they get 7 days of LOP.

And the fifth violation gets them a trip to segregation.

Because of the gradual increase of LOP each time they violate the policy, it is called progressive discipline. I call it being so ridiculously lax that it takes more officers to continually enforce policies than would be necessary otherwise.

If you are going to have a discipline policy, there should actually be some real discipline. Maybe take away their radio and television. Make them read a book and do a report on it before they get out of their cell again. You're right. That would be too harsh. We would get too many calls from their lawyers and mommies complaining about cruel and unusual punishment.

LOSS OF PRIVILEGES

The little handbook given to inmates when they enter the institution states: Loss of privileges means the loss of recreation and some social activities. It may also consist of confinement to one's own cell/room/bunk during non working hours, etc. What this amounts to is they get a little more time to watch television.

SECURITY CENTER OR ESCORTED OUT

There are holding cells in the security center. Inmates are held in these cells for many reasons.

If they are leaving the prison for a medical reason;

If they are going to court;

If they can't get back to the block in time for count;

If they need to take a UA (Urine Analysis);

If they need to be searched;

If they are not in control of themselves;

If so many inmates were being sent to segregation that they had to let some out in order to fit more in, some could be held in the Security Center holding sells until they had cells for them in segregation;

If the Watch Commander wants more information in order to decide what is to be done with the inmate;

If it is easier to put them there until officers can get them back to segregation;

And who knows how many other reasons.

If I state that an inmate was escorted out, they generally went to segregation and sometimes to the Security Center. If they went to the Security Center, they generally went to segregation later after things settled down or after reports were handed in. The way I conducted my business was to make sure if I pushed that button on my radio to have someone removed from the area, they were not coming back. I gave these guys every break in the world to comply with policy or correct their behavior. I could have someone hauled out if they disobeyed my orders just one time. I generally would not push the button until they had refused my directives at least three times. That equaled, slam dunk baby; you're going to the hole.

SEGREGATION

If I stated that they went to segregation that is generally where it ended for me. More often than not, I would not know what happened to the inmates after that. I could have called officers assigned to discipline, but that would've been a nuisance to them and frankly, I didn't have the time. Also, my job was to document what I observed; whatever happened after that was not up to me.

Once they are taken back to segregation, they are charged with policy violations or crimes.

The last time I was assaulted, the degree of the assault was severe enough for the inmate to be charged with a crime. The inmate was held at Oak Park Heights until his trial at the county court house. Two things happened with this guy that extended his stay in prison.

He lost all of his good time for the assault. In Minnesota, if you get a 30 year sentence, you will only do 20 years if you don't create any problems. Basically, your sentence is two thirds of your sentence. The other third is incentive to behave.

He pleaded guilty to the assault charge. That got him more time added onto his previous sentence.

Typically, these guys get off pretty easy when they assault an officer. It is generally more frustrating to hear about the light sentences that these guys received than to hear nothing at all.

As an officer working in this place, we just have to accept that we are at the bottom of the ladder. The inmates have more rights than us. In Minnesota the public rules. The public knows more criminals than corrections officers. That gives the criminal more power. It is good to know that is the way it is when you accept a job here, but you don't find that out until later.

There was a time when I submitted a report to the Watch Commander. The report was on an inmate that was a major pain in the ass. The Watch Commander asked me what I wanted done with the guy. I told him that wasn't up to me. I said, "I just write the reports. Do what you feel is right." I would've loved to see this guy in front of a firing squad, but that was never going to happen.

Another time, an officer from discipline called me up and was apologizing to me for him giving an inmate a very light sentence for what he had done. I told the officer that there was no need to apologize. I told him that I had the ultimate respect for him. I told him that anything he did was not necessarily what he wanted to do, but what he had to do and I understood that. I told him to never worry about what I thought about any decision he had to make.

As time passed and I saw how the system worked, I realized that as the report writer it was best if I was not involved in the sentencing process. These inmates would be coming back into my block. I would have to work with them again. By not being involved in their discipline, they had less to be angry about with me.

I would explain that they chose to violate a policy. They chose to not take adequate precautions to prevent me from catching them. My job was to report what I saw. That was all I did. Other officers follow guidelines in administering discipline after that. I was not involved. Everything centers on choices that inmates make. They knew exactly what I would do in most any situation. If they didn't want me to write a report on them, they shouldn't violate policies when I was working.

HEARINGS

There were times that an inmate would dispute the charges levied against him. In a case like this, there would be a hearing inside the prison that I would have to attend and be a witness. I did not have to attend many of them.

Anything I put in a report was the facts. It's hard to dispute the facts. Anything I put in the report was something I saw or heard. If I wasn't sure of something, I would not write the report.

This made it so that the only guys to dispute my reports were liars, people trying to manipulate a way out from under what they had done and those wanting to have fun with playing jail house lawyer.

One time a guy lined up witnesses to testify for him. It was very funny. These guys were all scum, just like the one trying to evade the charges.

A couple of them saw me before they were to go in to lie for this guy, changed their mind and wouldn't testify.

Another guy went in to testify to what he had seen, but he hadn't even been around. He was caught at his lie. He was also there to speak up as a credibility witness for the guy being charged. He had already destroyed his credibility, so that didn't work.

The inmate that I wrote the report on got the maximum sentence on all charges.

Another time a guy was trying to get out from under his charges. He was very decent about it. He didn't try to discredit me. He was asking me a lot of questions trying to present a case. He wasn't getting anywhere with it.

I asked if I could ask him a question. He was fine with that. I said, "Is there anything in this report that is not true?"

He said, "No." The hearing was over.

I could respect a guy trying to avoid a sentence by presenting a case rather than by lying. There was an omnibus program where legally trained people would come in and assist these guys with their cases. Inmates that used these people saw them as a way to try to beat their charges rather than legitimately having a case. It wasn't very successful. Funding was cut for it so it was eliminated. The institution provided council for the inmate by asking for volunteers from us corrections officers.

This may seem a bit strange to have the people that write these guys up representing them, but there are a lot of officers in this place that see things as I did. Right is right and wrong is wrong. If there are grey areas or extenuating circumstances or a corrupt officer, we would be able to help them gather information and coach them on the merits of their case.

I volunteered to do this. No one ever used me. My reputation for catching people and making it stick was part of the reason. The other reason was that I was honest and I let it be known that I would help anyone that felt they were being unjustly charged, but If they wanted to win their case by lying, I wasn't who they wanted.

I did have a lot of guys come to me unofficially for advice. The first thing I would tell them was that they had to make a decision on whether to sign off on the charges or fight them. There are sentencing guidelines for every charge on how much time in segregation they should do for each charge. A discipline officer goes back to segregation and offers them a reduced number of days in segregation other than the recommended guidelines. This is to try to get each case out of the way with as little time involvement and cost as possible. Also, if they sign off on the reduced time, it helps to get these guys out of segregation sooner as seg just wasn't big enough to handle the number of inmates that create problems. The sooner they were out of seg, the better the possibility of having a cell available when the next guy got hauled back.

If they didn't sign off and didn't have a legitimate reason to beat the charge, they would generally get the maximum time according to the guidelines.

I would tell them that if they signed off on the charge, they were admitting to doing it. Even if they didn't do it, if they signed off on it to get the reduced charges, it would be on their record that they did it. If they went to a hearing and lost, they would get the maximum time, but at least, if they were innocent, they wouldn't be admitting to something they didn't do.

Most of these guys signed off, because they were guilty. Most of the guys that went to a hearing were just trying to beat the charge.

TECHNIQUES FOR REDUCING VIOLATION REPORTS

I was working the bubble when the door officer noticed an inmate from up on the top gallery going into a cell on the flag. He called me and had me watch that cell. Three officers went to see what was going on. There were seven inmates in that one cell. They were all patted down and all of their cells were searched. Three of the inmates had been locked up previously for an unauthorized gathering. We locked them up for that again.

Only the person assigned to a cell and two others are allowed in any cell at one time. Seven inmates in a cell at one time is not a comfortable situation. They had to be crammed in there like sardines. The biggest possibilities for seven in one cell would be to be planning something, assaulting someone or intimidating someone. It could even be something as simple as a group of guys getting organized for going out to recreation to play a game.

There were times when I found four guys in a cell hanging out. It is generally obvious if they were up to something, because those guys will give you attitude. Instead of writing up these guys that were just socializing and passing the time of day, I would start counting; one, two, two and a half, three. They would laugh and one would step out into the doorway.

Even though I wrote a lot of reports, I avoided writing a whole lot more by using these kinds of methods.

PROGRESSIVE DISCIPLINE & LOP

Everyone looks at some of these policies as a nuisance that creates more work for them. The officer enforcing the policy has to check the inmates file to see if there were any previous warnings for that specific violation within the last 90 days. If not, the officer documents it as the inmate's first verbal warning for that violation. If you warn any inmate about any violation and don't document it in his file, it doesn't count as a violation. There will be no consequence. It doesn't exist.

If the inmate has a documented violation within 90 days, the officer has several things to do:

Go back to the inmate's cell

Lock him in

Inform him of his policy violation

Document the violation in the inmate's file

Write a report

Turn the report into the watch commander and wait for his signature or any questions from him

Print off copies (one for the inmates file, one for a clip board in the block for all officers working that area to review and be aware of, the original goes back to the watch commander, sometimes they need a copy to go to the discipline office, and I always made a copy for myself)

Mark down the cell number on a list kept at the officer's desk as to who is locked in so they don't get let out and so they get meals ordered for them and delivered to them

Notify Health Services in case they would have to bring the inmate any medications

The next day, the block lieutenant has to take time to review the report, get an officer to get the inmate and bring him to the lieutenant's office, have a conversation with the inmate to hear his side of the story and inform him of the problems he will incur if he continues to violate that policy.

The lieutenant has to explain the progressive discipline policy also. The first violation is a verbal warning; second is 3 days of LOP (Loss Of Privileges); third is 5 days of LOP; fourth is 7 days of LOP; and the fifth violation within 90 days gets them relocated to segregation.

As you can see, there is significant time consumption any time a report is written; no matter how insignificant the violation.

The officer getting time to write the report and take care of business is often difficult. Another officer has to cover that officer's post while the report is getting written. There is a lot of computer work that needs to be done, so you have to try to find a computer that is not in use. Many officers aren't very cooperative in letting you use a computer when you need to write a report, unless it is a major violation or an inmate they don't particularly care for.

A lieutenant, when I transferred into his block, told me to enforce policies that he was not asking the other officers to enforce.

I said, "I'll do exactly as you ask, but don't ask me to enforce any policy that you don't intend to make every other officer follow. I went through that in B-West. It put me on the top of the hit list."

OAK PARK HEIGHTS

SEND ME NOW

An inmate had been placed in segregation on quiet status. This means he was in a cell with a solid door. A camera was in the cell, so he could be watched at all times. The inmate protested that he should not be on quiet status and that he knew the DOC policy. He said, "I have not threatened anybody, masturbated or damaged anything. I will do what I got to do; to whoever I got to do it to so I can get to Oak Park Heights!" He then demanded to talk with the Watch Commander. The Watch Commander was notified of the inmate's behavior and threats to staff. She reported to segregation and spoke with him regarding his quiet status placement and threatening behavior. After speaking with the lieutenant, he seemed to calm down and said he would cooperate and follow the chain of command regarding his complaints by writing a kite to the segregation lieutenant.

When I first started working at Stillwater, I would use the threat of sending these guys to the Oak Park Heights prison to try to get compliance. Boy was this off base. Many of these guys preferred Oak Park to Stillwater. It was cleaner, quieter and safer. The temperature was controlled better. If you behaved, you received plenty of privileges. It did not take me long to discover that the tactic of threatening to send guys to the Oak Park Heights Prison was a dud.

A TYPICAL DAY
ON SECOND WATCH

Actually, there is no such thing as a typical day in this place. But with so many whack jobs incarcerated here and working here the following will give you a general idea of how things would go.

START GETTING READY THE DAY BEFORE

When I got home from work, I transferred the hardware from the shirt I wore that day to one that I had ironed after I had laundered it. The shirts were supposedly permanently pressed, but I never thought they looked quite good enough without being ironed. I laid all my clothes out, so I would be ready for the next day. Getting up at 4am was not conducive to quick thinking. I was super prepared. This was so I could get ready for work in my early morning zombie state until I was able to start functioning normally. I wanted to eliminate any stress that I could control in my day. There would be enough stressful situations that would creep into my day once I got to work.

TRAFFIC

Traffic at 5 in the morning was busier than rush hour when I first started to drive; of course, I'm no spring chicken. Before I got this job, I was used to going to bed at 2am or later, now I was getting up at 4am. My body even had to acclimate itself to a different point in time to do some ah, reading.

Just because there were fewer vehicles on the road, didn't mean that it was any safer than the rush hours. I had to brake often for deer jetting across the road in front of me. One officer hit a deer two times on the way to work within about 5 years. No, it wasn't the same deer.

A semi came flying up behind me one morning. I was driving a little old junky Mitsubishi Colt that I had picked up for a few hundred bucks. It may have looked like crap, but it started every day, even in the winter when it was below zero. I was going the posted speed. He wouldn't back off or go around me, so I slammed on my brakes real quick and then canned it. The semi driver started swerving all over the road. When he regained control of his truck and trailer, he stayed way back from me. There are a lot of jerks and idiots on the road at any time. At this time of the day that is about all there is out there; me included. I won't poke buttons, but I refuse to let mine be poked. Hey, if I were normal, I wouldn't be going to work at a place like this every day. Frankly, you normal people could not handle this place. You must have some severe dysfunction to be able to tolerate the goings on in a prison.

DON'T FRONT THEM OFF

Once I got to the prison, I would observe officers getting newspapers from the paper box in front of the prison that we were not to take into the inner part of the prison where we performed our duties. This was a lax rule that wouldn't be enforced unless someone had a chip on their shoulder that day or if someone were blatant about it. If you put the paper down when higher ups came around, they generally didn't say anything. Our rules and the inmates' rules were the same. If you were doing something that you shouldn't do, but it was something that really didn't matter at the time and place you were doing it, it was OK if you just stopped doing it when someone came by that it was their job to tell you not to be doing it. In prison jargon, don't front them off.

FIRST SALLYPORT & VENTING

When we got inside we went through the first two electronic sliding gates, or the first sallyport, where the officer controlling the gates would verify that we were people authorized to enter the institution.

I always found the word sallyport strange and somewhat annoying. Once again it is the English language using Latin. It seems like we would've been better off just using Latin instead of this ridiculous English language someone made up just to be different and to make life more difficult.

It's kind of like all of these made up religions that pop up. They take a little bit from this religion and a little bit from these other religions and feel like they are special because they made up their own thing. No, you are just an idiot that plagiarizes. It would be different if you created something better, more accurate or more complete, but no, you just muddied the waters.

In this case, sally isn't a woman. A sally or sortie is a military maneuver made by a defending force. The easy part is that port refers to a door. So the name could've been Sortieport. I guess they both sound stupid.

There, I've vented. It has to be done once in awhile. I would allow inmates to vent on me once in a while. Some needed an outlet at times in order to stay sane. I realized it was too late for me, but at least I could help them out.

I passed by a cell on the second tier while on a security check one day. The inmate in that cell started going off on me, yelling at me. He was complaining about a multitude of things that he had jumbled up all together into one.

There were not a lot of inmates out of their cells at this time, but those who were, congregated on the flag down below to see and hear what was going on. They were surprised to see me taking this from anyone and for so long. The guy in the cell was ranting at me for a good 15 minutes when he finally started winding down. I asked him what all of that ranting was about. He told me that things had been piling up and actually had nothing to do with me. I told him, "That's your one." Meaning that was the one I was letting go with no consequences to him. I told him just not to try that with any other officer or he might find himself in segregation and going through a psych evaluation.

I wound up saying, "That's your one." often to other inmates in order to give guys a break. One time after I said that to a guy, he told me that was about the fifth time I had given him that line. I said, "Just don't go for a sixth."

Some inmates never got that break from me because they were too ignorant, stubborn or defiant to realize that I was just seeking compliance. They would push it to another level and force me to write a report.

Many of the things I enforced, I could care less about, but my bosses did. I'd flat out say, "Not on my watch." If other officers chose not to do their jobs the way that I perceived it to be, that was their choice. If it was policy, I'd enforce it first with a heads up verbal notification and later if not corrected I'd enforce it by writing a report. I needed a paycheck, so I enforced policies I did not agree with so I could keep my job.

How did we wind up here? Back to, after getting through the first sallyport.

SECOND SALLYPORT

From this next area you could access a meeting room, the visiting room, a couple of holding cells, and a locker room with lavatories. You could go downstairs to the employee lunch room by going through the locker room. The lunch room had food, beverage & snack machines, a couple of microwaves, a water cooler, a telephone and a television, in addition to plenty of seating. This area is where First and Third watch got briefed at the beginning of their watches.

There was a blind man that came in to restock the machines during most of my time there. One winter, when he was out in front of the building walking on the handicapped ramp, he slipped on some ice, smashed his head and never returned. He was a friendly guy that did a great job. He was missed by all of us.

Some days, after entering the second sallyport, there would be surprise searches on us officers. These searches were rare. Lieutenants would have to come in early to conduct these searches. They would look through whatever we brought in; have us empty our pockets; take off our shoes and pat us down. Of course, during the pat down, officers would be moaning with satisfaction, as that is our mentality. After that, they would ask the lieutenant if it was good for them too.

Not that I liked going through this, but I feel it should've been done more often and at times a few days in a row. The results would've been worthwhile. I looked at it as just being part of working in a place like this.

GEAR & MACE

We got our gear from our little square locker. This gear varied at times. When I first started, it consisted of a utility belt with a radio holder and a little pouch to put surgical gloves in. We had to use these gloves when shaking down cells, cleaning up bio hazards (generally blood) and other such things where we could get a disease. Most of us bought special leather gloves with a special lining to help prevent exposures when breaking up fights or other volatile situations where those thin surgical gloves would disintegrate.

In time, mace and a small mouth shield in a pouch for protecting ourselves if we had to give someone mouth to mouth were added. I did not like having these items added, but I kept them on my belt. I never used the mace, but I observed others using it effectively to end violent situations.

When we were first assigned the mace, anyone that used it got investigated. That helped deter me from using it.

Off and on, there were instances of abuse or horseplay with the mace. I was working the B-West bubble one day when an officer was in there with me fiddling with his mace. He accidentally set it off, or so he said it was an accident. He quickly ran out embarrassed and laughing. The bubble could never be left unattended. I was assigned to it and he got out first, so I was stuck in there dealing with it until it dissipated. I saw the humor in it, as did the other officer, even though it wasn't appreciated.

Another time, an officer and a sergeant were goofing around with mace back in segregation. They had been squirting it at each other in various situations. Finally, the officer decided to spray some on the sergeant's food. First off, we are not to be eating the food on trays that comes back to seg to be served to the inmates, but it always happens. Second, that tray wound up getting served to an inmate. They were both suspended and the sergeant was demoted.

Eventually, after most officers refused to carry the bulky cumbersome mouth shield, we were instructed to get rid of them.

MORNING BRIEFING & SOILED BRIEFS

We went into the visiting room for our briefing. We talked about what we had been dealing with, what was going on in the world and cracked jokes until the Watch Commander came in to brief us.

This was also the time and place that some of the more inappropriate officers would release some gas; and I'm not talking about the gas from their canister. I'm talking about the gas from their can. This would initiate oohs, evacuations from the area, laughter by some and anger by others.

When I really hated it was when someone knew they had some awfulness going on inside of them on a day I was working in the bubble. They would come into the bubble, drop it, try to have a contest to see if I or whoever else was in there could guess what they ate and then run out laughing with me stuck in there. Spray some mace instead. That wasn't as bad.

Maybe these things go on at other types of jobs, but I never ran into anything to this extent at any other job I ever had.

Anyway, the Watch Commander would brief us on what had been going on in the prison, the last 24 hours; inform us of policy changes, acknowledge officers for a job well done and chastise us when procedures weren't being followed.

THIRD SALLYPORT

When we were released to go to our posts, we had to go through another sallyport. Start to finish, there were a total of four doors that we had to pass through in order to get inside the institution. Doors 1, 2 and 4 were controlled electronically by officers in the bubble. The third door was controlled by an officer with a key.

From here on, anywhere else we had to go to, there was at least one more door to gain access through. Depending on where you had to go, there could be many more.

BLOCK OFFICER

There are many different parts of the institution to work: Security Center, Laundry, Canteen, Health Services, Education, Industry, Visiting, Kitchen...... I worked as an officer in a cell block most of the time.

Assignments were chosen within the block by those officers with the most seniority on down. These assignments varied somewhat from block to block, as they were all somewhat different. There was a desk officer, door post, shower post, kitchen coverage, rounds to be done, cell checks......

When we got to our block, we got our radios. Morning radio checks were conducted right away. Each radio was assigned a number. An officer in the Security Center would call each number. The officer with that radio would have to respond. This was to make sure the radio was working properly and that all officers were accounted for.

Two officers would go up on the tiers and conduct a security check.

Once this was complete without any problems and officers were at their posts, the inmates could be let out block by block to go for breakfast.

After breakfast, some inmates would go to work outside of their cell blocks, some would work in their cell blocks and others would return to their cell to be locked in.

After all of this movement, there would be what was called a lay in round. This was like a full count of the institution without all of the inmates in their cells. Everyone had to be where they were assigned. If someone was not accounted for, a quick search would be conducted. If there was a discrepancy, it was often some type of a paperwork error that was quickly and easily found. If there was still a problem, every inmate would have to return to their cell for an emergency count.

There are so many scheduling variations throughout the institution and different cell blocks that it would be real boring to read about all of them. I was never fully aware of some of the areas that I was never assigned to. Day by day and hour by hour the scheduling varied throughout the institution.

Inmates went on passes, to recreation, library, laundry, entering the institution, leaving the institution......

Officers had to maintain security, assist inmates, discipline inmates, cover their posts......

You probably noticed me typing in a lot of ...... Reading this book will fill in the wide variety of situations, scheduling...... that exist.

This will be more interesting and informative than trying to list every possibility, because as I stated, there really is no such thing as a typical day in this place.

IT'S A CRIME, INMATE MENTOR

It's a crime that my best mentor in this place was a serial killer.

This chapter is not just my experiences. It has a few of the teachings, thoughts and experiences of my Inmate Mentor. I cannot verify the accuracy of his statements; only that these are things that he told me. Are some of these stories made up by him? Have some thoughts become clouded by time? Is everything 100% accurate? If so does this clear up inaccuracies in his bio? Does this solve other crimes?

All I can say for sure is that his influence was a big factor in my approach to the job. He got me up to speed real quick on the knowledge of the job. I learned to keep my mouth shut about so many things that I learned from him, because when you say you learned how to do your job from a serial killer, it may not be taken well by some, especially the big shots.

I can say too that with better training and support in this job, turnover would go way down. There would be fewer mistakes that would need to be fixed. There would be more consistency on how to do the job. Staff would have fewer problems with each other because of better training and more well defined procedures. There would be fewer problems with inmates because with everyone doing everything the same way, they would know what they could and couldn't do; they would know that where the line was drawn is where the line would stay. All of this would make for a more efficient, smoother running system.

HOOCH TIP

Report: *While following up on the swampers, I saw two laundry bags by the washers and dryers. Our laundry swamper was finishing up for the day. I asked him about the two bags. He informed me that people frequently leave bags down there. I checked out the bags. One was light with clean clothes in it. The other was very heavy for it's' size. It contained a sheet on top and a pair of jeans on the bottom with a plastic bag inside of them. There was just under two gallons of orange based hooch with bread in it inside of the bag. I disposed of it.*

Someone had been leaving a laundry bag in Inmate Mentors area with hooch in it. This way it looked like laundry that needed to be washed. This way, if the hooch maker's cell was checked while he was gone to work, it wouldn't be found. Inmate Mentor didn't like the guy, wanted it out of his area, and didn't want to be accused of having it and who knows what other reasons, so he gave me the heads up on it. I took it, wrote up the report and was congratulated by the lieutenant. I let the lieutenant know that there are people that would be giving me the heads up once in a while, because I take care of things as discreetly as possible.

It was necessary to phrase the report like this for the safety of Inmate Mentor. I did not recruit information, but by these guys knowing they were safe in filling me in, I received more information than most. I always researched the information myself. I never went straight on any one man's' word; officer, inmate or big shot.

Guys that recruited information in exchange for giving these guys favors received all kinds of inaccurate or conjured up information in order for these guys to get more favors.

DECISION MAKING

My Inmate Mentor may have told me a lot of things, but I decided whether it was worth putting into my memory bank to use. Coming into this place at 47 years of age, my ideas and values were set. His information gave me another tool as to the who, what, where, when, why and how to apply my decisions. I've always looked at problems as the more information you have, the better decision you can make. You just have to hope that you are not missing a critical piece of information.

Did his teachings make me swing decisions in his favor? No. Every decision I made was based on several questions that I would ask myself. Is this right or wrong? Is it just? Is it policy? What is my job responsibility? What would I do if the warden was watching me? Knowing God is watching; what should I do?

It does however make it more difficult to not favor those who help you out. You do feel obligated to swing their way. When I had these feelings, I just had to ask myself those series of questions in order to make the proper decision.

WHO TO LISTEN TO

When we graduate out of the academy, we are assigned a mentor. The definition of mentor is a wise and trusted counselor or teacher, usually a more experienced person. My officer mentor was a good officer that people said was on the fast track to the top. They called him the Golden Boy. I figured I got lucky. Luck and I have never been buddies, so I should've known better. We had hardly got acquainted when I found out he was gone, finished here. What I heard was that he was working in segregation when one of the inmates squirted baby oil on the gallery. When he walked by, he slipped in it and hurt his back when he went down. He had a lot of pain and missed a lot of time. All of a sudden, he wasn't the Golden Boy anymore. When you get hurt here, you are no longer of any use. You are a nuisance, even if you were one of the most promising people to ever come along.

The turnover in the prison is so high that the officers get sick and tired of rookies coming in without enough training to function. The rookies have to ask a lot of questions to get by. Sure there are the ones that think they know it all and don't ask, but then it's an even bigger problem to fix their mistakes. It is difficult to get a straight answer out of most people, so you stop asking, get in trouble and get fired.

At times, someone would explain something to me that I already knew. I'd just let them fill me in because at least they were trying to help. Plus, who knows, maybe I'd find out a few more details, a better way to do something or that I was totally misinformed. Frequently we would get lied to just to screw with us.

There were officers that I watched and liked their style. If I had a question, I would search one of them out. This made it so that I actually had more mentors than just the one assigned to me. This made it easier to get a hold of someone when I needed information. Also, I felt more secure in getting a competent answer than if I actually had a mentor. After my mentor left, the person in charge of the mentoring program asked if I wanted another mentor; I told her no.

When I got to B-West, Inmate Mentor was there. When he got transferred to A-East, I wound up over there. You could say that I did most of my time right along with Inmate Mentor. He was a swamper in both cellblocks and I was the swamper boss in both cellblocks, so we had a lot of interaction with each other on a daily basis. He would come and talk with me a lot when I worked the door post.

Inmate Mentor wound up being my best mentor in this place. Better than any officer I ever worked with, and I worked with some good ones. I learned more from him than I did from going through the academy. Some of the things I learned were from him trying to pull stuff over on me. An example was the first time he thought he would use this rookie. He was listed as a clerk in B-West. I was working the door post which was by the lieutenant's office. He said he needed a few sheets of paper and that he always got it from the lieutenant's office. He asked if he could get some. I knew he was the clerk, so I let him. I was leery, but a few sheets of paper either way didn't seem like a big deal and I could verify it with someone later. He came out with a package of paper instead of just a few sheets. I let it go because this taught me a lot. I now knew his game. I quickly learned that anything he told me or anyone else told me for that matter, I had to verify with at least one other source. At least he taught me things and those things were invaluable to doing my job. His advice was also valuable. He would give me the inmate's perspective on different situations. He knew how the politics of this place worked. He was a master manipulator of this. If you got on his bad side, you were in trouble.

GENIUS

I was told that he had an IQ level that was in the genius range. He was proud of that. He was very knowledgeable about most everything. It was amazing at times the wide variety of detailed information that he had stored in his brain. Once in a while, I would research what he had said and it was always spot on.

We were talking about IQ's one day. He said he used to be 168. He figured that now he was about 120. I told him that I'd never been tested and didn't even know what the average was. He said average was 100 and that he thought I would fall in at about 115

STAYING HEALTHY

In his younger years he was said to be super strong. I was told by others and himself that he would do one arm pull ups endlessly on his cell bars. How long endlessly was, I have no idea; but for me, endlessly would be about a grand total of one effort.

Even at 80 years old, he was still a very powerful man. When troublemakers were placed in Inmate Mentors cellblock, he sort of took them under his wing and "talked to them." He still had the size, power and wisdom to make them listen.

Inmate Mentor informed me about a mild stroke that he had once. He told me that you have to be able to take care of yourself in here, because he couldn't get any health care until 13 days later.

This place can get to anyone at times. He stated to me on Christmas 2001 that he believed he would be dead by March. I retired in May of 2008 and he was still doing OK; just not as well as when I met him almost eight years earlier, but who would be?

One of Inmate Mentor's jobs in the prison was to distribute food to inmates that were locked in their cell for disciplinary reasons and those that were physically unable to go to the dining hall. Inmate Mentor was allowed to have his food delivered because the timing of him delivering food to others just made it more practical. As Inmate Mentor got older, slower and started using his cane more, he would've qualified anyway.

GETTING TO KNOW HIM

Much of what follows is what Inmate Mentor told me. It could be fact or fiction or somewhere in between. This was two guys passing the time of day. Some I could verify through public records and some may have been created to make interesting conversation. Only he will ever know for sure.

Records show that he first committed murder while in the military. He told me that this was actually his second murder.

He told me that the first murder he committed was not known to many. He said that his father had been raping his older sister. She needed help in stopping this incestuous behavior, so she enlisted his help, even though he was just a little kid. The only details he told me were that they blew him away with a shotgun when the father came for her with what would be the last time. He was put in the same prison as his sister so she could take care of him because he was so young. They were released and their record expunged before a year was up. It was ruled a justifiable homicide. This was in the mid 1930's when he was 8 years old.

Information I found on the internet stated that he was sent to live with his aunt and uncle in North Dakota over this time period. This could be the time when he was actually locked up with his sister.

Early in his life, he had a lot of problems fitting in. As time went on, he became larger and stronger. He had a lot of anger built up in him from the way his life had been so far. He used these traits to take control. Instead of getting beat up, he became the person beating up others. He said that when he throws a punch, he doesn't just try to hit the person, he punches through that person. He isn't trying to just win a fight; he wants to make sure the other person does not get up. He wants to hurt them as bad as he can.

In reform school he eventually became known as "The Duke." People knew not to screw with him or to challenge him. The ruthless reputation he built up became a coat of armor for him.

Records show that for seven years, from 1939 through 1946, Inmate Mentor was in reform school.

He told me about when he was in a boys home when he was a kid. The older boys would try to rape him. He fought them off, so he was constantly being beaten by them. His skin always had large spots of purple and yellow from the bruising. As he got older and grew, he was able to beat them up. Because of this, he was shipped out to be housed with a tougher group. When they tried to rape him, he resisted, so they busted him up so bad it took 8 months for him to recover.

At one point he was staying at a place where he was being molested daily by two older ladies. One would approach him in the morning and one in the evening. One was an old lady with gray hair tied back in a bun. Every day she would suck on him for an extremely long time. To this day, if he sees any gal with her graying hair tied back in a bun, it drives him nuts.

The other lady was younger, about 40 years old with red hair. She made him do her every day. She gave him a round suction kind of a thing and made him rub it up and down on his penis. It was supposedly a cock enlarger. He said that it didn't actually enlarge his penis, but that it caused the weaker areas of his penis to bulge out in those areas. The bulges made it look strange, but the irregularities made for greater pleasure for the women he was with.

He stated that later, when he was staying in an apartment or motel or some such place, and he got someone in the sack, they would tell other women how great it was. He would wind up satisfying most of the women in the building. He said that even with this, he would rather have his penis back to normal.

I didn't ask him why the two women were able to take advantage of him. I can only assume that his age and the need for a place to stay made for a situation not as repulsive as getting done by a group of guys. He would be quiet about it, so doing him was a safer situation for the women than involving any of the other boys.

We had a nurse in the prison whose hair like the older gal with the graying hair tied up in a bun. I had been told that when Inmate Mentor got upset, he would start to twitch and pull on his face. If this happens, you better be ready for trouble. This nurse came to the door when I was working the door post and Inmate Mentor was talking with me. She had to come in the block to deliver pills to guys that were locked in their cells. When he saw her, his demeanor changed instantly. He stopped talking. His eyes were fixed on this nurse. He started twitching and pulling on his face. It appeared as though he was ready to go off. I stepped up to the door and told the nurse to hold on a minute. This was enough time for Inmate Mentor to rein himself in a bit. He left and went to his cell. I let the nurse in and got an officer to escort her through the unit to the cells she had to deliver medications to. Inmate Mentor didn't get this way often, but whenever he did, I found that if I could divert his attention, he was able to regain enough composure to leave the area.

He said his mother signed off on his emancipation. This was important so he could get married to the mother of his child. It made it possible for him to be able to work in a piano bar playing guitar and piano where his wife was a singer. At times I would hear him playing his guitar in his cell. I played guitar myself, so I know how difficult some of the music he was playing was to play.

At one point in his life, he was making $800 per month and his wife was making $2400 managing 8 supermarkets. The boss tried shafting her by cutting her pay. Inmate Mentor showed up. He decked him, knocked his teeth out and kicked him a bit. The guy quit. Inmate Mentor's wife got a raise.

He told me that incest was normal for the farmers in the Dakotas. They needed to have a lot of kids to help work the farm and they wanted them for sex when their old lady didn't want to give it up anymore. As the girls got older and moved away, the fathers would move on to the next oldest daughter. He said the wives were glad for the break and that they were probably conditioned for abuse as they were probably raped by their father. He said this cycle of incest was normal in the Dakotas.

He said that he knew of a guy that would go to Burma, buy babies, have sex with them until they died and then go back and buy another one.

He told me about one day when he was burglarizing a house. He went to try on a coat. It was so big that the shoulders of it came down to his elbows. He is 6'2" and was 73 at the time of telling me about this. He still had enough size so that he didn't get hassled by anyone. He was in the house of a giant and figured he better get out of there. Just then, three large guys came in and caught him there. They were three Minnesota Vikings. They didn't turn him in. They made him kneel down and pray with them. He said, "Boy did I pray."

At one time Inmate Mentor was a contractor. He did primarily basements and was good at waterproofing. He used hydraulic cement that would expand. He discovered that by putting a plastic mixture in the cement that the cement became better than the way others made their cement. Because of his top quality product, he made a lot of money with his cement work. At one point he had built up $160,000 in the bank. He took on a girlfriend at this time. They spent $1000 a day on drugs and things. This went on for 160 days until the money ran out.

When explaining to me the difference between him and me, he told me that people like me walk along, see a fence and stop because we see something that is somebody else's on the other side of the fence.

He said that him and others like him walk along, see a fence and get angry because a fence is in their way of getting to whatever they want; that they are entitled to everything; that everything they want is theirs.

Grass Analogy: We don't see anything wrong with reaching for the grass on the other side of the fence. (The grass being things that are considered to be taboo by people who are considered to be normal.)

He once told me that I was the best officer he ever knew. He said, "There has never been any officer like you and there never will be again."

An officer filled me in on a time he was chatting with Inmate Mentor. He had read about a place where two bodies were dug up that were said to be two of Inmate

Mentors victims. The officer asked Inmate Mentor about this. Inmate Mentor said the people that dug them up were stupid, that if they would've dug down further, they would've found four more bodies.

We were talking about nutrition one day. He said that Goliath was actually only 6'4" and David was 5'4". Goliath lived in an area that had better food. He said that in the 1940's the average height of someone going into the army was 5'10" and that today it was 6'4".

Not in Stillwater, but some other prison or prisons he was in, he said the following:

If your pants are hanging down = you're a girl

Blue hanky in right rear pocket = you're a guy looking for a steady girl

Red hanky in left pocket = you're a girl looking for a guy

Blue in right & red in left = you're looking for anything

2 packs of cigarettes would get you head

3 packs would get you head with hot oil in their mouth

When I started, Inmate Mentor wore suspenders that he made. Later, he stopped wearing them. This was quite disappointing. The last thing you ever want to see is the butt crack of a 75 year old serial killer. Guess that's something that never crossed my mind as a vision I could one day experience.

Inmate Mentor saw a bible lying on the desk by the door while I was working the door post. He opened it up, closed it and threw it in the trash saying, "Well, they smoked all the front pages out of this one." This was typical of the way he would inform me of things. The pages in a bible worked great for rolling tobacco or pot in them. Tobacco was banned before I started and of course, pot had always been contraband.

He told me of a girlfriend of his named Irlene. They were having relationship problems and Inmate Mentor wanted to talk about their relationship. A scuffle ensued. She tried running away from him. She got outside. He threw a clump of dirt at her, but it just disintegrated when it hit her. There was a curved hook that was used for pulling corn out of a corn crib. He threw it at her. It entered her temple and curved into her head. She was still trying to get away, but this slowed her down enough so that he could catch her. He was trying to hold her down. There was a metal post in the ground that had a guide wire fastened to it. It just so happened that he was holding her head down over this guide wire post. It went through her head. Irlene was dead.

He wrapped her body up in a U-Haul moving quilt and put her in the trunk of his car. He got a couple of girls to drive while he slept in the back seat. He dumped her body in a pit around Milaca. It was on his conscience that he hadn't buried her. He went back to take care of this. He saw a guy hauling her body out of the pit, into the woods and onto the edge of a corn field. Just then another guy came walking out, so the first guy went running off. This guy started checking out the body, every orifice. Finding nothing in any orifice he wrapped her up in the quilt and took it with him.

Inmate Mentor spoke a little about being locked up in Alcatraz, Leavenworth and Walla Walla. He did not care for the Birdman of Alcatraz. He said the Birdman was nothing; that people jumped on the birdman hook and created him.

The Birdman, Robert Stroud, gained his reputation with birds while in Leavenworth. He was transferred from Leavenworth to Alcatraz where he was not allowed to have birds. He actually should've been labeled the Birdman of Leavenworth.

Inmate Mentor told me that he had written a manuscript on his life. He said that a trusted friend has it and will get it published either when Inmate Mentor says to or when he dies. This should be a very interesting book. It could answer a lot of questions about him at the same time as creating more mystery.

Inmate Mentor said he had a deal struck with the FBI to get only 10 years. He could name where he would do his time. If he said to build a pool in the prison they would do it, it was almost that good of a deal. His lawyer blabbed the deal to the local courts. The FBI was forced to back out of the deal due to public pressure. His lawyer blew the deal. Inmate Mentor received life plus 40 years.

A book was written about him. Inmate Mentor was real upset about it. He said it was full of lies. However, I knew of officers that would bring a copy of it in for him to sign. If he was on good terms with the officer, he would sign it. It wasn't permissible for officers to do this, but a few officers chanced it anyway.

I can't reveal much about the book as it would reveal his identity. Officers knew him more by the nickname the author labeled him with rather than his actual name. Most people in the prison knew enough to not let him hear them refer to him by that nickname. Word around was that he would go off on you if he heard it. He hated being referred to by that nickname.

Inmate Mentor said that people who read the book about him thought they knew him. He said they don't. He told me, "You do because you actually took the time to find out. Some who have heard about me or read the book come in and call me Inmate Mentor. I say, to them, it's Mr. Inmate Mentor".

He was a respected inmate and was allowed in areas that others were not. He had a sense of humor that I could relate to. One day I went into the office to get my coat and leave.

I asked him if he had to get in the office for anything before I locked it up.

He said, "It's too late now. Someone took their coat before I had a chance to go through the pockets."

We had our differences, but overall we had a good relationship. There will be more about Inmate Mentor in other chapters where situations caused him to conspire against me. This was his world and I was just a visitor, so I could understand his position.

PHONES

STILL ABLE TO VICTIMIZE

These guys were given the privilege of using telephones. The abuses of these phones were crazy.

In this instance a mother called about her daughter receiving a phone call from an inmate. The daughter was a victim of this inmate and had a restraining order against him.

Here she thinks this guy is behind bars and can't harass her anymore. Then he reaches out from behind these walls and is allowed to victimize her some more.

In this instance he probably was restricted from the phones for a while. But our overly lenient system would probably let him use phones again.

Guess what? I guarantee this guy would continue to harass this gal at any opportunity that came his way.

My opinion: You abuse any privilege in this manner, slam dunk, you never get it back.

NO PHONE LIST

Every cell block is issued a "NO PHONE LIST." This lists the offenders in that block that are not allowed to use the phones due to some infraction involving the phones. If we catch them on a phone, we write them up and their loss of phone time is extended. Typically, someone who abuses this privilege will abuse it again and again.

PHONE ALARMS

If any officer telephone is ever not set in place correctly or is off the hook, an alarm goes off. A call is made over the radio to the staff member or officer in that area; at the same time an A-Team officer is dispatched to that location. Even if someone in that area responds stating everything is OK, an A-Team officer has to visually check it out to make sure.

An inmate could be holding a shank and forcing someone to say everything was OK.

This is also the procedure if the alarm on a radio is set off.

PROTECT YOUR PIN NUMBER

An inmate reported to me that his PIN (**P**ersonal **I**dentification **N**umber) number to the phones had been stolen. He said that all of the money in his account was gone and that he suspected one of our swampers as being the thief.

This became way too common of a problem. Every inmate is assigned a PIN number to use to access their phone account. Dollars they earn or that are sent to them, that they can never see or touch, can be directed into this account by them to use for making phone calls. They must guard their PIN number so that no one else knows what it is. Anyone knowing that number can make phone calls and use the money in that account.

The smart ones will cover up the buttons when they punch in their number. Still others are dumb enough to let others use their PIN number. In this place, no one is to be trusted. It's like you see on the court television shows. If someone can't afford something themselves, don't you be the fool to get used.

GANG CONTROL

It is common in prison for gangs to try to control a phone or bank of phones. They will not let anyone other than one of their gang use those phones. Anyone else attempting to use those phones will be taken care of when they are not in view of an officer or camera.

If we are given the heads up on phones being controlled, we can keep an eye out for that happening. Inmates may inform us. Officers may identify the problem.

Also, investigations may give us the heads up. They record all phone calls and can listen to them at any time. A lot of restricted and criminal activity gets discovered this way. We were informed in May of '07 that the Vice Lords were attempting to take over phones in B-West by investigating officers listening to phone calls.

GOTTA STEAL SOMETHING

Phone books were available to us in every part of the institution. If an inmate wanted to sign one out, we were to let them and to make sure it was in good condition when it was returned. However, if someone tore a page out, it was almost impossible to know. Because of this, if we had to use these books, the information we sought may have disappeared.

CAREER CRIMINAL
IN TRAINING

Because hamburgers were being served for lunch, most of our unit went to lunch. This was a very popular meal. Many inmates were wandering around the dining hall talking to their friends. They were not in their assigned area. Most of them followed my directives to return to their table and be seated. Due to the large number of inmates in the area it made for an unstable situation.

One inmate that was not in his assigned area was talking with people at a different table. I directed him to go back to where he belonged. He did not do so. I took his ID, told him to go back to where he belonged and to switch in when he got back to the unit. He followed me to my post and wanted to talk. This guy was generally quite pleasant during our discussions, as we had already had many of them. He liked to keep talking rather than do as he was directed to do. This time I told him to walk away or I would have him escorted to segregation.

This guy was a chronic trouble maker. He was a young guy that seemed a bit naïve to the system when he came into the prison. He hooked up with a gang shortly after he got here. He changed from this talkative con man type into an angry defiant criminal that constantly created problems.

He was living on the top tier in my block. He was there because he had requested to live up there. Other officers and I had been writing him up frequently. Finally, one day after I had to write him up, I informed him that he needed to stop getting in trouble or I would move him down to a cell on the flag. He told me that I couldn't do that. I told him that the way he was going, he'd be going to the hole soon and I wasn't going to be hauling all of his property down from the top tier when he went. He said that I wasn't his dad and couldn't speak to him like that. I told him that I was glad I wasn't his dad, but that if I was, he never would've wound up in here. He walked away steaming.

It wasn't long before I had to write him up again. When he stepped out of the lieutenant's office after being reviewed for his violations and receiving some LOP, I told him to pack up his property and move to a cell on the flag that was ready for him. He started yelling at me and said I couldn't make him do that. I told him it was happening now. He flew back into the lieutenant's office to complain to him. The lieutenant backed me up and told him that if I told him to move, that is what he was going to do.

The inmate came back out and started ranting on me. Most inmates were out of the block at the time, so I let him get it off of his chest. After a few minutes, he still wasn't winding down, so I asked him if he was done yet and if that had made him feel any better. He responded negatively to both questions. I informed him that he was done with his ranting and to start moving. He wanted to rant some more. I reaffirmed that he was done and that if he didn't stop hollering and move immediately that he would be going to segregation immediately. He walked away grumbling and moved to his newly assigned cell.

Shortly after this, he wound up in segregation.

He eventually wound up in Oak Park Heights.

His time eventually expired, so they had to let him out.

He had good time hanging over his head. Any violation of terms of his release would get him tossed back in prison to do the rest of his time. He stopped reporting to the outside officer he was assigned to. Whether he was on the run or wasn't reporting for some other reason, I wasn't able to find out. I do know that they eventually caught up with him, because the last I knew he was on "Intensified Supervised Release."

This is a program that provides intensive supervision of inmates seven days a week, 365 days a year - including four face-to-face contacts weekly, electronic home monitoring, mandatory work or school, daily curfews, mandatory restitution and random drug testing. Specially trained corrections agents whose caseloads are 15 or less supervise inmates that have been released and are considered to be high-risk to the public.

Good Time - Offenders serve 2/3's of their sentence. If an offender is sentenced to 3 years, they only have to do 2 years. That other year is time they do not have to serve if they follow prison policy and do not get into any trouble. It is an incentive to do good time. That third is called good time. If they act up and get tossed in segregation, they lose good time and must stay in longer. If they act up a lot, they could lose all of their good time and do the entire 3 years. Any time they serve in segregation, makes them serve more of that 3 year sentence. If they lose 6 months of good time from being a jerk, they will be released in 2 years and 6 months. That means they will have 6 months of their 3 year sentence that they do not have to serve, UNLESS they have a parole violation. Then they return to finish the rest of the 3 years.

INFAMOUS –
CRAIG BJORK & EDWIN CURRY

When I started working in the prison, a law suit was heating up. Lawsuits are very common in this place. Many of these guys like to kill time by being jail house lawyers. I guess it's better for them to be killing time instead of people.

Some of these guys have legitimately been screwed over and work for justice.

Some have relatives that are after an easy buck. You can see how the mentality of someone in prison developed at times due to the people they were related to. How's that saying go, "The apple doesn't fall too far from the tree?"

Most of the following information was taken from court documents along with what I heard working in the prison.

EDWIN CURRY

Edwin Curry was 41 years old and serving time for rape when Craig Bjork murdered him inside Stillwater Prison.

Harold Lowell Curry, an heir of Edwin's, filed suit against Warden David Crist and other prison officials on September 28, 2000. He alleged that they violated Curry's Eighth Amendment rights by failing to protect him from the fatal assault. He said it was known that Bjork had committed multiple murders and shouldn't have been permitted around Curry. Well, duh! It's prison! This is where we collect people that commit felonies. If you don't want to be among felons, don't become one. Guess he figured he may as well try to get some cash out of this useless convicted rapist's murder. The lawsuit was denied as Warden Crist had immunity because he had followed procedures.

CRAIG BJORK

Craig Bjork murdered Edwin Curry in the Stillwater prison kitchen on Thanksgiving Day in 1997. He was transferred to a federal prison due to it being difficult to protect him in any Minnesota State prison where other inmates knew of him. This was also done to try to prevent further lawsuits.

Bjork tried to get his conviction of murdering Curry overturned on the grounds that the judge did not allow the introduction of evidence concerning the violent nature of the prison environment they were in and that the judge excluded evidence of assaults by inmates in the prison that did not involve Bjork and Curry.

Bjork didn't mention that he was serving consecutive sentences for three separate first-degree murder convictions plus a separate consecutive sentence for second-degree murder and was not eligible for supervised release on those convictions until 2056.

Craig Bjork was born on September 14, 1959. In 1982, he was living with a girlfriend. When she was gone to work, he brought a prostitute home, killed her and stuffed her under the bed. The girlfriend came home. She was going to go back to work, but he didn't want her to. He killed her and put her under the bed. His two boys came home from school. He killed them and put them under their beds. He then got a sandwich and played a Black Sabbath album.

He was sentenced to three consecutive life sentences for first degree murder and another consecutive 242-month sentence for second degree murder.

After he was sent to prison for doing these murders, his wife was found decaying in Iowa. Iowa did not prosecute him for this murder due to the expense and the fact that he was already doing time for the other four murders.

During the 1980s, Bjork was a difficult inmate, and other inmates harassed him for being a child killer.

In March of 1984 Bjork had threatened to kill a prison officer and commented, "What can they do, give me more time?"

He was eventually transferred to the Montana prison system, from which he tried to escape. He was returned to Minnesota in 1989 and spent five years in the Oak Park Heights Prison. Bjork received above average work evaluations and no disciplinary reports in 1991, 1992, and 1993 and was transferred to Stillwater in 1994. He received three or four disciplinary reports and segregation sentences in 1994 and 1995 for disorderly conduct, disobeying orders and substance abuse.

In May 1996, Bjork was sentenced to seventy-five days in segregation for threatening to throw hot water on two correction officers. On July 14, 1996, while in segregation, Bjork sent a kite to Warden Crist stating that "Stillwater is not a healthy environment for me." Bjork described himself as "homicidal" and depressed. He stated, "I'm very close to committing mass murder in Stillwater. Trust me; there'll be a minimum of 3 bodies. I'd go for 10 & come real close. So how do we handle this? (I'm for real) I'd like to work it out. But you can blow me off."

Warden Crist immediately referred the threatening kite to investigations. Case Manager Debra Nelson interviewed Bjork. She reported that he appeared capable of following through on his threat and requested a psychological evaluation. On July 30, Nelson issued a formal Notice of Violation for Threatening Others, which prevented Bjork's release from segregation. A staff psychologist interviewed Bjork on August 1. Bjork denied threatening anyone, said "he was merely trying to get people to take him seriously," but also "indicated that some officers might get hurt because of their attitude." A few days later, Bjork wrote Crist a lengthy kite explaining that his July 14 kite was "an emotional release and cry for help," not a threat; complaining that further segregation was unnecessary, that he had not been properly charged; and stated, "I really want to stay at Stillwater, so let me show you how I want to do my time quiet and easy." Warden Crist responded in writing that the "Threatening Others" charge was deserved but would be withdrawn because of undue delay in bringing it through the legal process.

Bjork was then released to the general prison population. In January 1997, Bjork was assigned to work in the prison kitchen with Curry. All kitchen workers are housed in D-Hall due to its close proximity to the kitchen.

In October 1997, at his request, Bjork was moved to a different tier in Cell Hall D. Soon after, he asked to move again, complaining that other inmates controlled the use of the telephone on his new tier.

On November 12, Bjork sent a letter to Crist complaining of the telephone situation. The complaint was investigated, and two inmates who were controlling the use of the phone were moved to another tier. Bjork's request to move again was denied because if everyone were allowed to keep moving whenever they wanted, it would never end and create security problems.

When Crist spoke to Bjork briefly on November 21, Crist did not perceive that Bjork was distressed or noticeably angry with prison staff or other inmates. Unit Director Tim Lanz spoke to Bjork about the telephone situation on November 26 and did not perceive that he was distressed or agitated or felt he was being treated unfairly. Lanz was "extremely shocked" when Bjork murdered Curry the next day with a pipe he had gained access to.

Smoking was banned in August of 1997. Bjork said that the stress of this and being upset over not having easy access to all of the phone time he wanted contributed to his actions.

THE KITCHEN MURDER

Bjork and Curry were workers in Stillwater's' kitchen. Bjork's duties usually involved cleaning garbage cans and

Curry's involved recycling. At approximately 10:00 a.m. on November 27, 1997, corrections officer John Sward found Bjork alone in the kitchen's basement recycling area using a hose to wash away what appeared to be large amounts of blood on the floor. Bjork was breathing hard. Sward noticed him soaked in blood and blood splattered all over the place including the walls.

Sward asked Bjork, "What is going on?"

Bjork replied, "It's these beet cans making a big mess."

Sward told Bjork that the mess did not appear to have been made by beet cans.

Bjork dropped the hose and said, "I got to get out of here," and left the area.

Sward let him leave and radioed the A-Team. Bjork was found in the dining hall, eating a candy bar and drinking a cup of milk."

Instead of pursuing Bjork, Sward had followed a set of drag marks on the floor, leading to an overturned garbage cart in a room referred to as the garbage room. Lifting the garbage cart, Sward found Curry with a plastic bag partially covering his face, lying in the fetal position, covered with blood and struggling to breathe. The area was secured and Curry was transported to Regions Hospital, where he died at approximately 1:10 p.m. that afternoon from being beaten with a pipe.

As Bjork was escorted to the prison security center, he made the following statements: "You are lucky a guard came when he did otherwise there would be three more bodies laying there." "I told those motherfuckers they should get me out of D Hall. None of this would have happened if they would have got me out of D Hall like I told them to." At the security center, Bjork said to one of the corrections officers that "it was nothing personal but a few minutes more and you would have had a dead guard on your hands also."

When the corrections officer replied that he might someday have to repeat Bjork's statement, Bjork replied,

"Well, that is okay, I'll see you in court, because I don't care."

Bjork was first interviewed by a corrections department investigator. When asked what happened in the basement, Bjork did not respond directly to the questions, but instead complained that he had been denied telephone privileges by the way other inmates managed telephone usage. Bjork also referred to killing a corrections officer, and said he wanted to do it on Thanksgiving because Christmas would have been too late.

That afternoon, Bjork was interviewed by investigators from the Washington County Sheriff's Office and the Department of Corrections. The interview was audio taped, transcribed, and played for the jury. In the interview, Bjork stated that he was angry with staff because, although he had asked to be moved to a different cell on a different tier over seven weeks earlier and had recently been told that he would be moved before Thanksgiving, they had failed to move him. Bjork said he knew when he went to bed the night before and when he awoke that morning that he would kill someone and that he had intended to kill a staff member. By doing so, that day, Bjork hoped to send a message to Stillwater's administration not to "play games" with people. According to the statement, he wanted "enough dead bodies to get media attention." He indicated that although he did not like Curry, the attack was not personal and Curry was just in the right place at the right time. He also indicated that after killing Curry, he had hoped to kill other inmates.

When Bjork was asked if he attacked Curry just because he was closest, Bjork responded, "There's a saying in the business world, location, location, location, huh, location is everything." While giving the statement to the Washington County Investigator, Bjork repeatedly asked about Curry's condition, stating that he did not care if Curry died. Before finding out that Curry had died, Bjork stated, "I wish the son of a bitch was dead."

When asked about the murder weapon, Bjork said that shortly before Thanksgiving, he had found and hidden a three-foot section of pipe in the kitchen's basement. He had also hidden a shorter section of pipe that he had planned to use to kill staff members. He referred to this shorter section of pipe as the "staff killer."

Bjork described killing Curry as follows. Earlier that morning, while in the kitchen, he observed the corrections officer on duty for a while, then went to the basement. While Curry was at the recycling sink removing can labels, Bjork retrieved the three-foot section of pipe from its hiding place, approached Curry from behind, and hit him in the back of the head as if swinging a baseball bat. Curry was temporarily knocked into the sink, but he stood back up. Bjork then hit him in the head at least another eight times before crushing his windpipe. He had to keep whacking him over and over again because Curry wouldn't die. When Bjork was convinced that Curry was dead, he dragged Curry's body into the garbage room and covered it with a garbage cart. He rinsed the pipe, washed himself off, changed into a clean shirt he had brought along, placed the shirt he had been wearing in a bag in the garbage, and began hosing down the floor, at which point Officer Sward arrived.

The Bureau of Criminal Apprehension was called to process the crime scene. BCA agents found a three-foot section of pipe, partially covered with blood, standing in one corner of the recycling area and a shorter section of pipe in a milk crate. A paper bag containing a bloody shirt was discovered in a garbage cart. The recycling sink and the surrounding area were heavily spattered with blood. Blood spatter analysis established five impact sites, the first was sixty inches high and directly in front of the sink, the others were further from the sink and lower to the ground. Shoe prints recovered from the floor matched the shoes Bjork was wearing when he was taken to the security center. Bjork's left shoe contained bloodstains consistent with being a mixture of Bjork and Curry's blood. The three-foot section of pipe and items of Bjork's clothing, including the shirt found in the garbage cart, were all stained with blood consistent with Curry's. A search of Bjork's cell produced a notebook, the first page of which was captioned "November" and contained an entry, written in red and underlined, for the 27th that read "Should have moved me, punks."

An autopsy revealed that Curry died from head and neck injuries caused by blunt trauma. Curry suffered fourteen major injuries to his head, including multiple skull fractures. Blunt trauma to Curry's neck caused a massive hemorrhage in the airway and fractured the thyroid cartilage, the superior horn, and the hyoid bone. Curry also suffered twenty less serious injuries to other parts of his body and face, at least six of which were consistent with defensive wounds.

At his trial, Bjork's testimony was significantly different from the statement he gave to the Washington County Sheriff's investigator.

Bjork testified that he had known Curry for a little more than one year, that they both held service jobs in the prison kitchen, and that for a period of time they lived in the same cell hall. Approximately two weeks before the murder, Curry started calling Bjork a "sissy boy" and a "punk," and saying that Bjork needed a "daddy." Bjork took those comments to mean that Curry was suggesting that he could not take care of himself and that Curry would protect him in exchange for sexual favors. The Thursday before Thanksgiving, Curry pressed the issue while he and Bjork were working in the basement. Eventually, Bjork told Curry he would not be Curry's "punk," and Curry knocked him unconscious. When he came to, he was alone and his pants were down, exposing his buttocks.

The following Monday, while Bjork was at his work station, Curry came up behind him, grabbed him by the hair, and threatened to cut his throat with a can lid if he moved. When Bjork said he would not move, Curry unsnapped Bjork's pants, inserted his finger into Bjork's rectum, and then rubbed his penis on Bjork's buttocks, causing Bjork to be terrified. The encounter ended when Curry simply walked away. Afterwards, according to Bjork, Curry continued to humiliate him by calling him "punk" and "bitch."

According to Bjork, he went to work on Thanksgiving morning hoping to finish his duties in the basement as quickly as possible. Before he could finish, however, Curry entered the basement and approached Bjork, saying that he was going to sexually assault Bjork that day. Bjork asked Curry to leave him alone, but instead Curry punched Bjork in the stomach three or four times and hit him once on the head. Feeling scared, Bjork retrieved a three-foot section of pipe he claimed that he had left in the basement in case he should someday need a weapon. When Curry lunged at him, Bjork swung the pipe without making contact. Curry then said to Bjork, "I'm going to fuck you and cut your fucking throat," ran to the recycling sink and started removing a can lid. While Curry was retrieving the can lid, Bjork came up behind Curry and hit him on the head, causing Curry to momentarily bend over the sink and then stand back up. Bjork next hit him on the shoulder to make Curry drop whatever he was holding. This blow caused Curry to fall. Afraid that Curry might get up and kill him, Bjork continued to hit Curry until Curry stopped trying to get up, at which point he panicked and dragged Curry's body to the washroom and hid it under a garbage cart. Bjork then cleaned up and changed into an extra shirt he claimed he kept in his work area because of the dirty nature of the work. As he began hosing down the blood on the floor, he was confronted by Officer Sward. In his testimony, Bjork admitted giving the statement to the Washington County Sheriff's Investigator, but claimed he had contrived the story he gave during the statement because telling the truth would have demonstrated weakness to the other inmates who would then have subjected him to further abuse.

At trial, Bjork sought to introduce evidence of the violent nature of the prison environment at Stillwater, as well as general evidence of prison assaults. His purpose in having this evidence admitted was to give the jury insight into the violent nature of prison life in order to assist the jury in understanding why his reaction to Curry's alleged assault on November 27, 1997 was genuine and reasonable. The trial court permitted the introduction of some general evidence about what happens to snitches in prison and about the dangers of prison life, but it limited the evidence regarding prison assaults to those involving Bjork and Curry.

This last story at his trial is a believable situation; however, it is not consistent with many things he stated earlier. It is more consistent with trying to create Curry as the predator rather than himself. The entry in his notebook pretty much negates Curry being the predator.

Bjork was serving a life sentence in an undisclosed location. However, in 2013, he wound up in The Oregon Department of Corrections in Salem. Guess what? They placed this murderer of 5 people in a cell with another felon. Guess what? You guessed it. Bjork allegedly murdered that guy; allegedly strangled him in August of 2013. That's allegedly 6 and counting.

As far as the sex angle on this story, a lifer once told me that they know they will never have sex with a woman again, unless they are able to get a female officer. He told me that they will take anything they can get because of that fact. That if they decide they want someone and get the opportunity, they will take it; damn the consequences. Non consensual sex or coerced sex in prison adds to the violence. Retaliation adds more violence.

An example of a victim that retaliated is Clyde Barrow of Bonnie and Clyde fame. Clyde was 20 years old in 1930 when he was locked up in Huntsville, TX, in Eastham Prison Farm for burglary and auto theft. This prison was identified as one of the most brutal prisons in America. Clyde was being raped by one of the inmates. He was eventually able to devise a plan and kill his abuser in the shower. The degradation he felt was said to have changed him drastically. His escalated violent nature was attributed to this. It was said that Clyde went from being a school boy to a rattlesnake. He vowed to never go back to prison or be taken alive, mission accomplished.

He vowed to get even with the place by freeing all of the prisoners and killing all of the guards. In January of 1934, Clyde executed his plan. He returned to that prison and was able to free 5 prisoners and kill 1 guard before having to make his exit.

Three Department of Correction employees are mentioned in the court documents that I got a lot of details from. I left their names in because they are in the public records. They are all people that I knew. They are all people that I held in highest regard. They are all the kind of people that should be allowed to run the prison system without interference from elected officials.

PAT SEARCH ROUTINE

You too can conduct professional pat downs at home. Playing correctional officer and inmate could be the start of an enjoyable evening with your partner. The policy lists the following steps to conduct a thorough pat down.

1. Put on protective gloves.
2. Inform offender-you will be conducting a pat search at this time.
3. Instruct offender to remove coat, gloves, hat and any items in his shirt and or pants pockets and place items on table or floor. Search removed clothing/items to ensure no contraband is hidden. Check coat collar, seams, pockets, and unroll and check all hemlines. Do not return items until after the search is complete.
4. Visually inspect offender for contraband looking for bulges or odd hanging clothing.
5. Tell offender to turn around, facing away from you with his legs shoulder width apart. Hands pointing out, arms perpendicular to the ground, elbows above shoulders. Offender should remain in this position until pat search is completed.
6. Begin pat search by inspecting the collar/neck area of the garment. Place thumbs inside collar and with a light pinching motion move fingers around the entire neck area of the garment.
7. Move hands out and over the shoulders and then move slowly down each arm using both hands, and then back underneath arms and into armpit area.
8. Move hands over the torso, beginning with the upper chest, being sure to check shirt pocket. Work down to the beltline in front, checking waistband. Inspect beltline by placing thumbs inside beltline and with a light, squeezing motion inspect the entire beltline from front to back (If offender is larger, you may need to do one side at a time)

9. Move hands over back from neck down to waistline being sure to check the small of the back.

10. Inspect one leg at a time. Start with one hand on buttocks, just below beltline and one hand in front just below beltline. Pat down above crotch and buttocks area both at the same time. Pat down each leg on all sides to the foot using both hands.

11. Upon completion of search, return items to offender.

Note: Be aware of anything unusual in shoes. At your discretion the offender may at any time be required to remove shoes or medical devices if possible. Offender shall not walk away until officer determines search is complete.

Tip: Position self in a safe position at all times. Courtesy and conversation can make these searches a means of good security as well as a chance for staff-offender communication.

This is according to the book. Anyone actually doing pat downs to this extent, would be the only one and would be written up for sexual harassment.

This would actually be a good way to start off a romantic evening with your significant other. I bet you never thought that reading this book would replace your Kama Sutra manual. Feel free to improvise, but remember, we are not issued Billy Clubs.

WHEN PRISON BUDDIES SQUABBLE

While I was working the B-West shower post on this June afternoon, an inmate came to chat with me. Guys coming to chat were especially appreciated while working such a boring post as the shower post. No matter what you are doing, you have to stay alert to what is happening around you.

While we were conversing, I noticed two inmates start to scuffle and push each other up against some cells roughly 100 feet away from me. They started exchanging punches.

I grabbed my radio and called for an A-Team response as I hopped up and started running toward them. By the time I got to them, the stockier inmate was on top of the more slender inmate punching him. I grabbed onto Stocky trying to pull him off as I directed him to break it up several times.

Screwmaster was an acting sergeant at this time. He came running and with all of his force flew into Stocky. Stocky was like a hamburger patty spurting out from between a bun, with Slender being the bottom of the bun and me being the top.

Stocky received a cut above his right eye when he slammed into one of six stools that were welded to a large table. Screwmaster put a choke hold on Stocky while I got Slender up and over by the cells. Slender was very shaky but responded to my directives.

The A-Team arrived, cuffed the guys up and escorted them to segregation.

When the A-Team got them back to seg, checked them over and took pictures of their wounds, they found that Stocky had bitten Slender on his left chest close to his shoulder.

Stocky had a broken wrist. Sometime later, when Stocky was back in B-West with a cast on, I asked him how his wrist got broken. He said that when he had Slender up against the cells, one of his punches missed and he hit the wall. That's when his wrist broke.

He was so angry that he kept punching Slender even with his wrist broken.

I asked him what the fight was about and if things were settled. He told me that they were very good friends, and that they just had a disagreement.

I guess that means you would want to avoid having a disagreement with these guys.

The guy that I had been talking to when the fight erupted came up to me afterwards. He said he was standing there talking to me and all of a sudden I was gone and he was talking to an empty chair. He hadn't been aware of anything going on and was surprised with how fast I disappeared.

We have a lot of slow boring times in this place. We get paid for staying ready and alert to be able to respond to any situation in an instant.

MORE PUZZLE PIECES

FIRST STOP

Other than being born in a hospital or where ever they popped out; other than the jail they were first taken to; other than the courtroom they were convicted in; other than the bus they were shipped into St. Cloud Correctional facility in; St. Cloud was their first stop. OK, most of them probably had a long line of other crimes, jails, courtrooms and the such leading up to this point, but this is their first stop in Minnesota's Correctional System; this time anyway.

Every state felon starts out at St. Cloud. This is where they get oriented into the system. This is where they get assessed to determine which prison they will be shipped to. Depending on their crime, incompatibilities, gang affiliations, cooperation, threat to society, risk of them attempting escape, space availability and many other considerations, this is where it is determined which state prison they will be shipped to. Some will stay at St. Cloud where the state's license plates are made. Their assessment may take a few months. If they act like an idiot here, they may wind up in a more restrictive facility than they would have otherwise.

When they get transported to their next prison, they get to wear that bright orange jump suit and have their hands and feet shackled. Of course, any time they get moved from one place to the next, they get the privilege of at least a pat down if not an unclothed body search.

TOUGH GUYS WILL COMPLY

Some of these guys try to play tough guy right from the start. They have not realized that only negative consequences come from that behavior.

25 inmates were being shipped out to Stillwater. One of them thought that he could continue living by the rules he established on the streets. He had not come to the

conclusion yet that there would now be a lot of people telling him what he could and could not do.

While these inmates were being body searched, an officer noticed one that had his shirt hanging out. He told him to tuck it in. The inmate became argumentative.

Later, they were all directed to keep quiet while the officers conducted ID verifications. It wouldn't be good to transport the wrong people. The big mouth refused to shut his yap.

"Ain't no one tellin' me to shut up! I'm a grown man! I'll talk whenever I want to talk!"

He was told several more times to be quiet.

"Man, ain't no one tellin' me nothin'!"

When they got him to Stillwater, he was searched by Stillwater officers and placed in restraints. He was being removed from the intake area to segregation when he spit at a sergeant. An officer took him to the ground. Several officers assisted in controlling him and putting a spit mask on him.

He yelled, "I'll spit on that mother fucker again!"

He wasn't able to do that very well from a quiet cell in segregation.

WISDOM FOR THE INCARCERATED

An inmate's words of wisdom on how he gets by in prison: I stay out of others business for 12 hours and mind my own business the other 12.

IDIOTS CAN BE FUNNY

CO 1 Idiot had just come down from the academy. He was a bit of a wise guy. No matter who you are, you need to put some time in before you start making wise cracks. After you've paid a few dues and made a few connections, you should've learned who will take your crap and who won't.

This idiot went into the watch commander's office. Upon not seeing anyone there, he sat down, put his feet up on the lieutenant's desk and kicked back.

Guess who the watch commander was that day, Psycho LT! He walks into his office and saw this idiot sitting there.

Psycho LT asked, "Who are you?"

The idiot said, "Bill Clinton. Who are you?"

For some reason unbeknownst to me, that guy was never seen around again.

THE TERMINATOR

B-West double bunking caused things to change drastically for me. Because I was not intimidated by these guys, I was able to continue doing my job. With so many angry men in one place, there was a lot of defiance in this block.

The inmates in this block were the trouble makers of the prison. I was the guy to stand up to because I was enforcing the policies. I was good at spotting abnormal activity. These factors caused me to write a lot of reports. This is where I truly became an author.

Because I saw so much going on and wrote it up, many of these guys went to segregation because of my documenting their activity. Some guys would get out of seg, come into the block, see me, refuse placement and go right back to seg.

I would catch some of them committing a violation as soon as they came in from segregation. My reports put them right back in seg the same day.

Some of these guys refused to leave seg because they knew they had to come to my block and they knew they couldn't get away with their games while I was there.

When I took academies on a tour of the prison, I would take them back to seg. After B-West was double bunked, segregation would erupt when I went back there. A large percentage of the inmates were back there because of reports that I had written. I would have to stay out of seg and have an officer assigned to seg give the academy students that part of the tour.

By 2002, the nickname "Terminator" had evolved. I would hear inmates talking to other inmates. They wouldn't say, "That's Basham." They would say, "That's the Terminator."

CHANGED

An inmate came back to my block that had been gone for a year and a half. He said, "You've changed from when you were first here."

I said, "I haven't changed. My job has changed. The number of guys trying to create havoc in this block has gone way up. Take a longer look and you will see what I'm talking about."

A few days later, he came to me and said that he understood now.

OUT, BACK AND OUT AGAIN

Officers Smiley and Moody were in B-West when I bid in. They bid out before double bunking hit, came back later in order to get better days off and found out it wasn't worth the grief, especially with the lieutenant and unit director that we had at this time. Smiley quickly bid out to B-East. Moody was upset about it because he bid back in to B-West because Smiley convinced him to come over so these two buddies could work together again. Moody bid out real soon after Smiley left.

CAPTAIN RESPECT

Our captain on second watch was gone for an extended period of time. He had to have some surgery done that would require extensive recuperating time.

Lieutenant Respect was chosen to be captain while the captain was out. This was a great choice. This guy did a great job.

He was lieutenant in B-West when B-West got double bunked. There was nobody else in this institution that was competent to handle the bizarre situations that double bunking created other than him. Without him in charge, I am convinced that there would have been a riot.

He treated officers and inmates fairly. If he said jump, I would say how high. Anything he told me to do, I would feel confident that it was the right thing.

He entered the cell block one day. I saw the captain hardware on his lapel. I said, "Captain Respect that looks real good on you."

He said, "I wouldn't have these if it weren't for you."

DON'T WISH ME A MERRY CHRISTMAS

An inmate was locked up for writing a kite to female Officer Cutter wishing her a Merry Christmas. This is not allowed. Plus, I think this inmate needed either a psych evaluation or eye glasses. What is it that makes some of these guys go after someone with such a repulsive personality and such a hideous appearance? There were plenty of female officers here that looked better and had better personalities; all of them. I guess he went for the one he felt that would appreciate his attention the most and not report him. This was the wrong choice in so many ways. She wrote him up immediately.

LEARN ENGLISH

An inmate came down for laundry exchange and was missing one of his towels. We have to charge them $3 for each towel they do not return. This policy went into effect, because of so many towels disappearing or being destroyed. This guy couldn't speak English, so his buddy stepped in to interpret. This communication and explanation took awhile.

Later in the day, the guy discovered that he had left the towel in the washing machine. He brought it to me, so I was able to tear up the charge slip.

TALK ABOUT BAD LUCK

There was a woman that a sergeant had been dating. They were both drunk when they were riding home on his motorcycle. They went off the road. He was killed. She flew clear and lived.

Sometime later, an officer was drinking in the same place she was. He decided to leave. She asked him for a ride home. He was reluctant, but eventually he gave in. She was on the back of his motorcycle when she passed out, fell off and was run over by a car. She was smooshed, causing her to expire. He received one year in the workhouse.

The same woman was involved in two motorcycle accidents; one sergeant dead, her dead and one officer in the slammer. Beware of bar flies wanting a ride, especially if you've been drinking and came on a motorcycle.

INMATE OBSERVATIONS

Smart inmates have very good observation skills, because they have the time. The more they are aware of and can accurately formulate their observations; the better their lives may be in prison.

An inmate, who had been locked up here for quite some time, decided to share an observation he had made about correction officers and their gender. Not an earth shattering observation, but an interesting one that I had never noticed.

He said that fewer female officers work on Easter and Christmas than do male officers. He concluded that family time meant more to the women, so they found people to switch days off with. He said that male officers liked to find a way out of going to family gatherings, so they would take those shifts.

He said fewer male officers worked on New Year's Eve and New Year's Day. His theory was that male officers were more inclined to switch for those days off so they could go out and get hammered. He mentioned that the college bowl games were another reason the guys wanted off.

His conclusions may not have been totally accurate, but they did have merit.

After this, when I worked those days, I did notice that there were fewer females working on Easter and Christmas and fewer males working New Year's Eve and New Year's Day.

I asked him about an observation that I made. In springtime, the block smelled like a sewer had backed up, but I couldn't find any problem. He told me that this always happens this time of year. He said there were a lot of farms on the other side of the river in Wisconsin. It was a nice spring day, so farmers were out fertilizing their fields. There was a wind blowing from the east, so we got that smell.

He told me that larger items get smuggled in under guy's bellies or on their thighs. He said that those areas are typically the areas the officers are most reluctant to be touching.

PEG LEG PETE

Peg Leg Pete was a one legged inmate. He was lazy and preferred to lie around all day doing nothing other than trying to create problems. He was a loud mouthed obnoxious pain in the rear.

He was assigned to work in G-Shop. This is where inmates refurbished computers for schools. He refused to go to work. He said he wanted to go to the hole instead.

The extent that he went to in order to avoid having to go to work was extreme. He wrote a snitch kite on himself. He tried to disguise the handwriting and left the name off of it. The kite said that he had a shank in his cell. An officer was told to check out this guy's cell. The inmate had made it easy to find. The officer started spazzing out as if he had made the greatest find in history. The inmate got his wish. He was taken to segregation and did not have to work. Mission accomplished.

WHERE'D THE MEMORIES GO

There are times, while writing this book that I discovered my notes were insufficient to write about something and not leave a lot of questions hanging; or not get it right. This is when I would have to delete what I had. I just thought that this would illustrate that if I couldn't get it right, it didn't go in the book.

GOING STRAIGHT

Inmate "Out To Nail My Ass," was a Vice Lord. He thought he was a bad ass. While in B-West he had been a real pain. He was constantly creating problems. I caught him violating policies many times. I don't know how many times my reports sent him to the hole. He tried to get rid of me by lying to my superiors. When I was in A-East, he got transferred to A-East. I thought, here we go again. Instead, when he saw me, he came up to me and apologized for his past behavior and lies. We shook hands and I never had to write him up again as he behaved as a model inmate.

ONE PISSED OFF INMATE

There was an inmate, Frustrated, that I had a very good rapport with. He went to segregation from A-East before I went over there. He was released to B-West after I left B-West.

When inmates get out of segregation, they can get back the property that they had in their cell when they got hauled out. Officers have to pack it up, label it and turn it in to laundry where it is stored. When he went down to get his property, his television was missing.

Fred called me from B-West to see if I knew what happened to it. I couldn't find any paperwork on it. I was able to find out who packed the cell. That officer told me he took everything down to laundry. Laundry was saying that they never received it.

One of two things could've happened to it. Either someone stole it when the officer packing the cell wasn't watching or the high odds were that it was misplaced in the area where everything was being stored.

Frustrated was getting no results. He was getting the run around. Everyone was passing the buck. He was frustrated and decided to take matters into his own hands.

There are metal rods fastened to the outside wall vertically and horizontally which make it possible to open the four levels of windows with a crank when you are standing on the flag. He climbed up these rods and stopped across from the third tier. He sat there, tied one end of a sheet around his neck and the other end around a metal rod.

He stated that either he gets his television and no discipline for what he was doing or he was going to hang himself.

The watch commander had someone pull a lift around the outside of the building. Her plan was to cut through the bars and window and pull him in. What? Where did this come from? The guy would either jump or move before anyone could get through.

This guy wasn't loony tunes; it was just his way of trying to get some action. All he wanted was his TV. He wanted something to keep his mind occupied while he was locked in his cell most of the day. Maybe he was missing his favorite soap opera.

If I would've been there, I could've prevented the whole thing, because he trusted me to take care of business.

Miss Arrogant was there. She had been a case worker when I started. She was a black woman on the rise despite the fact that she escalated more problems than she solved. I don't know of anyone who had anything good to say about her. She tried to talk Frustrated down, but he hated her with a passion.

He said, "Get that fuckin' bitch away from me. Why are you here? You were an asshole a year ago and you ain't changed."

A new lieutenant tried to talk him down.

He was eventually talked down by Officer Savvy. He was just one of us hack officers that weren't good for anything except to cover a post.

The reason I say that is that they gave the credit for getting Frustrated to come down to Miss Arrogant and the lieutenant.

If it weren't for Officer Savvy, the problem would've escalated. Officer Savvy was straight up. Frustrated could trust him.

The typical thing the institution does is to give credit for the things officers do to honchos.

When it was announced about Miss Arrogant saving the day, there was an uproar from officers. Officers had seen and heard what had gone down. To have a jerk such as this gal getting the credit when she created so many problems was unacceptable. Officers had seen what had gone on. Eventually it was announced that Savvy helped.

It was great that officers spoke up. The one being disrespected should not have to be the one to speak up. It is up to everyone else to speak up and set the record straight. Unfortunately, it is easier to say nothing. This is one of the few instances in my lifetime that I experienced people being so upset that they spoke up for someone else.

WHEN GEESE ATTACK

An inmate, that had a friend locked up in Lino Lakes Prison, shared an experience with me that the friend conveyed to him in a letter.

He said that there were a lot of geese that flew into the prison at Lino Lakes. Inmates liked seeing the geese so they would feed them. This caused more geese to fly in for the easy pickings. This became a huge problem. The geese were getting in the way, excreting their slime on the ground and getting violent at times. Everyone was told to stop feeding the geese.

An inmate had to transport meals from one building to another three times a day. The geese could smell the food inside the covered trays.

Hundreds of geese had accumulated one day when an inmate started pushing his cart of trays outside. The geese came for the food. The inmate tried to chase them off, but there were too many of them. The geese attacked the inmate that was pushing the cart full of food trays. The geese had him down on the ground pounding their beaks into him and biting him. Officers had to run out, get him and take him to Health Services. The officers were being attacked by the geese while they were rescuing the guy.

The geese got all of the food.

TRYING TO MAKE IT BETTER, DESPITE THE SYSTEM

Officer Screwmaster had transferred out to industry. There was an inmate that had been a model inmate for me. I don't know what happened for Screwmaster to be able to toss him in the hole, but that's what happened.

I had to pack up the inmate's cell. Because he never created any problems, he had a lot of canteen items in his cell; over 5 bins full of canteen. All of it gets tossed or else they have to pay to send it out. Actually inmates working in the area that the bins get sent to scavenge whatever they can before it gets tossed, so long as they are not caught.

Before I took all of his stuff down to be stored or tossed, I went back to seg to talk to him about it. He wanted me to let a friend of his hold the bins of canteen items for him instead of it getting dumped.

In order to cover my ass, I had him sign a piece of paper stating that was what he wanted done. He was very happy about me doing this and surprised that anyone would.

Modified lockdown is when so many officers call in sick, that there are not enough officers in the prison to maintain the institutions security guidelines. Predetermined blocks, on a rotation basis, are chosen to run with fewer officers. Inmates in those blocks are placed on Modified Lockdown status. They get out of their cells for chow and passes, but no flag time.

There was a time that we were placed on modified lockdown and I was OIC. I requested permission from the watch commander to let the inmates out of their cells from the time they got back from recreation until count. He said that as long as we had four officers in the block, it was alright with him. The inmates appreciated it and didn't create any problems.

Another time, when modified lockdown was announced, three inmates got in my face, but all of the others obeyed. With the cooperation of the officers in the block this day, I was able to allow the inmates some flag time from 1123 to1200. Later, a group was allowed to go play a softball game. When they got back they were filthy. They had beaten a team in B-East that hadn't been beat in two years. They came back hootin' & hollerin'. They asked if they could take a shower. This was not allowed according to modified lockdown policy. I knew I could allow this without any of these guys creating a problem. Someone needed to be at the shower post according to regular policy, so I covered the post. They were very appreciative.

WHAT COUNTRY AM I IN

We have a problem with too many officers that can't speak English. Communications in the prison is a big problem; from the poor speaker system, one person saying one thing and someone else saying another, to morons hiring people that cannot speak our country's language. Excellent communication in an environment like this is critical!

HORNY INMATE

An inmate was assaulted. He was afraid to identify his attacker. There was a video tape of the assault, but nobody could identify who the assailant was.

The assaulted inmate called his aunt who called the institution complaining. She called a lot of people in the government. I'm not sure if she got a hold of the governor, but if one of them wasn't him, one had to be awfully darn close. Orders were coming down from above to get this solved instantly.

I was working with two on the job trainees from the academy when discipline called and asked if I could come down and take a look at the tape. I took the trainees with, so they could see another side of what goes on here.

The tape was run back and forth a couple of times. You could see the predator go into the assaulted guys cell and come out shortly afterwards. The predator then went to a group and high fived them.

The camera was far away from him, but in one shot where the predators head was turned just right, I caught the identifying factor. He had a shaved head with unique tattoos on it. He actually had horns tattooed on his head.

The assaulted inmate's aunt called discipline again while we were viewing the video. Due to identifying the assailant and moving the assaulted inmate to a different cell block, the aunt settled down a bit; but just a little bit.

SO THAT'S HOW YOU DOIN' ME

There was an inmate that I had always gotten along well with. One day, I saw him violating a minor policy. As per my rule, if I see it, I say it. I mentioned it to him.

He blew up at me and said, "So that's how you doin' me?"

This was out of character for him, so I asked him what was up with him. It took a bit of talking, but he eventually said, "Someone told me that you're out to get me."

I asked him if he had ever seen me out to get anyone.

He stated that he hadn't.

I told him to consider the source, try to figure out why they would want to create a problem between us and then he would know I wasn't out to get him.

A few days later, he told me he figured it out and apologized.

I never asked him who it was or why they wanted to get something started. If he wanted me involved, he would tell me.

KICKING A SIGNIFICANT VIOLATION

One of my swampers had been smuggling food into the unit when returning with the floor scrubber. I had received a tip, but he would never try bringing it in when I was around, so I gave our blocks most experienced officer the heads up.

This officer was unable to catch him even when he smuggled in a large amount of onions, cheese and green peppers.

One day, the swamper in charge of the supply closet gave me the heads up. The smuggler had hidden the food in the closet. This swamper didn't want to get blamed for it. The smell of onions was so strong, it couldn't be missed. Even with the smell that strong, it still took me a while to find its exact location.

Sgt. Two Face was passing by, so I showed it to him and filled him in. He kicked the violation instead of nailing him.

Later I found out that the smuggler kept a large push broom in his cell and used it to pull items out of other inmate's cells; items like tennis shoes.

Because the sarge had kicked the smuggling charge, I gave the lieutenant the heads up in hopes that he would do something. He said he might look at tapes if he got a chance; fat chance on that one.

There are primarily two reasons that both of these guys would let these types of violations slide. Laziness, which was a slam dunk; and that the smuggler was probably a snitch for Sgt. Two Face.

CAN'T SAY WE DIDN'T TRY

Inmate Arrogant, and others, came out of segregation to B-West. I gave them the opportunity to find someone they wanted to live in the same cell with.

Arrogant informed me that he wanted a single cell. I informed him that I checked the computer and he had no restrictions, so being in a single cell was not an option for him. Arrogant looked around and came back later requesting me to find a cell for him. After placing him, he came back to me informing me that the man in that cell was gay and that he wouldn't live with him. He again requested a single. I again informed him that was not an option. I moved him to a different cell. He came back telling me that he couldn't get along with that man and that he wanted a single. I informed him that if he gave me a kite with his signature and the signature of a man wanting him as a cellmate that I would do that. Later he gave me a note with the requested information. I moved him. He came back when Officer Future LT was assisting in the bubble. Arrogant informed him that he could not live with that man because he knew his case and he wanted a single. Future LT checked with me. I let Future LT know that I already had put him in 3 different cells. Future LT told Arrogant that he was staying where he was. I could hear yelling and cursing from Arrogant. Future LT called for a 10:14 and had Arrogant removed from the unit. Future LT called the watch commander to fill him in. Arrogant went back to the hole.

SOME SENTENCES ARE NOT LONG ENOUGH

Every once in awhile, someone gets released and shortly after that you see them in the news for having committed another crime. This one guy, that was a rather smarmy character, was one of them.

This guy came to Stillwater in 2003 for third-degree criminal sexual conduct. He had knocked up a 15 year-old girl. The opportunity was presented to him when the mother let him stay in her home.

Here it was less than 3 years later and he was out and preying on young girls again.

He had met this one girl a few times close to the Dorothy Day Center in downtown St. Paul. When he ran into her at a McDonalds, he got her to come with him by telling her he had a friend that needed a babysitter. He drove her to a house in Frogtown, a ratty section of St. Paul.

When she got inside the house, the woman in there told her she had been brought there to "ho" for her.

The girl was pistol whipped to get her compliance. She was kept in a closet for weeks with little or no clothing and forced into prostitution.

She was continually ordered to sexually satisfy men that were brought into the house. If she did not cooperate, she was pistol whipped or beaten with a belt by the woman or the convict.

When not getting raped, she was forced to do housework and babysit the woman's kids.

She escaped once, but the woman caught up with her, aimed her gun at her and told her to get in her mini-van. She escaped two weeks later and reported to police.

The convict was captured and immediately sent back to prison for violating the terms of his release by having direct or indirect contact with a minor and for using intoxicants.

This guy only received 9 years for kidnapping, prostituting and assault; doesn't that sound lame to you? He's proven to be a repeat offender. Some of those 9 years were probably time riding on him from his previous sentence.

The woman holding her captive, prostituting her and beating her only received 9 years. That meant that she would only do 6 years if she did good time.

A second girl was found that they had done this to also.

Are these the kind of people we really want out committing crimes against others? Some sentences need to be much longer.

NOT YOUR CHOICE

A new inmate to Stillwater refused to go on his pass to orientation, so he was placed in segregation. I guess this guy chose a different method to get orientated to the prison; it's called trial and ERROR!

REBEL FILMWORKS

A company called Rebel Filmworks wanted to make a shoot a film inside of the prison. They were granted permission for November 7th and 8th of 2005, from 7am to 7pm. It was a special project made up 100% of people from Minnesota.

Background checks needed to be done on anyone entering the prison. Anything being brought in had to be checked. These things are routine procedures for anyone entering the prison.

They were escorted through the institution twice before shooting, so they could plan out their shots. Areas that they chose to film were the turnkey, yard, Cell Hall D (Doghouse), Atlantis (the chemical dependency unit) and the main corridor.

The plot of the film was that two inmates would cross paths in a prison. One would be entering the prison and the other would soon be released from prison.

The company would be donating $250.00 to the recreation fund. They would give the institution a copy so that it could be shown to the inmates and the staff.

I retired two and a half years later without hearing another word about it.

DENIED

When I requested to go inside and take pictures for these books, my request was denied by an Associate Warden.

Rebel Filmworks was granted access to film there.

A past warden of Oak Park Heights was granted permission to go inside that prison and take pictures for his book.

What's with that? There would be no security problem with the pictures that I wanted to take. They would've been great for readers to see the areas that I have written about. Maybe I can get a better contact later, so I can put some pictures in the upcoming books; but I won't hold my breath.

I wrote and tried to get permission to include some articles from the inmates' newspaper, "The Prison Mirror." I never received a response. That same Associate Warden that denied me access told me what to do. Maybe she intercepted that request. I can only speculate, but things just don't add up with this situation.

I NEED HERB

Just before I escaped my self-incarceration in Stillwater Prison, an update was released as to where inmates could buy herbs or tea. Six herb vendors were authorized that inmates could order from; two in Minnesota, and one each in Missouri, Massachusetts, Pennsylvania and South Dakota. These six were probably accepted by the DOC because they were probably willing to abide by security restrictions that weren't necessary to be followed when selling their products to normal buyers.

You're probably wondering why this was allowed. That was a big question that I had when I first found these items in a cell when shaking it down. I had never been told about this before I discovered it.

Native Americans had won the right in the courts on religious grounds. Witches, (Wiccans), were allowed these items under that ruling. Other groups had formed and more were forming. They claimed that they needed to have these items in order to practice their religion. These religions were formed so they could gain access to these items.

With the growing number of inmates feeling they deserved these items, even though they were never religious before entering the prison, would never be religious after leaving and really weren't religious in any way while being in prison, the DOC had to meet their demands.

Let's remember that these are felons. They are in prison to deprive them of privileges that law abiding citizens receive. However, some morons in the Supreme Court decided to make our justice system a joke and grant ridiculous privileges as this.

If I were tossed in the slammer, I could create my own "Basham Order of Idiotic Religious Ceremonies." I could state that I needed items not allowed in the prison but not illegal. I could say that I needed to heat up a concoction of lizard spit, bat dung and elephant testicle powder to pray over. I could create a song to sing while I rubbed it all over my body in order to drive all negativity from my soul. The DOC would have to find vendors for me to access these items and approve of the ones that would cooperate with their policies. They would have to build me a shack equipped to accommodate this ceremony, because the Native Americans are granted this right.

I think you get the drift. I could go on, but I'll get back to the details.

The policy allowed inmates to purchase sage, sweet grass, cedar, bitter root and bear root for use at religious ceremonies and as one of the five religious items allowed in their possession.

Because the number of different groups had grown and demanded other items, the DOC was adding chamomile, lemon balm, peppermint, mugwort and jasmine.

Ooh, but there were some guidelines. Inmates could buy up to two ounces of a single herb once a month and have up to two ounces each of five different herbs in their possession. They could only buy from the approved vendors; however Canteen would have new varieties of teas to choose from.

With all of these restrictions, who would ever want to wind up in a Minnesota prison? I know they would certainly deter me from committing a crime. Isn't sarcasm wonderful?

GATE MONEY

"Gate Money" is the money that an inmate saves up that he gets back when he is released and walks through the gates to the outside world. This is money that he can use to try to get by on until he gets a job; money that is to be used to get by on so he doesn't have to commit a crime and wind up having those gates slam behind him again.

When I started, the amount they had to try to save was $100. Sometime in 2006, someone in the Department of Corrections realized that $100 in this world equated to next to nothing. The policy was changed to increase the amount gradually. On January 1, 2007, the minimum amount of gate money an inmate had to save up went to $200. January 1, 2008 it went to $300, 2009 was $400 and 2010 was $500.

How do they accumulate this money? The state deducts money from what they earn working jobs in the prison and place it in this account until it reaches the required amount. The inmate accumulates interest on this money.

If an inmate has not accumulated the required amount by the time they are to be discharged or paroled, the state gives them whatever amount is necessary to get them to the required amount. If the inmate has $300 in their gate money account in 2010, the state adds $200. The purpose is to try to make it so they do not return.

Sadly, $500 in this day and age will only get them a purchase from a drug dealer, so they can return to prison.

Lifers are not required to have gate money accounts, as they will never need it.

INDIGNANT INDIGENTS

What's that? An indigent inmate is an inmate that is not assigned to a job and has less than $1.00 in their spending account, less than $1.00 in their voluntary savings account and $500.00 or less in the gate savings account for at least one pay period.

These people are allowed to receive free basics like toothpaste, soap, toothbrush, etc. These items would be like a sample you would get outside of these walls. They would be like travel size items of this sort that you could buy at Target or Wal-Mart.

Indigent inmates would also get postage paid envelopes. This is where the mail room supervisor was alert and found an envelope scam going on. It doesn't sound like that big of a deal, but once you get some of the details and multiply the waste by all of the institutions, you will be thanking her, because that is our tax dollars.

An inmate had a large indigent envelope that he had filled with eight magazines that he was sending to a pen pal in Africa. The postage on this was fifty dollars. The mail room supervisor refused to send it and had it returned to the inmate.

The inmate complained that she was violating an indigent policy by, "not providing him with his community ties". She stood up to him as eight magazines sent to Africa was hardly a violation of this policy. We tax payers being responsible for something like that is ridiculous, especially when most of us could not afford to do that ourselves. Of course the bozos in the courts would probably have us pay for this guy to visit his pen pal.

After this, she started monitoring the large envelopes. Once she eliminated paying for the ridiculous, the cost to us taxpayers went down from fifty dollars per day to four to five dollars per day.

She then started monitoring the small envelopes. The indigent inmates would trade their envelopes for other items, favors or to be left alone. Others would just have them taken from them.

On a day where she checked out 80 envelopes, roughly half of them were from inmates that were not indigent, so she returned them. She estimated that by watching for abuse of these envelopes, fifteen to twenty thousand dollars would be saved at Stillwater alone.

35W BRIDGE COLLAPSE

At 6:05pm on Wednesday August 1, 2007, the 35W Bridge that goes over the Mississippi River collapsed. It made the national news. 13 people were killed, 145 were injured and many more were freaked out.

This area became an attraction that many people were trying to get close to. Personnel providing security were needed to keep people away for their safety and so that emergency personnel could perform their duties. This would be necessary until the bridge was removed from the river, as it was a unique situation that people would never see again. It was like the Haley's Comet of Minneapolis.

If the Minneapolis Police Department and State Patrol were unable to cover the security of this area themselves, we would be contacted to see if we had any volunteers.

The institution accumulated a list of officers that were interested in volunteering. They would be paid overtime for working the bridge detail.

The first day, three officers worked the collapse site. This was on an overnight shift. They did not get back to the prison for their shift until 10am. Their prison shift was to start at 6am. This created a problem. Officers working in the prison on first watch had to stay over onto second watch to cover for these guys and receive overtime pay. This situation made it so officers were only permitted to volunteer on their days off.

Request for officers would be on short notice. The shifts would be primarily on overnights and weekends. Especially corrections officers with families would be jumping at the opportunity to get a few extra dollars.

I never volunteered for this duty. The extra money would've been nice, but going to work in the prison as refreshed as possible was imperative to me. I had to be ready for conflicts with inmates and staff. Also, I was never at peak health until a few months after I retired.

The major from the State Patrol reported that some staff members from the Department of Corrections and other state agencies were reporting to the collapse site and attempting to use their state identification to be able to enter the secured perimeter. They were denied.

Dudes and dudettes, if you wanted to get up close, you should've volunteered. If you didn't want to do that or couldn't, you could've seen it on television, the internet and in newspapers. It was a lot quicker, easier and you could've seen a lot more.

GOOD HIDING PLACE

An officer was inventorying an inmate's cell, because the inmate had been taken to the hole. The officer removed a piece of tape from the wall. He found a razor blade behind the tape.

STUCK FOR YOU

The Stillwater Lift Bridge spanning the St. Croix River between Minnesota and Wisconsin would get stuck in the up position every once in a while. This bridge is how the staff that lived in Wisconsin would be able to get across the river to get to work. This is an old historic bridge that was opened in 1931.

When it got stuck, staff would have to drive south to Hudson, Wisconsin and get across the river on the Interstate 94 Bridge. This would add 18 miles and 40 minutes to their drive time. The bridge getting stuck was one of the few reasons anyone would not get written up for being late.

However, the bridge would get closed down when the river rose so high that it was unsafe to cross the bridge or that the water level went over the bridge. This was more predictable and would not be an excuse for being late.

People hassled over building a new bridge for four decades, from the time one was proposed until one would be open. One is scheduled to open in fall of 2016. It is just south of the Stillwater Lift Bridge and is high enough to eliminate problems with the river rising, baring anything Noah had to contend with, with his ark.

INFAMOUS –
LARRY DONNELL HILL

An officer that I had a brief acquaintance with had been escorting a blind inmate, Larry Hill, to get a glass eye replaced when he and the other officer he was with had a surprise attack mounted upon them. This officer was large and strong. He took plenty of good natured ribbing for being overcome by a blind man. This incident was put forth to us in the academy as, if this could happen to someone the size and strength of this officer; this could happen to any of us. This officer left the job shortly after I started.

Larry Hill was convicted of second-degree murder and given 27 years for strangling his girlfriend in 1982. He had a long history of violent crime. He had been convicted of two rapes, robbery, criminal sexual conduct, burglary and illegal possession of a handgun.

Hill was blind. Two officers took him to a medical office outside of the prison to get a glass eye replaced.

He had met Willie Johnson in prison while Willie was doing 5 years for aggravated assault.

Willie had a handgun and met Hill at the doctors' office wearing a Halloween mask. Willie tied up the officers and the doctor.

Willie and Larry went to the townhome of a woman in Apple Valley.

She had corresponded with Hill in prison. She supposedly stopped communicating with him 18 months before this when she found out that he had strangled his last girlfriend.

Why do some women "Look For Love In All The Wrong Places?"

Police tracked Hill and Johnson to the woman's home where a two day standoff began. Eventually there were over 100 officers surrounding the townhome.

Larry and Willie held the woman, her 6 year old daughter and 8 year old son hostage.

During the standoff, the woman was tied up and sexually assaulted by these two scum bags.

The woman left the house to start a car for the men to attempt to escape. This was the second day. The police seized her. She was taken to a hospital for treatment for exhaustion.

It was arranged for drinks to be delivered to the door. One of the children came to get the drinks. At this time, officers threw in two stun grenades. The grenades create loud blasts meant to disorient those nearby momentarily.

The police entered. Hill grabbed the little girl and held a knife to her throat. The police shot him.

Willie Johnson surrendered. Willie Johnson, 47, was convicted of 13 counts and sent back to prison.

GOOD, BAD, UGLY ME

FIRST INCIDENT REPORT

Head Banger was the first report of any kind that I ever had to write.

I was working in B-East standing by the center stairway when it was announced to the block that the door was open for anyone signed up and wanting to go to the Pipe and Drum Ceremony to leave now. Most everyone that was going was out of the block had left. The door would soon be locked.

An exuberant young native was rushing down the stairway to try to catch up. Instead of just running down the stairs, he jumped off a top stair. He was watching where he was going to land rather than the I-Beam above the bottom stair. He smashed his head on the beam and fell to the floor. The impact made a very loud clunk. I asked him if he was OK and he said he was.

He got up and started walking toward the door. He then noticed blood starting to come from his head and came back to me. I instructed him to sit down and got some toilet paper that was handy to cover his wound.

Toilet paper was handy because when I started working at the prison, it was common to see rolls of toilet paper scattered around the cell blocks. They were used instead of boxes of Kleenex.

While he held the toilet paper on his head, I moistened some paper towels with cold water. He put these over his wound. When the bleeding stopped, he said he was OK and wanted to go to the Pipe and Drum Ceremony. I told him it was too late for that and that I needed to escort him to Health Services. I informed the nurse of how hard he hit his head.

Once he was taken care of, I had to lock him in his cell on ICR. He thought he was being punished and couldn't understand why. I had to explain to him that it wasn't for discipline. It was for his safety. First off, the lieutenant had to check into what happened and make sure it was just an accident. Health Services needed him locked in so he wouldn't be wandering around and pass out from a concussion.

He was young and had a lot of energy, so he didn't like it but realized he had to accept it. I told him to relax and take it easy. I told him that for his own good he was being forced to take it easy and that the institution had procedures that had to be followed to make sure he was alright.

AN UNSAVORY EDUCATION

Within about a week of starting to do my time in Stillwater Prison, I learned that I was going to get a constant unsavory education. I learned that my path in this place would be a solitary one.

I was working back in segregation. There was a young black kid locked up back there that was very friendly and smiled a lot. He spoke and acted in a childlike manner.

Politically correct ways of referring to him would be slow or mentally impaired.

More than likely he had been referred to as "Retard" as often as anyone ever used his name. However much humiliation and abuse he had gone through in life, he still was not an angry kid. His mental capacity was so low; he didn't seem to have those emotions. He could probably not comprehend them.

With a mental capacity this low, people were able to get him to do most anything. Reasoning and right and wrong were not a concept he could relate to. It was easy to manipulate and use him, which is probably how he wound up in prison.

One day, after he was released back into population, I saw him in the dining hall and noticed that his eyes were all bloody. When I asked him what happened, it took awhile, but eventually I was able to piece together that he was taking a shower and got soap in his eyes. Later, I found out that there is lye in the soap that is handed out to the prisoners.

I asked him what he had done to take care of his eyes. He wasn't able to communicate what if anything he had done.

I asked him if he had flushed his eyes out with water. He didn't have the mental capacity to even think about this.

I asked him if he had seen a doctor. He said that he had not. I found out that an inmate had sent notification to Health Services for him. He had received no response from Health Services even after a couple of days had passed.

When I asked him if his eyes still hurt, he said that they hurt a lot.

I notified the officer in charge. He told me he would make sure the kid was taken care of.

The next day, I had to escort an inmate through a cellblock to get him to Health Services. I noticed the kid with the bloody eyes in one of the cells and asked him if he had been helped. He told me he had not. The officer that said he would take care of it just said he would in order to get me to move on and did nothing.

While at the doctor's office, I tried to get this kid some help. Knowing that his request for help had been ignored, I had to feign ignorance in order to try to get this kid some help. I asked the nurse if this kid had been seen. She said that she had no idea.

The doctor showed up. I asked him about it. He said he was told about it but thought they had been joking. I told him it was no joke.

The doctor had to go back to segregation, so I escorted the doctor to the kid with the bloody eyes. He took a look at the kid and told me to get him to Health Services right away.

This was not my cellblock. I was not allowed to do this. An officer assigned to this block needed to use his keys to get this kid out of his cell and escort him to Health Services.

The doctor and I went to the OIC (Officer In Charge) and made the request. He told the doctor to tell someone on the next shift, because he was leaving soon.

This kid's eyes are bloody and he's worried that he might wind up being here a couple of minutes longer. I had to believe that now the doctor knew this was no joke; and that by his reaction when he saw the kid; that he would tend to business.

The next day I stopped by the block to ask if this kid had been taken care of. The OIC said he had no idea, refused to allow me to check on him and would not do it himself. He then ordered me out of his block.

On my way out of the block, an officer that I believed was straight up and gave a damn about things noticed my frustration and asked me how things were going. I filled him in.

He told me I had done the most that I could and that I would have to leave it at that. He said there was no way I could change the system or the people in it. He said that if I did anything else, I would be stepping on the toes of people that would make it tough for me here.

I ran into the kid about a week later and found out that he had received the help that he needed.

If I had not been so new to the job at this time and knew how this place worked, I would've went straight to the Watch Commander, informed him and not left until this guy had been properly taken care of. It is one of my regrets that I didn't do this anyway. This is one of my experiences that evolved my style into being that officer that pissed off lazy good for nothing officers.

I learned a lot from this situation.

I learned that I wasn't able to overlook these kinds of problems.

I learned that people here are afraid to offend someone that is not doing their job.

I learned that there are a lot of people here that are too lazy or unwilling to do their jobs; many just don't care.

I learned that I could never trust getting the truth from anyone in this place.

I learned that 24 hour health care sounds a lot better than it is.

I learned that I would have to play stupid many times about policy and procedures in order to get problems like this solved without appearing to be that bull in the china shop that I was. People here can accept stupidity and ignorance better than someone that is aggressively doing their job.

I learned that there are people here that are incapable of helping themselves.

I learned that things like going into another cellblock to make sure a problem was taken care of, was something I would be doing a lot.

I learned that I would be stepping on the toes of a lot of people and they would be making my life extremely difficult.

I learned that because of this, the old boy network would try to drive me out or get me fired.

I learned that every day was going to be a battle.

I learned that dealing with distasteful situations like this would be the norm and not the exception.

I learned that even some good officers don't have the balls to do what is right and necessary at times; and that they would have to disassociate themselves from me in order to not incur the wrath of the corrupt in this place.

I learned that if I was going to maintain the standards and values I had set for myself over the years, more often than not, I would have to stand alone.

I presented this story as a speech at one of my Toastmaster clubs. I received a note from someone. It read, "I am "SO" glad that was not a true story!"

This is the reality of the prison system folks.

A COMPLIMENT? IN THIS PLACE?

After being on the job three months, the segregation lieutenant came to speak to me. I thought, "Oh. Oh. What did I do wrong?" He complemented me on the job I was doing. He said he appreciated the attitude that I had and wished that he had more around with that attitude. I couldn't even detect any alcohol on his breath.

REVIEWED

We were supposed to get reviewed every two months during our first six month stretch in the prison. I received it at the end of my 7th week. My rating was fully satisfactory. Not just satisfactory, but fully satisfactory. It was a generic type of a review. This is the type of a review that is done because they have to give you one. They don't want to put any time into it, so they just mark everything right down the middle. If not a real evaluation, why give them? Nobody even checked to see what I had been up to. Generally you talk with people during a review. Nothing was said except, "You can read this if you want and then sign here."

The lieutenant could have put in the review that I have never been late, never missed, never been less than 15 minutes early, have always been ready for the day and have always been cooperative on changes.

It could be in there that I assisted a fellow academy member by changing shifts with her when nobody else would.

By talking to inmates I found out things that helped to deflate situations.

Maybe they could've put in there that I found out that the inmates have discovered a new easier and faster way of making hooch.

Finding out that an officer in St Cloud had been teaching PPCT, Pressure Point Control Tactics, to inmates would've been a worthwhile item to put in my review.

I compiled a list of job responsibilities in the segregation bubble as there was so much to do in there and no one person knew what all had to be done. This left everyone doing different things and never a complete job getting done. I typed it up and laminated it so it could be posted in the bubble as a checklist. The sergeant thought it was great and asked me to make copies that he could put in the post order book. Do you think that was something that should've been acknowledged?

On just my second day in the bubble, they raved about how well I did. They liked it when I got assigned to the segregation unit. If things got hectic in the bubble they called for me to help get things caught up and in order. Maybe that is something that would be deserving of better than a fully satisfactory rating.

All of us new officers put up with the demeaning attitude of officers that make like we have a problem when it is their poor communication skills that cause them to be unable to explain what they want done. Then they try to pawn problems off as it being the fault of a new person.

I have the knowledge that I have gained from being a resource volunteer at Lino Lakes Prison.

I gave the speech at the graduation of our academy.

I applied to be an academy trainer.

There was a trend that I identified of assaults happening right after pipe & drum ceremonies.

It had not been necessary for me to have written any one up. This was not due to not finding anything, but it was due to researching the full situation, acting and explaining accordingly. I didn't try to demean the inmates; instead I treated them with respect. I found that I didn't have to pull a power trip on these guys to get their cooperation.

These are the types of things that could have been put in my review. I found out that this was primarily the type of review that most people always get unless you suck up to the boss. I found out that this is primarily the type of review I would continue to get. I did have a couple of lieutenants that put a little more effort into it, but even with the best lieutenant that I ever had, reviews were not a high priority.

Some suck ups said they got better reviews, but nobody ever showed me one.

FIRST DISCIPLINARY INCIDENT REPORT I WROTE; THE DEVIL MADE ME DO IT

My plan was to never have to write a disciplinary report. I had the farfetched idea that no matter what, I could reason with these guys and get compliance. This goes to show how naïve I was. The following report is the first disciplinary report that I had to write. I gave the guy every opportunity to follow procedures, but he just seemed to want me to write him up. The rest of the inmates in the institution should know that this is the guy that opened the flood of reports that flowed from my fingers over the years. From this point on, this guy was always giving me that inmate stare. I'm sure it didn't help, but whenever I saw him playing that attempted intimidation game with me, I just couldn't keep from laughing.

THE HISTORIC FIRST

Incident: Formal Discipline
12-29-00 0730 B-West Door Officer Basham
Flood Gate OID#XXXXXX B-West Cell 530

While checking inmate ID's, as they were leaving the block to go to the dining hall for breakfast at the above date and time, I, Officer Basham, could see no ID on Flood Gate. I pointed to my chest and ID and stated, "ID?" He looked away. I stated, "Sir, I need to see your ID." He mumbled something as he past me, making no effort to show me his ID. I gave him a direct order to stop. He ignored me. I again ordered him to, "Stop now." He then stopped, put his hands on his coat and told me he had it. I gave him a direct order to come back into the block. He stood there looking at me. I stated, "Get back in here now." He came back in, at which time he opened up his coat, so that I could see his ID clipped to his T-shirt in the upper right corner of his stomach. I informed him that it had to be visible in his chest area and clearly showed him on myself the entire acceptable area. He proceeded to try to argue with me that this area of his stomach was his chest. I took his ID and gave him a direct order to go back to his cell.

Flood Gate is being charged with #16 Disobeying Direct Orders and #32 Disorderly Conduct.

HE HAD MY BACK

An officer that I enjoyed working with wrote the next report. He had been aware of what was going on at the door with Flood Gate and me. The combination of the two reports really sealed the deal on these guys.

Some guys didn't like this officer, but I found him to always be pleasant, a hard worker and alert and savvy to what was going on. He was also one of the few officers in this place that helped new officers like me learn how things worked in this place. Good officers seem to ruffle the feathers of the bad officers in this place.

He transferred out of B-West and out of Stillwater a few months after this. He transferred to the Moose Lake Facility. His leaving opened up the position that I took that got me off of First Watch. When I bid into B-West, I didn't know I was taking his place. One of the reasons I bid into B-West was that I thought I would be working with him.

Incident: Formal Discipline
12-29-00 0735 B-West Flag Officer Good
Other Staff: Officer Basham
Flood Gate (XXXXXX), Inciter (XXXXXX)
B-West Cells 530 and 516

While walking down the B-West Flag toward the shower post, I overheard a loud conversation between Flood Gate and Inciter. Apparently, Flood Gate did not display his ID properly while on

*his way out of the unit for breakfast, and then refused to stop when
ordered. (See report by Officer Basham).*

*Flood Gate stayed out on the flag and complained to Inciter. A
page was then made over the unit PA for Flood Gate to switch in.
Not only did Flood Gate still not switch in as ordered, he began to
disrupt the unit by stating in a loud voice to Inciter, "That fuckin'
dude just havin' a power struggle, trying to use some power he ain't
got!"*

*Then Inciter replied, "That dude's an asshole! What a fuckin'
hillbilly! He can't do that shit! He can't tell you to switch in just
because you didn't have your ID on your chest! You know what
I'm saying?!"*

*All of these statements were made in a loud and disruptive
manner.*

*Flood Gate and Inciter are in violation of rules:
30 (Abuse / Harassment) and 32 (Disorderly Conduct)
[Flood Gate only: 16 (Disobeying a direct order)]*

Officer Good turned in the reports to the Captain. The
captain put them on ICR (Investigative Cell Restriction).
This is where they are locked in their cells until there is an
investigation and determination of guilt and punishment.

This was too lean for their offences. The discipline unit
was surprised that they hadn't been sent to segregation. The
sergeant in B-West called the Captain and diplomatically
got him to admit he blew the call.

The captain sent in four members of the A-Team to haul
them off to segregation. Flood Gate was giving them his
attitude, flapping his jaw and moving in slow motion. Two
members of the A-Team each grabbed an arm and hauled
him to the hole.

For every two days he spends in segregation, an
additional day will be added to his sentence.

Inmates and officers were glad that we got these guys
out of their unit. Inmate Mentor, an old lifer for mass

murder who is well respected, asked if there were any way we could keep them from ever coming back to the unit.

The Lieutenant came up and commended us on the job we did. Basically we were very thorough, professional, allowed Flood Gate to dig a big hole for himself and through good teamwork sewed up a tight easy case to eliminate these guys from being a nuisance to all but those in segregation, for a while anyway.

LABELED A SNITCH

I was working the dining hall. The other officers that were supposed to be posted up on my side of the dining hall were not there. One that did report to the dining hall was up front chatting with other officers and not paying any attention to what was going on. If he had been standing where he was supposed to be, officer presence alone would've chilled things out a bit. The inmates seeing only one officer doing his job decided that they could get away with a lot.

When I worked the dining hall, I enforced the policies consistently. When someone had a violation, I'd ask them for their ID. I would put it in my pocket so I could use the information off of it to call the inmate's cellblock and have them locked in their cell when they returned. The information was also necessary for the accuracy of my reports.

Before I left the dining hall that day, I had 12 inmate ID's in my pockets from three different cell blocks. My pockets were bulging from all of the ID's. Lunch ran long. I had a dozen inmates to lock up and write reports on and I was supposed to be back in the block to take the door post.

I called the door post and told the officer there that I would be late. I tried to come up with a way to not punk this guy out any longer than necessary.

My sergeant radioed me. I called him on the phone from D-Hall. He was upset that I wasn't back yet. After I explained the situation, he told me to get back as soon as possible.

The inmates were from three different cell blocks. I figured that if I stopped at the different cell blocks, explained the policies to these guys and got their word that they would comply with these policies, at least when I was working, it would be quicker than writing reports.

Nine of them accepted my terms and gave me no attitude, so I gave those nine their ID's back, took them off lock up and told them no report would be written on them. These guys were appreciative of how I handled the situation.

I was glad that at least 9 of these guys had the sense to lie to me. The fact was however that I never had another run in with any of those 9 ever again. I was impressed with that.

Now, I only had to write reports on the three that were uncooperative and gave me attitude. Three was better than 12 any way.

To me the job wasn't about discipline, it was about getting compliance.

As usual other problems ensued. A fight broke out when I was by A-East. I had to help break it up and cuff up a guy.

My lieutenant, Psycho LT, was covering for the B-East lieutenant while that lieutenant was on vacation. Psycho LT had stepped out of B-East to see what was going on. When he saw me, he directed me to come into the B-East lieutenant's office because he wanted to speak to me; or more accurately bitch me out about some Mickey Mouse crap. This guy was always on my case for something. While I was in the office with him, my sergeant radioed to me again. I called him on the phone. He was steaming. I told him what was going on. He told me to report to him as soon as I got back to the block.

He was in the bubble when I entered the cell block. The door officer that I was to have relieved by now was pissed off and told me I was in trouble with the sergeant.

The sergeant started to chew me out. I hollered back. He settled down enough for me to explain. I reinforced how often I had told him that I was alone on my side of the dining hall. He backed off from me a bit. He asked me who was supposed to be down there with me. I told him that I did not know, even though I did. I didn't want to front anyone off.

Life in this place was tough enough without fronting off another officer. My sergeant was determined to solve this problem and make sure that officer was dealt with. He called A-West, spoke to that sergeant and found out that Officer Slacker was supposed to be assisting me in the dining hall.

My sergeant went to talk to the Watch Commander about it while I wrote up reports. Then the Watch Commander and my sergeant spoke to the Captain. This was actually bad for me, because the next day before starting work, this instance was brought up during our briefing. I was identified and Slacker was identified. Everyone was put on notice that they had better be doing their job down there or they would be disciplined. That made me real popular. Hope you caught the sarcasm of that statement. The harassment I had to put up with after that made me wish that I had identified that lazy jerk.

Officer Slacker started the rumor that I wrote him up. When I went to the break room, everyone got up and left. Officers would not speak to me.

The officers in my block saw what was going on and tried to get the truth out. Officer Slacker was part of the "Old Boy Network," so their efforts didn't yield much result. Most officers were afraid to buck those guys.

I spoke to Officer Slacker and told him I never mentioned his name; that I tried to keep his name out of it. My sergeant is an excellent sergeant and did what he was supposed to do though.

Officer Slacker kept spreading the rumor and embellishing it.

My lieutenant told me to notify him if I got harassed. I didn't tell him a thing, as that would've made matters even worse.

That lazy jerk continued to badmouth me to everyone he worked with the entire time I was there. Even after he transferred out to industry, he bad mouthed me to the old timers out there that didn't even know me. Every once in a while I would have to work with an industry officer. When they heard my name, they would say, "I've heard about you." Sometimes it was about good things and sometimes it was about me being a snitch. I would hear comments like, "Oh, so you're Basham." and "Officer Slacker told me about you." Sometimes they wouldn't say anything; they would just stare. Yep, I sure wish I would've identified that asshole.

Officer Slacker started other rumors about me. One that was so far beyond the scope of reality was that he told people that Lt. Solid and I were watching videos of officers smoking in the parking lot. This was something that would never happen, yet many officers bought it. That shows the low intelligence of some of the people they hired in this place.

STEVEN SEGAL

An inmate informed me that they looked at me as a Steven Segal type of character. I guess that's not a bad way to be perceived. It's better to be looked upon that way than like Barney Fife.

ASSAULT AVERTED

There was a time when the discipline lieutenant got a tip that an inmate was going to be assaulted. This lieutenant was intelligent, hard working and knew a lot of how this place worked. He knew about me and the protection order. He came to me and asked if I would be able to stop the assault. I told him that I didn't know, but that I would check into it. He said it had to be quick, because it would go down soon. The inmate that was to be beaten was currently in his cell, but would be coming out soon.

I approached my contact. We started our non-committal phrasing dance. I asked if he knew of this guy with a hit put out on him.

He asked, "Why?"

I said, "A lieutenant came to me and wanted to know if I could get it stopped."

He asked, "Do you want it stopped?"

I said, "It would be best if it didn't happen."

"Do you want it stopped?"

"I would never ask for any favor."

"I know that, but do you want it stopped?"

"Yes, I would like it if it were stopped."

"OK. It won't happen. Have the guy stay in his cell for at least a couple of hours, because it will take time for word to spread."

"Alright, I appreciate that."

I contacted the lieutenant and informed him that the man would be safe if he didn't come out for a couple of hours. He thanked me.

I had to go to the guy's cell and explain that he should voluntarily stay in his cell for a couple of hours and the longer the better to play it safe, but by supper time he would be safe.

The man never had a hand laid on him. He was verbally harassed, but he knew he wouldn't be beaten.

I never knew why the hit was put on; I just followed the lieutenant's request. The lieutenant never asked my source or anything other than to just try to stop the assault. This place would run a lot smoother with mutual respect and trust like this.

Toward the end of my time, this inmate gang leader wound up in my block. I went to him and told him that I was sure he had heard a lot of negative things about me since he left B-West. He verified that was a fact. I wanted to assure him that I hadn't changed. He said he knew that too. He said he always considered the source and that plenty of people filled him in on the positive things too.

This was one of those conflicting mind control things I had to deal with. This was an inmate that I had more respect for than most anyone else in this place. It had become increasingly more difficult to treat this guy the same as everyone else.

PUPPET FOR PROMOTION

Our lieutenant was the same way as this unit director, only he wasn't so nice about it. He would call us into his office for a meeting. It was more of a bitch session for him. When it came time for us to be able to make a comment or ask a question, it had better be something he liked or wanted to address or he would come down on us. He would become loud, stern, demanding and talk over us before we even made our point. I learned to not even speak up in order to have these sessions end. Another guy would just compliment him on what a great job he was doing. He would do this with sarcasm and humor and it would generally end the meeting.

This lieutenant was actually a decent guy. The problem was he was smart enough to know how to play the game. He wanted to rise up the so called ladder. He knew you could do this only by being a puppet to the people above if you were a white male. Talking with him before he came to my block, I was thinking this guy would be a good fit. Do what had to be done. Back up officers that did their job.

I believe he knew the right thing to do, but he wouldn't make that choice. If he had at least stated his piece once in a while rather than just saying yes sir to the higher ups all of the time, I could have respected that. That is probably what he didn't like about me. He probably had some choice words to describe me.

The unit director came into the block at about the same time as the new lieutenant. The unit director bought into every manipulative inmate that wrote a kite complaining when we did our job. The higher ups didn't like kites complaining about officers. More often than not, they viewed that officer as harassing the inmate. It was easier to come down on the officer than to get the inmate to follow institution policies.

JUST FOLLOWING POLICY

Let me say that I found many of these rules to be counterproductive. Inmates would tell you that I enjoyed enforcing these rules. They felt that I reveled in catching inmates violating policy. That I was bucking for a promotion. Nothing could be further from the truth. I was only there to do my job and that involved enforcing lots of policies that I didn't agree with. Kind of like the lieutenant being a puppet to the higher ups, it probably appeared that I was the same way.

One of my problems was that I always told the truth. I had no problem telling anyone how I felt about policies that I didn't believe in.

Also, as far as me bucking for a promotion, it wasn't going to happen. Sure I would've taken promotions if I was going to be there for a long time, but I started when I was too old.

Sergeant is a seniority position and there is no way I would have a shot at it before I retired. Even if an opportunity arose before I'd retire, I'd be exiled to work different watches. I liked the 6am to 2pm shift. There would be no reason to change my life for a few months in order to be a sergeant.

This lieutenant had tried to help me out with the politics of the place, but that isn't who I am. There were a couple of times that I was called into his office and asked about a situation. He would say, "Did you do that. Say no." I always admitted 100% to anything I did. If I said or did something, there was a reason for it. If someone didn't agree with how I handled a situation, it didn't matter. I had to make decisions on what information I had and how I evaluated the situation. I would take into account what was just and what I felt my job responsibility dictated. If my bosses saw things differently, they had the right to coach me on how they saw things, how they wanted it handled the next time or they could fire me if they thought I was that far out of line.

I didn't get fired, even though there were people there that wished they had something on me in order to get rid of me.

These people were upset with me doing my job thoroughly. They didn't want to put out the effort to do their job thoroughly. They wanted me to be like them. Some felt that my job ethics and standards made them look bad. By doing my job, it created more work for some of them. It was easier to ignore violations than to confront people on them and do paper work on them.

Some higher ups flat out told me to ignore certain policies. I told them that if they wanted me to not enforce a policy, that's what I would do. But I told them that I needed it in writing. This was to cover my ass in case anyone above them tried to discipline me for it. Not a single one of them would put it on paper. I learned in this place that if it isn't documented, it doesn't exist.

ENOUGH IS ENOUGH

There was a lazy swamper in charge of the supply closet. He closed it down before he was supposed to. We had a lot of inmates in this block that wanted to clean their cells. They needed ample opportunity to accomplish that. Inmates were coming to me complaining that they couldn't get cleaning supplies. I told them that I would find out what was going on and that they would be able to get supplies to clean their cells. I checked with the swamper whose job that was. He said he was done for the day. I told him to open it back up and informed him that I would now notify him when it would be alright to lock it up.

FIRE EYES

Both the lieutenant and unit director were in the unit and a lot of inmates were out.

One of my lazy swampers was trying to get by without doing his job again. This guy was always complaining. I told him he was going to do the job properly or he wasn't going to have it. He said he was going to complain to the lieutenant. I told him to complain all he wanted to whoever he wanted; the fact was if he wanted to keep the job, he would have to do the job.

He turned to the lieutenant and started complaining. The lieutenant was buying into his BS.

I wanted the lieutenant to wise up and realize this guy was playing him. I told the inmate that I was through taking his crap.

The lieutenant told me to go away. Later he told me that I was not appropriate and that fire was shooting out of my eyes. He said he thought I was going to kill the guy. I smiled and said that was good. What I was trying to portray came through. I needed the lieutenant to know what this guy was pulling and that he should be backing me.

Later, the lieutenant had the sergeant speak to me about it. The sarge was laughing while telling me the directives that he had been given to convey to me as this was totally ridiculous.

BEING BLIND SIDED

The next day, the lieutenant came to me and said to come with him. I asked where we were going. He wouldn't respond. A lieutenant coming to a cell block to escort an officer somewhere is not a good sign. They generally call and tell you to report somewhere.

He was making like he was my buddy. He was doing some small talk. This was quite strange. We were not buddies. I was only a pawn in his game to getting a promotion. He didn't give a damn about me or anything I had to say. Especially after yesterday, I knew something was up.

He escorted me to the unit director's office. This was a really bad sign as I had never even been to any unit director's office before. His motive was becoming very clear. The lieutenant and I sat in chairs in front of the desk. The lieutenant sat with his back to the wall and played bad cop. My back was to the door. The unit director was sitting behind his desk. He played not quite as bad of a cop. There was no good cop routine going on in this room. The double team attack was on. I was not allowed to speak.

When you have a unit director and a lieutenant verbally attacking an officer and not letting the officer explain his position, you know that troubles a brewing.

The following pages will explain how this unit director and lieutenant blindsided me.

ORGANIZED INMATES, A BAD THING

They told me they were getting a lot of complaints about me from the inmates. That would be a good thing if these honchos would ever stop by and actually see how I did my job. The inmates that wanted to get away with things wanted me out of the block. This letter writing campaign was their attempt to get me fired, transferred, stop me from doing my job or any change that would allow them to get away with whatever they wanted to. All that the honchos had to do was to look at the discipline records of those who were writing the letters. This would slap any intelligent person in the face with what these guys were trying to pull off. Unfortunately this unit director decided it was easier to let the inmates run the asylum in this instance and the lieutenant was following his lead. The lieutenant was bringing up the subjects and speaking harshly. The unit director was talking about them, emphasizing the points, smiling and joking off and on. It was quite strange.

SKILLED OMISSION

They had a kite from an inmate accusing me of locking him up without any reason. This was an inmate lying about me. They believed the inmate and already had me convicted.

What had happened was that this inmate wanted to move to a different cell. I informed him that moves were done for the day and to put in a kite requesting the move and it would be considered the next day. He didn't like this answer. He wanted it to happen on his terms. I informed him that wasn't the way it worked. He became irate and started yelling trying to incite the inmates around him to help raise a little hell. I told him to switch in or I'd have him hauled out. Another officer escorted him to his cell as he still wanted to get others involved. This was B-West during double bunking. We never really had enough officers to handle everything that went on in this block with them putting the worst trouble makers in that block. I was super busy, so if I could get out of the bubble and talk with the guy, I might be able save some time by not having to lock him up and write a report. An officer that I respected came in the bubble. He asked if I would like it if he went to speak to the guy so I could continue what I was doing. I would've liked to handle it myself, but time was against me and he was a good officer, so I agreed. He spoke to the guy and let him off the hook. I figured this was a done deal until I got blind sided with it in this meeting.

I've never regretted writing a report; only not writing a report. I should've locked up this scum bag instead of giving him a break.

After explaining what had gone on, the lieutenant said, "How can I believe you over them?"

Did this fool actually verbalize that statement?

I said, "Ask me; I don't lie."

My question to them would be, "How can you believe them over me?"

Of course, I didn't say that, but I sure wish I would've. I also wish I would've said that I don't lie like the two of them do.

THEY'RE AFRAID, THEY'RE VERY AFRAID

One of the most bizarre comments I ever heard was in this meeting. My block was the block that anyone coming out of segregation would have to come to at this time. They would be unemployed. If they got a job, they would get transferred to the block that housed people that worked in the type of job that they had been accepted for.

The lieutenant told me that people were refusing to come out of segregation because they were afraid of Basham. He said this with a straight face. I started to laugh. It was impossible not to. They saw nothing funny. They were actually buying this load of crap.

I told them that it was because I actually do my job and the inmates know it. The inmates know that I will catch them at violating policies that they refuse to follow.

I was flattered by the comment, but I knew where it was coming from. For murderers and gang bangers to be afraid of me would be a good thing. I am not a weak man, but as I have had to accept with age, there are a lot of people in this prison that could hurt me. Especially if I were ganged up on, I would be in trouble. I'm five foot ten, had been varying mostly between 220 and 240 pounds and was in my 50's. There are many inmates here that are lot larger and fitter than me that had plenty of time to work out on all of the weight lifting equipment in this prison. The reality is that anyone believing that people would refuse to come out of segregation because they were afraid of me would have to be mentally deranged. It was, to me, a good thing to hear anyway.

The lieutenant said that when I got mad, fire would shoot out of my eyes. He said he had seen it and he wouldn't want to be on the other end when I got mad. He brought up yesterday's incident as an example.

If he had ever learned anything about me, he would see that I had a background in standup comedy, improvisation and acting. Obviously I'm a much better actor than I thought if I could make that strong of an impression. My friends know me as someone who doesn't show much emotion. Most inmates know this too. I used acting in my job frequently in order to get compliance with a situation. It made the job much easier. The part of acting that this lieutenant saw was something I've heard called "The Art of Intimidation." This works especially well if you can't be intimidated yourself. The only thing anyone here has to fear from me is me catching them in some sort of violation and writing a report on it.

RESTRAIN THYSELF

Needless to say, I was quite frustrated with these honchos being ignorant enough to believe this line of malarkey. I'm thinking that they have me in this office conjuring up this crap in order to fire me.

They wanted me to back off on doing my job. I told them to put it in writing and I would. Of course, they weren't willing to do that. Now I was angry. I felt cornered. Feeling the frustration of dealing with idiocy like this took everything I had to restrain myself.

When I was younger and more physically powerful than I was at this time, I found I could easily hurt people if I released my frustrations. I didn't want to end up living in a prison, so I had to learn to contain it. I was now a professional at not showing my feelings in any way. What people saw was what I wanted them to see.

At the end of this attack, they told me that there would be no report written on this meeting. Obviously that was more for their benefit than mine.

I thought, "Write me up you assholes. I did nothing wrong. I'd like the chance to front you morons off. If anyone should be written up, it should be you two idiots."

It's got to do with integrity. Who has it and who doesn't. A convict that has done nothing except create problems and lie about it or an officer that works his tail off and will have any superior officer he has worked for verify his integrity, even one that doesn't like him.

Even after what I had experienced with these guys, it was still hard to believe that they were that stupid.

TIME TO LEAVE

I had been thinking about bidding out of this block to get away from these two numbskulls before this, now it was a top priority to find a different home.

At this point in time, I had been in the B-West block much longer than anyone. When most officers had bid out of the block when it got double bunked, I stayed. Officers would bid into B-West for better days off and hours than they could get anywhere else in the prison. This was possible because people with higher seniority would not bid into the B-West hell hole. When anyone bid into the block, they left soon after they found out what it was like in there. I had seen many officers come and go.

I went into the lieutenant's office shortly after the surprise meeting and told him I was going to be bidding out. He looked surprised, said he didn't want me to go, but he knew I had been in this block a long time.

What's this? You complain about the way I do my job. You haul me into the unit director's office and chastise me. You take trouble maker inmate's words over mine. You show me no respect and you want me to stay. Guess I wasn't as bad of an officer as he made me out to be. After this, he treated me totally different. He was pleasant to me and would even compliment me at times. After what had happened and how long I had been in this block, it was time to get out.

BURNED BRIDGES

A job opened up in segregation that I knew I could get. The problem was that I had an altercation with the sergeant there some time back. He had called me when I was working the B-West bubble and was telling me what to do. He was loud, rude and demanding. I informed him that I was performing my duties as I had been directed to do them. Wrong answer! He started yelling at me warning me that he was a sergeant and that I better do as he tells me. I informed him that he knew nothing about how this block ran; that he did not make policy in this block and should he have a problem with how I do things, he should speak to my superiors. I then hung up on him with him yelling that I was in big trouble. He tried to make trouble for me, but nothing changed.

I couldn't bid into segregation with him there. At least not the way things were between us. So I went back to talk to him. He was surprised when I asked to speak with him. You could tell he was ready for a confrontation. I was expecting it too. I explained that I was considering bidding into his block, but that there was no way I would do it if he had a problem with it. I explained that our altercation before was due to me following my orders. He said he respected that I came to him and that he was impressed by that. He said he had no problem with me coming in as long as I did what he told me to do. I informed him that was why we butted heads before; I was following my boss's orders. He said he would be glad to have me. Time was tight. There were duties I still had to perform on this day. I had delayed too long in trying to get all of my ducks in a row and missed out on the bidding deadline. Plus I didn't push it too hard because a friend of mine with lower seniority really wanted the job, so I passed on it. An opportunity came up in A-East with better days off shortly after, which I did take.

REQUESTED

The lieutenant in A-East had seen my interaction with inmates, heard about me and read my reports. One day when he saw me, he came over to have a chat with me. He said, "You're the kind of officer that I want." He asked me to bid into his block. This happened to me several times during my time in Stillwater Prison.

CAPTAIN SCREW OFF

It was a Saturday, sometime in 2002, shortly after we got to the cell block to start our shift; sometime around 0630. I was working the bubble. Luckily, a good officer and a fun guy to work with has been assigned to B-West. I'll just call him Officer Screw Off. He knew when to have fun and when to take care of business.

He went in the sergeant's office, picked up the telephone and punched in a phone number. From my position in the bubble, he was right in front of me only lower. My phone in the bubble rang.

When I picked it up, the voice on the phone asked, "Is Officer Screw Off there."

I said, "In body, but not his mind. He's still hung over from last night."

I could see Officer Screw Off laughing.

He said, "Is he busy."

I said, "Officer Screw Off is never busy. He's just in the can jerking off."

He said, "When he gets through, could you have him come to see the captain."

I said, "Sure, it will probably be a while though. He has a hard time getting off, because he really isn't his type."

He said "OK." and hung up.

There was a problem with this. Officer Screw Off didn't hang up. He kept talking and laughing. When we were having our conversation, before I hung up, whenever the voice on the phone was talking, Screw Off was talking. After anything I said, he was laughing. I thought maybe he is continuing to screw with me. I started to get that panicky feeling. I realized that I had actually been saying all of those things to the captain.

When Screw Off got off the phone I waved him into the bubble.

I said, "The captain called and wants you to go see him."

He asked, "Why?"

I said, "I don't know, but you better be ready for anything."

I explained what had transpired. He seemed a little upset with me. Who wants to talk to the captain for any reason after something like that?

Officer Screw Off reported to the captain. When he got back, he was laughing. He had explained everything to the captain and the captain wasn't upset. The reason the Captain wanted to see him was nothing bad.

Boy was I relieved. From that time on, I called Officer Screw Off, Captain Screw Off.

Later in the day, I had to take some paperwork to the security center. After dropping off the papers, I entered the sallyport to go back to my block. The captain stepped in. I apologized to him. He just smiled and said, "Oh well, It's a Saturday."

From that time on, I was extremely careful with anything I said on the phone.

OFFICER THOUGHTFUL

Some officers are really decent people and much more thoughtful than I was brought up to be. Below is an email he wrote, sent to my superiors and copied to me.

WELL I HAVE TO WRITE AND GIVE AN ATA-
BOY TO THE OFFICER IN THE BUBBLE TODAY.
OFR BASHAM HAD ALL OF THE WORK DONE IN A
SUPER TIME LINE. IT WAS NICE TO GET ALL THE
WORK DONE EARLY SO I CAN ACTUALLY GET
SOME THINGS DONE AROUND HERE THAT GET
NEGLECTED, PLUS I HAVE A MEETING WITH THE
WARDEN.
NOT ENOUGH GOOD WORK GETS RECOGNIZED
AROUND HERE SO FOR WHAT IT IS WORTH I
THOUGHT I WOULD DROP YOU A NOTE.

LETTER OF APPRECIATION
David Basham
April 20, 2004

I wanted to take a moment to express my sincere appreciation for your contribution to the development and implementation of double bunking at MCF Stillwater.

This has been a major undertaking for the Department of Corrections as well as MCF-Stillwater. Planning for this initiative began in the spring of 2003 and ultimately culminated on March 24, 2004 with an overall facility schedule change. This included changes to the Canteen and linen exchanges schedules; weekend and holiday meal schedule changes; changes in living by assignment designations; controlled movement schedule and finally, changes to the hours of work for staff.

In CHB-West, (Cell Hall B-West) the Double Bunking Project is nearly halfway completed. One hundred fourteen cells are capable of double bunking with one hundred of those cells already being double bunked. CHB-West has gone through some major changes not only in clientele but also in procedure.

You were very much involved with the process from ensuring that cells were vacated in a timely manner so that

315

the work on these cells could proceed uninterrupted to implementing and enforcing new unit rules.

Through your hard work and efforts, CHB-West has made this transition with very few issues and I want you to know how much your efforts are appreciated.

A/W Operations (Associate Warden of Operations)

(This was probably a form letter that was sent to everyone that was a B-West block officer during the double bunking process, but it was nice to get.)

INTAKE PACKET

Every state prison has an "Offender Handbook" with information specific to their institution. They give each inmate one of these handbooks upon their entry to their new home. These handbooks are similar, but differ in how each institution is run. Department of Correction policies are the same, but each institution has their own types of problems to address due to their layout, programming and security level. Each institution has different people to contact should the inmate have a problem. This handbook is a guide to assist them in knowing how to get by in the prison without getting into trouble and what to do if they should have a problem.

Every cell bock is different. A few of the things that differ between cell blocks are the physical layout, the programming and who is employed where.

Because of this, each block needs a list of rules and regulations specific to their block. These are to be given to each inmate when they are transferred into the block. This is why it is called an "Intake Packet."

The intake packet has important information in it that is from the Offender Handbook. Many inmates will never read the handbook due to it containing much more information than the intake packet. That is another reason for the intake packet, even though many will ignore that too.

Things change over time and things are different in each cell block. When I went to B-West, their packet was not current to their situation. I typed up the B-West intake packet, updated it and saved it to a word file. This way I could make changes whenever they occurred and adapt it to different cell blocks when I switched cellblocks. Eventually, other officers in other cell blocks found out about my file. I would get calls to send it to them so they could tweak it for their cell blocks.

When B-West double bunked, we were fortunate to have a very intelligent lieutenant with common sense running the cell hall. He took one of these intake packets and adjusted it for double bunking. The smart thing he did was give it to an intelligent inmate with common sense. The inmate worked on it from the inmate perspective. They then worked together to develop an intake packet that would best fit this awful situation that we were all in together. With an intake packet that combined the concerns of the institution and the inmates, we were set up to go forward as best we could.

The following is a combination of what they created along with some other information from other cellblocks. Combining them was necessary to give you as much basic information possible without having the redundancy of intake packets from numerous cellblocks.

INTAKE PACKET

Any violation of B-West Unit Rules and Regulations may result in possible disciplinary action.

This packet is for all new offenders entering B-West. Your assignment status dictates the B-West rules that will apply to you. Your assignment status will be one of the following:

UI: Unemployed Idle

This status will be no longer than 60 days in length. UI's are on that status for 60 days after a segregation sentence or termination from an assignment.

You are not allowed to bid on jobs, once you have been UI for 60 days, you will become TU and will be able to bid on jobs

All B-West rules apply to you. No special rules.

Out for meals, 1 hour of flag time per day, recreation per unit schedule, allowed phones during flag, also allowed are visits-canteen-other activities

TU: Temporarily Unemployed

This status is the final status before being assigned. All B-West rules apply to you. However this status depending on your seniority, allows you to move to a single cell in B-West (space permitting). When cells are available, some T.U. offenders may be placed in other units to wait for assignment. This is the only status in which you may seek employment. You are allowed to bid on jobs.

Out for meals, 1 hour of flag time per day, recreation per unit schedule, allowed phones during flag, also allowed are visits-canteen-other activities

B-West currently is not designed to be a permanent residence for offenders other than Cell Hall Workers. Depending on your assignment status, you will transition out of the unit.

The assignments are made by the Assignment Committee, depending on work experience and MCF-STW seniority T.U. status. These assignments are posted on Fridays at the bulletin board in the front of the unit on the wall. (Keep in mind that you may only apply for 2 assignments per week).

TRV: Technical Release Violators

This status is for offenders who are release violators. *(Tossed back in the slammer due to a parole violation)* All B-West rules apply to this status. An offender may not seek employment on this status.

No special rules apply to T.R.V. offenders.

LOP: Loss of Privileges

This status is the result of (In House) informal discipline. You are allowed 1 shower per day. No flag, no recreation, no library, no phones. You are not allowed to go on any passes other than Health Services, Laundry or Property. If you are double bunked and your cellmate has a pass or is out for any reason, you may not be out of your cell when your door is open, only for meal feedings.

LOP will generally be assigned in the following progression: 1st violation-verbal warning, 2nd-3 days LOP, 3rd-5 days LOP, 4th-7 days LOP, 5th & subsequent violations-formal discipline, a trip to segregation.

IHD: In House Detention

This status is temporary. When an offender is under investigation or waiting for discipline action, they will be placed on this status. There will be no recreation or flag time; a shower will be given every 3 days. Meals will be brought to the offenders in their cell. You are not allowed to leave your cell.

IHS: In House Segregation

Segregation is overflowing, if there were room in seg, you would be there. This status is for offenders completing their segregation sentence in population *(In a cellblock)*. The rules on this status are limited to the following:
* Recreation. If you remain report free for a period of 15 days once you have been assigned to B-West, you will be allowed to go to recreation. All rules and regulations must be adhered to, there are no warnings. This privilege will be assigned by the Unit Lieutenant only. Send a kite requesting this privilege.
• No Passes (No evening programming)
* You will be allowed to sign up for library twice per month. This privilege will be assigned by the Unit Lieutenant. You must be report free for a period of 15 days once assigned to B-West.
* You will be allowed non-contact visits after 3:30pm on regular visiting days. These visits must be scheduled through the visiting department 24 hours in advance by having your visitor call 651-748-7909.
* You will be allowed canteen privileges consistent with B-West general population offenders.
* You will be allowed to receive all of your property including your television.

* ANY and ALL reports will be formal and referred to the Discipline Unit. You will be charged with violating special unit rules. Any privilege earned will be forfeited.

* You will continue to accumulate Extended Incarceration (EI) as if you were in the Segregation Unit; one day of EI for every 3 days of Segregation time.

IR (Investigative Restriction): (Formerly **ICR** Investigative Cell Restriction) This status is a temporary no privileges status until you are reviewed by the Unit Lieutenant after the investigation of your rules violation. You are not allowed to leave your cell until you are called for review. Meals will be delivered to your cell. If you are double bunked and your cellmate has a pass or is out for any reason, you may not be out of your cell when your door is open. This includes meal feedings.

Activities: There is a sign up area for activities such as religious services and library in the front of the unit.

B-West Bulletin Board: At the front of the unit is the Bulletin Board. On this you will find the most recent memos, chow menus, current activities, employment postings, etc. Between the 2 Bulletin Boards is the sign-up area for activities such as Religious Services, Library etc.

Count: You must be standing facing the cell bars with your light on.

Health Services: If you have a health issue that is not an emergency, fill out an offender kite with your issue. A Health Service mailbox is located at the front of the unit next to the door.

Job Applications: must be in before switch in Sunday night.

Job Openings: are posted on Friday.

Library: UI's & TU's are allowed to sign up and go to the library; IHS & LOP are not. If you need to go to the Law Library, send a kite to the librarian for a pass.

Mail: An outgoing mailbox is located by the B-West bubble.

Medical Authorizations: must be posted in the gray square. *(There is a 3' x 3' gray square painted on the wall of each cell which is the only area an inmate is allowed to post anything.)*

Name Plate: A state issued name plate will be issued and displayed on either your cell bars or your locker. Your mail will not be delivered without having your name plate.

Notary: If you need a notary, send a kite *(inmate letter within the institution)* to the unit lieutenant.

Passes: All passes are indicated as either "direct order' or "optional." You have the right to decline an optional pass by giving it to the officer at the officer's desk by noon that day. Failure to cancel a pass and not attend that pass will result in progressive discipline and could also lead to restriction from activities.

Property Pick Up: Property will issue a pass when your property is available. It may take up to 7 days for your property to be available. Do not ask the officers when you can get it. You will be notified when a pass is issued. Laundry will issue a pass the next business day after you are released from segregation.

Religious Services: TU and UI offenders are allowed one religious event per week. Event sheets are posted in the sign up area. If you sign up for more than one, you will not be allowed to go to any. You must sign up to receive a pass. IHS may send a kite to the chapel for your religious needs.

Visiting: All institutional visiting rules are posted on the Unit Bulletin board. If your visitor arrives during meal feedings, you make the choice of eating or visiting. B-West officers are not liable for a substitute or reserved meal if you choose to go to your visit. IHS is the same as segregation; your visitor must call and make an appointment.

Yard & Recreation: TU's & UI's are allowed to sign up. IHS & LOP are not allowed to go.

All Unemployed Must Report Directly To Their Cells Upon Returning To The Unit.

UNIT RULES AND REGULATIONS

• Canteen & Linen Exchange will be on Tuesdays.

• It is your responsibility to thoroughly check your cell when you move in, complete the cell inspection form and turn it in to staff. After that, you will be held accountable for any damage or contraband found in the cell.

• Headboards are not allowed. Items used as headboards or to obstruct the view may be confiscated. *(Footlocker lids were commonly used as headboards. This helped to keep their pillow from falling off the end of their bunk. However, it also obstructed part of the view into their cell.)*

• Nothing is to obstruct the officer's view into the cell. The walkway between the cell door and the back of the cell is to be clear.

• Anything covering any cell bars is strictly prohibited.

• Beds must be made daily and blankets tucked under the mattress (no overhang). Beds and Bedding are to be used only for their intended purpose.

• Nothing may be hung from or attached to the cell bars or electrical conduit at any time. "Clothes lines" are not permitted for any reason.

• Nothing can be hanging on the walls except in the painted gray square area. Hangings may be one layer thick only. Frames and backings are not permitted. Staff must be able to lift each item up to see completely behind the item. Religious items may not be displayed.

• Colored or painted light bulb and homemade lampshades are not permitted.

• Vents between tunnels and cells must remain unobstructed at all times.

• Table covering and rugs are not permitted.

• All appliances and lights must be turned off when your cell is unoccupied

• Mops, buckets and checked out cleaning supplies are not allowed to be left in cells when not in use and must be returned to the supply cell.

• Televisions will be stored on the TV shelf only.

• Headphones are to be plugged in and worn when operating your television or radio. They may not extend outside the cell, be used as speakers or be altered in anyway. No audio volume is to be heard outside of your cell.

• Television cables may be no more than 18" in length and are not to be altered.

• Cells must be kept clean and orderly. Items not currently in use are to be put away. Clothes are to be stored in footlockers or hung inside your wardrobe closet. You must sleep on your bunk and not on the floor. Mattresses may not be placed on the floor.

• Store your items in 2 footlockers and your wall locker, not in boxes or bags

• All items must be in their original containers. Once the container is emptied, it is to be properly disposed of.

• Mattresses and trash containers are to remain in the cell when you move out. The keys to the padlocks and mirrors are to be turned into the staff.

• Do not keep food trays & lids in the cells. Place them on the bars or outside of cells when meal is finished.

HYGIENE & DRESS

• All individuals are expected to maintain a socially acceptable level of personal hygiene, cleanliness and neatness.

• Pajamas and robes may not be worn outside the cell except when going to and from the shower.

• Shirts and shoes are to be worn outside the cell except when going to and from the shower.

• Shower shoes are not permitted to be worn outside the living unit.

• Sagging is not allowed *(Pants hanging below waist)*

• Garbage should be disposed of daily in the trash containers located on the Flag.

• Headgear and gloves that are issued for a specific work assignment will only be worn during that work assignment.

• Do-rags may only be worn in cells.

• Plastic caps and curlers may not be worn outside the living unit.

• Headgear, ball caps, stocking hats, sunglasses etc will only be worn outdoors.

• Religious headgear as approved by the Religious Coordinator may only be worn in cells and authorized religious services.

• Wearing any necklace outside of your cell is not allowed.

• Athletic headbands must be white and may only be worn during recreational activities.

• Sunglasses may not be worn indoors without medical authorization.

• Sports gloves may only be worn for weight lifting, racquetball or handball.

• ID Cards must be worn on the outer clothing clipped visible on or near the chest level at all times when out of your cell.

• Hobby craft items may not be worn or displayed.

• Sexually explicit pictures are prohibited.

UNIT GUIDELINES

• Climbing on, jumping from, throwing or hanging items from the tiers is not allowed.

• Crossing the black line by the door until directed to do so by the door officer is not allowed.

• Yelling or screaming and excessive noise is not allowed.

• Only 3 people are allowed in any cell at one time. You must live on the tier of the cell you visit. No one is allowed in anybody else's cell when they are not in their cell.

• Windows may only be opened or closed by staff and will not be opened when the heat is on.

• Offenders are not permitted to do another offender's laundry unless the unit has an authorized laundry worker.

• ID Cards must be displayed in the phone ID slot when using the phone. Only offenders using the phone are allowed in the area. You must be seated on the stool while on the telephone and telephones must be hung up after use.

Sharing of telephone calls and PIN numbers is not permitted.

• Items may not be hung from tier railings.

• No slamming of game pieces such as cards and dominoes.

• All cell hall lights are considered security devices and may not be tampered with.

• Cell lights must be on during stand up counts.

• Offenders are to be standing in their cells after the count tone rings.

• Mirrors may not be used for spotting. They are to remain in the cell.

• Any item that is altered from its intended purpose is considered contraband.

• All offenders are expected to comply with one for one linen exchange (1 pillowcase, 2 sheets, 3 towels) on the designated linen exchange day and return directly to your cell

• Loitering in the canteen area is not permitted.

• Unit games may not leave the unit.

• You must report directly to your cell at the first count bell and close your cell door. All doors must be closed by the time the second count bell rings.

• The unit warning bell rings 5 minutes prior to switch-in. You must be in your cell by the following bell with your door closed or you will be subject to disciplinary action.

• You have less than 5 minutes for mass movements. If you miss your work ring out, you will be on Unauthorized Lay In Status and be locked in your cell all day.

ARE WE REALLY DEALING WITH THIS SHIT

IT'S THE JOB

Just one of the many television channels these guys receive was not coming in. One of our pain in the buttocks inmates approached the sergeant at 1530 to inform her of this and that he needed it fixed by 1900 because there was a program on at that time that he did not want to miss.

Really! You came to prison so you could expect better service than those outside of these walls that haven't committed crimes. (Or at least haven't gotten caught committing crimes.)

The sarge called the watch commander who informed her that nothing could be done about it until Monday. She informed the inmate of this.

The inmate went to another officer and complained to him at 1810.

"Channel 23 still isn't working. WWE Smack down comes on at 1900 and I can't miss it."

"Did you speak to the OIC about it?"

"She basically said, 'Fuck you' and 'I don't give a fuck.'"

"Is that what she really said?"

"No, she said she would call someone, but the way she said it, told me 'Fuck you' and 'I don't give a fuck. I'm going to miss my show. It's essential that I watch it. New developments happen every week! When do you get off the door post?"

"1900."

"Can you get it fixed?"

"I'll call the watch commander."

The watch commander told him it had already been reported and once again that Monday was the soonest we could get someone out to repair it. The officer relayed the information to the inmate.

"I tell you what I'm gonna do. I'm gonna call MY people and they'll call Direct TV and fix this!" He then walked away.

The officer placed him on ICR for using vulgar language and making false claims about the sergeant.

The next day the inmate was spoken to by a lieutenant and released from his cell. He assured the lieutenant that he could keep from losing control of his mouth. He then went to the same officer as he had the day before.

"Will you refer me to a psychiatrist? You're the first officer that I'm taking this to, because the sarge wouldn't understand."

"Why do you want me to refer you to a psychiatrist?"

"My mouth keeps getting me in trouble because my moods are up and down. I'm not suicidal or homicidal."

"Are you sure you are not going to harm yourself or anyone else?"

"Definitely not. I just need some pills to solve my problems with mood swings and irritability."

The officer submitted a Mental Health referral to the watch commander.

That evening, the inmate was complaining to the lieutenant that another inmate stunk.

The officer assigned to check out this situation found no hygiene problem. He did find out that the complaining inmate had gone into this guy's cell without permission a couple of weeks ago and was told by that inmate to leave him alone. The complainer was locked in his cell for misrepresentation and harassment.

Three days later, he still had not been seen by a psychologist or even heard that he had an appointment. This is not acceptable in a place like this with people like this.

He approached a different officer that checked out and confirmed that the referral had been submitted. He called the psych office and was told he could make a referral.

What's with this crap? At this point there should not need to be another referral, one had already been submitted. Someone should've gotten off their ass, come into the block and spoken to this whacko!

Sure, this guy was a pain in the ass. He was more often than not like the "Little Boy Who Cried Wolf." But these are the kind of people you have to keep a close eye on. You never know what is fact or fiction. You have to check out everything this guy said to play it safe, because many times this particular inmate did have great information.

It's the job!

VAPORS

We received a kite from an inmate stating that he smelled "Vapors" and that they "are a danger to a person's life."

The sarge went to speak to him.

"What specifically are these "Vapors" that you smell?"

"Hot sauce and arm pit odors. I think they are coming from the cell either above mine or below mine. Someone is cooking noodles with hot sauce and fanning the odors out of their cell. I have a very sensitive nose. The odors are making me constipated."

"Lots of inmates cook with hot sauce. There is nothing I can do to change that. Changing cells probably wouldn't help at all. Lots of these guys use that stuff. What do you suggest I do?"

"You are right. There probably is nothing that can be done. I had the same problem when I lived in a different cell block."

"You could check with Health Services and see if there is anything that can be done about your sensitive nose."

The sarge submitted a psych referral on this guy.

DRAMA QUEEN

A problem inmate went to a female sergeant. She had problems with this guy before. She told him she would not talk to him without a lieutenant present, so he went to a different officer. He told the officer that two mental health referrals had been put in on him in the last 5 days and still no one from psychology had come to see him. He said he needed to talk to someone right away about something "very private and personal." If he could not speak to a psychologist right away, he wanted to talk to a nurse. He said he was not suicidal. The watch commander was informed. This was eight thirty at night, shortly before the prison got locked down for the night.

This was one of those guys that everything was always urgent. He was always sticking his nose in others business. He would make up lies to try to get his own way. We had to take care of business, but it got frustrating because he was always being a drama queen.

PLAYING DUMB WHEN YOU ARE DUMB

Some of these guys are really dumb, but some show how utterly stupid they are when they try to play dumb. Those are the really dumb ones.

An inmate on In House Segregation status went up to a fellow SUR 13 member's cell on galley seven.

(SUR is short for Sureno. SUR 13 is a Mexican gang that is generally associated with the Mexican Mafia. Mexican gangs will fight each other, however within the United States prison systems they find it beneficial to get along. There is power in numbers.)

A sergeant saw him and asked him where he lived.

"On the flag," was the response.

The officer told him to report to his cell. When the officer checked his cell a few minutes later, he was not there. The sarge had him paged to his cell.

When he showed up, the sarge asked him why he did not report to his cell.

"I don't know."

"Do you know you are on IHS status?"

"Yes."

"Then what were you doing on gallery seven?'

"I don't know. I don't know nothing about rules."

"You've been here long enough to know the rules."

"I forget. I need another copy of the rules."

The sarge locked him in his cell. Policy dictates that anyone on IHS status having any violation of any type, is to go right back to the hole. That is probably what happened when the Watch Commander received the report.

HE IS OUT AMONG US

An inmate in segregation on quiet status (locked up in a cell with a solid door) wanted to speak to someone in Administration. He had a lot of things to complain about. (As many do) He said that the officers in Doghouse (D-Hall) lied about him threatening them. He said he was disrespectful, but not threatening.

He had been written up several times in the past few months for threatening staff.

He said that his discipline record from a previous incarceration was being used against him and that he was dealing with the Commissioner on that issue.

He stated that he had some demands.

He was asked what he was going to do if they were not met.

He said he would make a political issue out of it by going on a hunger strike. He said that would get him media attention and put pressure on the politicians to meet his demands.

This guy was in for arson. He did not accumulate any good time in prison, so he was doing his full bit. By the time you read this, he will have been released.

He is 59 years old with nowhere to go. Oh, lucky us!

DOUBLE VIOLATION

The dress code policy had been violated by an offender that acquired "Round Spacers" and worked them into his ear lobes. First, ear rings were not allowed and second, the spacers were contraband. He hadn't thought it through.

I WANT TO JOIN THE TALIBAN

There was a request by an inmate to move into a detention cell, so he could be alone in a cell. That was not allowed. When he was informed that what he wanted was not allowed, he started on an entertaining little rant.

He said, "Well, you're a government worker, right? I want you to go out and call the police and tell them I want to join the Taliban. I hate this fucking country. I'm not even an American. I want you to call and have me transported to Guantanamo Bay. I want to join the Taliban. In fact, I want to bomb America. Actually, I want to bomb Stillwater. I want to bomb this facility. Better yet, I "AM" going to bomb this facility."

His request for a single sell was granted, in segregation.

CHRONIC WEENIE PAIN IN THE ASS

A chronic weenie pain in the ass that would be chewed up and spit out by most anyone in this place, liked to be a nuisance to officers. This was because we were the only ones that could not physically retaliate. This was probably the only way he could feel like a big shot. We were OK with it because when it came down to it, we had the final say, "To the hole with ye, ye rat bastard! I'm going home."

Obviously, we never said that, at least most of us didn't. I always wondered where that term "rat bastard" came from. Seeing this guy, I knew. He looked like a bastard from a rat.

Anyway, he had four footlockers and was only allowed to have two. He was directed to take two of them down to the door.

He said that he was going to bed and would do it later.

He was again issued the same directive.

He again stated that he would do it later. He sat down on his bunk and said, "If you want them down there, you can do it yourself if you think you are so tough."

"To the hole with ye, ye rat bastard! I'm going home."

ADULT SIZED CHILDREN

Some of these guys never developed past the childhood phase of their lives. Once you realize that, it is easier to understand what is going on; that makes it much easier to do your job.

A prime example of this is this inmate that was out of his cell when he was not supposed to be out. His cellmate was moving; that is why the door to his cell was open.

An officer saw him out of his cell and motioned for him to come to him. The inmate turned away. The officer got another officer and went to the inmate's cell. As the inmate had returned there once, he knew the officer was coming for him. When the officers got there, the inmate was lying on his bed faking like he was sleeping; just like a little kid would do. When the officer "woke" him up, he denied being out of his cell.

This adult size child would be speaking to the lieutenant the next day.

FRIEND'S FUN

There were two inmates that were friends. They enjoyed goofing around with each other. In the prison we call this horseplay. At times, horseplay gets out of control; especially in a place like this.

One inmate was walking by his buddy's cell. His buddy was sleeping. He reached through the cell bars and slapped him on the face to surprise him.

The sleeping inmate was a bit more than surprised. The slap turned out to be much harder than the slapper realized. When you are tired and get woken up with a slap in a place like this, it can be very disconcerting.

They both wound up going to the slappers cell. The slapped picked up the slapper and threw him on the bed. They started wrestling. As the slapped was a bit irritated, the wrestling got out of control.

They stopped their wrestling and began to talk about it as an officer was nearing their cell.

"You didn't have to hit me."

"You're stupid."

"You didn't have to slap me, that hurt. I should beat you up for that."

After hearing that, the officer locked them up in their separate cells for the lieutenant to speak to them.

My brother and I had exchanges like this all of the time. If caught, we would get a talking to from our parents.

This was a different place with a different person giving the talk. Everything in this place needs to be documented and incompatibility waivers need to be signed.

These kinds of situations were very common inside these walls.

ELEMENTARY PROBLEMS

Is this grade school? While passing out food trays in the unit, one inmate cut in front of another in line.

"What's your problem?"

"Nothing."

The cuttee gave the cutter an elbow. "What did you say?"

The cutter turned around to face the one he had disrespected and said, "I did not say anything."

An officer stepped in and directed the one that was cut in front of to step back.

He said, "Just hand me my tray."

The officer directed him to, "Step back."

"All you have to do is hand me my tray."

The officer called for a 10-14 and started escorting him to the door.

The inmate kept saying, "All you have to do is hand me my fucking tray."

The A-Team took him to the Security Center and then returned for the cutter.

The incident was sorted out with the inmates locked in holding cells.

TAKE MY SHIT, PLEASE

An inmate reported that a small book containing his pin#, social security numbers of himself and his family and other important information was taken from his cell.

By asking this guy questions, I found out that he routinely left his cell door open when he was not in there. In this place, that is like saying, "Take my shit, please." The joke was on him.

NOT SMART TO CUSS OUT A COP

A rookie officer was doing an excellent job by enforcing the policy that during feeding in the cell block, the only thing any inmate is allowed to do is to come down to get their food.

An inmate went to the sink by the ice machine on the front flag and started getting water.

The officer told him that he could not get water at this time and that the water in his cell would have to do.

The inmate told the officer that he had to take medication and that he couldn't drink the water in his cell.

Folks, it's the same damn water. It comes through the same pipes from the same place.

The officer gave him numerous direct orders to keep moving, but he did not comply. It was only after the officer told him to turn over his ID that he moved on.

The officer saw him on his tier, shaking his head and saying, "Bitch ass mother fucker."

I went up to the third tier to get his ID and lock him in his cell.

The sarge instructed the new officer to place him on ICR by writing a report and turning it into the watch commander.

INEFFECTIVE LIAR

An effective con these guys would try to pull on us was to dump water on their floor, tell us their toilet overflowed and that they needed to get a bucket and mop to clean it up.

With this guy on this day, it worked, for a while. 30 minutes later he was seen on the phone and had never gone to get a mop.

The officer locked him up for being in an unauthorized area and misrepresentation.

PUNKS RETURN

The sergeant and another officer were conducting cell shakedowns (cell searches). One double bunked cell they had to search had one inmate in it and the other one was missing. The sarge had the bubble officer page the missing inmate several times.

They directed the inmate in the cell to step out and go down a few cells, so they could conduct their search.

During the search, he kept coming back to his cell to try to see what they were searching through.

The sarge told him to sit at the first table on the back flag. When the search was complete, the sarge noticed that the inmate was not sitting at the table. He was in an unauthorized area on the flag.

The sarge patted him down and locked him in his cell.

The inmate began yelling, "You're a fucking asshole sergeant! Why don't you be a real man, you pussy? I'll kick your ass, you pussy mother fucker."

His missing cellmate was found and taken to the Security Center by A-Team officers.

An A-Team officer came to get Mr. Foul Mouth Tough Guy and heard the comments he was yelling at the sarge. He directed the inmate to approach the door to be cuffed up. The officer began cuffing up the inmate. The inmate attempted to turn and pull away. The officer kept hold of the cuffs and applied pressure to the cuffed wrist to gain control of him. The inmate stopped pulling away and the officer placed on the second cuff.

The inmate started mouthing off to him. "Don't go pulling on me! You think you're tough don't you. You're a pussy too!"

As he was being taken from the back of the cell hall to the Security Center, he was yelling and trying to incite the other inmates that were out of their cells into action. "I'll be out in a couple of days and we'll see how tough you are then. You see how these pussies are? That sergeant thinks he's tough. That's alright! We'll see!"

As they entered the Security Center, the count officer asked for his name and number.

"I don't remember my name. Fuck you!"

The officers took him to seg and conducted an unclothed body search on him.

They then went back to the Security Center to conduct an unclothed body search on his cellmate. He was not cooperative.

"Fuck this shit!"

When directed to bend over and spread the cheeks of his buttocks, he refused. He was directed to do this several times and refused.

"You fags like to look at guy's asses don't you? Fuck this shit."

He eventually complied with the search and went to the hole.

Both inmates were charged with failure to comply, disobeying a direct order, interference with security procedures, disorderly conduct and abuse and harassment.

Both of these guys were chronic trouble makers and should never have been in general population, but they were consistently returned.

One of these guys has since been released, only to murder someone and get tossed back inside to do life without parole. This was entirely predictable.

The other one, at the time I am writing this, will soon be released. I predict the same for him.

TEMPTATION

An inmate housed on the flag had a mop in his cell. He said that it was to mop up spilled coffee. As a couple of officers passed by, the inmate asked, "Could I get out to get a mop bucket?"

"I can have a swamper bring you one, because it is now another galleries flag time."

About five minutes later, they saw him throw the mop out into the middle of the flag.

One of the officers went to retrieve the mop and get the inmates ID.

"Give me your ID. I'm placing you on ICR for throwing state property."

"No! I'm not going on ICR. I refuse to go on ICR."

Comments like this are quite comical. We just write a report and they are on ICR. There is absolutely nothing that they can do about it.

This officer paged the other officer. When the other officer arrived, the inmate was packing up his property. This is an indication that they are going to escalate their level of stupidity and go to the hole.

"Give me your ID."

He ignored the directive and continued to pack up his property.

'I'm giving you a direct order to give me your ID."

"No."

When the inmate heard him call for the A-Team, he said, "I'm gonna do you." He looked at the other officer and said, "I'll do you too."

He said to the first officer, "Rambo, we know each other personally now. You're not man enough to come in and get me yourself."

Frankly, there is nothing many of us would like to do more than to let these guys bring it on. There is a problem with that. We could wind up being cellmates with these guys. Being stupid like some of these guys is just not worth it. I'll do as I'm told here, get a paycheck and be able to do as I please for the other 16 hours of the day.

BRING IN MY MA

During a lockdown, inmates were complaining that they did not get bread or desert with their meal. They were complaining about only getting TV dinners and milk. Many began yelling and throwing items at windows, breaking them.

When I was a kid, I didn't know what desert was. If I would've complained about anything, I would've been hit so hard and fast, I would never have seen it coming. I would've gone flying off of the chair onto the floor and not be allowed to eat.

Too bad my mother is dead. We could use her here.

LITTLE CONSEQUENCE

The sergeant had given an inmate a warning to put his ID on a half an hour ago. He now saw him without it again.

"Why aren't you wearing your ID?"

The inmate wanted to argue.

"Report to my office." The sarge wanted to speak with him.

The inmate refused and went to the ice machine.

Sarge called for the squad to remove him.

When they arrived, the inmate walked toward the sarge and in a sarcastic manner said, "Ooh, you gonna send me to seg?"

"Yes."

"Well, I'll see you in two days."

This was a big problem in the prison. These guys create problems and there is very little consequence for it. They keep doing the same things over and over. There needs to be a greater consequence in order to correct their behavior.

This lack of consequences is again displayed in this incident.

An officer noticed an inmate on the phone without his ID displayed and told him he needed to display it.

He was ignored.

"You need to have your ID displayed."

The inmate took the ID out of his pocket and threw it up to where the ID's are to be displayed. It landed face down. The ID's are to be inserted into a slot. This is so that we can see the inmate's picture. This way we can quickly verify that is or isn't the inmate who is allowed on that phone.

The inmate yelled, "I am on an important call."

The officer took the ID and checked the inmate's file. He had a previous violation a month ago.

The officer returned, told him to hang up and that he was being placed on ICR.

The inmate ignored him and kept talking.

The officer gave him three more directives to hang up and switch in.

The inmate stood up and continued to talk on the phone.

The officer called for a 10-14.

The inmate was taken to seg where he wouldn't be using a phone for some time.

MUST LIE BETTER

An inmate on LOP was not found in his cell. The sarge was in the bubble and paged him to his cell.

He reported to the bubble with his hair half braided and said, "Sergeant, this is the only time I got to have my hair done."

"Switch in immediately."

"But sergeant, may I just go finish my hair. I only have three rows left."

"Are you on LOP?"

"Yes."

"I am placing you on ICR for violating your LOP."

"Why are you being so mean?"

"Switch in immediately."

When he reported to his cell, the officer said, "Give me your ID."

The inmate lied and said, "I already talked with the sarge and it's all good."

"Hand over your ID. I spoke with the sarge and she informed me that you are ICR'ed.

These guys are good at playing one officer against another, but it didn't work this time.

JUVENILE BEHAVIOR

The door officer noticed an inmate walking around the block that he had let back in the block from a pass ten minutes before. The inmate was supposed to go directly back to his cell. The officer called the offender to see him at the door.

"Why are you out of your cell?"

"I just got back."

"That was ten minutes ago. I'm placing you on ICR."

The inmate became loud saying, "Whatever!" He started clapping and cheering in an effort to draw in other inmates and stir them up. Things had been getting increasingly tense in the block for some time. It would not take much for the place to blow up. The inmate said, "You're a sorry mother fucker." He then went to his cell and was locked in.

WE ARE HERE TO HARASS

Inmates are not to hang anything from the conduit in their cells as it may pull the conduit off of the walls and ceiling. The sarge noticed clothing hanging from the conduit in a cell.

"Whose clothes are hanging from the conduit?"

"They are mine. Do you have a problem with that?"

"What's your name?" The sarge had to ask this three times before getting an answer. A smart ass remark followed.

"What do you do; come to work to harass people?"

The inmate was becoming aggressive. He was escalating the tone and level of his voice.

The sarge had him hauled out. The Watch Commander had him taken to segregation.

IT'S PART OF THE JOB

During feeding, the sarge noticed a group of inmates accumulating by the cell hall door. She went to that area and told them to disperse. All moved except one. She stood by him and told him to move up the stairs.

"I'm waiting for someone!"

"Keep moving."

"Why are you being so disrespectful? This is bullshit!"

She reinforced that he had to move as he had been standing there for some time.

He continued to argue.

She told him to give her his ID.

"It's my cell! You know my name!"

"What is your cell number?"

"You know where I live!"

She instructed another officer to hold him at the top of the stairs so she could call the watch commander. The A-Team was dispatched to pick the guy up.

She again asked him for his name.

Now he stated his name and cell number.

Comments that he made to her were, "You must be on your period. Are you on your period? I know you're on your period!'

She told him his comments were inappropriate as the A-Team arrived, cuffed him up and removed him from the unit.

How would you like to put up with this every day at work?

THE ANSWER'S THE SAME

When you ask someone something and you don't get the answer you want, you ask someone else and when you still don't get the answer you want, you ask someone else and when............

An inmate ordered a television and had not received it yet. He went to the sarge, who was sorting mail to be delivered to the inmates, to see if she would call down to canteen and find out why.

She referred him to the sergeant in the bubble as he was by a phone. He went to the bubble and said, "Is the canteen still open and if so could you call down to find out why I didn't get my television during canteen?"

"You need to write a kite and address canteen that way."

The inmate went to the first sergeant that he had spoken to and said, "He said to write a kite. I don't understand why I can't have my television. I paid for it. The money came out of my account already."

She had him switch in, but she had just finished sorting the mail, so she called down to canteen. They informed her that this guy had already gotten several people to call them this day. He was told this morning, by canteen staff that he could not have his television yet, because he had been written up for having a television that did not belong to him.

If I remember correctly, if you are caught with a television that is not yours, you are not allowed to have one for a year.

The canteen sergeant came to the block and along with the block sergeant spoke with the inmate and gave him a direct order not to have any more staff calling on his television. He was instructed whom to write to in order to resolve his issue.

He was angry and argumentative and said, "Don't go putting words in my mouth! That's not what I told you! I never told you to call down and ask about my television! You better stop putting words in my mouth."

She said, "I did not put words in your mouth. It is what you asked both of us sergeants to do. This conversation is over"

He continued making inappropriate comments by calling her a liar.

She locked him up for disorderly conduct toward an officer.

POWER PLAYS DO NOT WORK

The sarge was switching in inmates from their flag time. An inmate said, "Are you going to shut my door?"

She directed him to close his door.

"That's your fucking job."

"It is not my job. Close your door now."

His roommate said to him, "What's your problem. Just close the damn door."

"What's your fucking problem? That's her fucking job to close our door!"

She placed him on ICR.

GO AHEAD AND FREEZE

A night sergeant was very aware of inmates throwing items at windows and trying to break the windows.

At 2158 he turned the lights off in the unit to make it better for sleeping.

It all started 2 minutes later. A carton of milk hit a window and broke it. An officer cleaned up the glass.

17 minutes later, 2217, another crash was heard but the officers could not find any broken glass, only a bar of soap. The glass could've fallen behind a metal panel under the window.

28 minutes after that, 2245, the sarge saw a carton of milk hit a window and bounce off without breaking it.

27 minutes after that, 2312, another crash was heard. It was successful. A leaking milk carton was found on the flag along with the glass from the window.

This kind of behavior went on night after night when B-West was double bunked, especially when the inmates were on lockdown. Rarely can anyone be identified and held to task.

The down side of this, for the inmates, was that the block would get very cold in the winter with all of these windows broken. That is when prison justice would take place. It's not smart to inconvenience your fellow felons.

WHAT DID WE LEARN

A female sergeant was getting verbally harassed by two inmates. She had been putting up with it for a month.

They made comments like "Crack Bitch" and "Crack Ass." They would say, "Don't even look at her. She is a crack ass bitch."

They denied saying anything to her and said they were hollering to their friends up on a different gallery.

She told them it was extremely coincidental that each time she was in the immediate area, she would hear their comments. She informed them that she would not tolerate

345

such disrespect of an officer and ordered them to cease this behavior.

On this evening, during feeding, she heard one of them say, "That's an ugly ass haircut!"

They both began to laugh. She went to their cell, stated that this type of harassment wound not be tolerated.

They began to argue and denied saying anything. They became loud and disruptive.

She told them to give her their ID's. They refused. It took several more directives before they complied.

As she walked away, she heard them yelling to her, "Fucking ass bitch, crack ass bitch."

What did we learn from this? And let this be a warning to everyone. You can call a woman most anything, but never insult her hair.

LAUGHABLE IDIOTS

A major pain in the ass, lying troublemaker that was constantly in unauthorized areas came to the bubble and said to the sergeant posted in there, "Pop 125" which was his cell. This was in B-West where cell doors could be opened by pushing a button in the bubble. He then walked away. He stood at his cell waiting for the sarge to pop the door open. The sarge waved him back to the bubble so he could ask him some questions.

"Why were you on the front flag during galleries 3 and 4's flag time?"

"Just pop my cell open."

The sarge tried again to get him to answer his questions.

"I'm not going to listen to anymore of your fucking bullshit. Pop my cell open."

He then walked away giving that inmate stare that says, "You better do as I say and buy into my acts of intimidation or I'll come for you. I know that you know that I'm always violating policy, but you better not do anything about it."

I always had a difficult time keeping from laughing when idiots gave me that stare.

The sarge had him taken to seg.

I DON'T LIKE YOU EITHER

One of the items that inmates in double bunked B-West had delivered to them as part of their meal was an ice cream cup and spoon. An officer saw an inmate throw the ice cream cup and spoon out of his cell and onto the flag. The officer had always noticed a mess outside of this inmate's cell.

She asked him why he was throwing garbage out onto the flag.

He refused to answer.

She asked him again.

"Because I don't like you. I hate you with a passion. I'm just being honest."

He was placed on ICR for unsanitary acts.

As many times as inmates expressed displeasure with me or called me names, I can never remember ever giving a damn about it. More often than not, I found their antics humorous.

LIFE OF A CHILD MOLESTER

A cell close to the feeding line in the block contained a well connected inmate. Because many inmates would stop to talk to him and give him things, it disrupted the feeding. Also, if officers would toss everyone that stopped, inmates would stop stopping.

The sarge had what was called a vulnerable inmate approach her and request a cell closer to the bubble to decrease the amount he was getting harassed. He was a wimpy white guy that was a child molester. He had been inappropriate with a little girl. How inappropriate and how little, I do not know. It was listed as Criminal Sexual Contact 1 and the girl was 12 or younger.

He couldn't handle himself with the big boys and would come whining to officers all of the time, but he thought it was alright for him to force himself on a little girl.

Anyway, the sarge decided to have the two of them switch cells in order to solve both problems with one move. When she told the connected inmate he was moving, he was not happy about it.

When he asked why, she told him about the disruption with people stopping. He told her that she should just write them up.

She told him that she was solving it with the move.

When he was moving, she saw him switching mattresses. This is not allowed. Mattresses are assigned to the cell, not the inmate. When she told him to leave the mattress in its proper cell, he became mouthy and uncooperative.

An inmate living on a tier above them hollered down to him and said, "Bro, that dude has to be moved closer to the bubble because he is a PC (Protective Custody) inmate. He made you move. He got AIDS too!"

The sarge reiterated her reason and made him complete the move.

The baby raper created problems for himself by making the request to move and having it granted. He wrote the following note.

Terroristic Threats

The guy in cell XXX who used to be in YYY threatened my life by saying, "F_ _ K around with me and get vaporized." Forty-five minutes later, the guy leaned on the wall in front of my cell trying to intimidate me. I heard him say, "When that S.O.B. in cell 5YYY comes out, I am going to beat the S_ _ T out of him and F_ _ K him up." Please have all guards keep an eye on me. I'm not safe here. If he can't get me, he will have his friends attack me. If he or his friends get to me, I will be severely beaten. I take the threats to be very serious. If or when the attack happens to me, I have already packed up everything I own so that the cops won't

have to worry about packing my things up for me. It is so dangerous for me to go out to meals, so I won't be doing that. Please let my best friend and body guard ___ ___ come with me once a week to canteen so I can pick up 1 weeks' worth of food that I ordered so that I may eat in my cell every day.
God Bless You

Protecting these guys from each other, no matter what they did is our job.

Nine days later, the baby raper was writing again.

To B-West SGT

A Native Indian who lives on galley 2 about 4 or 5 cells down (from me) threatened my life when we were both in A-East. He tried to use extortion on me to make me pay $40 every week for protection. This happened about 4 months ago. He has friends everywhere in B-West. He or his friends could attack me at any time. His name Is ___ ___. This guy in 506 who has threatened my life has friends everywhere in B-West. I have no intention of being attacked again. As long as my life is in danger of an attack, I'm not leaving my cell. I will cancel all future passes. I will do all of my laundry in my sink. I will not come down for any meals as long as I am in this unit. I will never leave my cell. I don't feel safe in this unit at all. I will go out of my cell when I move out of this unit. Until then, I'm staying locked up in my cell for my own protection and for my own safety. When I have money, I will buy enough food for a whole week for breakfast, lunch and dinners at canteen. Going out to canteen once a week for my meals is a lot safer than going out of my cell 3X a day for meals ever day. ___ ___ hasn't said anything to me yet. But I'm not willing to take a chance because of the threats and extortion that he tried to use on me in the past. Until I leave this cell and this unit, I'm not going out of my cell. My life is too important to me to go out into a dangerous situation.
P.S. Don't need to see LT. I would tell him everything the letter already says. Decide how to keep me safe.

My response would be, if I were allowed to call it like I saw it rather than what my responsibility dictated, "How do you think that little girl felt and feels now and forever. Sounds like you made a choice. There is no need for us to intervene."

The baby raper was being moved to segregation. The A-Team needed everyone switched in to try to prevent attempts to get at this inmate.

One of the inmates needing to switch in was not happy about this and yelled out, "You guards are a bunch of pussy motherfuckers! All this for one guy!"

When the sarge was checking to make sure the big mouth's cell was secure, he called him a "fucking faggot."

Once the baby raper was secure back in seg, this jerk was taken back to seg.

HOW TO FLOOD

Flooding cells has generally been reserved for being in segregation. Now that B-West was basically the new seg, a few guys decided to try to flood B-West.

One guy clogged his toilet with a wash cloth. The other two were in a cell together and jammed toilet paper in the pipes. When they clog the toilet they keep flushing it. When they clog the sink, they leave the water on.

They were on gallery 7 which is basically the third story. The water runs over the galleries and onto the flag like a waterfall.

They were moved to different cells and charged with destruction, damage or alteration of property.

DEFIANT INMATE'S PLAN

A call had been made to get an inmate removed from the unit due to him refusing to switch in. About 20 other inmates gathered around the area of that inmate's cell.

They were told to leave the area and find something better to do. Arguing and giving their opinions about the B-

West officers for calling to get the disobeying inmate hauled out would not be tolerated.

One inmate that was hanging out at a table in the area said, "I ain't got to do nothing. This is my flag time and I can hang where ever."

He continued his protest as more officers entered the unit. When directed by one of the officers to cuff up, he refused, and crossed his arms.

A different officer directed him to cuff up. He said that he would cuff up for that officer.

He had time to think and realized that any further negations would lead to him being sprayed with mace, taken to the ground, physically hauled out of the unit to seg and strapped nude on the board. He knew just how far he could push it before he went all of the way down that path.

DISRESPECTFUL INMATE, WELL DUH!

An inmate returned from a pass and decided to loiter rather than return to his cell, even after two directives.

From gallery two, he asked an officer if he could go check and see if he had any mail.

The officer refused the request reminding him that he had already ignored two directives.

He went toward his cell and loudly said to those in the cells he was passing, "Bitch ass rookie."

The new officer directed him to report to the door so he could try to resolve the issue.

He started to walk toward the stairway and again loudly said, "Bitch ass rookie." He yelled down, "What you want?"

The officer told him that he was not going to speak to him while he was on the gallery and to please come down to the door.

"Man, I need to go lock my door then."

He went to his cell, grabbed some items and tossed them down to an inmate on the flag. He was making unintelligible comments the entire time, before arriving at the door. That is expected from the unintelligent.

The officer asked for his ID and asked why he found it necessary to shout the comments the way he had.

"Man, I wasn't talking to you."

"Who were you referring to?"

"Man, I wasn't talking to you, was I? Man, I'm gonna take my ID and go back up there."

"Your behavior has been disruptive and verbally harassing toward me."

"What then; you gonna write me up? Well then if you're gonna write me up; I'm gonna write you up."

The inmate began to walk away and then made some comments to an inmate waiting to get out on a pass. The inmate backed away as he did not want to get sucked in with this inmate's inappropriate disruptive behavior. He made more comments to inmates in the cell next to him before switching in.

The officer placed him on ICR. I guarantee that he would not be that disrespectful when the lieutenant called him down to speak to him the next day.

HARASSMENT

Finding different ways to harass people in here seems to be the goal of some of these guys.

An inmate informed officers that, the day before, someone went into his cell and dumped water all over his bunk and pillow when he went down to pick up his meal. Today when he was out getting his meal, he returned to find milky white salad dressing on his linen.

Discipline was informed about this so that they could view video tape to catch who was doing it.

When you have over 400 delinquents housed in one block like this, you get a wide variety of goings on.

SOME NEVER LEARN

Fat boy; tell them to open my cell."

An old pain in the butt inmate kept repeating this to an officer. This officer wasn't at all fat, but that is beside the point. It was his style of being a pain in the butt and if you let one get away with it, you will have a lot more joining in.

If this guy would have called me that, I might have thanked him for the compliment. That comment might have down sized me and it would've shaved off a few decades.

The officer said, "What are you calling me?"

"Fat boy; what is it with you?"

The officer placed him on ICR. When his cell door was opened, so his cell mate could come out and get his morning meal, "Pain in the Butt" came out of the cell.

The sarge saw him and said, "No, you are on ICR. I need you to switch in now."

The old inmate started to swing his arms in the air with his fists clenched, but returned to his cell.

A bag breakfast was delivered to his cell.

"NICE ASS" FROM AN ASS

Some of these guys just can't control their mouths. Lack of appropriate control is what lands guys in here. An inmate was passing by a female officer when he said, "That's a nice ass."

She asked, "What did you say?"

He said, "I asked how you were doing," as he looked her up and down.

Need I say that she locked his ass up?

KEEP THEM IN SEG

Stupid little games that some of these guys play are supposed to piss us off. All they actually do is give us officers some good entertainment and something to talk about when it is slow.

Inmates are supposed to have their ID displayed on the phone they are using. An officer noticed that an inmate had not done this and directed him to do so.

The inmate refused this order and two others, so the officer told him to give him his ID.

The inmate put the ID on the phone rather than giving it to the officer.

He was told to hand it over another time.

"Get it yourself."

The officer again directed him to give him the ID. The inmate would not give it to him, so the officer reached for it. The inmate quickly grabbed it first and tossed it on the floor at the officer's feet.

"What was that all about?"

"You wanted it."

The inmate then grabbed the ID before the officer could get it.

The officer took it from the inmate and locked him up.

These types of things happened all of the time, generally from the same small group of inmates.

I always said that this job would be a lot easier if the chronic trouble makers were kept locked up instead of continually letting them back out into the general population.

DISRUPTIVE RELIGIOUSLY

The sergeant had an inmate that was ICR'ed for a pass violation, report to him to for the formality conversation that would get him taken off of ICR. When the sergeant was explaining pass procedures to him, the inmate became loud, argumentative and kept interrupting the sarge. The sarge had him go back to his cell and lock in.

The inmate did this, but then started chanting loudly. The sarge went to investigate with another officer. The inmate had his arms in the air with his eyes closed and was chanting real loud, words that made no sense. After the sarge called out his name several times and was ignored with the inmate continuing to chant, he called for the A-Team to remove a disorderly inmate. The A-Team came and ordered the guy to cuff up. He ignored them and continued with his chanting. The sarge radioed the watch commander. As the watch commander was on his way, the inmate stopped chanting. He said he could not stop his prayer until he finished because of his religion.

He was then cuffed up and hauled out.

This is just one of the ways that these guys try to inject religious freedom into being disruptive. It didn't work for this Hispanic chanter.

NOT A MODEL CITIZEN

Inmates are always looking for an angle to play, then again isn't almost anyone?

When an inmate is hired for a job, their status does not change until we notify them that it has changed. They see on a job sheet that gets posted in the cell blocks, who got hired for what jobs.

If they see their name on the list, some feel they have the privileges that a working inmate has. Their status does not change until the day they start. They know the rules but try to play dumb. Actually, playing dumb is one of the best ways to get away with something.

However, it is just like outside of these walls, ignorance is no excuse. If you didn't know it was against the law to kill someone and you do kill someone; tough luck Charlie, you're toast.

Two inmates that were to start jobs on Monday, stayed out of their cells this weekend. When one was caught, he didn't create a problem. When locked in his cell he just yelled out, "They say I gotta keep my ass in all weekend!" Sure he wasn't happy about it, who would be? But he was smart enough to follow the rules when he found out he couldn't get away with breaking them.

The other guy was a different story. He was confrontational. He displayed characteristics that you would not want in a good employee.

He was not very cooperative. That means he was making our job difficult and was threatening about it.

His comments of "This is bullshit" and "Y'all kiss my ass" help to verify his demeanor.

He was placed on In House Detention. That meant "No Job," "You're going to seg," "You're starting all over waiting for a chance at a job" and "You exiled yourself to a lot more time in your cell for a longer period of time."

I guess this guy wasn't in here for being a model citizen anyway.

I JUST TELL MYSELF, I GET PAID BY THE HOUR

An inmate was on IHS status in a cell by the shower post. He had an officer get his cell popped open to come to the bubble to check on a pass. The officer should have refused his request as this inmate was a chronic pain in the ass. It was his way of getting some time out of his cell. After speaking to me while I was working in the bubble, he stopped to have a conversation with another inmate. About a minute later, he slowly went down the flag and stopped to talk to inmates by the exercise equipment. He leaned up against a piece of exercise equipment. I waited several minutes before paging him to his cell to lock him in for being in an unauthorized area. He then slowly headed down the flag again and stopped to talk to some other inmates. I paged him in again, at which time he very slowly complied. I locked him up for being in an unauthorized area and disobeying. Once again, he would've gone to seg if there was room, or if he were violent, room would be made for him. Just being a nuisance would not warrant a trip back there during these times.

NOTE FROM A SARGE

Hello,

Many inmates are hoarding toilet paper. I've seen and confiscated 20 rolls of TP out of one cell. No inmate should have more than 2 rolls a piece. If an inmate runs out, he should bring the empty cardboard roll to get a new roll; the same applies on 3rd watch on Sundays for the weekly issue. Bottom line is only 2 rolls of toilet paper in an inmate's possession and only replace the TP when the inmate produces the empty roll. This should help our TP issue. Any questions let me know. Thanks for your help.

STRANGE IS NORMAL

An inmate reported to me at my door post stating I had called him to the door. I informed him that I did not page him and that he could go back to his cell.

He started complaining loudly saying, "Why you keep wasting my time?"

I informed him three times to just report back to his cell. He did not comply. I directed him to take a seat, which he also chose not to comply with. I called for a 10-14. The A-Team was there immediately to escort him to the security center. The lieutenant spoke to him a short time later and resolved the issue. Sometimes I think I'm working in a psych ward and not a prison. I learned that no matter how ridiculous something seemed in this place, I better take it seriously.

PEER PRESSURE WORKS GREAT

Working inmates in the block had been complaining to me that the unemployed in this block were loud at night. Some requested to move to the back half of the unit where there weren't any unemployed.

After count, I could hear yelling on the flag. When I went to check it out, I caught an inmate yelling to an inmate in another cell. I directed him to quiet down and not to be yelling to people in other cells.

He was loud and argumentative. A few of his comments were, "You gonna send me to seg for talking?" "You talk to your wife like that?" "You talk to your dog like that?"

I informed him a couple of times that the charge would also be disobeying my directives.

He continued to be loud and argumentative until shortly after I walked away. I locked him in his cell so that he could have his chat with the lieutenant the next day. I spoke to four others that quieted down after I spoke to them. I issued them warnings and notified all block officers of the problem and that these were inmates to be watched.

I watched for this problem constantly and was on anyone the instant they started yelling. Once I had the instigators identified by catching them yelling, I yelled out their names when I told them to quiet down. I yelled it so loud that all of the other inmates in this area now knew who was creating the problems. This put major pier pressure on them. Boy, were they pissed off at me for doing that. I then moved them to cells on opposite ends of the tier. They were refusing to move until I told them one way or the other, they were moving. Their choice would be where I told them to go or the hole. They decided to go where I told them. In the days that followed, I had inmates coming up to me and thanking me for solving the problem.

ASSAULTS – EXTORTION – INTIMIDATION

ASSAULT BY OTHERS

A trouble maker inmate was walking around the unit telling others that an inmate he had a beef with was "5-0." This meant that the guy was a cop. That is a good way to get someone ostracized or assaulted.

EFFICIENT ASSAILANT

During breakfast ring out, an inmate reported to me at the door that he had been assaulted. He stated that it happened while he was walking down the flag toward the door. He was punched under his left eye which knocked his glasses off. He was only able to identify the assailant as being a white inmate. He was escorted to the security center where an unclothed body search was conducted on him to see if there were any more injuries. None were found. After viewing tapes, the assailant could not be detected due to the large number of inmates out and blocking what had happened. This time the perpetrator got away with it. Nothing further happened to the assaulted inmate.

ALWAYS KEEP AN EAR OUT

While working the A-East doorpost, I observed two inmates passing by cell XXX. The A-East painter was painting the floor in that cell.

He asked where they were going.

The response was that they were going to Rush City.

The painter said, "Rush, boy that sucks."

The response was, "I'll just smash a few heads and go to Oak Park."

Two officers came to the block to pick up the two inmates for transportation. I informed an officer of what I had heard. I informed her which inmate I believed to have made the statement, but that I could not be 100% sure.

Whenever anyone gave me a tip like this, I appreciated it. It's good to know the mindset of people like this, so you can be extra aware of the higher possibility of assault to yourself or others.

Either this guy was all blow and no go or he chickened out, because nothing happened.

TIPS APPRECIATED

An inmate informed me of an assault that had taken place. I was working the shower post at the time, so I went up to check it out. The man that got assaulted had a split lip. He told me that he had a seizure and fell. I locked him in his cell for his protection and told him we would get him medical attention as soon as possible.

I then went to the assailant and asked to see his hands.

He said, "Man that was quick."

His hands were slightly red and his right eye was a little puffy. The one assaulted was taken to Health Services. The assailant was taken to segregation. I cleaned up a trail of blood that was on the tier. I also accumulated a large bag of bloody clothing and bedding from the cell of the man who was the victim.

CLUMSY

Another clumsy inmate, if you can believe that. Officers on a security check noticed cuts and abrasions on an inmate's face. He was dabbing them with a wash cloth.

"How did you get the injuries to your face?"

"I fell in my cell."

"How many times?" This would seem like a crazy question and it was. It was actually a bit of a humorous question. The officer knew the inmate was trying to cover up a fight he had been in or that he had been assaulted. He knew the injuries could not have been sustained from just one fall.

"I fell" is the common response we get to try to cover up an altercation.

The inmate responded with, "Two times; I have a bad leg."

The officer had him removed by the A-Team and then conducted a search of the cell. Blood was found on the desk and on the floor by the toilet. A bloody wash cloth was on the desk.

The inmate had been released from his cell 90 minutes before to report to the lieutenant's office to be reviewed for a violation that he had been ICR'ed for the day before. He was placed on ICR again.

ATTEMPTED MURDER

Three inmates were fighting close to the bubble. An officer saw it and called for the A-Team. Two black inmates were beating a white inmate. The officer shouted for them to break it up. They ignored him.

Two officers were in the sergeant's office. They had heard the squeaking of inmate's tennis shoes and came out to assist. One of those officers yelled for them to stop and when they did not, he sprayed the two aggressors in the face with his chemical irritant.

The first officer tried to grab one of the black inmates. Before he could, the guy picked up the lid to a trash receptacle, raised it over his head and slammed it down on the white inmate. Seven officers worked on restraining the fighters.

The black inmate that smashed the white inmate with the trash container lid shouted, "What the fuck is wrong with that white boy?" while he was being cuffed up.

They were taken to seg.

None of these guys were speaking up as to the reason for the altercation; however, by the comment by the assailant, we could determine that the "white boy" refused to be intimidated. The "white boy" was not severely injured.

You should know that these trash bins that are scattered throughout the cellblocks are made of thick plate steel. They are large and heavy. The edges are sharp, not like the blade of a knife, but the edges are not rounded. That combined with their weight make the edges a wicked weapon. These trash bins seem to have been a welding project that was given to industry. You won't find anyone picking these things up and hauling them around. A strong person could get one on a cart by themselves. Most people would get someone to help them get the trash can on a cart to take them to the shower to clean them. The lid itself is very heavy. To pick one of these lids up and smash someone with it, I would call that attempted murder.

After this incident, maintenance was made to come in and fasten the lids to the bottom container with steel cables. This way no one would be able to throw a lid again.

INMATE CONNECTIONS

Beware whose kids you pididdle. You may be housed with them some day.

I have no idea if pididdle is an actual word. Spell check did not like it. Whether I heard it or made it up, I think you get the general idea without being graphic.

An inmate reported to officers that he was assaulted by his cellmate.

"What happened?"

"I don't know. I was watching TV and my cellmate hit me in the face and head."

When the sarge asked the assailant why he whacked the guy, he said, "He's a fucking chimo! He molested my friend's kids."

I guess you know where this guy wound up going.

THREAT TO ACHIEVE A GOAL

A couple of ways to try to get in a cell by yourself is to act crazy or threaten your cell mate. An inmate stated to his cell mate, "You are a young punk ass bitch. I'm going to kick your ass. I'm not just some old man. I'm going to teach you a lesson."

There were no cells available in B-West, so the inmate threatening violence was moved to D-Hall and locked up, which is probably just what he wanted.

HISPANIC GANG WAR

In B-West, a lieutenant spoke with two Hispanic inmates that lived in the same cell. One was a known "Latin King" and the other was a known "Sur 13." They both said they had no gang affiliation and that they had no incompatibility issues. This was quite suspect as word around the prison was that these groups were gearing up for a fight for Hispanic power. In a little over an hour from the time of this interview, the war was on.

It started with two of them fighting on the fourth tier. When they finished fighting, they went to get their people together.

Quickly, one guy was attacked from both sides on tier three. One of this guy's affiliates saw him being teamed up on. He lived on the second tier, so he ran up to a friend on the third tier, obtained a ten inch steel shank from him and ran to the rescue. By this time, it was four against one.

When officers arrived, they saw the guy with the shank and his buddy standing up to a group of 6. The group was backing up, as they didn't want to get shanked. They were all looking for an advantage. The shank created a stalemate.

Officers directed them all to get on the floor. There was no compliance, so officers started spraying their chemical irritant at them. The officers went in on the group. They were met with resistance, but over took them.

The inmate with the shank was coming at an officer. The officer directed him several times to drop the shank as he was spraying the inmate in the face. The inmate leaned over the railing and tossed the shank to the tier below as he lay down on the tier. The shank landed in a cell on the second tier.

The inmate that had the shank was being taken back to segregation through A-West. An A-West inmate saw him and attacked. He threw a punch at the restrained inmate's face. One of the officers deflected most of the punch with his elbow. The assailant was then cuffed up and added to the collection of inmates being processed for new homes in segregation. A minimum of ten inmates had been involved in these fights.

An inmate in the cell that the shank landed in informed an officer that it was there.

Another inmate went up to an officer and said, "I was involved. Take me to seg." He also told them to look at the tapes. He was obviously afraid to stay in the unit with fewer of his gang available to him.

It is only a little over a month from Christmas and these guys seem to have forgotten about "Peace on earth and good will toward men." Actually, they probably don't even care about that on Christmas Day.

NOT ALL PENS ARE USED FOR WRITING

In "Doghouse," an inmate was laying on his bed reading shortly before the institution was going to be secured for the night. He had not secured his door.

Why these guys don't secure their doors is beyond me. There is always someone in this place that given the opportunity will wreak havoc on you for whatever reason.

Two inmates entered his cell and started stabbing him. The shank was some kind of a pen. After they left, the victim left his cell and tried to get some help. As he passed by his assailant's cells, one of them came up behind him, held him against the rail and again began stabbing him again with a pen. The assailant also tried to throw him over the top railing of the fourth tier.

An officer noticing called for an A-Level response. As some officers were going up the stairs approaching the victim, the victim was saying, "Help me! Help me!" He was covered in blood. As they saw him only from the front at this time, they observed that he was bleeding from his chest and head.

An officer saw one of the assailants walking away from him. He ordered him to stop. He complied, was cuffed up and taken to segregation.

The institution response was upgraded to a B-Level, so they could have more officers there to get the block switched in, secure cells and search for the weapon.

The victim had been cuffed up and was taken to Health Services. He said that they were trying to kill him. By trying to get away and twisting, he received stab wounds in his back and extremities. They were stabbing him where ever they could to try to kill him. He had 38 stab wounds in addition to getting beaten.

He was able to identify the assailants. An officer went to the remaining inmate's cell and checked his hands and knuckles. His knuckles were cut up from beating the guy. He was cuffed up and taken to segregation.

While responding to the fight, an officer had seen the weapon fly over his head and out the window. It was found outside in the window well.

The victim needed to be taken to the hospital in an ambulance.

One of the assailants was a murderer set to be released in 2112. The other was in for assaulting someone with a knife and has been released.

SOME WATCH THEIR LANGUAGE

Generally, inmates are not dumb enough to let officers hear them threatening someone or let them see them preparing to attack someone. However, on this day, a couple of officers were escorting the nurse through the unit while she delivered medication to those who needed it. They heard yelling coming from a cell. They saw one inmate cowering near the sink in the back of a cell. They saw two other inmates' just inches from this guys face. One said he was going to "fuck him up." The other one did not use that foul of language. He said he was going to "mess him up." I guess that predator had a better upbringing than the other one.

The consequence for all of them was to be removed from the unit and be kept separated.

PINBALL WIZARD

An inmate notified an officer that an inmate that lived on the top bunk in a cell in B-West had a problem with his face. Both sides of his face were swollen, both eyes were purple and the left eye was almost swollen shut. There was bruising on the bridge of his nose and scratches on his lower forehead.

The officer checked it out. He asked how it happened.

"I hooked my foot on my bed and fell on the desk."

He was escorted to see the nurse. When asked by her what happened, he said, "I was getting up to go to the toilet. My foot got caught up in the blanket. I fell out of the bed and hit my face on the desk and then the floor."

There were no other marks any place else on his entire body.

OK, who votes for assault and who votes for believing his story?

Sure, it's possible that he fell, but he lives in B-West and it's 1030am. There has been ample time for someone to get to him. Did I forget to mention that he said his roommate never woke up as his face was pin balling around the room? Is it possible that he made no noise at all when this happened? Is it possible that his roommate found him annoying?

He said he didn't have any pain. With your face looking like this, would you have any pain? Is it possible that Hitler was a humanitarian?

You be the judge.

PMB VS NAZI LOW RIDER

The breaks were released back in segregation one evening for the inmates to be able to come out for recreation. This makes it possible for them to interact with 15 other inmates on their half of the tier as these areas are all fenced in and sectioned in half by gates.

As soon as the inmates were able to get out of their cells, loud yelling was heard to be coming from the front half of the second tier. An inmate was being attacked in his cell. The attacker was holding his victim against the wall with his left hand and stabbing him with his right. The victim fell to the floor. The assailant kept punching him while he had him down.

When officers got to them, the officers yelled, "Get down on the ground!"

Both inmate's followed the directives with the aggressor being a bit slower, so two officers helped him out.

The victim's face was covered in blood, so the officers put a spit mask on him to help protect themselves from any possible exposure to a disease. It appeared as though he was bleeding from his abdomen, mouth and chest.

The attacker was yelling, "I was set up! You fucking set me up! (The sergeant) set me up by putting me on the same gallery as that guy. He's a PMB (Prison Motorcycle Brotherhood) and I'm a Nazi Low Rider. That's just asking for trouble." Of course it wasn't his fault that he planned an attack and executed it.

He had small cuts on his hands. He said, "I got these cuts from the knife I had when I broke it in half and flushed it down the toilet."

A U shaped piece of metal was found in the toilet of the victim's cell. It was sharpened on one end and had strips of fabric torn from a sheet wrapped on the other end. The fabric was stained with blood. Obviously, the assailant had not broken the knife. He had only bent it. It had not gone down when the toilet was flushed.

He also had two sets of clothing on to help protect him a bit from any retaliation.

The aggressor was yelling, "That's how we do things in South Central! We kill motherfuckers! 213 South Central L.A.! That's how we do it in the 213 area code! You crackers need to represent!"

The assailant was locked up in a quiet cell.

The victim was put in another quiet cell to be worked on. Two of his teeth had been knocked out. They had to cut his clothes off. One officer could see blood coming out of at least five puncture wounds on his left bicep and at least six from his left chest area. There was too much blood flowing out of his body to detect anything else. Officers were applying pressure to as many wounds as they could. He stated that he felt like he was going to pass out. There was a lot of blood in front of three cells in the area of his attack. He had lost a lot more blood since then. Staff elevated his legs to try to keep him conscience. As soon as the ambulance arrived the EMT's took over and rushed him to the hospital.

ENTREPRENEUR

One inmate was extorting others for specific canteen items. He had lists of every inmate he was extorting, the items he required them to give him and prices listed for those items. With those items he was running a store. This means he would sell those items to other inmates for other items or favors. Of course he would save as much of it as he wanted for himself.

VIOLENT HOCKEY GAME

An inmate was found in his cell washing his face. The sarge detected something was wrong. He directed the inmate to turn on his light and come and talk to him. He refused the orders for a while, but eventually complied. When he did, the sarge noticed that his face was very swollen. When he asked how it happened the inmate said it was during hockey. There was no report on it and a beaten face is not consistent with a hockey injury. He was taken to the security center to be checked over by a nurse. Officers found two bloody T-shirts, a bloody pair of sweat shorts and a bloody shoe in his cell.

It's amazing how violent hockey has become in prisons. With hockey injuries like this, it seems necessary to assign every participant a goalie mask.

REQUEST TO BE BEATEN

It is my distinct opinion that an inmate decided that he wanted other inmates to beat him up. Why do I believe this?

He went up to an officer and said, "I want to see the Watch Commander."

The officer asked him what his issue was.

He complained about water being on the flag by the ice machines. He was getting very worked up over it. He said, "None of these fucking swampers do their job. They are fucking lazy." He pointed to gallery two and said, "It's that fat fucker that lives on two who won't do his job."

Many inmates were in the area observing and hearing this. Breaking the inmate code of not fronting off other inmates will get one broken up. This guy blurted it out for all to hear.

The officer told him he needed to observe the chain of command and speak to the sergeant. The inmate walked away, but came back. The officer told him that he would probably have better results if he wasn't disrespectful, yelling, swearing and pointing fingers at people.

The count bell rang. The inmate turned around to go to his cell. As he was turning around, he shouted, "These fucking CO's don't do their job either. They're fucking lazy."

Lucky for this guy, he was escorted to segregation before anyone was released from their cells after count cleared.

DON'T FLUSH THE EVIDENCE

An inmate living on gallery 7 came to an officer seeking help.

"Someone is out to get me."

"Why?"

"Someone placed a note on my bed that said I was going to be thrown over the railing."

He avoided the question as to why someone was after him. He said he flushed the note down the toilet, thus destroying any evidence, if there ever was a note.

With this situation, the best that could be done was to lock him up by placing him on ICR and having him discuss it with the lieutenant the next day.

CONSENSUAL BEATING

During a security check, officers noticed an inmate kneeling on the floor between the sink and the bunk. He had several abrasions on the left side of his face and was dabbing his ear with a wet towel. The floor was wet.

The inmate stated that he was cleaning his floor, became light headed, lost his balance, knocked the back of his head on the sink, fell forward and hit his head on the edge of the steel bed frame.

One of the officers checked the bed frame and did not find any blood. As they spoke, the officers noticed scratches on the right side of his neck and his left ear was turning purple.

The inmate was escorted to Health Services where he was treated for his injuries. They determined the injuries to be consistent with those resulting from an altercation or assault.

During an unclothed body search, more scratches were found on his neck. Pictures were taken and entered into evidence. The inmate was taken to seg for his safety.

The next day, video tape was viewed. This inmate and another were identified. They met and had a discussion in the brake area between gallery's 3 and 7. They went up to the brake area between gallery's 4 and 8 where they were less likely to be seen due to extra fencing in that area. They squared off and started fighting. They took each other to the floor. After 3 to 4 minutes, they separated. A few minutes later they went at it again and went to the floor again. Eventually, they stopped fighting and went their separate ways. Shortly after this, the officers were viewed entering the inmate's cell.

The inmate that the officers found on the floor in the cell had gloves on during the fight. This indicated that he was expecting some sort of altercation. Wearing gloves protects your hands from abrasions in case officers come around checking them. It's apparent that either one of them could've avoided the fight and didn't. Their wounds would have plenty of time to heal relaxing in segregation.

REQUEST DENIED

An inmate kite was as follows:

"I am in B-West as a regular transfer from St. Cloud. I have to keep my B-West cell hall worker job for 90 days before I can get a job in a different cell block.

I've been threatened before. I was again threatened at the supper meal today as I was doing my job on the landing between gallery three and seven. Another inmate, who witnessed this, told me this guy is known for assaulting people for no reason. I do not wish to go to "P.C." (protective custody), but don't think I should be forced to stay in this unit either."

This kite was given to an officer to give to the unit lieutenant. The officer placed both inmates on ICR. The predator was a major trouble maker in the prison.

QUICK TRIP TO THE HOLE

An officer noticed an inmate spotting, so she took his mirror and labeled it to be returned to him in one week.

Fourteen minutes later, he threw a bar of soap at her. It missed and banged against the bubble.

He said, "I'm going to get you."

He threw a juice box at her and hit her in the waist.

Guess what? Threatening, disorderly conduct and staff assault got him a quick trip to the hole.

TWO FOR THE PRICE OF ONE

During the evening feeding, an inmate going through the line demanded that the server open another bin of bread and give him some from the middle of a loaf. He said, "The next time you try to give me the ends of bread, I'm going to pop you in your jizzle." Deciphered, this means punch you in the jaw.

The officer witnessing this told the inmate that he was not to be threatening other inmates.

He said, "Whatever" and began to walk away.

The officer directed him to come back and finish talking with him.

"What do you want? Do you want to go? What are you going to do? What are you going to do, huh?" The inmate turned around and put his tray on the table readying himself for an altercation with the officer.

The officer called for a 10-14. He directed the inmate to turn around and put his hands behind his back.

"You better not touch me." he warned as he started walking toward the A-Team officers that came to get him.

Another inmate decided that he wanted to leave too. He said to the officer, "That was bullshit! That was trumped man. I saw the whole thing and that man didn't do anything wrong."

One of the A-Team officers said something to him. What, I don't know, but this officer was a member of the SORT team, (Special Operations Response Team), and wasn't into putting up with any nonsense.

The inmate said, "Don't touch me."

He spun around and was postured to strike the officer.

Wow! This was two hot shots going to the hole with one push of the button. Wise guys never know when to shut their yaps.

SNITCH OR NOT

An inmate hollered to a sergeant from his cell that he wanted to speak to her. She went to see what he wanted.

"I don't feel safe on my gallery."

"Why?"

"When my gallery was let out for feeding, someone punched me in the arm."

"Do you know who it was?"

"No, but because my cellmate went to seg and I did not, everyone thinks I'm a snitch."

He wanted to be moved.

The sarge ICR'ed him so he could have this conversation with the lieutenant the next day.

SORTING IT OUT

The door officer's attention was directed to an inmate in a cell on the flag close to the door that was waving a bloody shirt out of his cell. The officer went over to investigate. When asked what had happened, he said that someone had entered his cell and assaulted him. He stated that he did not know who it was. The sergeant was called along with the A-Team. They had to handle the situation as the officer had to handle the door post. The assaulted inmate was taken to segregation. Inmates don't always end up in seg because they did something wrong. They may be put there for their safety. They may be put there to give staff time to investigate so they can make the best determination possible. Just because we are told something, that doesn't necessarily mean that is what happened. An incompetent predator may wind up looking like a victim.

SLEEP TIGHT

An inmate reported that his cellmate had threatened him. The inmate said, "This dude said, I need to move or I might not wake up in the morning."

How would you like going to sleep with a criminal in the room that said that to you?

ASSAILANT LOSES

An inmate reported to the bubble officer that he had just gotten into it with his cellmate. I find this one rather funny. The reporting inmate had bite marks on his wrist and forearm.

When officers asked the cellmate what happened, he said, "Right before lunch, he got off the bed and started hitting me."

Why do I find this humorous? I see it that the attacker got what was coming to him and then was himself afraid instead of intimidating the other guy. He felt he could establish dominance over his cellmate by attacking him. He found out it was more like attacking a wolverine or a bear that was cornered. That's a wicked situation. The fists came flying and the teeth started chomping. Dominance was established by the one who was to be the victim. The attacker was now afraid of retaliation and had to go to officers for protection. I like stories like these.

PAINFUL WEAPONS

An inmate received information that another inmate was going to throw hot water on him. He found this credible as that inmate had previously spit on him. He would not divulge what started these actions. He stated that he did not want any trouble, but would defend himself if he were attacked.

The lieutenant had the other inmate placed in a cell that would ensure that he could do no harm until he was able to speak to both inmates.

Heating up water in a micro wave and tossing it on someone has been done before. I would rather take a beating than have the pain that comes with an assault of that nature.

WIENER

An annoying mouthy inmate, the kind that never grew out of that stage of being a wiener, was whining again. He was a white guy that had been a wiener to a black guy.

Who started this is impossible to know for sure. Wiener may have made some stupid comment or the other inmate may have been having fun bugging the wiener.

In any case, it seems as though Wiener threw orange juice on the other guy. The other guy was able to reach through the bars enough to slap Wieners face.

Now, if you know wieners like I know wieners, slapping their face probably would not have been satisfying enough. You just have to do something else because you know that forever, they are going to be an annoying wiener.

The other guy tossed some kind of a liquid into Wiener's cell and onto his bedding.

That is when Wiener started whining. More often than not, wieners start something and then call for help to have someone finish it for them.

The officer told the other guy to return to his cell. As he walked away, he said, "When I get flag with that dude again, I'm gonna kick his ass."

When Wiener was let out of his cell to get his supper, he tried inciting any black inmate that could hear him by yelling out, "I'll write kites on all you fuckers and have the whole gallery placed on ICR. I've done it before. I'll do it again."

He may have written kites on guys and got some locked up once in a while, but not an entire gallery. Also, once someone establishes themselves as wieners, they become like the little boy who cried wolf. We have to keep them safe, because that is our job, but you just wait for the day a little prison justice comes their way.

THE SIGN WAS THERE

A bubble officer noticed one inmate following another. As they walked by a wet floor sign, the inmate following the other picked up the sign and began striking the other with it. The victim tried to get away. The aggressor dropped the sign and continued the beating with his fists. The victim tried running away and made it into the barber cell, where the aggressor kept punching him. An officer sprayed him with chemical irritant in order to put an end to the attack. Once the squad hauled the inmates out, officers had to clean up the blood. The victim was never seen throwing a punch, so he would return after he was cared for and things were sorted out.

IT'S NOT SMART TO FOOL WITH THE SARGE

During linen exchange, an inmate protested to the sergeant that an officer was charging him for not turning in a sheet. The sarge checked and found out the inmate only turned in one sheet, so he told him he was being charged for the one he did not return.

The inmate said, "I'm not paying for shit!" At this point, the inmate pushed his left shoulder into the sergeant's chest trying to push the sarge out of the way.

Not a smart move! This is an officer assault. This got the jerk a quick trip to segregation with a charge that would most likely get him a quick trip to the Oak Park Heights Prison.

Are you old enough to remember seeing that commercial where Mother Nature is saying, "It's not nice to fool with Mother Nature?" Well, I have one for the inmates; "It's not smart to fool with the sarge."

NOT SO SMART

Cell hall workers were allowed to live in single cells.

A cell hall worker was asked to do his job. He stated that it was not his "Motherfuckin' Job."

The officer again told him to accomplish the task.

The inmate stated that he was going to complain to the lieutenant.

The officer told him that was his right, but that he still needed to do the task. He did it, but later, when a lot of inmates were around, he created a scene.

He yelled out that he did not need that "Motherfuckin' Job" and that he was going to quit. He said to the officer, "I won't work for a mother fucker like you."

The officer had me report to his location to take the guy to his cell and lock him in. Whether he really wanted to quit or not, he effectively was now unemployed and would be moved into a double bunked cell.

He later was heard issuing threats concerning that officer.

Now, wasn't that smart of him? He went from living comfortably in a single cell with a job that allowed him to be out of his cell all day to being locked up most of the day in a double bunked cell waiting to be escorted to segregation. Guess he showed that officer.

SOUTHERN EXTORTIONIST

Another extortionist was dumb enough to have written a note to one of his victims. This extortionist was more like a loan shark. Information in the note exposed that this guy was getting items and also trading items. The note stated, "I will be at yawl's gym on Friday and Sunday, so make sure that you bring some shit with you. I got some more for you, but I got to see if you keep your word and get me together by Sunday."

PART OF THE GAME

Intimidation tactics really don't work on most officers. A couple of officers were escorting an inmate to segregation.

The inmate was yelling, "You guys only searched "my" cell and are out to get me. I'm going to get you for harassing me. What are your names?"

I loved these guys. They were punks that got caught. They weren't real men. They have slid by all of their lives by being big mouthed idiots. That is how they landed in here. There was no way to have any respect for this type of a person. I could respect the inmate that tried something, got caught and took ownership of it. It was part of the game in this place.

PREDATOR

An officer received the following kite that caused two inmates to be secured away from each other.

You will see, "Extortionist", as I do not use people's real names as they generally are of no consequence.

You will see "property." This refers to the officers at Oak Park Heights that are responsible for checking inmate's property lists when inmates enter or leave the institution. If someone buys something, they enter it on that inmate's property list. This way they make sure that whatever an inmate enters with and also buys, the inmate leaves with.

Inmates are not allowed to buy, sell or give anything to other inmates.

To B-West staff: I am having a problem with an inmate who I was at Oak Park Heights with. His name is Extortionist. The problem occurred today during our flag period, where Extortionist made several threats, even death threats, saying I owed him more for some tennis shoes he had of mine at the other prison. Extortionist was extorting money from me and when I transferred from Oak Park Heights to Rush City prison, the Oak Park Heights "property" went and retrieved my Addidas I bought for $100.00 and Extortionist got at Oak Park Heights. Now Extortionist came to me today and claimed he got in trouble for that and demanded I pay him for those shoes and I must pay him more later on. He claimed if I get the CO's involved he will have me killed he said (death threats he made). Please see me as I believe I will have serious problems If I do not be separated from him. Thank You!!!

More often than not, if an inmate is being extorted threatened or harassed by any other inmate, if they notify an officer, it will stop. Both inmates will be called in to speak to a lieutenant. This shows that it is known what has been going on and if the intimidator knows what is best for him, it will stop immediately.

INTIMIDATION DENIED

An inmate was transferred into B-West. I assigned him to an upper bunk in a cell on the flag. He reported back to me that the inmate in that cell was refusing to let him come into that cell. I radioed this situation to the OIC. The A-Team soon extracted the disruptive inmate out of the unit.

With the extremely high volume of inmates being transferred in and out of this unit, when we tell an inmate something is going to be a certain way, they better have a very good explanation if they want it changed. This guy just tried intimidating the inmate that I sent to his cell. That would not be tolerated.

RUSH CITY ASSAULT

Anything can be a weapon. Where do we draw the line on what these guys are allowed to have?

They have razors that they use as weapons against other inmates, themselves and officers. Officers can get cut on them when searching cells.

They walk around with pens and pencils behind their ears that can be pulled down and used against anyone at any time.

They have microwaves. The use of these as a weapon are not as frequent, but very harmful when they are used.

We were alerted to an incident that happened at the Rush City Prison located about an hour north of Stillwater Prison.

A sergeant was attacked by three inmates. They threw boiling hot coffee on his face. They teamed up on him kicking and hitting him. One of them took his mace, sprayed him with it and sprayed the officers arriving to help the sergeant.

Every inmate in the unit was out of their cells. They were cheering as the assault went on.

The sergeant would eventually recover, but that always sounds better than the truth. The truth is that after something like this, there are generally scars, chronic pain forever and who know what all else the victim will have to deal with. There are lasting mental repercussions from attacks that few officers are ever able to avoid while doing their time in a prison.

REASON FOR ZERO HORSEPLAY TOLERANCE

While securing the front flag from linen exchange, I observed an older crotchety inmate in his sixties with his arm up by the laundry officer's shoulder. This looked a bit strange, but especially with inmates that officers have known for quite a while, a camaraderie displaying itself in horseplay can develop. The officer was backing away from the inmate. I made eye contact with the officer. He gave me no indication that he was in trouble, so I continued on. That instant, I heard him make a call on the radio that he had just been assaulted. I turned around and went to him as did two other officers. We were there instantly and stood between the inmate and the officer. One officer spoke to the inmate to try to get him to back off, but the inmate kept pushing towards the officer. The inmate had to be restrained by holding his arms behind him and pushing him toward the front of the block for the A-Team to take him to segregation.

MAIL

A FOR EFFORT & CREATIVITY

An inmate had a package addressed to him. The "From" address was Meshbesher & Associates, Attorneys at Law.

Enclosed was a stack of inkjet printed papers approximately 1 ½ inches thick. They looked like they had gotten wet and were stuck together. The pages would not separate easily. The officer bent the pages to try to separate them. When he did this, it came apart enough to reveal a secret compartment that had been cut out of the center. The area cut out was about 4 inches by 7 inches. A vacuum sealed bag filled with marijuana completely filled the cavity.

This is not saying that this package was from Meshbesher & Associates. Anyone can address a package to be from anyone. It would be assumed that a package from a prestigious law firm would be under less scrutiny that one addressed from Charles Manson. That is not the case. If we are doing our jobs properly, every package is treated the same, suspiciously.

Hopefully that covers my ass from those lawyers coming after me and suing me for everything thing I have. That would be a waste of their time and the joke would be on them as I have nothing of value. My will consists only of how to dispose of my body.

Of course I'm not saying it wasn't from them either. Oh, oh; did I get myself in trouble again?

Actually, they should pay me for mentioning them. There are thousands of guys locked up in prison that would seek their services now.

Hey, guys! What's my commission on something like that? If I accept a cut, would I wind up living in prison or can you create a good enough shelter so that no one would know?

REOFFENDING IS FOR SURE

An inmate asked an officer to help explain some words in a legal document that he received. While the officer was helping him in understanding what the document was stating, the inmate said, "I know this is for my civil commitment hearing. I don't know why they are wasting their time with this. If I don't get civilly committed when I am released, I will reoffend without a doubt."

MAIL REFUSAL

Inmates generally love to get mail. One inmate chose to refuse legal mail from the Ramsey County Attorney's Office Child Support Enforcement Division.

I wonder why.

OMBUDSMAN

A nongovernmental complaint investigator: somebody, responsible for investigating and resolving complaints from consumers or other members of the public against a company, institution, or other organization.

The Ombudsman Program was created after the riots at the prison in Attica, New York. It may have been needed back then. I don't know, because I wasn't working here then. If I had been, I would be a totally whacked out basket case by now.

There was an ombudsman program in effect when I entered the prison. When the state hit a budget crisis in 2003, it was eliminated.

When it was eliminated, the prison had officers volunteer to assist inmates with their complaints. I volunteered.

Because the inmates knew me for knowing and following institution policy, no one ever used me, officially that is.

Many of them sought my advice on the side. Giving advice was not my role. Informing them of policy was. If they had officially sought my help, I would've been allowed to investigate for them. No matter how much time I spent explaining policies to these guys, they would keep pressing me to find some way out of the predicament they created for themselves.

There was not a single inmate that came to me because they were innocent of the charges against them. Every one of them was looking for a loop hole out of what they had done.

There are plenty of groups, organizations and people just waiting for an opportunity to assist the poor mistreated inmate. Some people out there thrive on an opportunity to spout off about what they know nothing about.

The contacts of the inmates threaten negative publicity to politicians. They threaten to go to the press if their precious mistreated little boy is not coddled whenever he whines. This is generally enough to let the inmate get his way.

For those legitimate problems, there are plenty of us officers that would go to bat for an inmate to get them justice.

Working here, we know what it is like. Speaking up for one's self generally does not get action. Others speaking up for you will help to get the unjust to back off.

I saw some articles by a reporter that was pitching the great need for the ombudsman program to return. I'll grant him his opinion no matter how ill informed it is. However, this reporter owes it to the public to get it right; that is his job. Unfortunately, this reporter works for a newspaper that I find highly credible and that gives him credibility that he does not deserve.

"The poor mistreated inmate needs our protection" is always the pitch in articles like this. These people believe everything an inmate tells them. Hey you morons that go about sticking your nose into something you know nothing about; leave managing inmates up to the professionals. We work with these people. We know who is credible and who isn't. Even if we don't trust someone, we investigate and get the facts. We are locked in with them. We are here. We are competent. We do our job. You are just a busy body wanting attention and trying to feel important.

We are here doing our job every day and not seeking any recognition. We are the people that try to keep things calm and just in this place. We are the people that you don't even think about. We are keeping you safe from the people that are locked up here.

These people always get their facts wrong or make them sound bad. Your supposed facts are useless. They are not correct. Many things go unreported by inmates and staff. Your letters are generally from the whiney inmate that was babied by their mother. The inmates that are adult and take responsibility for what they did are overall decent people that went down the wrong path. People die in prison. People are killed in prison. People kill themselves in prison. People are raped in prison. People are beat up in prison. These people are inmates and officers.

When you put 250 inmates in a cell block with 5 officers, there is only so much we can do. But you don't want to pay to have more officers in there with them do you? Then shut your yap and tend to what you are good at, if there is anything other than being a know it all that knows nothing.

It may sound like I am against an ombudsman program. I am not, but I am against wasting money. There are plenty of people in the prison system that could better handle these complaints without spending more money.

A past ombudsman said it was impossible for us officers to conduct impartial investigations. This person also said they served as a safety valve for staff as well as inmates.

Do you detect a conflict of interest here? Maybe you detect a conflict of interest in my view point too. I strongly believe that everyone employed by the state should be followed up on, but the fix must come from the top on down, not the bottom on up. And unless you thought otherwise, corrections officers are the bottom. An inmate has more rights than we do!

RACISM

9-11

9-11-01 I was conducting a security check when the 9-11 travesties transpired. The inmate in a cell close to the door told me to take a look at what was on his television. This was right when the planes had flown into the towers and it wasn't known what was going on yet. This inmate was shocked by it.

As more information was received or hypothesized, other inmates were hooting and hollering. Most of these guys celebrating were Muslim. They were all for our country being invaded and for any non Muslim being killed.

RACIST INTIMIDATION TACTIC

An inmate worker called me to the supply cell to inform me of problems he was having doing his job as the second watch supply cell swamper. He was upset about inmates coming into the cell, taking supplies and his inability to stop them. He was very loud and was unwilling to inform me of the problems as they occurred or who the problem people were. I informed him that he had three options. Enforce the requirements of his job, move to a different swamper position if I could find someone to take his position or to quit. At this point he called me a racist. I never took kindly to this manipulation tactic. Many inmates tried to use this on me and others in an intimidation tactic to scare us into not doing our jobs. I was solid on my actions, speaking and mindset never being anything close to being a racist. That was definitely not the way to get me to see things their way, so I gave him several directives to switch in before he finally complied and then I fired his racist ass.

LITTLE HITLER, TRAINING BY A RACIST

Sometimes I wonder how some of these jerks ever got hired. It could be understood that a bad apple sneak in here or there, but the number of bad employees we got stuck working with was ridiculous.

Luckily, I didn't get stuck working with Little Hitler very often because he worked first watch, 10pm to 6am. It was my first time on first watch in D-Hall. The kitchen workers were housed here. Some had to get up and be at work by about 4am. One of the guys alarm went off. He didn't wake up. Little Hitler told me to put a warning ticket on his cell bars. I didn't agree with it, but I just figured this was procedure in this block. At this time, I was not aware of this officer's reputation.

It is important to know that the inmate was a black man. Also, unbeknownst to me at this time, Little Hitler was a racist. I believed this guy was training me in on procedures on this watch.

Before the inmate left for work, he came to me irate about the warning ticket. I couldn't defend myself for doing it because I didn't agree with doing it in the first place.

A few weeks later, while I was working in the kitchen at 4:30am, this inmate and I had another couple of run ins. He was still upset with me because of the warning ticket and once again Little Hitler was there using me to enforce policy that others had not been enforcing and that he was afraid to enforce.

The report I wrote went as follows:

Workers are to check in with the kitchen officer upon arrival to the kitchen and put their ID in the rack. He refuses to do so. Yesterday when he had to pass by me I asked him for his ID. He ignored me and kept going. I was dealing with other workers at the time, so I was unable to pursue him. He dropped it off later. Today he never checked in either. When spoken to, he comes off with a major attitude. This has been an ongoing problem every time I have opened the kitchen. I was instructed to file this report now and not say anything to him at this point in time due to his temper. The issue will be handled later when more staff is present.

He wound up in the hole for a short time because of this, but got his job back when he got out. The next time we ran into each other, he came up to me. He said that while he was in seg he found out some things and pieced them together. He realized that Little Hitler was with me each time. He remembered that I was being trained in on the overnight shift. He had seen me a bit before I was moved to first watch and we had no problems. He said, "Little Hitler told you what to do didn't he."

I said that he did, but I had to admit that I wasn't happy about the attitude he had been giving me.

He apologized and said he let his anger get the best of him. From this time on, we had a great friendly relationship.

LITTLE HITLER'S COWARDICE COMES THROUGH

Little Hitler worked first watch because he was afraid of the inmates. Part of the reason he was afraid of them was because he was a jerk to them. However, even without that, I believe he was afraid of them from day one. That is why he worked first watch. Most of them were locked up and sleeping during this watch.

The one place that they weren't locked up was outside the walls in the Minimum Security Unit, MSU. This is where we had our major altercation.

We were running short of staff. There are supposed to be two officers out at MSU over night. We only had one and it was Little Hitler. He was out there alone with over 100 inmates. This didn't set well with him.

I was assigned to car patrol. The car patrol officer is supposed to cruise around the exterior of the institution all night. He is also supposed to pick up the count slip from MSU and deliver it inside the institution to the watch commander at midnight and 4am. When we are short staff, the car patrol is to do a thorough round of the outside of the institution, checking all locks, gates, nooks and crannies and anything appearing out of the ordinary and then report to MSU for the rest of the night.

When I had just started doing my security checks, Little Hitler was on the radio telling me I had to report to MSU. I responded that I had to do security checks first. He responded that I should make it quick. Before I finished, he was on the radio again yelling for me to report to MSU. I knew my responsibilities at this point. I responded back that I would be there upon completion of my rounds, which I was close to finishing. He told me to hurry up. As I was pulling up to the MSU building, he was radioing me again screaming at me. I did not respond. I was there. He was at the entry at the top of the stairs. This guy was scared out of his mind and trying to cover it up by yelling at me. He knew he couldn't get away with yelling at all of those inmates. He found out that he couldn't get away with it with me either.

I went swiftly up the stairs at him, stopped right in front of him and yelled back that I was doing my job the way I was instructed and that I would not tolerate anyone yelling at me. He backed up quickly and ran into the building. He had the inmates inside that he was afraid of and me in front of him that he was running from. He was really afraid now in order to be running back toward the inmates. He tried to cover his fear by telling me to step out to the parking lot to fight him. I laughed at him. If I would've done it we both would've been fired. This really pissed him off. He was spazzing out, yelling and shaking, angry and afraid. He told me he was going to call the watch commander. I told him to go ahead. He called the watch commander and complained to him about me. As he was hanging up, the lieutenant was on the radio directing me to pick him up at the front of the institution. As I was heading out the door, I told Little Hitler to have fun being alone with all of the guys.

When I got to the front of the prison, the lieutenant was standing at the top of the stairs waiting for me. He was a new transfer to this prison from Oak Park Heights. He got in the small pickup truck and told me not to go to MSU yet; to just drive around awhile. He told me that upon hearing Little Hitler's radio transmissions, officers inside had already informed him about this guy being a problem many times before. While driving around, he had me fill him in on the details. When I finished, he wanted to know if I wanted to write him up. I told him, not unless I have to; and that I would just like the problem taken care of and not have to deal with this guy's inappropriate behavior again. He was happy with that. He appreciated not having to do any extra paperwork.

When we got to MSU, he talked to Little Hitler. He chastised him a bit and then was real easy on him. He was patronizing him. He almost laid the problem on me now that we were in front of this guy; almost but not quite. I wanted to see this guy get his ass reamed. Nothing close to that happened. Because the lieutenant was filled in on this guy and wanted the night to go smoothly, he was almost kissing his ass. I'm thinking, let him blow up at you so you can fire him, I have no problem being out here alone. I can understand why he handled it the way he did, but now I wish I would've written the guy up.

For some strange reason, I never had to work with him again.

RACIST GETS HIS COME UP-UNS

There was an officer on first watch that when we worked together we had a great time. Officer Banger and I saw the job the same way. We worked hard and took care of the inmates needs. He was a black man about my height, but without as much fat. Knowing he is black is necessary to know about when we get to the conflict between him and Little Hitler.

Officer Banger was a former gang member from Chicago. There was a guy in Chicago that was a big problem for the police. He was bad mouthing Banger to other people. Banger smashed down the guy's door, shot him in the leg and left. A lot of the guy's friends were there at the time. Banger called the guy and told him that if he gave him up to the cops, he would come back and finish the job. While the cops were there, the guy's friends were saying, "It was Banger." The guy that got shot kept saying, "No, it wasn't Banger." The cops eventually had a chat with Banger. Instead of him getting in trouble, they told him it was a good job.

After I was no longer on this shift, I was told that Little Hitler and Banger had to work together one night. Obviously Little Hitler couldn't keep his mouth shut. Racial slurs were used. When they got off work, Little Hitler went to his car to leave. Banger went to Little Hitler's car too. He pulled Little Hitler out of his car and finished the night's conversation with an exclamation point, his fists.

I heard that Bangers final days came from not showing up consistently and that Little Hitler's final days came around the same time because of him using racial slurs. These may have been the reasons used, but also they may have found out about their fight after the fact and wanted to get rid of them whichever way they could.

RACIST MUSLIM

A-East had a barber of black and white origin that wasn't very good and was creating problems. He didn't like my rules, so he got A-West to hire him. Shortly after he had transferred over there, he wanted me to hire him back. I just smiled and stated the old saying, "The grass is always greener on the other side, isn't it." I told him that I didn't need the problems that he would bring with him and it was nice having him gone. That didn't set well with him, but at least he knew not to keep pestering me about it.

I had been in A-East about nine months without having a decent barber. I was then able to get Inmate Smooth

Head, a black barber I had worked with for about three years in B-West. It took about five months to get him. That satisfied a lot of people, but I still needed a good "white or other race" barber.

I had a Hispanic barber lined up that the white guys requested. I had to try to steal him from B-East. It took about four months to get this lined up. Unfortunately, events transpired that made it best for him to stay in B-East.

I had allowed an inmate of Middle East origin to take his place on a trial basis, Inmate Racist Muslim. I tried him out because he told me he could cut well and that he had cut in the army back in his country. He was awful! The army that used him to cut hair must have been the worst looking army ever. He was never hired as a barber. I let him function in that position until I could find a guy that could cut hair well. Next is the straw that broke the camel's back.

On the days from 12-17-06 through 12-20-06 I spoke to Inmate Racist Muslim about securing the barber shop when he leaves it. I also spoke to him about not leaving the barber equipment unattended in the barber shop. He argued about it. He did not agree with these security policies and found them a nuisance.

After this, while I was off on 12-22 & 23, Officer Future LT found Inmate Racist Muslim leaving the barber shop open with the barber equipment unattended again. I found this out when I returned from my days off.

As it was obvious that he did not intend to comply with security policies, I informed him on 12-24-06 that he would no longer be a barber, that I was moving him to a utility position. He became very upset. He began arguing with me. He stated that the barber job was his and that I could not remove him from that position. I told him it was my responsibility to do so. He stated that I could not fire him. I told him that I could fire him, but at this time I wasn't going to; I was just moving him to a different position. He was yelling. He refused to listen. Eventually he went down the flag telling inmates that I had fired him because Inmate Smooth Head, our other barber, had snitched on him.

Inmates were coming up to Smooth Head and me informing us of what Racist Muslim was saying. Soon after this, Racist Muslim came to me to yell and complain to me again. I told him that what he had done was unacceptable, that he was putting Inmate Smooth Head in a dangerous position and to stop this at once. I informed Inmate Smooth Head that for his safety, I could lock both of them up for incompatibility issues. He stated that he felt safe. He stated that no one would be coming after him. As I had told Racist Muslim that Smooth Head had nothing to do with this, he had backed off on trying to create trouble for Smooth Head and was focusing his anger on me.

Later others came to me professing what a fantastic barber Racist Muslim was and that if I wouldn't let him cut, they would write grievances on me and speak to the lieutenant about me. I went to Racist Muslim and informed him that I would not tolerate him stirring things up, recruiting his Muslim buddies to threaten me and that if he continued this behavior; I would have to lock him up. I informed him that if he had a complaint to handle it in the proper manner on his own instead of recruiting others. He was calm at this point and was writing a kite.

The next day, Christmas, inmates were continuing to come to me complaining. Some threatened to write me up if I didn't put Racist Muslim back on as a barber.

Eventually it came out from talking to these people that Racist Muslim was telling people that I was a racist. He was telling them that he was Muslim and that I was Jewish and that is why I fired him. I had never spoken about my religious views, so there is no way he would know if I was even a Jew, a Muslim, a Christian, a witch ...... or anything.

Since Racist Muslim came to A-East as a swamper he had been uncooperative. He started out doing the stairs and would not clean them as I had directed him to. He would argue with me. He cleaned them his way which was not good. It was a struggle to get him to do his job completely. I would have to call him back out of his cell to redo his job at times.

The cleanliness in our barber shop had not met my expectations for some time, even before Racist Muslim. It got worse when Racist Muslim started cutting.

He constantly complained about not having proper equipment. Even after we got a lot of new equipment, he continued to complain. He did not clean and maintain the equipment properly before or after we received the new equipment.

I knew Smooth Head to be an excellent barber, a good worker and a team player. He got the barber shop and equipment cleaned up and in order. He had to give a lot of haircuts in order to get caught up with all of the people that had been waiting to get a decent hair cut. He tried working with Racist Muslim to get him to be a better barber and to maintain the barber shop and equipment. Racist Muslim would not cooperate. I asked Smooth Head if he could handle the position by himself until I could search out another good barber. I told him that we had one swamper going home in a month, so we could get one hired then. He said he preferred it that way. He stated it would be easier handling the barber shop himself rather than having to deal with Racist Muslim and clean up after him.

Racist Muslim had bid on a barber job in B-West that he did not get. After talking to him, he informed me that they had a posting again and that he was bidding on it again.

Another reason for moving Racist Muslim to the utility position was that we had been using some unemployed inmates for temporary swampers. However, most of them seemed more interested in just getting out of their cells rather than actually doing a job.

One temporary swamper started out doing a very good job but slowly did less and less. One of our regular swampers needed help, so I positioned Racist Muslim to back him up. With this move, there was no need for any temporary swamper.

Another inmate was used a couple of times. The first time was to get cleaned up quick after our lockdown. He later lied to officers when I was not there, telling them that I said he could be out of his cell. I never committed to anything on any shift other than mine and only when I was there. I was informed that he gave a kite to the warden stating that I wouldn't let him out on third watch. I always made it clear that if I had anyone out, I could only commit to them being out on my watch when I was there. I also found him to have a television in his cell that wasn't his, a weapon and he accumulated numerous continuous cell violations. When he wasn't able to manipulate things his way, he became loud, disruptive and verbally abusive. It was necessary for me to write repots on him twice that caused the watch commanders to have him escorted to segregation.

Situations like this made it necessary to use temporary swampers as little as possible and to put Racist Muslim in a utility position.

Eventually I had enough documentation on Racist Muslim to fire him. He complained to all of the big shots. Again, he told them I was a racist against him because I was a Jew. His appeals were eventually denied after I put the word out that if I wasn't backed on this move; I would resign as swamper boss.

As an unemployed, he was soon transferred to another cell block. He wrote numerous kites and grievances on me. I got a lot of heat from big shots that were crapping in their boots because he was claiming me to be racist against him. There were no grounds for this and I had pages of violations on him. The big shots caved into him and gave him a job in the dining hall. These lily livered honchos were afraid that some civilian know it all would jump on the bandwagon, support this guy and try to get them all canned. Racist Muslim wasn't happy with his new job and arrangement and neither was I. He should've been in segregation, but at least he wasn't my problem anymore.

I got an inmate from our block to volunteer to help out Smooth Head temporarily until I could hire a good barber. This was another black man. No man of any other race would volunteer. Oh, one Hispanic guy, but he was hauled off to segregation before we could even check him out.

White supremacists didn't like that there were two black barbers, so they tried to get them fired. They put up a sign in the block stating "Haircuts $3" to make it seem like the barbers were charging for their services, as this was not allowed. A white supremacist guy that was getting shipped out to Faribault, wrote a kite stating he was getting charged $2 and that the barbers were refusing to cut any hair other than black guys. The lieutenant had called me into his office to find out the scoop. I filled him in on the white supremacists campaign. Shortly after this, a white guy volunteered that I could trust, so I put him on as another temporary barber.

HOW MANY MORONS CAN I PISS OFF

"I'm a Nazi! I'm a Nazi."

Inmates on TU status (temporarily unemployed) are to go to canteen during the day. Those who are at work during the day are to go in the evening. This makes for a better flow rather than everyone going down to canteen at one time.

Mister Nazi got caught going down in the evening. When informed of the rules by the sergeant, he said he had been going down at that time for weeks. He said he did not want to hear that shit and then asked to be let into his cell because he was locked out. He then started to walk away from the sarge who was posted at the desk.

An officer called him back.

Mister Nazi said, "Get out of my face."

The officer called to get him hauled out and cuffed him up.

The inmate started yelling that he was a Nazi and began resisting. A different sergeant and the officer took him to the floor to more easily control Mister Nazi.

This was one of the few times an inmate was literally hauled to segregation. He continued his fighting back in seg, so he was stripped and placed on a restraint board until he could wear himself down and realize that his efforts were futile.

Maybe this intellectual idiot's mind was so under developed and childlike that he just wanted to be carried and have some other people take off his clothes, so he didn't have to do it. It was probably something he missed from back when he was a baby. He still wanted to be able to act like a baby and be treated like a baby, because intellectually he still was a baby.

In this day and age, anyone believing in Hitler's philosophies must have an under developed mind. Am I pissing off Nazis now? Probably, but if they have the right to believe they are superior to others, I have the right to believe their views are retarded. Oops, there I've pissed off another group. Not those with mental impairments, but those that try to make an issue about a specific word and try to twist the meaning of how it was used.

But there really shouldn't be a problem with any of this anyway. None of the people I am slamming would ever be reading a book anyway, so don't tell them. This will just be between you (those who read) and me.

CULTURE?

Over time I learned to expect certain things from the black race. These things were not exclusive to the black race, but primarily traits that if you heard of it, it probably came from a black man. I have not read any studies on this; it is just from my experience in this one prison in Minnesota.

This incident portrays what I am writing about.

An inmate that was out of his cell waiting to be seen by the lieutenant for a disciplinary problem yelled to the officer working the door post. The officer could not make out what the inmate was trying to communicate, so he called him over. The officer was not allowed to leave his post to approach the inmate.

The inmate came to him and in a loud voice stated that he was just talking to him like a "Motherfuckin' Man."

The officer asked him not to use that language.

The inmate asked when he could see the "Fucking Lieutenant" because he was getting tired of waiting.

The officer told him that he had to be patient and that he would be called when the lieutenant was ready for him.

The inmate called the officer a "Motherfuckin' Asshole" and tried walking away from him while attempting an intimidating stare.

It didn't work. The officer called for the A-Team to remove him. This eliminated the need for the inmate to speak with the lieutenant.

Point one is that more often than not, if you hear the word "Motherfucker," in this prison, it came from a black man.

Point two is that more often than not, if someone states that they are a man, in this prison, it came from a black man.

This probably has to do with culture, environment, slavery or some such thing.

If you want a more accurate educated explanation for this, you'll have to find a book about it from a psychologist, preferably a psychologist that is a black man.

MISTER INNOCENT MUSLIM

Another Muslim problem! There were Muslims in this place that I got along with very well, however, as a group, ratio wise, they were a major pain in the ass. For such a religious group, it was surprising how many were liars, thieves, intimidators, extorters, trouble makers, self righteous, etc.

In this instance, a Muslim was refusing to let another inmate be bunked in his cell with him. He thought he was Greta Garbo, "I vant to be alone."

Sorry, you lost that right when you committed a felony.

The sergeant and lieutenant had a chat with him in the lieutenant's office. After having the consequences of not allowing the other inmate in his cell laid out for him, he stated that there would be no problem.

About 10 minutes later, an officer informed the sarge that the two inmates said it was not going to work out.

Mr. Innocent Muslim said, "I am not refusing to have him move in."

The other inmate said that Mr. Innocent Muslim told him things that made him very upset and that he knew this was not going to work out. He asked to be moved in with anyone but Mr. Innocent Muslim.

The new inmate was placed in a different cell and Mr. Innocent Muslim was called to the lieutenant's office again.

He said, "I told him that he must know that I pray 5 to 6 times a day and that when I pray I need all the floor space and that he is not to disturb me when I pray."

I guarantee that is an extremely watered down and sanitized version of what he actually said.

It was explained to him that this is a double bunking unit and that the cell must be shared.

He said, "You can't stop me from my religious rights!"

There were no consequences for this jerk. During his time in prison, he got his way most of the time. I guess he was good at threatening and intimidating the big shots.

FAILING WITH USING THE BLACK CARD

When someone is in the block on In House Seg status, it generally means they are a big trouble maker. It means that their sentence in segregation was so long, that they still had time left to serve in segregation when other inmates had to be placed in seg. IHS means their time wasn't up, but they had to be moved out to make room for other jerks.

A couple of officers were directed to shake down this guy's cell. The cell was chosen randomly by the computer. After they completed the shakedown and were placing the inmate back into the cell, he yelled, "These guys just called us a Nigger."

He was unable to stir up any immediate action against these officers; however, inmates would come up to them and ask them about it.

They never made any such comment. They would have had to been morons to say anything like that. Not that some morons haven't been hired, but these weren't them and even a moronic officer would have better sense than to make a comment like that.

This charge would get this jerk high priority for going back to the hole.

ADVERTISING RACIST

A white power dude decided to accumulate more than just a spotting violation when he stuck his mirror through his cell bars. He wrote some information on the back of the mirror. Written on it were "WHITE POWER" and a Swastika. It seems like he wanted to get attacked by some of the black gangs, Hispanic gangs, Asian gangs or non affiliates that were not considered to be white. White guys would even be upset with this racist, because they would not want to be seen as being associated with the racist just because they were white too.

The mirror was confiscated and he was locked in his cell to speak to the lieutenant the next day. I am sure that there were many others looking forward to having a more physical meeting with this guy.

WHY WIGGERS WHY

During dinner feeding, an officer noticed a fresh tattoo on an inmate's forearm. He saw another inmate go into that guy's cell.

After feeding was complete, two officers went to shakedown that cell. They found a half gallon of ketchup based hooch behind the guy's footlocker. He had tattoo drawings, one with a Swastika.

The roommate had tattoo drawings. Under his mattress on the bunk was written "Die niggers die."

White power drawings were on the walls along with swastikas.

The guy with the fresh tattoo was taken to seg and the cellmate was placed on ICR.

COUNT HIM RACIST

A racist black inmate had not switched in by the time the second tone sounded for everyone to be in their cells for count.

An officer asked him for his ID.

As he was walking away, the inmate yelled to the block, "That's white out there man; made his fucking day."

The officer went back to the guy's cell and told him that the comment was not acceptable.

The inmate mumbled a few more things as the officer walked away. His racist ass was escorted to segregation.

ACCURATE QUOTES

When you use that word nigger, you are using fighting words. When you use that word in the presence of any black man, you are asking that black man for a reaction. It is a call to arms, because when that word is used in the presence of a black man, he has an obligation to do something about it, to say something. He has a duty, in most situations, to confront the declarant. No one, no black man can hear that word without getting upset.
Christopher Darden

"There are a lot of black people who are unintelligent, who don't have success. It's best to knock a successful black person down 'cause they're intelligent, they speak well, they do well in school, and they're successful. It's crabs in a barrel. ... We're the only ethnic group that says, 'hey, if you go to jail, it gives you street cred.' "
Charles Barkley
(Crabs in the bottom of a barrel will try to pull down the crabs that are closer to the top.)

TIPS

GOING THROUGH THE MOTIONS

I received an anonymous note stating that an inmate had offered drugs to him. It stated that the drugs were in a Jet magazine. Another officer and I shook down the cell belonging to the inmate that supposedly offered the drugs. A white powder was found wrapped in plastic in a Jet magazine.

Discipline was called to get the powder analyzed. The Watch Commander was called to get the inmate UA'ed. The powder analysis came up inconclusive. The UA came up negative. The powder was placed into evidence and the inmate was locked in his cell without being able to use his powder.

Nothing would come of this, because there were too many variables. The informant may have put the powder in the guy's magazine in an attempt to get the other inmate in trouble. Most likely the powder was not a drug, but none the less would be a minor violation to have possession of it. If the guy was trying to sell it as a drug, it would be next to impossible to prove. Overall a lot of time would be wasted to have nothing come of this, but it had to be investigated just in case it was a drug.

ASSAULT PLANNED

I received information that an inmate had a paint handle that he intended to shank another inmate with when that inmate came into the unit to do linen exchange. The inmate targeted to be shanked was a laundry worker. I informed the lieutenant. Our unit painter stated that no paint cans had come into the block with handles the entire time he had been a painter. While investigating this situation, I was informed that the shank was a paint brush handle and that the inmate with the shank dumped it, but still intended to attack the other inmate. Another officer was checking out the trash cans and shaking down the unit. No shanks were found.

We never know how accurate our information is. We have to take everything as being the truth and properly investigate to try to keep these guys safe.

OBSERVING & LISTENING

Early on, I stopped informing the big shots of things I was informed about that were going on in the prison. I stopped doing this because I was being ignored. If they did not want to listen, I couldn't make them. Back when I had informed them of a group of officers smuggling in pot, I was ignored because it seemed unbelievable to them. Officers in discipline and investigations knew of me and would check with me from time to time if they needed information to work off of.

One day an investigations officer asked me if I knew anything about an incident of a gathering in the yard. I knew it happened, but wasn't positive of what it was about.

Two inmates from A-East were involved. I knew them to be involved in gambling and both to be Mickey Cobra Stones. I knew them to be on good terms with members of other Security Threat Groups, STG's.

I informed the officer that the incident in the yard probably had to do with gambling. I told him that I would check into it.

Upon investigating, I observed that many of the more powerful members of other STG's were no longer in the unit. The organizing inmate had come back into the unit recently. The other inmate was his enforcer. From observing them, it seemed as though they were in control of gambling in the unit.

One day, while I was at the shower post, I observed an inmate put a note pad in the enforcer's cell. Shortly after, I observed another inmate put some canteen items in that cell. When our unit went to the morning meal, the organizer and enforcer stayed in the unit. I observed them coming down the flag and go into the enforcer's cell. The organizer was loud and animated as he was speaking to the enforcer.

I informed the captain and the watch commander of this. I informed them that they keep score on paper now rather than having the canteen items at the table. I was instructed by the captain to get the score pads. When I went back to the unit, I took three sheets of paper with numbers on them from a table on the front flag. That table was occupied primarily by white and native inmates.

Another officer was with me when I took a lined pad with numbers on it and a small unlined pad with numbers on it from two different tables on the back flag. Both of these tables were occupied by all black inmates.

Several inmates started yelling. I informed them that I was doing as instructed, and that they didn't want to raise this to another level. They all settled down at this point.

One inmate asked if they could copy down the numbers. I told them, "No."

The other officer and I left the area. The inmates at all three tables disbursed.

Shortly after, the organizer came to the desk to protest. Without me saying anything about the sheets, he stated that they had nothing to do with money, that they were just playing spades. He continued being loud and confrontational.

I stated, "Thou doest protest too much."

He looked confused, so another inmate explained it to him. He then he left without incident.

An inmate from the first table came and asked me if they were going to the hole. I stated that I did not know, but that I doubted it. I notified the Watch Commander and placed the papers into evidence.

The next morning, while on a security check, I observed the organizer and the enforcer in the enforcer's cell. I heard the organizer say to the enforcer, "We gotta do this for the power."

He seemed to be working with the enforcer on their point system for keeping track of the gambling. The organizer was being very loud and forceful.

He had been getting quite pushy with people lately. An example on this day was when he tried getting pushy with a powerful old timer inmate. The old timer sets out the food for all of the inmates that get food delivered to the unit.

The organizer asked him, "You got any extra milk."

He said, "No."

The organizer said, "Yeah, right. I know you do."

He walked away grumbling. Later, I observed the enforcer at the phones with another inmate. I have no idea what this was about, but the other inmate was one of the people that seemed to be trained to be at a table when the other two weren't there. The enforcer was pointing out something in a little black book that he had.

With all of this information, the investigations officer that had approached me asking me if I knew anything; now had plenty to work with. I also gave him a list of names. The organizer wound up being shipped out to do the rest of his time at Oak Park.

FLOOR WAX THIEF

The sarge in A-East received a tip that one of the swampers was stealing floor wax and selling it. When he shook down the cell, he found a handmade rope almost five feet long. This was a worse violation that the floor wax situation, so he was taken to segregation.

VISITING

FEMALE MALE RATIO

Working the hours in the visiting room were great for officers that liked to sleep in. They were 12 to 8 on Wednesday, Thursday & Friday and 9 to 5 on Saturday & Sunday, when I started working in the prison.

The problem in the visiting room is that female officers don't have to do shakedown, even though that may have been a preference for some of them. This leaves the guys with much more nuts & butts time then there ought to be. If everyone working visiting were treated equally, shakedown time could be divided equally between everyone. If the females can't do the entire job, then they shouldn't be in there.

This was a good place for the females to bid into. By not having to do shakedown, they did not have a lot of close inmate contact.

A female sergeant ran the visiting room when I got forced to work there. Luckily I was able to bid out and only got stuck there with it being my daily job for two weeks. Seven people work the visiting room. At least two of them must be in shakedown, two in the visiting room, two working the front desk and the seventh floated around helping out wherever needed and covering for people to take their breaks. Of the 7 needed, at least 2 are always female and sometimes as many as four. This made it so the male officers had to work shakedown much more often than if only males were allowed to work visiting, as I believe is the way it should be. You can see how a guy in this area would get more than his fair share of inspecting nude dudes with bad odor problems and shit stained underwear in a poorly ventilated area.

Later the hours were changed to 10 to 8 Thursday through Sunday. This was done to create a four day work week which they thought might help entice some male officers to bid into that position. It worked and the amount of time one would have to be in shakedown decreased at least a little bit.

VISITING ROOM

Upon entering the visiting room, the visitors went to a place marked on the floor close to where an officer was sitting. The inmate that they came to see met them at that spot. They were allowed to hug, no groping or inappropriate touching. They were allowed to kiss on the cheek, no lips as drugs could be passed that way. They then were allowed to sit in rows of chairs across from each other and conduct their visit. They had to maintain a gap between them to help us identify if someone were trying to pass contraband.

The two officers working this area sit on elevated platforms watching for anything suspicious or any rules being broken. Should these officers suspect the passing or attempted passing of anything, the officer has to request that we conduct an unclothed body search of the visitor. If they refuse, they are banned forever from the visiting room.

The inmates are allowed to hold a small child. This gives them a great opportunity to get contraband out of a kids diaper or some clothing.

Sometimes inmates lose their visiting room privileges. They may not have followed the visiting room rules, created havoc in the visiting room or numerous other reasons; whatever the reason, at times they are banned.

Sometimes they are just banned from contact visits. This is generally if they are serving time in segregation. The rules get pretty involved depending on the violation and how long they have been in seg. If they are in seg and are allowed a visit, it is behind glass with a telephone.

The visiting room is the place where most drugs enter the institution. Why aren't all visits behind glass with the telephone in order to stop drugs from coming into the prison? I don't know. It makes no sense to me. I guess that is just one of the reasons they don't have me running this place. The state wants this to be a kinder gentler place of incarceration. A lot of problems would be eliminated by having all visits being non-contact visits. Don't like that; don't commit a crime.

FRONT DESK

When you enter the institution, you turn to the left and enter the area that visitors coming to see the inmates wait. They must register with officers at the front desk. The officers have to inform visitors of the rules and check them over the best they can for contraband. They have to run everyone through a metal detector. If someone is found trying to smuggle anything in, they call the Bayport police and have them arrested.

Once they are cleared to enter the visiting room and the inmate is in the visiting room waiting for them, they have to pass through a series of three doors controlled by the officer in the bubble.

VISITING ROOM BUBBLE

Working the bubble in visiting was the busiest most hectic position in visiting. I was good at it and I liked it because the time passed much more quickly in there than in many other areas. An officer that worked the visiting room all the time was very bad at working the visiting room bubble. Another new guy and I always had to fix up his mistakes. Most officers weren't good at the bubble and hated it, except on the slower days. I hated it on the slower days, but not as bad as shakedown

When working this area, we had to direct the flow of people in and out of the visiting room. We had to make sure that only the people authorized to go in and come out, went in and came out. This had to be done smoothly and efficiently. We had to work in close communications with the front desk officers in order to help control the flow. We could control the start of the visit, but not when it ended.

When someone was ready to go in, an officer at the front desk would push a buzzer to notify the officer in the bubble. If the middle door was closed, we could open the first door and let them in. Once the first door was closed behind them, we could open the middle door only if the third door was closed also. When they got through the second door and we closed that behind them, they had to give us their ID, generally a driver's license. It was held in the bubble until they came out. Once we had their ID and the second door was closed, we were allowed to open the third door so they could enter the visiting room and start their visit.

The small area the people passed through between the second and third doors had a brick wall on their right as they entered. To their left was a large mirror the length of this area. There was a small slot under the mirror in which to pass their ID through. They could not see who was working this area. We could see them as this was a two-way mirror. Most did not realize this was a two-way mirror. I realized this when I saw some of the things they were doing in there when they thought they were alone.

The guys typically checked under their arm pits, puffed up and picked boogers and flicked them away.

The women typically checked their make up, wiggled around adjusting their clothes and pushed up their breasts.

However, some of these females would put on a show or so it seemed. Whether they were oblivious to being seen or just trying to stir up whoever was behind the mirror, I don't know for sure, but I could've taped some of these gals and marketed it as an erotic video.

WHAT I HEARD AND OBSERVED

An inmate was telling me how he told his wife never to come to see him anymore. He had been in prison quite some time when it was noticeable that she was pregnant when she came to visit him. It was obvious that it wasn't his kid. He was embarrassed by people asking him about it.

A lady visiting with her little girl told me that she didn't want her to know where she was, so she told her that they were visiting her daddy in college. Now the little girl wants to go to college here too.

An inmate was in for raping his daughter. The mother and two daughters came to see him. The daughters, at this time, were 17 and 20. He was sentenced one year before this visit. The youngest daughter seemed extremely nervous. Why did the mother even bring her here?

I can just hear this sick mother before leaving home to come here;"Hey sweetie; it's time to go see daddy. You know how much he loves you, really, really loves you."

Even with all of the sick things I got exposed to working in this place, things like this still amazed me.

I found it amazing how many women showed up in this place for a visit that were dressed to heat up their man. Actually, I'm not talking about just heating them up; I'm talking about heating everyone else up too and having them boil over. If you're into strip clubs, you can forget about ever having to go if you are working the front desk in the visiting room. The smart ones could dress sexy for their man without being inappropriate. The inappropriate ones were not allowed to enter. Some would go to a store close by and buy something appropriate so they could be admitted. Others would go home, wait for their man to call and then complain to them about how we wouldn't let them enter for a visit for no reason at all. Then these guys would complain to us and start writing complaint letters of how unfairly they were being treated, their woman was being treated and that they were being singled out.

WHAT I WAS TOLD

An inmate once came into the visiting room with a razor blade in his mouth. When he went to give his visitor a kiss, he slashed her throat.

Another guy gave all of his things away before going to greet his visitor. This happens with quite a few of these guys when they intend to commit a violent act that will get them locked down for a long time or if they intend to commit suicide. When you see someone giving everything away and they are not being released in the next few days, it's time to notify the honchos.

When he got to the visiting room, he gave her a kiss, drew his fist back and smashed her in the face as hard as he could. He then just stood there and waited to be taken away. The gal he hit went flying against the wall. Blood splattered all over the place. The impact forced her contact lenses behind her eyeballs. Her face was split open and her nose was broken.

Strangely enough, she never came back to see him again. This is actually not sarcasm. Most of these women keep on putting up with whatever abuse is dished out.

DON'T VIOLATE VISITING ROOM POLICIES

The layout of the visiting room is lines of chairs. First there is a line of chairs against the wall. Then there is a line of chairs facing those chairs and relatively close together so inmates can be facing their visitors. There is another row of chairs behind that row facing the opposite direction. There is a gap between those rows so that people leaving can go through that gap rather than walking between people visiting and interrupting their conversations. This system repeats itself until the room is full of rows of chairs. There is a level to this room that is a couple of steps lower with the same set up.

As a courtesy, when inmates are in the visiting room with guests, officers give them a five minute warning, so they know to start wrapping up their conversation rather than abruptly saying their goodbyes.

The officer would get the inmates attention and hold up an open hand indicating that five minutes were left.

The officer walked to the area of an inmate with a constantly poor disposition and held up her hand. She thought the inmate had seen, but he had turned his head away quickly and gave her no nod or anything to indicate that he got the message. She held up her hand again. He glared at her, looked down and gave that head shake that indicates they are annoyed.

Visiting room staff constantly had to deal with this guy's negative attitude whenever they gave him the five minute warning or had to inform him of rules he was breaking.

When his visit was over, he stood up and walked down the aisle between the people who were visiting rather than the aisle where he would not interrupt anyone.

The officer saw this and called out to him. He continued down the path of being a jerk. His visitors went down the aisle where they wouldn't interfere with anyone.

The inmate walked past the officer that was speaking to him. He ignored her and continued on to a piece of red carpet where people are to say goodbye to each other.

The officer was trying to get by without locking this guy up by explaining the rules to him. He rolled his eyes at the officer, looked away and said to his visitors, "It's nothing important. It's just some bullshit rules."

"You should know the rules. It's rude to walk between people's visits. A warning is going in your file. If you can't adhere to the warnings, in the future your visits could be terminated."

"My visits always get interrupted!"

She sent him back to shakedown. She had forgotten to give him a warning about swearing so she called an officer back there to fill him in.

The shakedown officer gave him the swearing warning.

The inmate started yelling, "You guys are always ending my visits for some fucking bullshit rule! This is fucking bullshit!"

The officer told him his behavior was unacceptable. The inmate continued yelling and being aggressive toward him. He made a call to the A-Team to have him removed from shakedown and locked in his cell.

Warnings were entered in his file for walking between other's visits, swearing and creating a disturbance in the visiting room and in shakedown.

The lieutenant would have a chat with this guy the next day; however, guys like this rarely change their behavior.

COMING SOON – A BROTHER

The mother, brother and a female were visiting an inmate. The brother spit on the floor. The inmate and other visitors looked surprised. The inmate seemed to be chastising the brother. The observing officer went over to them. They had guilty looks on their faces and the visit was terminated.

Maybe the wrong brother is in prison. Actually, not. I knew this inmate well. They both belong locked up.

WHERE'S THAT TATTOO!

Following the conclusion of his visit, an inmate was being given an unclothed body search to see if he was smuggling in anything that his visitor may have brought him. The officer conducting the unclothed body search had been working this area for a long time. He knew these inmates very well, possibly too well. He discovered an undocumented tattoo on this guy. The new tattoo was on his genitals. I wonder who he was showing it off to. Sorry, I didn't bother asking what the tattoo was as I felt I had heard a little too much already.

INTIMIDATE TO MANIPULATE

Obnoxious criminals come to visit these guys. A lady... let me correct that. She was no lady. An intimidator of the female gender came to visit one of the inmates. As she passed through the metal detector, it went off. She was upset and started ranting about how she had been through the metal detector before with the same clothes on and it had never gone off.

The officer informed her of items like jewelry, belts, shoes and the like that could set of a metal detector. She placed these types of items on the counter and tried again. It went off again. She bitched again. "Just give me non contact then," she demanded.

The officer informed her that was not possible due to inmates from segregation in there having visits at this time.

Now, she really lost it. She was cussing about the metal detector and the prison. "I hate this fucking place. This is fucking bullshit. I've never had this happen. This is fucking ridiculous." Everyone in the lobby could hear her ranting.

Another intimidator of the female persuasion was with her. She told that person to go in and see the man without her. She failed to clear the metal detector also, even after several attempts.

They both left the institution. I assume that it was not quietly.

This is the type of behavior we run into when people are trying to hide something, when they are guilty of something and want to try to intimidate people into not checking further. They try to divert attention from them and onto something or someone else.

There were absolutely no other visitors the entire day that set off the metal detector; only these two Homo sapiens that as far as we knew did not have male genitalia.

AUNTIE LOVE

An aunt came to see her nephew in the prison visiting room. One way to pass drugs is to have it in your mouth and pass it when you kiss someone on the lips, so kissing on the lips is prohibited. She was seen kissing her supposed nephew on the lips.

OK, let's vote again. Who thinks this was actually his aunt?

This wouldn't happen in my family.

I guess if I was in prison and desperate for drugs, I might wind up tonguing a dog or a cow or something, but not a relative.

Not that their kiss was that involved, but ewe, your moms sister?

Not that this was an attempt to pass drugs, but really, your mom's sister?

I wasn't even into hugging much less kissing one of my aunts on the lips. There were a couple of cousins that looked pretty good, but a handshake is as far as I would consider going with any relative.

He was placed on In House Detention in his cell block. He received three months of non contact visits and she was suspended from visits for three months.

Did you notice something here? When he can have contact visits again, she can visit again and then they can hook up again. I wonder if his mother is jealous.

I SUGGEST NO CONTACT VISITS FOR THIS ONE

Some officers really have their act together. Knowing the rules are critical in this place. The visiting room sergeant saw an inmate and his visitor kiss on the lips as she was leaving. He informed the inmate that kissing on the lips was an offence that required him to go to segregation.

He said he was not aware of that policy and was sent to seg.

The sarge went up front and explained to the visitor that due to the kissing violation, she was banned from coming back for three months.

She protested that she did not understand that from reading the information on the internet. She said that was unfair as this was her first visit.

He informed her that our information packet stated that kissing was only allowed on the cheek and that this information was posted in every cell block for every inmate to inform themselves.

She asked for his supervisors name because she was going to contest the ban.

He gave her the information and informed her that she would have to appeal to him in writing.

She said she was going to exercise all of her legal rights and get the ban over turned. She left in a huff.

Maybe she belongs locked up in a prison too. We certainly wish we could lock up these jerks; in someone else's prison.

DISRESPECT OR CON GAME

An inmate was released from his cell to come to the bubble and pick up a pass to go to visiting. He picked up the pass, but did not go on it. The visitor was waiting so eventually an officer in visiting called the bubble to find out what was going on. The bubble officer was about to page the inmate again when he noticed him on the phone. They made eye contact. The inmate turned away and continued his phone conversation.

Getting out of your cell to go on a pass and not going was a common way for these guys to get extra time out of their cell to do what they wanted to do until we discovered their game. There was little if any consequence for it, other than writing them up for an unauthorized area violation, so it continued to be a nuisance.

VISIT OR CHOW

An inmate returned from a visit and asked for a bag lunch because he missed brunch. The officer told him that we do not provide bag lunches for inmates that choose to take a visit at meal time. That is their choice. It is their responsibility to provide a meal for themselves if they chose to have a meal. After the front half of the block returned from the dining hall, everyone was switched in. The officer saw the guy that went on a visit at the micro wave. She told him to switch in as it was not flag time. He ignored her. By the time she got to him, another officer was there. He had given the inmate the option to either switch in or continue to heat his meal and be ICR'ed. The inmate chose to be ICR'ed and continued cooking his food.

This was inappropriate for the second officer to change the directive of the first officer without her consent.

SEND HER TO SHAKOPEE WOMEN'S PRISON

Some of these people that come to pay a visit to the inmates should be locked up and kept away from the public as they are not fit to be out among decent people.

A female visitor was unable to clear the metal detector even after several attempts.

"I have staples in my stomach."

"You need a doctor's note stating where the staples are located. You can go in and have a half hour non contact visit if you want."

"I ain't doin' that! This is bullshit! I shouldn't have to take off all my fucking shit!"

She went back to her locker yelling, "Assholes! Pricks!"

Other visitors were waiting with small children to visit inmates.

An officer told her that she was now being denied a visit not only for failing to pass through the metal detector, but for her abusive language and disruptive behavior.

As the female was walking away, the mother said to the officer, "She is the most stubborn of my children. She has been banned from many places.

The female returned and asked to speak to the officer's supervisor.

The officer went and took the sergeants post in the visiting room. The sergeant went and informed her that she was banned for using abusive language.

The potty mouthed person accused the other officer of banning her only because she asked to see his supervisor.

Whoa! Red flag! We all know this is a lie. We are always more than willing to let someone else take over dealing with slime like this female.

The sarge reiterated that it was for her abusive behavior.

"He was mad at me for asking to talk to you. I only called him a prick."

"Any vulgar or abusive language directed at my staff will not be tolerated. You are being banned for six months."

"You're going to believe him over me?"

"Yes. If you want to argue the point further, you can write an appeal to my lieutenant."

"Give me the names of everyone and a contact number."

He gave her the information and then said, "You need to leave the premises now as you are banned and no longer allowed to be here."

"I'm going to wait in the lobby for my mother to come out."

"You are not allowed to be here. You have to leave."

She stared at him for a while and then grudgingly gathered her belongings and left.

Dealing with these kinds of people is part of the job. As you well know, everyone runs into these kinds of people once in a while. In this place, we have to deal with them all of the time.

NOT AS COOL AS HE THOUGHT

When these guys have a visit, a rule is that they must have their shirt tucked in. An inmate entered the shakedown area of visiting with his shirt hanging out. The officer told him to tuck it in. He complied. When he entered the visiting room, he pulled it out. His visitor was sent home without seeing him. He was placed on ICR for disregarding visiting room rules and disobeying a directive.

SEG CAN BE A GOOD PLACE

I received a call from an officer working visiting informing me that an inmate had created a disturbance there and was being sent back to the unit to be locked in. He said he would send me a copy of the paperwork after he got a chance to write it up.

The inmate came to the bubble to ask me questions. I informed him that he was on ICR and had to switch in. He refused. I directed him to switch in again. He went to talk with another inmate. I again directed him to switch in. He started walking up the front flag. He lived in a cell in the back of the cell hall. I called for a 10-14. He was escorted to segregation.

This guy's visitor must have given him news that he did not like. Things like this cause guys to behave even worse than normal. This guy decided to go back to segregation to chill out for a while. When I started, I use to think that going to seg was a bad thing. As time passed and especially when double bunking hit my block, I realized that being placed in the hole could be the desired result of a lot of these guys.

OFFICERS BLAMED AGAIN

OK! You are going to get a ration of my attitude toward the administration here. We were being blamed for inmates not showing up for their visits in a timely manner or even not going to the visit at all.

421

The way visiting works is that a visitor shows up. An officer working in visiting makes a page over the speakers in the cell block that the inmate receiving the visitor resides in. The inmate is to report to the door to be released to go to his visit. Simple, right!

Wrong, because we are expected to be baby sitters and not prison guards. This is actually where we should be allowed to be corrections officers, but are not.

Some reasons the inmate does not report:

Want to sleep instead

Want to take a shower first

Have an attitude that day and don't want to see that person

Just use the visitor for a reason to get out of his cell

Want to use the phone

Goes to socialize with other inmates

Impossible to know all of the reasons

The only reason it should be on us is if we are contacted and do not let the inmate out of his cell if he happens to be locked in.

If the inmate does not report to visiting within five minutes, we should be contacted so we can find out the circumstances. If the reason for the inmate not reporting is his cell door being locked, we can fix the problem promptly.

If the reason for the inmate not reporting is a policy violation, the inmate should be locked up. His visiting privileges should be revoked for a period of time. The visitor should be notified that the inmate established other priorities other than wanting to see them, even though the visitor made the effort to come to the prison to see him.

Is this common sense or am I just an asshole.

NUTS & BUTTS

NOT FOR ME

Shakedown is the small room where inmates pass through before and after a visit. A number like 7 is picked at the beginning of the day and then every 7th inmate is strip searched before going in for his visit. All are strip searched coming out from their visit. However, it is not politically correct to call it a strip search anymore. We have been directed to call them "unclothed body searches."

Talk about a crap job, this is it. Shakedown is also referred to as "Nuts & Butts." If I would've got stuck in there very often, I would've quit. You get stuck in there a bit when you first start. You better not complain about it or you will be placed in there more often. That is the mentality of people here. Of course if someone said they really enjoyed it, I might think twice or more about placing them in shakedown.

My idea of a job is not having someone bend over and spread their hind cheeks so I can look up his butt crack to make sure he isn't hiding anything up there. Or having them lift up their frontal package so I can look under it.

First off, I don't like looking at nude dudes. Nude females, oh yeah, some of them any way, but not nude dudes. Heck, I don't like seeing myself nude. When I shower I make sure the mirror is steamed up before I get out to avoid reality shock.

Another problem I have with this duty is the smell. Many of these guys haven't heard of personal hygiene and the ventilation in there is nowhere near sufficient. Some guys are very clean and won't go to their visit without first taking a shower. Unfortunately some of these guys never learned how to wipe. Some of them have solid smears of feces in their underwear; not just skid marks but chunks; and I had to thoroughly search all clothing and shoes by running my hands through them. At least we are provided with gloves like doctors and dentists use. Within a half hour, I'm gagging from the smell of poop, urine, body odor, bad breath and what ever foul gas is released from their rectum.

The inmates don't appreciate going through this process and I really hated it. I can see the need for it, but I'm not the guy to be doing it. This was an area where I could never be able to lay claim to having job satisfaction at the end of the day.

We also had to look over their entire body, in their mouth, under their tongue, the bottoms of their feet, they had to run their fingers through their hair, and anywhere that they could possibly hide anything has to be checked.

MENTALITY OF SOME

My first day in shakedown, I had to work with a really bad officer. He had the radio on, was reading a book, was making personal phone calls, wouldn't speak to me to inform me of what to do, and said he didn't give a damn because he planned on being gone in two years.

DINGLE BERRIES ON A BLACK MAN'S ASS

Training in this place could be much improved upon. But there are a lot of situations that can never be planned for and I seemed to hit a lot of them.

When we were in academy and got trained on what to do in shakedown, they didn't get too detailed. At least I would've liked a lot more detail. Maybe liked is the wrong word. I could've used a few more critical details.

A man was coming out of visiting and I was doing an unclothed body search. He was bent over with his cheeks spread. I thought I saw something up there, but had to get a better look. This generally is a quick look and done. I would generally say "OK" and that meant we were done. As it was taking me longer, the inmate was getting uncomfortable and stood up. I always try to do my job thoroughly, which can be a problem at times. This was a black man and I noticed something white up there. Most officers would've probably just passed it off, but not me. I thought this guy had keestered some cocaine or crack up inside his crack. Letting drugs into the prison was something I couldn't let happen. I was about to call over a more experienced officer, but figured I better make sure. When the inmate stood up, I informed him that I wasn't done yet. Boy, the looks I got from him and the awkwardness I felt made me positive that this would never be the job for me. I had a little flash light on my utility belt, so I pulled it out to get a better look. I just wanted to get this over with and hope this guy didn't start acting up. Maybe it was his first time too. To my surprise it wasn't a package of drugs, it was a white patch of dingle berries on this black man's ass. I smiled in relief. The inmate looked at me even stranger. It seemed like he just wanted to get the heck out of there. Some guy had just analyzed his butt crack using a flash light and was now smiling about it.

Remember the first title that I was going to name this book was "Dingle Berries on a Black Man's Ass?" This instance is why. There was no way to be trained thoroughly on everything, but training could have been a lot better. Officers and inmates are constantly being put into compromising positions. Simple things can turn into a big thing. Once any of us step through those gates, we all become victims of the system. The system can never be perfect, but it could be a lot better than it is. By the time you finish reading this book, you will see how this racist sounding title would have been a great title for this book.

UNABLE TO SHAKE IT

One mistake in this place and you will never hear the end of it. There was an officer that was working shakedown when he first started. He was very conscientious. He felt our training was inadequate. Granted it could've been much better, but in this instance, I believe he may have only caught part of what was being told to him. He was doing an unclothed body search on a guy coming out of the visiting room. These inspections become routine. The inmate and officer go through the paces and get the job done without much verbal communication. We are supposed to direct the inmate as to what to do and when to do it when this is not the case. The inmate was standing there facing him and had not lifted up his package for inspection. This officer reached out and lifted up the inmate's package for him. Whoa! Red Flag! We do not touch inmates unless it is in conjunction with arresting them, breaking up a fight or escorting them and we definitely would rarely if ever have a situation where we would have to touch their privates. We have to look at them but not touch them. This happened shortly before I started working in the prison.

He was unmercifully harassed by officers and inmates alike. He bid onto first watch to try to get away from all of it. First Watch is the 10pm to 6am shift where there are few officers and the inmates are all locked up and bedded down for the night. Thus this shift has a lot less interaction with people. I worked with him on this shift quite a few times. When I asked him about what had happened, he explained it to me. He said he didn't know how it was to be done for sure and he wanted to make sure he was thorough. By getting to know him, I know this was the way he was.

He quit within a year or so of me starting. He was an odd little man that was crazy about guns. He had many of them at home. He was always looking at gun magazines and talking about guns. The job he left the prison for was as a night watchman at an oil processing plant where a job requirement was for him to carry a weapon. He said this was his dream job.

It was several years later when I was setting up a room to teach a class when he walked in. He had been terminated from his dream job and needed to earn a living, so he decided to try corrections again. He thought that if he worked at the Oak Park Heights prison, people wouldn't know of his past. Some of his training would be at Stillwater as the two prisons are only a few minutes away from each other. He thought he would be able to do his job and not have to put up with the harassment he was forced to endure before. He was wrong. Word travels fast and stories like this never die. Before he finished going through the academy again, I heard that he was found dead in his car in the parking lot at the Oak Park Heights prison. He had committed suicide by firing a bullet into his head with one of his guns from home.

EAGER BEAVER

One story I heard was that an inmate's wife had continually been smuggling drugs to him by sticking them up her coochie. How's that for taming down the language. Spell check does not identify with the word coochie; even when I tried spelling it with a K. Well, anyway, his wife died. He needed someone else to smuggle drugs in for him, so he recruited his daughter. She was eager to please or it could've been a mother daughter competition thing, whatever the case she packed in a butt load of crack and pot. Actually she was able to pack in more than a butt load because she had a coochie. That's where the problem came in. Coochies hold more than keesters. The transfer in the visiting room slipped by without any officer noticing, but no matter how hard the father tried, he couldn't pack it all in. Part of a bag of marijuana was hanging out. Instead of having her take some back out with her, he hoped that the officer doing his unclothed body search on the way out would be too involved in the routine of the search to notice. This was wishful thinking on his part. The officer couldn't help but see this bag hanging out. When confronted about the irregularity, he didn't want to get his daughter in trouble, so he tried to put the blame on himself. He said with a smile on his face, "It's my fault. I should've trained her better."

TA DAH

At the end of one day, the final inmate had exited shakedown. The officer that I was with yelled out in relief, "Thank God! No more naked men!"

I said, "That's what you think." Then, I mooned him.

Okay, not really, "butt" I had a hard time resisting.

CHOW HOUND –
MY MOST BLATANT ENEMY

There was a fat officer; no an obese officer; actually a morbidly obese officer of the Native American persuasion. Knowing my excessive weight and the excessive weight of some friends, I'd have to guess him at about 400 plus pounds. His size gave him power and his high school wrestling background gave him the ability to know how to maximize the effects of his poundage.

He liked coaxing the immature fit officers into scuffling matches. With all of those pounds pressing down on those two feet of his, he could not be easily pushed around. He would do this out in the hallways where inmates could see these officers scuffling around. This was the same type of behavior that inmates would get thrown in the hole for.

He always had food stains on his shirt, even first thing in the morning. The number of stains increased continuously throughout the day. He worked on the A-Team, which gave him great flexibility of movement throughout the institution. He seemed to find his way to the kitchen frequently. The food down there was food for the inmates, not the officers, even though this was one of the most lacks rules in the joint. He took full advantage of the chow being constantly and easily available to him.

He was extremely friendly toward me, when I started. This was because he found out I was a standup comedian and he wanted me to tell him jokes.

He wasn't friendly toward me for very long. Once he found out I was an officer that did my job, followed the rules and played it straight, his attitude toward me changed in a flash.

One day, early on, the serving of lunch was completed and the inmates had returned to their cellblocks. My dining hall duties were completed and I was returning to my cellblock.

Chow Hound caught me alone just outside the dining hall. He said, "Hey, Basham. Come over here." I went to him. He said, "We need you to stop enforcing policies down here. You're creating problems. The inmates don't like it, so we don't like it. It's dangerous."

I said, "I'm just doing what I was told to do when I was trained in."

He said, "That's not how it is down here. You're stirring things up."

"I'm just doing my job."

"If you continue to enforce policies down here and anything goes down, no one will be there to back you up. You'll be alone."

"You know those paychecks that we get. I've never seen your name at the bottom. Until I do, I'll be doing things the way my bosses told me to and not what you tell me to do."

With this threat being issued to me, it was time to initiate CYA. I didn't know how to approach this issue. It would become worse if I outed him. The old boy network would be all over me. Those who didn't have the guts to stand up to the old boy network would be all over me. Those that stood firm by the code of snitching out any officer, even a corrupt officer would be all over me.

There was a sergeant that I felt I could trust, so I spoke to him. He gave me several options. One was to just let it go. Another was to write a report and turn it in to the watch commander. Another was to consult a lieutenant. He did say that someone should know in case anything further came of it.

I spoke to a lieutenant in a hypothetical manner. Without it being hypothetical, there would have to be a report for the lieutenant to cover his ass. There was a camera in the area, so it could be verified that there was a conversation between Chow Hound and me, but there was no sound. It would be his word against mine. The lieutenant said that writing a report or just dropping it would be the only thing someone could do in a hypothetical situation like this.

Writing a confidential report is something I could have done. This is a report that you give to the watch commander that no one else is to see; at that time. In a place like this, that doesn't happen. I knew that the warden was to get a copy of the report, but I don't know if an assistant warden would see it first. Then you never know if it gets talked about in the morning meeting with all of the lieutenants and other big shots. As you see, it just grows and grows. Kind of like the old commercial where one person tells two friends and they tell two friends and so on and so on. And all of a sudden I'm a snitch and breaking the code. Now, I'm not adverse to breaking codes, but I am adverse to compromising on what is right or just.

Unfortunately for me, in this environment, if it isn't documented, it doesn't exist.

Chow Hound knew how to play the game. Round one was his. A sergeant and a lieutenant were now aware, I informed a couple of officers that I felt I could trust and I documented this altercation at home in my computer. That is the best I could do; for now.

Later, I pieced together, from what inmates and officers told me, the reason for Chow Hound to come down on me like he did. By me enforcing policies in the dining hall, it got the inmates angry. Their job was to stop me from letting them get away with doing what they want to do. Their angle in this situation was to tell the officers that were taking food that they would rat them out if they didn't stop me from doing my job. Due to Chow Hound's massive consumption, he had the greatest motivation to keep the free food flowing, so whether he was chosen or just extremely willing to confront me, I do not know.

This was my first Easter in the institution and it was a turning point for me. This is when I became aware that I could not just come into work and do my job. I realized that passing through those four doors every day would be a battle with the old boy network; those officers that make up their own rules; those officers that would harass anyone who didn't do what they told them to do. Those officers that would do anything they could to get rid of an officer that didn't go along with them in their defiance of institution policy. Flat out, they had their own rule book and their own ways of doing things.

Chow Hound never gave up on trying to intimidate me into doing what he wanted me to do or trying to get me in trouble in order to get me fired.

He liked to try to stare me down. At times like these, I laughed at him and that perturbed him even more. He would try spreading rumors about me. Intelligent officers would either ignore them or check with me in order to verify their validity or not. It was amazing how many officers were stupid enough to buy into his bullshit.

When the B-West cellblock became double bunked, the inmates were quite upset. They were used to their own individual cell and didn't want to share. With their indifferent attitudes, their propensity toward violence and their numbers in this block almost doubling, trouble could start easily.

Chow Hound was well aware of this and used it as a tool against me. On this day he was the officer assigned to control movement in the institution. His job was to release one cell block at a time to go on their passes. When they got to where they were supposed to go and all doors were secure, he was to release the next cell block in order. This was to help prevent fights in case someone from one cellblock had a problem with someone from a different cellblock and saw the opportunity to bust him up a bit.

B-West was to get two opportunities for movement for every one of the other cell blocks. This was because we had so many more inmates piling up at the door waiting to get out on their passes. I was working the door post. Chow Hound saw this and chose not to release the inmates piling up at my door. I was not allowed to release them except on his direction. After he had skipped our turn a couple of times and I had inmates collecting at my door getting mad at me because I would not let them out, I stepped out into the hallway and asked him politely when we would be getting pass movement. He told me not to bother him and that he would call me when he was ready. He wasn't ready for a long time.

The sergeant of our block this day had stepped out to take care of some business and to get her break. When she got back, it had been close to an hour and a half that we had not been allowed to release any inmates to go on their passes. When she stepped into the block and saw all of the angry inmates collected around the door, she asked me what was going on. I explained the situation to her. She stepped out and asked Chow Hound why he had been skipping our block. He told her that he had been calling it, but that I must not have heard. He told her that we would be next.

Chow Hound had been trying to nail my ass for years when he let his frustrations and anger get the best of him. He made a couple of mistakes and fronted himself off big time.

There was a new academy going on. It was January 5, 2004. I was assigned one of the cadets to take to the dining hall with me and train him in. I always started off standing at the gate where the inmates came through with their trays of food. This is where I made sure they had their ID's clearly displayed. This was supposed to be accomplished by other officers before they got to this point, but most officers were too lazy, afraid or just didn't give a damn about doing their job properly to follow through. By making sure everyone had their ID properly displayed when they passed through the gate, I knew that if I did not see their ID on them later, that they were probably where they didn't belong or up to some other type of mischief. The cadet that was with me was alert and into doing the job properly. I informed him that it was OK to refer to the inmates as sir and to use please and thank you with them. I told him that some would try to get by without displaying their ID just to test us, others to be defiant, others to try to get away with things and that most of them had just forgot. He saw how most of the time I didn't have to say anything. He saw how by me just pointing to my ID and making eye contact that they would put their ID on.

There were other things to check, but on this day the item brought to the forefront was a Native American with his medicine bag hanging out. Displaying affiliation with any group, any religious items or gang colors of any kind was prohibited. I directed the inmate to tuck the necklace with the bag on it in under his shirt. He said he couldn't because his hands were full with his tray and beverage. I directed him to do it when he got to his table. I then informed the cadet that we had to keep an eye on him to see where he went and to see if he complied. We saw where he went and saw that he had not complied. The cadet asked what we were going to do about it. I told him nothing at this time. We knew who he was and what cellblock he was from, so we could lock him up later without creating a stir in the dining hall.

While we were posted up on the opposite side of the dining hall from this inmate, we noticed him standing up at his table with one foot on his chair leaning over with his arms resting on his knee and his medicine bag dangling in front of him for all to see. He was looking at us smiling.

The cadet asked if we were going over to enforce the policy. I told him that we were not. We still hold all of the cards. He stated that everyone is seeing that he is getting away with it and flaunting it. I informed him that later some will see him getting hauled out of his cell and taken to segregation. Others will see his cell getting packed up. Word will spread quickly. And if by the time they come back here for supper and still don't know what has happened, they will know when they don't see him here anymore, that he didn't get away with a thing.

This inmate started getting real cocky and thought he could get away with anything. He proceeded to start walking around the dining hall visiting with people at other tables. He was well out of his assigned area when I informed the cadet that now we had to do something, but we had to keep it as low key as possible. We had two officers and a cadet in the middle of 250 inmates. I told him that if both of us went over there every inmate would be keyed in on us and watching for something to happen. Most of them watch whenever I start to move around anyway. I told the cadet that I didn't want to get in a discussion with this inmate in the middle of everyone because he would just start to argue. He would have to stand up to me in front of everyone and things would go downhill from there. There was a sergeant at the front of the dining hall on the other side of the gate. I told him that I was going to direct the inmate to go to see the sergeant. This way the inmate would be isolated out of the large group and the sergeant could have the inmate escorted straight to segregation without sounding the alarm. I had the cadet go a different route to meet me by the sergeant.

Best laid plans can go awry. Most eyes in the place were on me as I approached the inmate. I did not stop and talk to him. As I passed by and headed up toward the sergeant, I directed him to meet me by the sergeant. This method surprised him and did not allow him the opportunity to be combative. He followed without incident.

As we approached the sergeant, things were stirring up behind us. I was explaining the situation to the sergeant as things were heating up even more. The other officer that had been working the other side of the room had seen someone flip me off behind my back. He went to that inmate, looked at his ID and spoke to him. He then came to the front to inform the sergeant while I was explaining my situation. By this time the inmates were getting quite rowdy. The sergeant called for the squad. The alarm sounded and the A-Team came running. This wound up stirring up the inmates even more. The sergeant had the squad look for the guy that flipped me off. He had moved to a different part of the room. The inmates were loving it; whooping and hollering. The squad was not having any luck in finding the guy. Eventually the officer that saw what happened, pointed the guy out. He was cuffed up and escorted out. My guy was also cuffed up and escorted out. Luckily, by this time, it was time for these guys to go back to their cellblock. Getting them out quick was the best thing that could happen before all hell could break loose.

Later, when I was leaving the dining hall along with the cadet, I heard a call over the radio for me to report to the security center. It was Chow Hound. When we got to the security center, he wanted me to go into the squad room with him alone. The cadet waited outside the door.

Chow Hound asked, "How do you want to handle this; formally or informally?"

I asked, "What are you talking about?"

"Formally of informally?"

"What do you mean?"

"Formally of informally?"

I have no tolerance for stupidity or games. I said, "Either you tell me what you're talking about or I'm leaving."

He said, "How you handle yourself in the dining hall."

I said, "Oh! Formally! Let's go see the lieutenant now!"

I turned, opened the door and headed toward the watch commander's office. Surprisingly he wanted a confrontation in front of the lieutenant. Great, maybe now this harassment thing will come to a head and be over.

All three of us stepped into the office. The lieutenant looked up somewhat bewildered. I said, "Chow Hound has a problem with the way I do my job."

He had us all step into a different office and closed the door. I informed the lieutenant of what had transpired in the dining hall. The cadet verified the information as being accurate. The lieutenant said, "Great job. That's exactly as I would've handled it. So, Chow Hound, what is it that you have a problem with?"

Chow Hound was never in the dining hall. He heard bits and pieces of what happened and formulated his own idea. He had probably been informed by his Native American buddies, old boy network buddies or both. If he heard Native American, dining hall and Basham that's all he needed to set him off. He told the lieutenant that I did things that I had never done. Thankfully on this day this cadet was with me, because he was able to say that these allegations were not true and that Chow Hound wasn't even there.

Chow Hound tried to discredit my methods. The lieutenant shut him down by saying that he likes how I do things. Chow Hound tried vast generalizations; like I targeted and harassed Native Americans. The lieutenant, a black man, stated that he had never seen anything to justify racism by me with any race.

Eventually, in frustration, Chow Hound gave up his fight. He was very angry. I held out my hand to shake his and said, "So can we put this behind us now?"

Obviously not, because he gave me a body block, knocking me into the wall as he passed through the door. He actually did this right in front of the lieutenant! The lieutenant said loudly and sternly, "Chow Hound, get back in here! Bash, you guys can leave."

What happened in that room afterwards, I have no idea. I can tell you that it was well over an hour later when I saw Chow Hound walking down the hallway with tears running down his face.

Did this stop his harassment of me? No. It just made it so he had to be sneakier about it.

Guess what? Chow Hound eventually was promoted to sergeant. How could this happen, you ask. Promotions to sergeant aren't based on competency or performance. It is strictly based on seniority.

Luckily, during my time in the prison, he was not able to gain enough seniority as a sergeant in order to bid into a cell block where I was working. When I retired, he was under discipline for some wrong doing with an inmate back in segregation. I never received accurate information on what exactly happened.

Next big surprise! Within a year and a half after I retired, Chow Hound was promoted to lieutenant! How could this happen? My sources hypothesized that one reason could be that during his disciplinary time he totally kissed ass and continued to do so. Now this could be that he just started following policy and that would be a good thing. But my information was that he was being a prick and that's not a good way to conduct business. Sounds like Chow Hound's head got to be as large as his belly.

Oh, sorry, I almost forgot, yeah right. He was a Native American. Unwritten policy in the prison had become to promote anything living and breathing that was not a white male; fortunately, some of them where highly qualified and well deserving. Unfortunately, many of them were not and some were horrendous.

For awhile people were getting promoted that weren't qualified strictly because there was no one qualified to fill the position. At one time, I was having a confidential meeting with one of the higher ups in the institution. He told me that there were only two people that were considered competent to fill the position at that time and that neither of them were sergeants. You have to have two years in as a sergeant in order to be able to be promoted to a lieutenant. He said one was a female and the other one was me.

During my time there I saw sergeants turn down the lieutenant job because they didn't want to put up with the politics of the position. A sergeant with good seniority and topped out on the pay scale can have a pretty decent time of things.

As far as Chow Hound's competency at being a lieutenant, all I can say is that I'm glad I'm not working there anymore. I got out in the nick of time.

Ooh, ooh! Guess what an officer friend of mine informed me of after I had retired? Chow hound had been such a jerk and pissed off so many people that he was now gone. What I heard was that the officer's grapevine had him being offered a demotion. Supposedly he didn't like that option and quit. This just shows the incompetency of those making decisions in this place. Not that he was forced out, but that he was ever promoted to even being a sergeant. He should've been fired when he was an officer. It took some time, but eventually somebody pulled their head out of their ass and got rid of this disruptive corrupt slug.

CONCLUSION

There actually is no conclusion.

New stories will continue to be created as time goes on. Others will have different perspectives than do I. Policies, people and buildings will change and that will change how things happen and what will happen.

There is much more to come in the next books. This piece has laid the groundwork for you to be able to enjoy the variety of upcoming pieces.

I have worked at not sensationalizing anything. That would be too easy. Working at just giving you the facts along with my opinions was the tough job. I have read books that clearly sensationalized events. My purpose is to accurately inform so that you can make your own decisions on the severity of each event.

If you didn't like this one, you won't have to waste any more time and money on the others. So, either you don't want to read anymore about this kind of thing, or it's on to volume 2...

CPSIA information can be obtained
at www.ICGtesting.com
Printed in the USA
LVOW11s2147250417
532182LV00001B/87/P